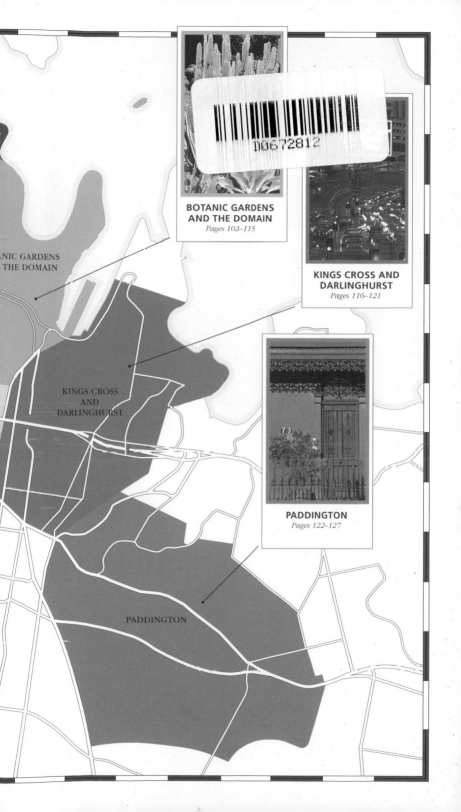

**BOTANIC GARDENS
AND THE DOMAIN**
Pages 102–115

**KINGS CROSS AND
DARLINGHURST**
Pages 116–121

PADDINGTON
Pages 122–127

ANIC GARDENS
THE DOMAIN

KINGS CROSS
AND
DARLINGHURST

PADDINGTON

00672812

EYEWITNESS TRAVEL

SYDNEY

MAIN CONTRIBUTORS: KEN BRASS & KIRSTY MCKENZIE

LONDON, NEW YORK,
MELBOURNE, MUNICH AND DELHI
www.dk.com

PRODUCED BY The Watermark Press, Sydney, Australia
PROJECT EDITOR Siobhán O'Connor
ART EDITOR Claire Edwards
EDITORS Robert Coupe, Leith Hillard, Jane Sheard
DESIGNERS Katie Peacock, Claire Ricketts, Noel Wendtman

Dorling Kindersley Limited
SENIOR EDITOR Fay Franklin
SENIOR ART EDITOR Jane Ewart
SENIOR REVISIONS EDITOR Esther Labi

CONTRIBUTORS
Anna Bruechert, John Dengate, Carrie Hutchinson,
Graham Jahn, Kim Saville, Susan Skelly

PHOTOGRAPHERS
Max Alexander, Simon Blackall, Michael Nicholson,
Rob Reichenfeld, Alan Williams

ILLUSTRATORS
Richard Draper, Stephen Gyapay, Alex Lavroff Associates,
The Overall Picture, Robbie Polley

REPRODUCED BY Colourscan, Singapore
Printed and bound by South China Printing Co. Ltd., China

First American Edition, 1996
06 07 08 09 10 9 8 7 6 5 4 3 2 1

Published in the United States by
DK Publishing, Inc., 375 Hudson Street,
New York, New York 10014

Reprinted with revisions 1997, 1999, 2000, 2001, 2002
(twice), 2003, 2005, 2006
Copyright 1997, 2006 © Dorling Kindersley Limited, London
A Penguin Company

ISSN 1542-1554
ISBN 978-0-75661-572-7
ISBN 0-7566-1572-0

Floors are referred to throughout in accordance with European usage;
i.e., the "first floor" is one flight up.

Front cover main image: Sydney Opera House and skyline

**The information in this
DK Eyewitness Travel Guide is checked regularly.**
Every effort has been made to ensure that this book is as up-to-
date as possible at the time of going to press. Some details,
however, such as telephone numbers, opening hours, prices,
gallery hanging arrangements and travel information, are liable to
change. The publishers cannot accept responsibility for any
consequences arising from the use of this book, nor for any
material on third party websites, and cannot guarantee that any
website address in this book will be a suitable source of travel
information. We value the views and suggestions of our readers
highly. Please write to: The Publisher, DK Eyewitness Travel
Guides, 80 Strand, London, WC2R 0RL.

CONTENTS

HOW TO USE THIS GUIDE 6

INTRODUCING SYDNEY

**A view of the Royal Botanic
Gardens and city skyline**

Tamarama beach and surf club

TRAVELLERS' NEEDS

Wattleseed, pepperberry and
lemon myrtle

SURVIVAL GUIDE

SYDNEY AREA BY AREA

Façade of Sydney Town Hall

Stained-glass window,
Queen Victoria Building

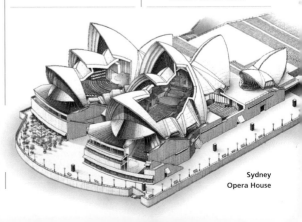

Sydney
Opera House

HOW TO USE THIS GUIDE

This guide helps you to get the most from your visit to Sydney. It provides both expert recommendations and detailed practical information. *Introducing Sydney* locates the city geographically, sets modern Sydney in its historical and cultural context and describes events through the entire year. *Sydney at a Glance* is an overview of the city's main attractions, including a feature on the city shoreline and Sydney's best beaches. *Sydney Area*

Strolling at the Royal Easter Show

by Area is the main sightseeing section, covering all the sights, with photographs, maps and drawings. *Further Afield* looks at sights just outside the city centre while *Beyond Sydney* explores other places close to Sydney. Carefully researched tips on hotels, restaurants, pubs and entertainment venues are found in *Travellers' Needs*. The *Survival Guide* contains useful practical advice on everything from the Australian telephone system to public transport.

FINDING YOUR WAY AROUND THE SIGHTSEEING SECTION

The centre of Sydney has been divided into six sightseeing areas. Each area has its own chapter and is colour-coded for easy reference. Every chapter opens with a list of the sights described. All sights are numbered and plotted on an *Area Map*. Detailed information for each sight is presented in numerical order, making it easy to locate within the chapter.

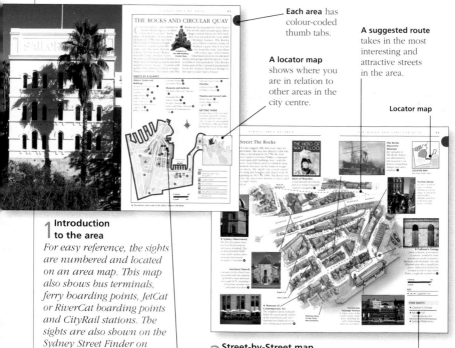

Each area has colour-coded thumb tabs.

A locator map shows where you are in relation to other areas in the city centre.

A suggested route takes in the most interesting and attractive streets in the area.

Locator map

1 Introduction to the area

For easy reference, the sights are numbered and located on an area map. This map also shows bus terminals, ferry boarding points, JetCat or RiverCat boarding points and CityRail stations. The sights are also shown on the Sydney Street Finder on pages 240–45.

The area shaded pink is shown in greater detail on the Street-by-Street map on the following pages.

2 Street-by-Street map

This gives a bird's eye view of the most important parts of each sightseeing area. The numbering of the sights ties in with the area map and the fuller descriptions on the pages that follow.

The list of star sights recommends the places that no visitor should miss.

THE HISTORY OF SYDNEY

The first inhabitants of Australia were the Aboriginal peoples. Their history began in a time called the Dreaming when the Ancestor Spirits emerged from the earth and gave form to the landscape. Anthropologists believe the Aboriginal peoples arrived from Asia more than 50,000 years ago. Clans lived in the area now known as Sydney, until the Europeans caused violent disruption to this world.

Sydney's coat of arms, Sydney Town Hall

In 1768, Captain James Cook began a search for the fabled "great south land". Travelling in the wake of other European explorers, he was the first to set foot on the east coast of the land the Dutch had named New Holland, and claimed it for King and country. He landed at Botany Bay in 1770, naming the coast New South Wales.

At the suggestion of Sir Joseph Banks, Cook's botanist on the *Endeavour*, a penal colony was established here to relieve Britain's overflowing prisons. The First Fleet of 11 ships reached Botany Bay in 1788, commanded by Captain Arthur Phillip. He felt the land there was swampy and the bay windswept. Just to the north, however, he found "one of the finest harbours in the world," naming it Sydney Cove, after the Home Department's Secretary of State. Here, 1,485 convicts, guards, officers, officials, wives and children landed. This marked the beginning of the rapid devastation of the Aboriginal peoples, as they fell to introduced diseases and battled an undeclared war against the settlers. Full citizenship rights were finally granted to the Aboriginal peoples in 1973, and their traditions are now accorded respect.

The city of Sydney soon flourished, with the construction of impressive public buildings befitting an emerging maritime power. In 1901, amid a burgeoning nationalism, the federation drew the country's six colonies together and New South Wales became a state of Australia.

In its two centuries of European settlement, Sydney has experienced alternating periods of growth and decline. It has weathered the effects of gold rush and trade booms, depressions and world wars, to establish a distinctive city marked by a vibrant eclecticism. The underlying British culture, married with Aboriginal influences and successive waves of Asian and European migration, has produced today's modern cosmopolitan city.

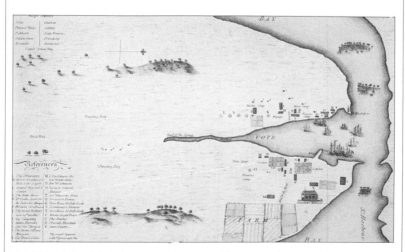

Sketch & Description of the Settlement at Sydney Cove (1788) by transported convict Francis Fowkes

◁ *Desmond, a New South Wales Chief* (about 1825) by Augustus Earle

Sydney's Original Inhabitants

Hafted stone axe

Anthropologists believe that Aboriginal peoples reached Sydney Harbour at least 50,000 years ago. One of the clans of coastal Sydney was the Eora. Their campsites were usually close to the shore, particularly in the summer when fish were plentiful. Plant and animal foods supplemented their seafood diet. Artistic expression was a way of life, with their shields decorated with ochre, designs carved on their implements, and their bodies adorned with scars, animal teeth and feathers. Sacred and social ceremonies are still vital today. Oral traditions recount stories of the Dreaming (see p19) and describe the Eora's strong attachment to the land.

Aborigines Fishing *(1819)*
Sixty-seven Eora canoes were counted in the harbour on a single day. Spears were used as tools and weapons.

Berowra Waters

This **Berowra Waters carving** is hard to interpret; experts believe that it may represent a koala.

Glenbrook Crossing
The Red Hand Caves near Glenbrook in the lower Blue Mountains contain stencils where ochre was blown over outstretched hands.

Glenbrook

The name **Parramatta** means place where eels lie down or sleep, or the head of the river.

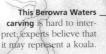

Parramatta •

Glenbrook Caves ochre hand stencils

Cabramatta •

Cabramatta means land where the *cobra* grub is found.

Red Ochre and Shell Paint Holder
Ochre was a commonly used material in rock painting. Finely ground, then mixed with water and a binding agent, it would be applied by brush or hand.

ABORIGINAL ROCK ART

There are approximately 5,500 known rock art sites in the Sydney basin alone. Early colonists such as Watkin Tench said that paintings and engravings were on every kind of surface. The history of colonization was also recorded in rock engravings, with depictions of the arrival of ships and fighting.

TIMELINE

43,000–38,000BC Tools found in a gravel pit beside Nepean River are among the oldest firmly dated signs of human occupation in Australia	**20,000** Humans lived in the Blue Mountains despite extreme conditions. Remains found of the largest mammal, *Diprotodon*, date back to this period	**11,000** Burial site excavated in Victoria of more than 40 individuals of this period
50,000 BC	**20,000 BC**	
28,000 Funerary rites at Lake Mungo, NSW. Complete skeleton has been found of man buried at this time	**18,000** People now inhabit the entire continent, from the deserts to the mountains	
23,000 One of the world's earliest known cremations carried out in Western NSW		**13,000** Final stages of Ice Age, with small glaciers in the Snowy Mountains

Diprotodon

Ku-ring-gai is named after clans who lived in this coastal district. It is rich in rock engravings.

Hunting and Fishing Implements

Multi-pronged Eora spears were used for fishing, while canoes were shaped from a single piece of bark. Boomerangs are still used today for hunting and music making.

WHERE TO SEE ABORIGINAL ROCK ART AND ARTIFACTS

The soft sandstone of Sydney was a natural canvas. Much of the rock art of the original inhabitants remains and can be found on walking trails in Ku-ring-gai Chase National Park *(see pp154–5)* and the Royal National Park *(p165).* The National Parks & Wildlife shop at Cadman's Cottage *(p68)* has a range of pamphlets about Aboriginal sites.

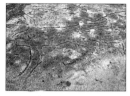

Gumbooya Reserve *in suburban Allambie Heights has a collection of 68 rock carvings. This human figure appears to be inside or on top of a whale.*

Fish Carving at West Head

This area in Ku-ring-gai Chase has 51 figures and is acknowledged as one of the richest sites in the greater Sydney region.

Bondi is from *boondi*, the sound of water crashing. This carving is of a shark and fish.

Shell Fish-Hooks

Introduced from the Torres Strait, these hooks were ground-down mollusc shells.

Coogee means bad smell of rotten seaweed washed ashore.

This python skeleton *is on view at the Australian Museum (see pp88–9), along with a large collection of Aboriginal artifacts.*

Maroubra comes either from the *merooberah* tribe, or means place where shells are found.

This carving of a leaping kangaroo is found in the Royal National Park.

Water Carrier

These bags were usually made of kangaroo skin. The skin was removed in one piece and either turned inside out or tanned with the sap from a gum tree.

Allambie Heights

Bondi

Coogee

Maroubra

Bundeena

8,000 BC The oldest returning boomerangs are in use in South Australia

5,000 BC Dingo reaches Australia, thought to have been brought by seafarers

Captain James Cook

AD 1606 Dutch ship, *Duyfken*, records first European sighting of the continent. Lands on the eastern coast of Gulf of Carpentaria

10,000 BC

AD 1

10,000–8,500 BC Tasmania is separated from mainland Australia by rising seas

Copperplate print of a dingo

AD 1700 Macassans search for trepang or sea slugs off Australia's north coast

AD 1770 James Cook lands at Botany Bay

The Early Colony

Hat made from cabbage palm

The colony's beginnings were rugged and hungry, imbued with a spirit that would give Sydney its unique character. Convicts were put to work establishing roads and constructing buildings out of mud, reeds, unseasoned wood and mortar made from a crushed shell mixture. From these simple beginnings, a town grew. Officers of the New South Wales Corps became farmers, encouraged to work their land alongside convict labour. Because the soldiers paid for work and goods in rum, they soon became known as the Rum Corps, in 1808 overthrowing Governor Bligh (of *Bounty* fame) when he threatened their privileges. By the early 1800s farms were producing crops, with supplies arriving more regularly – as were convicts and settlers with more appropriate skills and trades.

GROWTH OF THE CITY

☐ *Today*   ■ *1810*

Boat building at the Government dockyard

Pitts Row

First Fleet Ship *(c.1787)*
This painting by Francis Holman shows three angles of the Borrowdale, *one of the fleet's three commercial storeships.*

Government House

Scrimshaw
Engraving bone or shell was a skilful way to pass time during long months spent at sea.

A VIEW OF SYDNEY COVE

This idyllic image, drawn by Edward Dayes and engraved by F Jukes in 1804, shows the Aboriginal peoples living peacefully within the infant colony alongside the flourishing maritime and agricultural industries. In fact, they had been entirely ostracized from the life and prosperity of the town by this time.

TIMELINE

1787 The First Fleet leaves Portsmouth, bound for Botany Bay

1788 First white child born in the colony – and the first man hanged

Barrington, the convict and thespian star of The Revenge

1796 *The Revenge* opens Sydney's first, but short-lived, playhouse, simply named The Theatre

1785	1790	1795

Bennelong pictured in European finery

1789 The Aboriginal Bennelong is held captive and ordered to act as an intermediary between the whites and blacks

1790 First detachment of the New South Wales Corps arrives in the colony. Fears of starvation are lessened with the arrival of the supply ship *Lady Juliana*

1793 Arrival of the first free settlers

1797 Merino sheep arrive from Cape of Good Hope

The Arrest of Bligh
This shameful, and invented, scene shows the hated Governor William Bligh, in full regalia, hiding under a servant's bed to avoid arrest by the NSW Rum Corps in 1808.

The buildings may look impressive, but most were poorly built with inferior materials.

Male and female convicts housed separately

WHERE TO SEE EARLY COLONIAL SYDNEY

The Rocks was the hub of early Sydney. Wharves, warehouses, hotels, rough houses and even rougher characters gave it its colour. Dramatic cuts were made in the rocky point to provide building materials and filling for the construction of Circular Quay, and allow for streets. The houses are gone, except for Cadman's Cottage *(see p68)*, but the irregular, labyrinthine lanes still give the flavour of convict history.

Waratah *(1803)*
John Lewin, naturalist and engraver, drew delicate and faithful representations of the local flora and fauna.

Barracks housing NSW Rum Corps

Elizabeth Farm *(pp138–9)*
at Parramatta is the oldest surviving building in Australia. It was built by convicts using lime mortar from the penal colony of Norfolk Island

Experiment Farm Cottage,
an early dwelling (see p139), displays marked convict-made bricks. Masons also marked each brick, as they were paid according to the number laid.

Kangaroo *(1813)*
Naturalists were amazed at Sydney's vast array of strange plant and animal species. The first pictures sent back to England caused a sensation.

1799 Explorers Bass and Flinders complete their circum-navigation of Van Diemen's Land (now Tasmania), before returning to Port Jackson

1803 The first issue of the weekly *Sydney Gazette*, Australia's first newspaper, is published

1808 Rum Rebellion brings social upheaval. Estimated population of New South Wales stands at 9,100

1800	1805	1810

1801 Ticket-of-leave system introduced, enabling the convicts to work for wages and to choose their own master

1804 Irish convict uprising at Castle Hill

1802 Aboriginal leader Pemulwy is shot and killed following the killing of four white men by Aboriginal men

Love token

1810 New convict arrivals craft such items as love tokens

Victorian Sydney

Gold rush memorabilia

In the 1850s, gold was discovered in New South Wales and Sydney came alive with gold seekers, big spenders and a new wave of settlers. It was the start of a peaceful period of solid growth. Education became compulsory, an art gallery was opened and the Australian Academy of Arts held its first exhibition. The city skyline became more complex, with spires and "tall" buildings. Terrace houses proliferated. Victorian decorum and social behaviour borrowed from the mother country flourished, with much social visiting and sporting enthusiasm. It was an age of pleasure gardens and regattas, but also a time of unruliness and political agitation. In the 1890s, as the country moved towards Federation, fervent nationalism and an Australian identity began to take shape.

GROWTH OF THE CITY

☐ Today   ▨ 1881

The structure was built of hollow pine.

The dome was 30 m (98 ft) in diameter.

Mrs Macquaries Chair *(1855)*
This prime harbour viewing spot (see p106), with the seat carved from rock for the governor's wife, was "the daily resort of all the fashionable people in Sydney".

Boer War
The 1st Australian Horse division was praised for its bushcraft, horsemanship and accurate shooting.

THE GARDEN PALACE

Built in the Botanic Gardens especially for the occasion, in 1879–80, the Garden Palace hosted the first international exhibition held in the southern hemisphere. Twenty nations took part. Sadly, the building and most of its contents were destroyed by fire in 1882.

TIMELINE

Henry Parkes

1851 The discovery of gold near Bathurst, west of the Blue Mountains, sparks a gold rush

1868 The Duke of Edinburgh visits and survives an assassination attempt. The Prince Alfred Hospital is later named in his honour

1872 Henry Parkes elected NSW Premier

1850

1860

1870

1867 Henry Lawson born

1857 *Dunbar* wrecked at The Gap with the loss of 121 lives and only one survivor

Henry Lawson, notable poet and author of short stories

1869 Trend in the colony towards the segregation of Aboriginal peoples on reserves and settlements

1870 The last British troops withdraw from the colony

The Waverly
This clipper brig, with its extra sails and tall masts, enabled the fast transport of wool exports and fortune seekers hastening to newly discovered colonial gold fields.

The "Strasburg" Clock
In 1887, Sydney clockmaker Richard Smith began work on this astronomical model now in the Powerhouse Museum (see pp100–101).

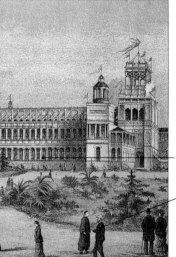

Some of the exhibits held in the Powerhouse Museum *(see pp100–101)* were rescued from this burning building.

The exhibition attracted over one million people.

Arthur Streeton
In 1891, Streeton and Tom Roberts, both Australian Impressionist painters, set up an artists' camp overlooking Sydney Harbour in Mosman.

WHERE TO SEE VICTORIAN SYDNEY

Sydney's buildings reflect the spirit of the age. The Queen Victoria Building *(see p82)*, Sydney Town Hall *(p87)* and Martin Place *(p84)* mark grand civic spaces. In stark contrast, the Argyle Terraces and Susannah Place *(p67)* in The Rocks give some idea of the cramped living conditions endured by the working class.

St Mary's Cathedral (see p86), *built in Gothic Revival style, is thought to be the largest Christian church in the former "Empire", outside Britain.*

Victorian terrace houses, *decorated with iron lace, began to fill the streets of Paddington (see pp122–7) and Glebe (p131) from the 1870s onwards.*

1880 The *Bulletin* is launched, and becomes a literary icon. Captain Moonlight, a notorious bushranger, is hanged

1890 First electric trams run between Bondi Junction and Waverley

Tivoli Theatre programme

1896 Moving pictures come to the Tivoli Theatre

1880

1890

1879 Steam tramway travels from the city to Redfern

Steam tram

1891 Labor Party enters the political arena

1877 Caroline Chisholm, a philanthropist who helped immigrant women, dies

1888 Louisa Lawson's journal *Dawn* published

1900 Queen Victoria consents to the formation of the Commonwealth of Australia. Bubonic plague breaks out

Sydney Between the Wars

Federation took place on 1 January 1901 and New South Wales became a state of the Australian nation. In Sydney, new wharves were built, roads widened and slums cleared. The 1920s were colourful and optimistic in "the city of pleasure". The skyline bristled with cranes as modern structures replaced their ornate predecessors. The country was hit hard by the Great Depression in 1931, but economic salvation came in the form of rising wool prices and growth in manufacturing. The opening of the Sydney Harbour Bridge in 1932 was a consolidation of all the changes brought by Federation and urbanization.

Vegemite spread created in 1923

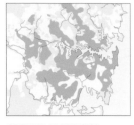

GROWTH OF THE CITY

☐ *Today*   ▤ *1945*

The poster depicts the youthful vigour of the nation.

Home in the Suburbs
The Federation bungalow became a unique architectural style (see p41). Verandas, gables and chimneys featured amid much red brick.

Surf lifesaver

Bronzed Lifesavers
No surf beach was complete without these icons, forever looking to sea.

"Making Do"
This chair, made in 1910, used packing case timber, cotton reels, fencing wire and the mouldings of picture frames.

SYDNEY CELEBR

MARCH 19ᵗʰ 1932

SYDNEY HARBOUR BRIDGE
After nine years of construction, the largest crowd ever seen in Sydney greeted the bridge's opening. Considered a wonder of engineering at the time, it linked the harbour's north and south shores.

TIMELINE

1901 Miles Franklin's *My Brilliant Career* is published

Miles Franklin

1912 High-rise era begins in Sydney with the erection of the 14-storey Culwulla Chambers in Macquarie Street. First surfboard arrives in Sydney from Hawaii

1920 Prince Edward, the Prince of Wales, visits

1918 Sydneysiders greet the Armistice riotously

1900   **1910**   **1920**

1902 Women win the right to vote in New South Wales

1901 Proclamation of the Commonwealth of Australia. Edmund Barton elected as first prime minister

1907 Trunk line between Melbourne and Sydney opens

Poster for telephone trunk line

1919 The Archibald Prize for portraiture is first awarded. Influenza epidemic hits Sydney

1915 Anzacs land at Gallipoli

Luna Park
This harbourside amusement park opened in 1935 (see p132). A maniacally grinning face loomed at the entrance way. Millions of Australians recall the terrifying thrill of running the gauntlet through the gaping mouth as children.

One million people crossed the bridge on its opening day.

Donald Bradman
The 1932 English team used "dirty" tactics to outsmart this brilliant cricketer, almost causing a diplomatic rift with Great Britain.

WHERE TO SEE EARLY 20TH-CENTURY SYDNEY
The years after Federation yielded stylish and sensible buildings like Central Railway Station, the Commonwealth Bank in Martin Place *(see pp40–41)* and the State Library of New South Wales. The suburbs of Haberfield and Strathfield best exemplify the Federation style of gentrified residential housing.

The Anzac Memorial *(1934) is in Hyde Park (see pp86–7). The Art Deco memorial, with its reflecting pool, commemorates all Australians killed in wars.*

The wireless *became almost a fixture in sitting rooms in the 1930s. This 1935 AWA Radiolette is held at the Powerhouse Museum (see pp100–101).*

Australian Women's Weekly
This magazine, first published in 1933, becomes a family institution full of homespun wisdom, recipes, stories and handy hints.

1924 Sydney swimmer Andrew "Boy" Charlton wins a gold medal at the Paris Olympics

Painted glass pub sign

1937 Heyday of painted glass pub art depicting local heroes

1938 Sydney celebrates her 150th anniversary

1939 Australia declares war on Germany

1930

1940

1928 Kingsford Smith and Ulm make first flight across Pacific in the *Southern Cross*

Kingsford Smith, Ulm

1932 Sydney Harbour Bridge opens

1935 Luna Park opens

1941 Australia declares war on Japan

1942 Japanese midget submarines enter Sydney Harbour

1945 Street celebrations mark the end of World War II

Postwar Sydney

1950s Holden sedan

The postwar baby boom was accompanied by mass immigration and the suburban sprawl. The hippie movement gave youth an extrovert voice that imbued the 1960s with an air of flamboyance. Australian involvement in the Vietnam War led to political unrest in the early 1970s, relieved for one seminal moment by the 1973 opening of the Sydney Opera House *(see pp74–7)*. In the 1980s, vast sums were spent on skyscrapers and glossy redevelopments like Darling Harbour, and on bicentennial celebrations. The city's potential was recognized in 1993 with the announcement that Sydney would host the year 2000 Olympics.

GROWTH OF THE CITY

☐ *Today*   ▨ *1966*

Drag queens pose in their Hollywood-style sequined finery or lampoon public figures of the day.

Sydney to Hobart Yacht Race
Australia's most prestigious and treacherous yacht race runs over 1,167 km (725 miles). Each Boxing Day since 1945, spectators have watched yachts jostle at the starting line.

Elaborate floats and costumes can take a year to make, with prizes given to the best.

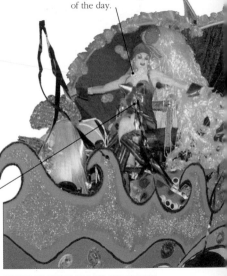

Bicentenary
The re-enactment of the First Fleet's journey ended in Sydney Harbour on Australia Day, 1988. A chaotic flotilla greeted the "tall ships".

NEW MARDI GRAS FESTIVAL

What began as a protest march involving 1,000 people in 1978 is now a multi-million dollar boost for Australian tourism. While the parade lasts for one rude and riotous night only *(see p49)*, the surrounding international festival offers a month of art, sporting and community events.

TIMELINE

1950		1960		1970	
1950 Petrol, butter and tea rationing ends	**1958** Qantas Airlines embarks on its first round-the-world flights		**1965** Conscription re-introduced; first regular army battalion sent to Vietnam	**1973** Official opening of the Sydney Opera House	**1976** Nude sunbathing allowed on two Sydney beaches
1954 Elizabeth II is the first reigning monarch to visit Australia	**1956** TV launched in Sydney. By the 1960s, the most popular show is *The Mickey Mouse Club*	**1959** Population of Australia reaches 10 million	**1964** Rocker Johnny O'Keefe, "The Wild One", continues to top the music charts	**1973** Patrick White wins the Nobel Prize for Literature	

Johnny O'Keefe

Patrick White

Green Bans
In the 1970s, the militant building union placed work bans on developments in the inner city considered destructive to the environment or cultural heritage.

The parade of ornate floats and showy dance troupes stretches for over 2 km (1¼ miles).

MR ETERNITY
Arthur Stace (1885–1967), a reformed alcoholic, was inspired by an evangelist who said that he wanted to "shout eternity through the streets of Sydney". "I felt a powerful call from the Lord to write 'Eternity'." At least 50 times a day, for over 30 years, he chalked this word in perfect copperplate on the footpaths and walls of the city. A plaque in Sydney Square pays tribute to Mr Eternity's endeavours.

Ned Kelly
This 1946 portrait of legendary hero Ned Kelly is by Sir Sidney Nolan (1917–92), an important postwar painter.

Arthur Stace and "Eternity", 1963

Floats are marshalled in Elizabeth Street, before travelling along Oxford and Flinders Streets.

Oz Magazine, 1963–73
This satirical magazine, which had a major international influence, was the mouthpiece of an irreverent generation. It was declared obscene in 1964.

Aboriginal Land Rights
In 1975, the first handover of land was made to Vincent Lingiari, representative of the Gurindji people, by Prime Minister Gough Whitlam.

1978 Brett Whiteley wins Archibald Prize, Wynne Prize and Sulman Prize for three works of art

Façade detail of the Brett Whiteley Studio (see p130)

1997 INXS singer Michael Hutchence commits suicide in a Sydney hotel

2000 Sydney plays host to the first Olympic Games of the new millennium

1980

1990

2000

1979 Sydney's Eastern Suburbs Railway opens

1992 Sydney Harbour Tunnel opens

2003 Memorial unveiled to the 202 people killed in Bali bombing (2002)

1989 Earthquake strikes Newcastle causing extensive damage

1990 Population of Australia reaches 17 million

SYDNEY AT A GLANCE

There are more than 100 places of interest described in the *Area by Area* section of this book. A broad range of sights is covered: from the colonial simplicity of Hyde Park Barracks *(see p114)* to the ornate Victorian terraces of Paddington; from the tranquillity of Centennial Park *(see p127)* to the bustle of the cafés and shops of Oxford Street. To help you make the most of your stay, the following 14 pages are a time-saving guide to the best Sydney has to offer. Museums and galleries, architecture and parks and reserves all have sections of their own. There is also a guide to the diverse cultures that have helped to shape the city into what it is today. Below is a selection of attractions that no visitor should miss.

SYDNEY'S TOP TEN ATTRACTIONS

The Rocks
See pp62–77

Royal Botanic Gardens
See pp104–5

Sydney Opera House
See pp74–7

Art Gallery of New South Wales
See pp108–11

Sydney Tower
See p83

Oxford Street and Paddington
See pp116–27

Darling Harbour and Chinatown
See pp90–101

Taronga Zoo
See pp134–5

Harbour ferries
See pp234–5

Sydney's beaches
See pp54–5

◁ Sydney Harbour Bridge, opened in 1932 *(see pp70–71)*

Sydney's Best: Museums and Galleries

Sydney is well endowed with museums and galleries, and, following the current appreciation of social history, much emphasis is placed on the lifestyles of past and present Sydneysiders. Small museums are also a feature of the Sydney scene, with a number of historic houses recalling the colonial days. These are covered in greater depth on pages 36–7. Most of the major collections are housed in architecturally significant buildings – the Classical façade of the Art Gallery of NSW makes it a city landmark, while the Museum of Contemporary Art has given new life to a 1950s Art Deco-style building at Circular Quay.

Bima figure, Powerhouse Museum

Museum of Sydney
The Edge of the Trees is an interactive installation by the entrance.

THE ROCKS AND CIRCULAR QUAY

Justice and Police Museum
This museum illustrates Sydney's early legal and criminal history. It includes some macabre relics of notorious crimes.

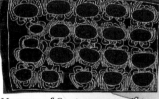

CITY CENTRE

Museum of Contemporary Art
The excellent Aboriginal art section at this museum includes Mud Crabs *by Tony Dhanyula Nyoka.*

DARLING HARBOUR

Australian National Maritime Museum
The museum is the home port for HMB Endeavour, a replica of the vessel that charted Australia's east coast in 1770, with Captain Cook in command.

Powerhouse Museum
This museum, set in a former power station, uses both traditional and interactive displays to explore Australian innovations in science and technology.

| 0 metres | 500 |
| 0 yards | 500 |

Art Gallery of New South Wales
The Australian collection includes colonial watercolours which, to avoid deterioration, are only shown for a few weeks each year. Charles Meere's Australian Beach Pattern *(1940) is among more recent works.*

Elizabeth Bay House
The dining room is elegantly furnished to the 1840s period, when the Colonial Secretary Alexander Macleay briefly lived in the house that ultimately caused his bankruptcy.

BOTANIC GARDENS AND THE DOMAIN

KINGS CROSS AND DARLINGHURST

Hyde Park Barracks Museum
Originally built by convicts for their own incarceration, these barracks were later home to poor female immigrants. Exhibits recall the daily life of these occupants.

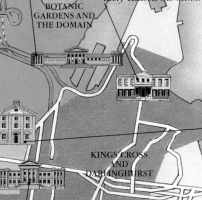

PADDINGTON

Sydney Jewish Museum
The history of the city's Jewish community is documented here. Included is a reconstruction of George Street in 1848, a major location for Jewish businesses.

Australian Museum
At Australia's largest natural history museum, dinosaurs such as this large mammal or "megafauna" Diprotodon skeleton are a major attraction.

Exploring Sydney's Museums and Galleries

Nautilus scrimshaw, National Maritime Museum

Sydney boasts a rich variety of museums and galleries that reflects the cultural, artistic and historical heritage of this, the country's oldest city – and of Australia as a whole. The growth of such institutions in recent years parallels a corresponding growth in public interest in all things cultural, a phenomenon that seems at odds with Sydney's predominantly hedonistic image. In fact, Sydney has a long-standing cultural tradition, one that has not always been widely recognized. It may even surprise some people that museums and galleries attract more people than do high-profile football matches.

Detail from *Window of Dreams* at the National Maritime Museum

Collage on one of the internal doors of the Brett Whiteley Studio

VISUAL ARTS

The traditionally conservative curatorial policy of the **Art Gallery of NSW** has been abandoned in recent times, and it now has one of the finest existing collections of modern Australian and Aboriginal art. Thanks to its former policy, however, it also possesses an outstanding collection of late 19th- and early 20th-century English and Australian works. Thematic temporary exhibitions are also a regular feature.

The far newer **Museum of Contemporary Art** (MCA) is best known for blockbuster exhibitions. Many of these take advantage of its prime harbour site to create a fine sense of spectacle. It also has a considerable permanent collection, and hosts mini film festivals, literary readings and talks.

The **Brett Whiteley Studio** opened even more recently. Housed in the studio of the late artist, it commemorates the life and works of perhaps the most celebrated and controversial Sydney painter of the late 20th century.

The substantial collection of Australian painting and sculpture held by the **SH Ervin Gallery** is supplemented by frequent thematic and other specialized exhibitions.

TECHNOLOGY AND NATURAL HISTORY

The undisputed leader in this area is the **Powerhouse**, with traditional and interactive displays covering fields as diverse as space travel, silent films and solar energy. The **National Maritime Museum** has the world's fastest boat, *Spirit of Australia*, as part of its indoor/outdoor display. Also part of their historic fleet are the destroyer HMAS *Vampire*, the *Onslow* (a submarine), and the *James Craig* (1874), a three-masted barque.

The **Australian Museum**, in contrast, emphasizes natural history with its displays of the exotic and extinct: from birds, insects and rock samples to giant Australian megafauna.

ABORIGINAL CULTURE

With more than 200 works, both traditional and contemporary, on display, the **Art Gallery of NSW's** Yiribana Gallery has the best and most

Jabarrgwa Wurrabadalumba's *Dugong Hunt* (1948), Art Gallery of NSW

comprehensive collection of Aboriginal art in the country. The **Australian Museum** has displays ranging from the pre-historic era to the start of European settlement. In its community access space, it also presents performances that celebrate Aboriginal culture and traditions.

The First Australians exhibit at the **Australian National Maritime Museum** includes audio and video material, with traditional tools made by Aboriginal communities.

The **Museum of Sydney** uses images, artifacts and oral histories to evoke the life of the Eora, the indigenous people of the Sydney region, up to the years of first contact with the European colonists.

The Georgian-style front bedroom in the cottage at Elizabeth Farm

COLONIAL HISTORY

The superb interior of **Elizabeth Bay House** has been furnished to show early colonial life at its most elegant, but while at first the house may appear to celebrate a success story, the enormous cost of its construction brought bankruptcy to its owner. Also built in grand style, **Vaucluse House** celebrates the life and times of WC Wentworth, explorer and politician.

Experiment Farm Cottage, Hambledon Cottage and **Elizabeth Farm** in and around Parramatta are testament to the crucial role of agriculture in the survival of a colony that was brought to the brink of starvation. The former has been restored as a gentleman's cottage of the mid-19th century, while the latter two have been furnished to the period of 1820–50. Parramatta's **Old Government House** was once the vice-regal "inland" residence when Parramatta had more people than Sydney. The colonial furniture on display predates 1855.

The **Museum of Sydney** is built on the site of the first Government House, close to Sydney Cove. On display are

Water dip at Experiment Farm Cottage

recently unearthed relics of that building, some of which are visible under windows at the entrance to the museum.

Susannah Place provides an insight into working-class life in the 19th century. **Cadman's Cottage**, also in The Rocks, is a simple stone dwelling dating from 1816 and the city's oldest extant building. Adjacent is the **Sailors' Home**, built in 1864 as lodgings for visiting sailors. It now houses permanent exhibitions detailing the area's architectural, archaeological and social heritage. The important role of gold in the history of Australia and how it determined patterns of migration and expansion are shown at the **Powerhouse Museum**. **Hyde Park Barracks Museum** evokes the often brutal lives and times of the convicts who were housed there in the early 19th century, while not neglecting its other place in history as an immigration depot.

Side view of the veranda at Elizabeth Farm, near Parramatta

SPECIALIST MUSEUMS

Author may gibbs' home on the harbour, **Nutcote**, has been refurbished in the style of the 1930s. The **Justice and Police Museum** examines a far less comfortable history, investigating Australian crime and punishment, while the **Westpac Museum** traces local financial transactions from first coins through to credit cards. Experiences of Jewish migrants to Australia and the story of the Holocaust are examined at the **Sydney Jewish Museum**.

Sydney's Best: Architecture

For such a young city, Sydney possesses a remarkable diversity of architectural styles. They range from the simplicity of Francis Greenway's Georgian buildings *(see p114)* to Jørn Utzon's Expressionist Sydney Opera House *(see pp74–7)*. Practical Colonial structures gave way to elaborate Victorian edifices such as Sydney Town Hall and the same passion for detail is seen on a smaller scale in Paddington's terraces. Later, Federation warehouses and bungalows brought in a particularly Australian style.

Contemporary
Governor Phillip Tower is a modern commercial building incorporating a historical site (see p85).

Colonial Convict
The first structures were very simple yet formal English-style cottages with shingled roofs and no verandas. Cadman's Cottage is a fine representative of this style.

Colonial Georgian
Francis Greenway's courthouse design was ordered to be adapted to suit the purposes of a church. St James Church is the result.

THE ROCKS
AND
CIRCULAR
QUAY

CITY
CENTRE

American Revivalism
Shopping arcades connecting streets, such as the Queen Victoria Building, were 1890s vogue.

Victorian
The Town Hall interior includes Australia's first pressed metal ceiling, installed for fear that the organ would vibrate a plaster one loose.

DARLING
HARBOUR

Contemporary Expressionism
Innovations in sports stadiums and museum architecture, such as the National Maritime Museum, emphasize roof design and the silhouette.

Interwar Architecture
Bruce Dellit's Anzac Memorial in Hyde Park, with sculptures by Raynor Hoff, encapsulates the spirit, form and detail of Art Deco.

| 0 metres | 500 |
| 0 yards | 500 |

Modern Expressionism

One of the world's greatest examples of 20th-century architecture, Jørn Utzon's Sydney Opera House beat 234 entries in a design competition. Work commenced in 1959 and, despite the architect's resignation in 1966, it was opened in 1973.

Australian Regency

During the 1830s, the best designed villas were the work of John Verge. Elizabeth Bay House was his masterpiece.

Early Colonial

The first buildings of character and quality, such as Hyde Park Barracks, were for the government.

BOTANIC GARDENS AND THE DOMAIN

KINGS CROSS AND DARLINGHURST

Colonial Military

Victoria Barracks, designed by engineers, is an impressive example of a well-preserved Georgian military compound.

PADDINGTON

Colonial Grecian

Greek Revival was the major style for public buildings, such as the Darlinghurst Court House, designed by the Colonial Architect in the 1820–50 period.

Victorian Iron Lace

Festooned with a filigree of cast-iron lace in a wide range of prefabricated patterns, Paddington verandas demonstrate 1880s workmanship.

Exploring Sydney's Architecture

Federation era
stained glass

While European settlement in Sydney has a relatively short history, architectural styles have rapidly evolved from provincial British buildings and the simplicity of convict structures. From the mid-19th century until the present day, architectural innovations have borrowed from a range of international trends to create vernacular styles more suited to local materials and conditions. The signs of affluence and austerity, from gold rush to depression, are also manifested in bricks and mortar.

Façade of the Colonial Susannah Place, with corner shop window

COLONIAL ARCHITECTURE

Little remains of the Colonial buildings from 1790–1830. The few structures still standing have a simple robustness and unassuming dignity. They rely more on form, proportion and mass than on detail.

The Rocks area has one of the best collections of early Colonial buildings: **Cadman's Cottage** (1816), the **Argyle Stores** (1826) and **Susannah Place** (1844). The Georgian **Hyde Park Barracks** (1819) and **St James Church** (1820), by Francis Greenway *(see p114)*, as well as the Greek Revival **Darlinghurst Court House** (1835) and **Victoria Barracks** (1841–8) are excellent examples of this period.

AUSTRALIAN REGENCY

Just as the Colonial style was reaching its zenith, the city's increasingly moneyed society abandoned it as undignified and unfashionable. London's residential architecture, exemplified by John Soane under the Prince Regent's patronage, was in favour from the 1830s to the 1850s. Fine examples of this shift towards Regency are John Verge's stylish town houses at **39–41 Lower Fort Street** (1834–6), The Rocks, and the adjoining **Bligh House** built for a wealthy merchant in 1833 in High Colonial style complete with Greek Classical Doric veranda columns.

Regency-style homes often had Grecian, French and Italian details. **Elizabeth Bay House** (1835–8), internally the finest of all John Verge's works, is particularly noted for its cantilevered staircase rising to the arcaded gallery. The cast-iron Ionic-columned **Tusculum Villa** (1831) by the same architect at Potts Point *(see p118)* is unusual in that it is encircled by a double-storeyed veranda, now partially enclosed.

Entrance detail from the Victorian St Patrick's Seminary in Manly

VICTORIAN

This prosperous era featured confident business people and merchants who designed their own premises. Tracts of the city west of York Street and south of Bathurst Street are testimony to these self-assured projects. The cast-iron and glass **Strand Arcade** (1891) by JB Spencer originally included a gas and electricity system, and hydraulic lifts.

Government architect James Barnet's best work includes the "Venetian Renaissance" style **General Post Office**, Martin Place (1864–87), and the extravagant **Lands Department Building** (1877–90) with its four iron staircases and, originally, patent lifts operated by water power. The **Great Synagogue** (1878), **St Mary's Cathedral** (1882), **St Patrick's Seminary** (1885), **Sydney Town Hall** and **Paddington Street** are also of this period.

AMERICAN REVIVALISM

After Federation in 1901, architects looked to styles such as Edwardian, American Romanesque and Beaux Arts from overseas for commercial buildings. The former **National Mutual Building** (1892) by Edward Raht set the change of direction, followed by warehouse buildings in Sussex and Kent Streets. The Romanesque **Queen Victoria Building**

The Australian Regency-style Bligh House in Dawes Point

(1893–98) was a grand council project by George McRae. The Beaux Arts **Commonwealth Savings Bank** (1928) features an elaborate chamber in Neo-Classical style.

INTERWAR ARCHITECTURE

Architecture between World Wars I and II produced skyscrapers such as the **City Mutual Life Assurance Building** (1936), by Emil Sodersten. This building exhibits German Expressionist influences such as pleated or zigzag windows.

Two important structures are the **ANZAC Memorial** (1929–34) in Hyde Park and **Delfin House** (1938–40), by the Art Deco architect Bruce Dellit. The latter, a skyscraper, features a vaulted ceiling and a granite arch decorated with an allegory of modern life.

MODERN ARCHITECTURE

Modern MLC Centre, Martin Place

From the mid-1950s, modern architecture was introduced to the city through glass-clad curtain-walled office blocks, proportioned like matchboxes on their ends. The contrasting expressed frame approach of **Australia Square** (1961–7) gives structural stability to one of the world's tallest lightweight concrete office towers. This city block was formed by amalgamating 30 properties. Harry Seidler's **MLC Centre** (1975–8) is a 65-storey office

FEDERATION ARCHITECTURE

This distinctly urban style of architecture was developed to meet the demands of the prosperous and newly emerging middle classes at the time of Federation in 1901. Particular features are the high-pitched roofs, which form a picturesque composition or architectural tableau, incorporating intricate gables, wide verandas and chimneys. The decorative timber fretwork of the verandas and archways and the leadlight windows reveal the influence of the Art Nouveau period, as do the vibrant red roof tiles. The patriotic references are seen throughout, and Australian flora and fauna are recurring decorative motifs.

"Verona" in The Appian Way, Burwood

tower comprising a reinforced concrete tube structure with column-free floors.

Jorn Utzon's **Sydney Opera House** (1959–73) is widely regarded as one of the architectural wonders of the world.

CONTEMPORARY ARCHITECTURE

The elliptical **Aussie Stadium**, or Sydney Football Stadium, (1985–8) and the **Australian National Maritime Museum** (1986–9), both by Philip Cox, make use of advanced steel engineering systems. Detailed masonry has made a return to commercial buildings such as the highly regarded **Governor Phillip Tower** (1989–94). The dictates of office design do not detract from the historical Museum of Sydney, ingeniously sited on the lower floors.

The **ABN-AMRO Tower** at Aurora Place (2000) was designed by Renzo Piano and was awarded the Sulman Prize for Architecture in 2004.

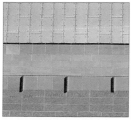

Masonry detail from the contemporary Governor Phillip Tower

Sydney's Many Cultures

Sydney has one of the world's most cosmopolitan societies, reflected in the extraordinary variety of restaurants, religions, community centres and cultural activities to be found throughout the city and its environs. Over 235 birthplaces outside Australia were named in the last census. Indeed, the Sydney telephone directory lists interpreting services for 22 languages, including Greek, Italian, Spanish, Chinese, Vietnamese, Turkish, Korean and Arabic, and many of these groups have their own newspapers. While immigrants have settled all over the city, there are still pockets of Sydney that retain a distinctive ethnic flavour.

Thai Community
Thai culinary traditions have caused a revolution in Sydney eating houses. The Loy Krathong Festival in Parramatta celebrates the transplanted Thai culture.

Thailand

Turkey

Auburn Mosque
This lavish mosque rises above the thriving Turkish businesses nearby. Halal meat markets and sweet shops are proof of their influence.

Cambodia

Cambodian
Cabramatta is the hub of the Cambodian community. Songkran, the three-day new year celebration is held at Bonnyrigg.

Vietnam

Filipinos
Over 60 per cent of this rapidly expanding migrant group arrive as the brides of Australian men.

Philippines

Lebanon

Vietnamese
This sculpture of a cow stands in Cabramatta's Freedom Plaza, an area offering all the sights, smells and street life of Southeast Asia.

Lakemba
A living monument to Islam, the fastest growing religion in Australia, this centre is a meeting place for local Lebanese people.

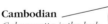
0 kilometres   4

0 miles   2

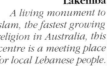

Irish Parade
Sydney's first settlers, many of them Irish, made their home in The Rocks. With its proliferation of pubs, it is the focal point for jubilant St Patrick's Day celebrations on 17 March each year.

Little Italy
Long home to the Italian community, Leichhardt evokes the flavour of Europe with its bars, cafés, restaurants and a sprawling annual street fair.

Jewish Delicatessen
The sizeable Jewish community in the city's eastern suburbs, about half of whom were born in Australia, is well served by kosher supermarkets and butchers' shops.

Ireland

Italy

China

Israel

Greece

Indigenous
Australia

Aboriginal Peoples
Redfern Park hosts a Survival concert every 26 January, the culmination of a week of cultural exchange.

St Nicholas Church
Marrickville's Greek Orthodox church is the home of worship for the community, mostly based in the southern suburbs.

Chinese New Year
Each year, revellers pack Dixon Street, at the heart of Chinatown, to celebrate with fireworks and Chinese dragons.

Sydney's Best: Parks and Reserves

Sydney is almost completely surrounded by national parks and intact bushland. There are also a number of national parks and reserves within Greater Sydney itself. Here, the visitor can gain some idea of how the landscape looked before the arrival of European settlers. The city parks, too, are filled with plant and animal life. The more formal plantings of both native and exotic species are countered by the indigenous birds and animals that have adapted and made the urban environment their home. One of the highlights of a trip to Sydney is the huge variety of birds to be seen, from large birds of prey such as sea eagles and kites, to the shyer species such as wrens and tiny finches.

Flannel flower

Garigal National Park
Rainforest and moist gullies provide shelter for superb lyrebirds and sugar gliders.

North Arm Walk
In spring, grevilleas and flannel flowers bloom profusely on this foreshore walk.

Lane Cove National Park
The open eucalypt forest is dotted with grass trees, as well as fine stands of red and blue gums. The rosella, a type of parrot, is common.

Bicentennial Park
Situated at Homebush Bay on the Parramatta River, the park features a mangrove habitat. It attracts many water birds, including pelicans.

Hyde Park
Situated on the edge of the city centre, the park provides a peaceful respite from the hectic streets. The native iris is just one of the plants found in the lush gardens. The sacred ibis, a water bird, is often seen.

Middle Head and Obelisk Bay

Gun emplacements, tunnels and bunkers built in the 1870s to protect Sydney from invasion by sea dot the area. The superb fairy wren lives here and water dragons can at times be seen basking on rocks.

North Head

Coastal heathland, with banksias, tea trees and casuarinas, dominates the cliff tops. On the leeward side, moist forest surrounds tiny harbour beaches.

Grotto Point

Bottlebrushes, grevilleas and flannel flowers line paths winding through the bush to the lighthouse.

Bradleys Head

The headland is a nesting place for the ringtail possum. Noisy flocks of rainbow lorikeets are also often in residence.

South Head

Unique plant species such as the sundew cover this heathland.

Nielsen Park

The kookaburra is easily identified by its call, which sounds like laughter.

The Domain

Palms and Moreton Bay figs are a feature of this former common. The Australian magpie, with its black and white plumage, is a frequent visitor.

Moore Park

Huge Moreton Bay figs provide an urban habitat for the flying fox.

Centennial Park

Open expanses and groves of paperbark and eucalypt trees bring sulphur-crested cockatoos en masse. The brushtail possum is a shy creature that comes out at night.

0 kilometres 4

0 miles 2

Exploring the Parks and Reserves

Despite 200 years of European settlement, Sydney's parks and reserves contain a surprising variety of native wildlife. Approximately 2,000 species of native plants, 1,000 cultivated and weed species and 300 bird species have managed to adapt favourably to the changes.

Several quite distinct vegetation types are protected in the bushland around Sydney, and these in turn provide shelter for a wide range of birds and animals. Even the more formal parks such as Hyde Park and the Royal Botanic Gardens are home to many indigenous species, allowing the visitor a glimpse of the city's diverse wildlife.

Colourful and noisy rainbow lorikeets at Manly's Collins Beach

COASTAL HINTERLAND

One reason Sydney has so many heathland parks, such as those found at South Head and North Head, is that the soil along the city's coastline is deficient in almost every known nutrient. What these areas lack in fertility, they make up for in species diversity.

Heathland contains literally hundreds of species of plants, including some unique flora that have adapted to the poor soil. The most surprising ones are the carnivorous plants, which rely on passing insects for their food. The tiny sundew *(Drosera spatulata)*, so called because of its sparkling foliage, is the commonest of the carnivorous species. This low-growing plant snares insects on its sticky, reddish leaves, which lie flat on the ground. You will often stumble across them where walking tracks pass through swampy ground, waiting patiently for a victim.

Red bottlebrush (Callistemon sp.)

Two other distinctive plants are casuarinas *(Allocasuarina species)* and banksias *(Banksia species)*, both of which attract smaller birds such as honey-eaters and blue wrens.

RAINFOREST AND MOIST FOREST

Rainforest remnants do exist in a few parts of Sydney, especially in the Royal National Park to the south of the city *(see pp164–5)*. Small pockets can also be found in Garigal National Park, Ku-ring-gai Chase *(see pp154–5)* and some gullies running down to Middle Harbour. The superb lyrebird *(Menura novaehollandiae)* is a feature of these forest areas. The sugar glider *(Petaurus breviceps)*, a small species of possum, can sometimes be heard calling to its mate during the night.

The deadliest spider in the world, the Sydney funnel-web *(Atrax robustus, see p89)*, also lives here, but you are unlikely to see one unless you poke under rocks and logs. A common plant in this habitat is the cabbage tree palm *(Livistona australis)*. Its heart was used as a vegetable by the early European settlers.

The soft tree fern *(Dicksonia antartctica)* decorates the gullies and creeks of moist forest. You may see a ringtail possum *(Pseudocheirus peregrinus)* nest at the top of one of these ferns at Bradleys Head. The nest looks rather like a hairy football and is found in hollow trees or ferns and shrubs.

Rainbow lorikeets *(Trichoglossus haematodus)* also inhabit Bradleys Head, as well as Clifton Gardens and Collins Beach. Early in the morning, they shoot through the forest canopy like iridescent bullets.

OPEN EUCALYPT FOREST

Some of Sydney's finest smooth-barked apple gums *(Angophora costata)* are in the Lane Cove National Park. These ancient trees, with their gnarled pinkish trunks, lend an almost "lost world" feeling.

Tall and straight blue gums *(Eucalyptus saligna)* stand in the lower reaches of the park, where the soil is better, while the smaller grey-white scribbly gum *(Eucalyptus rossii)*, with its distinctive gum veins, lives on higher slopes. If you examine the markings on a scribbly gum closely, you will see they start out thin, gradually become thicker, then take a U-turn and stop. This is the track made by an *ogmograptis* caterpillar the previous year. The grubs that made the track

Coastal heathland lining the cliff tops at Manly's North Head

become small, brownish-grey moths and are commonly seen in eucalypt or gum forests.

Grass trees *(Xanthorrhoea* species), also common in open eucalypt forest, are an ancient plant species with a tall spike that bears white flowers in spring. Lyrebirds, echidnas, currawongs and black snakes are predominant wildlife. The snakes, although beautiful, should be treated with caution.

A smooth-barked apple gum in Lane Cove National Park

WETLANDS

More than 60 per cent of New South Wales' coastal wetlands have been lost. This makes the remaining areas of wetland especially important. Most of Sydney's wetlands are mangrove swamps, with some of the best-preserved examples at Bicentennial Park and the North Arm Walking Track.

Mangrove swamps are one of the most hostile places for a plant or animal to live. There

A grey mangrove swamp near the Lane Cove National Park

is no fresh water and, unlike soil, the mud has no oxygen whatsoever below the very surface level. Mangroves have developed some fascinating ways around these problems.

First, excess salt is excreted from their leaves. Secondly, they get oxygen to the roots by pushing special peg-like roots, called pneumatophores, into the air. At low tide, these can be clearly seen around the base of most mangroves. They allow air to diffuse down into the roots so that they can survive the stifling conditions under the mud. The Sydney rock oyster *(Saccostrea commercialis)*, a popular local delicacy, is found in mangrove areas, particularly around the Hawkesbury and Botany Bay.

CITY PARKS

An amazing number of birds and animals make the city parks their home. Silver gulls *(Larus novaehollandiae)* and sulphur-crested cockatoos *(Cacatua galerita)* are frequent daytime visitors to Hyde Park, Centennial Park, The Domain and the Botanic Gardens.

After dark, brush-tailed possums *(Trichosurus vulpecula)* go in search of food and may be seen scavenging in rubbish bins. Also a night creature, the fruit-eating grey-headed flying fox *(Pteropus poliocephalus)* can be seen swooping through the trees. There is sometimes

The nocturnal grey-headed flying fox, at rest during the daytime

a temporary colony of these marsupials in the Botanic Gardens, where they hang upside down from trees in the park. Most of Sydney's flying foxes come from a large colony in Gordon, in the city's north.

Moore Park and The Domain are good places to spot flying foxes and they also have wonderful specimens of Moreton Bay and other fig species.

While paperbarks *(Melaleuca* species) are a feature of Centennial Park, a range of palms can be seen in the Botanic Gardens. The exquisite superb fairy-wren *(Malurus cyaneus)* can also be seen here, flitting between shrubs, while overhead honeyeaters dart after each other in the tree canopy.

STRANGLER FIGS

The majestic figs in the city parks hide a dark secret. While most of the Moreton Bay figs *(Ficus macrophylla)* you see have been grown by gardeners long past, in the wild these trees have a different approach. They start as a tiny seedling, sprouted from a seed dropped by a bird in the fork of a tree. Over decades, the pencil-thin roots grow downwards. Once they reach the ground, new roots are sent down, forming a lacy network around the trunk of the host tree. They eventually become an iron-hard cage around the host tree's trunk so that it dies and rots away, leaving the fig with a hollow trunk.

The Moreton Bay fig, with its massive spreading canopy

SYDNEY THROUGH THE YEAR

Sydney's temperate climate allows for the enjoyment of outdoor activities throughout the year. Seasons in Sydney are the opposite of those in the northern hemisphere. September ushers in the three months of spring; summer stretches from December to February; March, April and May are the autumn months; while the shorter days and falling temperatures of June announce the onset of winter. In reality, however, Sydney seasons often merge into one another with little to mark their changeover. Balmy nights, the sweet, pervasive scent of jasmine blossom and the colourful blooming of shrubs and flowers are typical of spring. Summer caters for sun- and surf-lovers as well as being Sydney's festival season. Autumn, with its warm days and cooler nights, is often perfect for bushwalks and picnics. And the crisp days of winter are ideal for going on historic walks and exploring art galleries and museums.

Reveller at the Mardi Gras

SPRING

With the warmer weather, the profusion of spring flowers brings the city's parks and gardens excitingly to life. Food, art and music festivals abound. Footballers finish their seasons with action-packed grand finals, professional and backyard cricketers warm up for their summer competitions and the horse-racing fraternity gets ready to place its bets.

SEPTEMBER

Spring display of tulip beds at the Leura Garden Festival

David Jones Spring Flower Show *(first two weeks)*, Elizabeth Street department store. Breathtaking floral artwork fills the ground floor.
Festival of the Winds *(dates vary)*, Bondi Beach *(see p137)*. Multicultural kite-flying festival; music, dance.
Primavera *(Sep–mid-Nov)*. Highly regarded talent-spotting show at the Museum of Contemporary Art *(see p73)*.
Sydney in Bloom *(dates vary)*, The Domain. Display gardens, with street entertainers,

sculpture exhibits and food stalls *(see pp104–5)*.
Spring Racing Carnival *(Sep --Oct)*. The horse-racing action is shared between Rosehill racecourse and the Royal Randwick racecourse.
Australian Rugby League Grand Final, Stadium Australia, Homebush.
New South Wales Rugby Union Grand Final, Sydney Football Stadium *(see p52)*.
Fiesta *(late Sep–early Oct)*, Darling Harbour *(see pp92–3)*. Fiestas, parades and festivals from all nations, including music, arts, dance, puppets and fireworks.

OCTOBER

Manly International Jazz Festival *(Labour Day weekend)*. World-class jazz at a variety of venues *(see p133)*.
Leura Garden Festival *(early Oct)*, Blue Mountains *(see pp160–61)*. A village fair launches the festival, when

magnificent private gardens featuring flower displays of a particularly high standard may be viewed.
Australian International Motor Show *(third week Oct)*, Sydney Convention and Exhibition Centre, Darling Harbour *(see p92)*.

NOVEMBER

Melbourne Cup Day *(first Tue)*. The city almost grinds to a halt mid-afternoon to tune in to Australia's most popular horse race. Restaurants and hotels offer special luncheons on the day.
Sculpture by the Sea *(early Nov)*, Bondi Beach. Hugely popular outdoor exhibition of fantastic sculptures on the path between Bondi and Tamarama beaches.
Sydney to the Gong Bicycle Ride *(first Sun)*. From Moore Park to Wollongong. Over 10,000 cyclists of all standards do this 92-km (57-mile) ride.

Sacred ibis stilt-dancer at the Sydney in Bloom festival

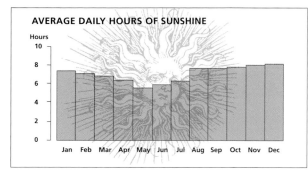

AVERAGE DAILY HOURS OF SUNSHINE

Hours
10

8

6

4

2

0

Jan Feb Mar Apr May Jun Jul Aug Sep Oct Nov Dec

Sunshine Hours

A sunny climate is one of Sydney's main attractions. There are very few days with no sunshine at all, even in the middle of winter. An up-to-date weather forecast is available by telephoning 1196. Coastal weather conditions can be obtained by dialling 11541.

SUMMER

Sydney turns festive in the summer months. Christmas pageants and open-air carol singing in The Domain mark the start of the season. Then there is the Sydney Festival, a month of cultural events and other popular entertainment, culminating in Australia Day celebrations on 26 January. Summer, too, brings a feast for sport lovers, with surfing and lifesaving events, yacht races and a host of local and international cricket matches.

"Santa Claus" at the surf: Christmas Day celebrations on Bondi Beach

DECEMBER

Carols in The Domain *(Sat before Christmas)*. Carols by candlelight in the parkland of the city's favourite outdoor gathering spot *(see p107)*.
Christmas at Bondi Beach *(25 Dec)*. Holidaymakers hold their own unofficial party on this famous beach *(see p137)*.
Sydney to Hobart Yacht Race *(26 Dec)*. The harbour teems with small craft as they escort racing yachts out to sea for the start of their journey.
New Year's Eve *(31 Dec)*. Street parties in The Rocks and Circular Quay and fireworks displays on Sydney Harbour.

JANUARY

Opera in the Domain *(throughout Jan)*, The Domain *(see p107)*. A free performance of highlights from productions by Opera Australia.
Cricket Test matches and one-day internationals held at Sydney Cricket Ground *(see p52)*.
Flickerfest *(early–mid-Jan)*, Bondi Pavilion *(see pp144–5)*. Festival of Australian and international short films and animation.
Symphony under the Stars *(throughout Jan)*, The Domain *(see p107)*. Free concert performed by the Sydney Symphony Orchestra.
Ferrython *(26 Jan)*, Sydney Harbour. Ferries compete fiercely for line honours, as do rigged competitors in the Tall Ships Race held on the same day.
Australia Day Concert *(26 Jan)*. Concerts take place all over the city.
Big Day Out *(usually 26 Jan)*, Olympic Park, Homebush.

Chinese New Year lion

Outdoor concert attracting huge crowds and hip acts.
Chinese New Year *(late Jan or early Feb)*. Lion dancing, firecrackers and other New Year festivities take place in Chinatown *(see p99)*, Darling Harbour and Cabramatta *(p42)*.
Festival of Sydney *(first week–end Jan)*. Fantastic music, theatre, sport and art events.

FEBRUARY

New Mardi Gras Festival, various inner-city venues *(see pp30–31)*. A month of events culminating in a flamboyant street parade, mainly on Oxford Street, usually held early March.
Tropfest *(third Sun)*, Darlinghurst and The Domain. Hugely popular short film festival.
North Bondi Classic Ocean Swim *(first Sun)*, North Bondi *(see p137)*. A 2-km (1½-mile) race. Any swimmer can enter.
Coogee Surf Carnival *(Sat in early Feb)*, Coogee *(see p55)*.

Australia Day Tall Ships race in Sydney Harbour

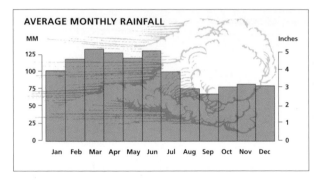

AVERAGE MONTHLY RAINFALL

MM / Inches

125 / 5
100 / 4
75 / 3
50 / 2
25 / 1
0 / 0

Jan Feb Mar Apr May Jun Jul Aug Sep Oct Nov Dec

Rainfall
Autumn is Sydney's rainiest season, with March being the wettest month, while spring is the driest time of year. Rainfall, however, can often be unpredictable. Long stretches of sunny weather are common, but so, too, are periods of unrelenting rain.

AUTUMN

After the humidity of the summer, autumn brings fresh mornings and cooler days that are tailor-made for outdoor pursuits. There are many sporting and cultural events – some of them colourful and eccentric – to tempt the visitor. For many, the Royal Easter Show is the highlight of the season. Anzac Day (25 April) is a national holiday on which Australians commemorate their war dead.

MARCH

Dragon Boat Races Festival *(late Feb–early Mar)*, Darling Harbour *(see pp92–3)*. Brilliantly decorated Chinese dragon boats race across Cockle Bay.
St Patrick's Day Parade *(17 Mar, or closest Sun)*. Hyde Park *(see pp86–7)* to The Domain. Pubs serve green beer on the day.
Sydney Harbour Week *(early*

St Patrick's
Day beer

Mar). A programme of more than 40 events, many free, including swimming, sailing, snorkelling, heritage tours and the Sydney Harbour Regatta.
Autumn Racing Carnival *(six weeks during Mar and Apr)*. Top-class races and big prize money, at Rosehill and Royal Randwick racecourses.

EASTER

Sydney Royal Easter Show *(one week before Good Friday)*, Olympic Park. Homebush. Country meets city in 12 days of ring events, livestock and produce judging, woodchopping competitions, sheepdog trials, arts and crafts displays and sideshow alley attractions.
Darling Harbour Hoopla *(Easter school hols)*, Darling Harbour *(see pp92–3)*. Circus acts and street theatre by magicians, acrobats, mime and other artists.

Woodchopping at the Easter Show

APRIL

National Trust Heritage Week *(dates vary)*. Celebration of the natural, architectural and cultural heritage of Sydney.
Archibald, Wynne and Sulman exhibitions *(until end of May)*, Art Gallery of NSW *(pp108–11)*. Annual exhibition of that year's entries in the portraiture, landscape, genre works and drawing competitions.
Anzac Day *(25 Apr)*. Dawn remembrance service held at the Cenotaph, Martin Place *(see p84)*, with a parade by war veterans along George Street.

MAY

Sydney Writers' Festival *(dates vary)*, State Library of New South Wales *(see p112)*.
Bridge to Bridge Power Boat Classic *(first Sun)*. Race from Brooklyn Bridge to Upper Hawkesbury Power Boat Club, Windsor *(see pp156–7)*.
Sydney Half Marathon *(fourth Sun)*, from Pier One, The Rocks. A 21-km (13-mile) run open to all standards.

Traditional decorative dragon boats on Darling Harbour's Cockle Bay

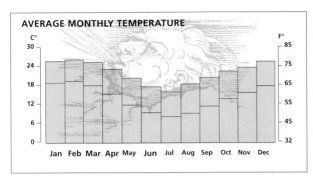

AVERAGE MONTHLY TEMPERATURE

Jan Feb Mar Apr May Jun Jul Aug Sep Oct Nov Dec

Temperature
This chart gives the average minimum and maximum temperatures for Sydney. Spring and autumn are generally free of extremes, but be prepared for sudden cold snaps in winter and occasional bursts of oppressive humid heat in summer.

WINTER

Winter in Sydney can be cold enough to require warm jackets; temperatures at night may drop dramatically away from the coast. The days are often clear and sometimes surprisingly mild. Arts are a major feature of winter. There are lots of exhibitions and the Sydney Film Festival, which no film buff will want to miss.

JUNE

A Taste of Manly *(first weekend)*, Manly Beach *(see p133)*. Annual food and wine festival.
Home Computer Show *(fours days over the long weekend)*, Convention and Exhibition Centre, Darling Harbour *(see p98)*. The very latest in personal computer software, hardware and entertainment.
Darling Harbour Jazz Festival *(Queen's Birthday weekend)*, Darling Harbour *(see pp92–3)*. Constantly changing line-up of jazz, blues, country, gospel and world music bands and performers.
Sydney Film Festival *(two weeks mid-Jun)*, State Theatre *(see p82)*. The latest short and feature films, as well as retrospectives and showcases.
Australian Book Fair *(dates vary)*, Convention Centre, Darling Harbour *(see p98)*. Australian book publishers' trade fair. Open to the public on the weekend, with author appearances, book discussion panels and lots of lively entertainment for children.

The familiar logo of the Film Festival

Australian soldiers or "Diggers" at an Anzac Day ceremony

JULY

Biennale of Sydney *(two months, mid-year)*, various venues. International festival, held in even-numbered years, encompassing many forms of visual art, from painting and installations to photography and performance art.
Yulefest *(throughout winter)*, Blue Mountains *(see pp160– 61)*. Hotels, guesthouses and some restaurants celebrate a midwinter "Christmas" with log fires and all the Yuletide trimmings.
Sydney International Boat Show *(late Jul)*, Convention and Exhibition Centre, Darling Harbour *(see p98)*.
NAIDOC (National Aboriginal and Torres Strait Islander) Week *(dates vary)*. Week-long celebrations to build awareness and understanding of Aboriginal culture and history.

PUBLIC HOLIDAYS

New Year's Day (1 Jan)
Australia Day (26 Jan)
Good Friday (variable)
Easter Monday (variable)
Anzac Day (25 Apr)
Queen's Birthday (second Mon in Jun)
Bank Holiday (first Mon in Aug: only banks and some financial institutions are closed)
Labour Day (first Mon in Oct)
Christmas Day (25 Dec)
Boxing Day (26 Dec)

AUGUST

City to Surf Race *(second Sun)*. From the city to Bondi Beach *(see p137)*. A 14-km (9-mile) community event that attracts all types, from amateurs to leading marathon runners.
Japan Festival *(dates vary)*, various venues. Ikebana, tea ceremonies, sports and music, with visiting acts of all kinds.

Runners in the City to Surf Race, surging down William Street

SPORTING SYDNEY

Throughout Australia sport is a way of life and Sydney is no exception. On any day you'll see locals on golf courses at dawn, running on the streets keeping fit, or having a quick set of tennis after work. At weekends, during summer and winter, there is no end to the variety of sports you can watch. Thousands gather at the Aussie Stadium (Sydney Football Stadium) and Sydney Cricket Ground every weekend while, for those who cannot make it, sport reigns supreme on weekend television.

CRICKET

During the summer months Test cricket and one-day internationals are played at the Sydney Cricket Ground (SCG). Tickets for weekday sessions of the Tests can often be bought at the gate, although it is advisable to book well in advance (through **Ticketek**) for weekend sessions of Test matches and for all the one-day international matches.

RUGBY LEAGUE AND RUGBY UNION

The popularity of rugby league knows no bounds in Sydney. This is what people are referring to when they talk about "the footie". There are three major competition levels: local, State of Origin – which matches Queensland against New South Wales – and Tests. The "local" competition fields teams from all over Sydney as well as Newcastle, Canberra, Brisbane, Perth, the Gold Coast and Far North Queensland.

These matches are held all over Sydney, although the Aussie Stadium is by far the biggest venue. Tickets for State of Origin and Test

Australia versus the All Blacks, SFS

matches often sell out as soon as they go on sale. Call Ticketek to check availability.

Rugby union is the second most popular football code. Again, matches at Test level sell out very quickly. For some premium trans-Tasman rivalry, catch a Test match between Australia's "Wallabies" and the New Zealand "All Blacks" at the Sydney Football Stadium. Phone Ticketek for details.

GOLF AND TENNIS

Golf enthusiasts need not do without their round of golf. There are many courses throughout Sydney where visitors are welcome at all times. These include **Moore Park**,

St Michael's and Warringah golf courses. It is sensible to phone beforehand for a booking, especially at weekends.

Tennis is another favoured sport. Courts available for hire can be found all over Sydney. Many centres also have floodlit courts available for night time. Try **Cooper Park** or **Parkland Sports** Centre.

Playing golf at Moore Park, one of Sydney's public courses

AUSTRALIAN RULES FOOTBALL

Although not as popular as in Melbourne, "Aussie Rules" has a strong following in Sydney. The local team, the Sydney Swans, plays its home games at the Sydney Cricket Ground during the season. Check a local paper for details.

Rivalry between the Sydney supporters and their Melbourne counterparts is always strong. Busloads of diehard fans from the south arrive to cheer on their teams. Tickets can usually be bought at the ground on the day of the game.

BASKETBALL

Basketball has grown in popularity as both a spectator and recreational sport in recent years. Sydney has male and female teams competing in the National Basketball League. The games, held at the Sydney Entertainment

One-day cricket match between Australia and the West Indies, SCG

Aerial view of the Aussie Stadium at Moore Park

Centre, Haymarket, have much of the pizzazz, colour and excitement of American basketball. Tickets can be purchased from Ticketek, on the phone or on the internet.

CYCLING AND INLINE SKATING

Sydney boasts excellent, safe locations for the whole fam-ily to go cycling. One of the most frequented is Centennial Park *(see p127)*. You can hire bicycles and safety helmets from **Centennial Park Cycles**.

Another popular pastime in summer is inline skating. **Total Skate**, located opposite Centennial Park, hires skates, and protective gear by the hour and offers tuition. **Rollerblading.com.au** runs tours starting at Milsons Point to all parts of Sydney. If you're unsteady, they also do group and private lessons.

For those who like to keep both feet firmly on the ground, you can watch skateboarders and inline skaters practising their moves at the ramps at Bondi Beach *(see p137)*.

Inline skaters enjoying a summer evening on the city's streets

HORSE RIDING

For a leisurely ride, head to Centennial Park or contact the **Centennial Parklands Equestrian Centre**. They will give you details of the four rid-ing schools that operate in the park. **Samarai Park Riding School** conducts trail rides through Ku-ring-gai Chase National Park *(see pp154-5)*.

Further afield, you can enjoy the magnificent scenery of the Blue Mountains *(see pp160-61)* on horseback. The **Megalong Australian Heritage Centre** has rides lasting from one hour to an overnight ride. All levels of experience are catered for.

Horse riding in one of the parks surrounding the city centre

ADVENTURE SPORTS

You can participate in guided bushwalking, mountain biking, canyoning, rock climbing and abseiling expe-ditions in the nearby Blue Mountains National Park. The **Blue Mountains Adventure Company** runs one-day or multi-day courses and trips for all standards of adventurer.

In the centre of Sydney, **BridgeClimb** offers a 3½-hour guided climb to the summit of Sydney Harbour Bridge.

DIRECTORY

Blue Mountains Adventure Company
84a Bathurst Rd, Katoomba.
Tel 4782 1271.

BridgeClimb
5 Cumberland St,
The Rocks, Sydney.
Tel 8274 7777.
www.bridgeclimb.com.

Centennial Park Cycles
50 Clovelly Rd, Randwick.
Tel 9398 5027.

Centennial Parklands Equestrian Centre
Cnr Lang & Cook Rds, Moore Park. **Map** 5 D5.
Tel 9332 2809.

Cooper Park Tennis Courts
Off Suttie Rd, Double Bay.
Tel 9389 9259.

Megalong Australian Heritage Centre
Megalong Valley Rd, Megalong Valley. *Tel 4787 8188.*

Moore Park Golf Club
Cnr Cleveland St & Anzac Parade, Moore Park. **Map** 5 B5.
Tel 9663 1064.

Parkland Sports
Cnr Anzac Parade & Lang Rd, Moore Park.
Tel 9662 7033.

Rollerblading.com.au
Tel 0411 872 022.

St Michael's Golf Club
Jennifer St, Little Bay.
Tel 9311 0621.

Samarai Park Riding School
90 Booralie Rd, Terrey Hills.
Tel 9450 1745.

Ticketek
Tel 132849.
www.ticketek.com.au

Total Skate
36 Oxford St, Woollahra.
Map 6 D4. *Tel 9380 6356.*

Warringah Golf Club
397 Condamine St, North Manly.
Tel 9905 4028.

Sydney's Beaches

Being a city built around the water, it is no wonder that many of Sydney's recreational activities involve the sand, sea and sun. There are many harbour and surf beaches throughout Sydney, most of them accessible by bus *(see p231)*. Even if you're not a swimmer, the beaches offer a chance to get away from it all for a day or weekend and enjoy the fresh air and relaxed way of life.

Scuba diving at Gordons Bay

SWIMMING

Harbour beaches such as Camp Cove, Shark Bay and Balmoral Beach are generally smaller and more sheltered than the ocean beaches. The latter have surf lifesavers in distinctive red and yellow caps. Surf lifesaving carnivals are held throughout summer. Call **Surf Life Saving NSW** for a calendar of events. District councils also provide their own lifeguards, who wear blue uniforms. Rules about swimming are rigorously enforced, so try to familiarize yourself with beach signage.

The beaches can sometimes become polluted, especially after heavy rainfall. The **Beach Watch Info Line** gives information about pollution levels.

SURFING

Surfing is more a way of life than a leisure activity for some Sydneysiders. If you're a beginner, try Bondi, Bronte, Palm Beach or Collaroy.

Two of the best surf beaches are Maroubra and Narrabeen. Bear in mind that local surfers know one another well and do not take kindly to "intruders" who drop in on their waves

or leave litter on their beaches. To hire a surfboard, try Bondi Surf Co on Campbell Parade, Bondi Beach, or Aloha Surf on Pittwater Road, Manly. If you would like to learn, there are two schools: **Manly Surf School** and **Lets Go Surfing** at Bondi Beach. They also hire out boards and wetsuits.

WINDSURFING AND SAILING

There are locations around Sydney suitable for every level of windsurfer. Boards can be hired from **Balmoral Windsurfing and Kitesurfing School**. Good spots include Palm Beach, Narrabeen Lakes, La Perouse, Brighton-Le-Sands and Kurnell Point (for beginner and intermediate boarders) and Long Reef Beach, Palm Beach and Collaroy (for the more experienced windsurfer).

One of the best ways to see the harbour is while sailing. A sailing boat, including a skipper, can be hired for the afternoon from the **East Sail** sailing club. If you'd like to learn how to sail, the sailing club has two-day courses and also hires out sailing boats and motor cruisers to experienced sailors.

SCUBA DIVING

There are some excellent dive spots around Sydney, especially in winter when the water is clear, if a little cold. More favoured spots are Gordons Bay, Shelly Beach, and Camp Cove.

Pro Dive Coogee offers a complete range of courses, escorted dives, introductory dives for beginners, and hire equipment. **Dive Centre Manly** also runs courses and introductory dives, hires equipment and conducts boat dives seven days a week.

DIRECTORY

Balmoral Windsurfing and Kitesurfing School
Balmoral Sailing Club, Balmoral Beach. *Tel 9960 5344.*
www.sailboard.net.au

Beach Watch Info Line
Tel 1800 036 677.

Dive Centre Manly
10 Belgrave St, Manly. *Tel 9977 4355.* www.divesydney.com
Also at Bondi and City.

East Sail
d'Albora Marinas, New Beach Rd, Rushcutters Bay. *Tel 9327 1166.*
www.eastsail.com.au

Lets Go Surfing
128 Ramsgate Ave North Bondi. *Tel 9365 1800.*
www.letsgosurfing.com.au

Manly Surf School
North Steyne Rd, Manly. *Tel 9977 6977.*
www.manlysurfschool.com

Pro Dive Coogee
27 Alfreda St, Coogee. *Tel 9665 6333.*

Surf Life Saving NSW
Tel 9984 7188.

Rock baths and surf lifesaving club at Coogee Beach

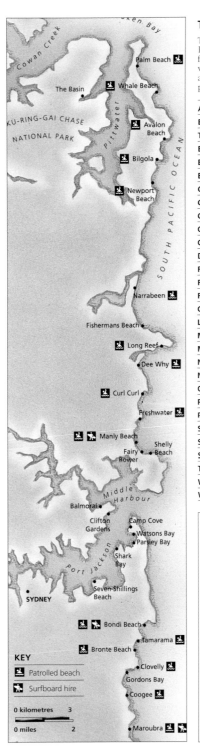

TOP 30 BEACHES

The beaches shown here have been selected for their safe swimming, water sports, facilities available or their picturesque setting.

	SWIMMING POOL	SURFING	WINDSURFING	FISHING	SCUBA DIVING	PICNIC/BARBECUE	RESTAURANT/CAFE
Avalon	●	●	●	●		●	
Balmoral	●		●	●		●	●
The Basin	●					●	
Bilgola							
Bondi Beach	●	●			●	●	●
Bronte	●	●		●		●	●
Camp Cove					●		
Clifton Gardens	●		●		●	●	
Clovelly					●	●	●
Coogee	●		●		●	●	●
Curl Curl	●	●		●			
Dee Why	●	●		●		●	●
Fairy Bower					●		
Fishermans Beach		●	●	●			
Freshwater	●	●				●	●
Gordons Bay					●	●	
Long Reef		●	●	●	●		
Manly Beach	●	●				●	●
Maroubra		●	●	●		●	
Narrabeen	●	●		●		●	
Newport Beach	●	●	●	●		●	
Obelisk Bay (naturist)							
Palm Beach	●	●	●	●		●	
Parsley Bay						●	
Seven Shillings Beach	●						
Shark Bay	●					●	●
Shelly Beach					●	●	●
Tamarama		●					●
Watsons Bay	●				●		●
Whale Beach	●	●	●	●		●	●

THE TYPES OF WAVES

Cresting waves *can be identified by the foam that is created as they break from the top. These waves are ideal for board riding and body surfing.*

Plunging waves *curl into a tube before breaking close to the shore. Fondly known as "dumpers", these waves should only be tackled by experienced surfers.*

Surging waves *are those that don't appear to break. They often travel all the way into the beach before breaking and can easily sweep a toddler or child off its feet.*

KEY

🏊 Patrolled beach

🏄 Surfboard hire

0 kilometres   3

0 miles   2

Garden Island to Farm Cove

Waterlily in the Royal
Botanic Gardens

Sydney's vast harbour, also named
Port Jackson after a Secretary in the
British Admiralty who promptly
changed his name, is a drowned
river valley which was transformed
over millions of years. Its intricate
coastal geography of headlands and
secluded bays can sometimes confound even life-
long residents. This waterway was the lifeblood of
the early colony, with the maritime industry a vital
source of wealth and supply. The legacies of alter-
nate recessions and booms can be viewed along the
shoreline: a representative story in a nation where an
estimated 70 per cent of the population cling to the
coastal cities, especially along the eastern seaboard.

The city skyline *is a result of random
development. The 1960s indiscrimin-
ate destruction of architectural history
was halted, and towers now stand
amid Victorian buildings.*

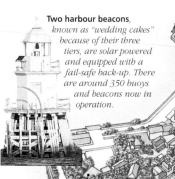

Two harbour beacons,
*known as "wedding cakes"
because of their three
tiers, are solar powered
and equipped with a
fail-safe back-up. There
are around 350 buoys
and beacons now in
operation.*

The barracks for
the naval garrison
date from 1888.

Garden Island
marks a 1940s con-
struction project
with 12 ha (30
acres) reclaimed
from the harbour.

Sailing on the harbour *is a pastime not
exclusively reserved for the rich and elite. Of
the several hundred thousand pleasure boats
registered, some are available for hire while
others take out groups of inexperienced sailors.*

Mrs Macquaries Chair *is a carved rock seat by
Mrs Macquaries Road (see p106). In the early
days of the colony, this was the site of a fruit and
vegetable garden which was farmed until 1805.*

| 0 metres | 250 |
| 0 yards | 250 |

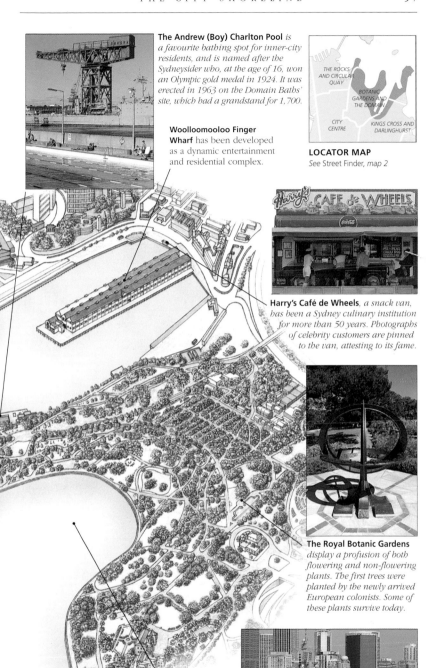

The Andrew (Boy) Charlton Pool *is a favourite bathing spot for inner-city residents, and is named after the Sydneysider who, at the age of 16, won an Olympic gold medal in 1924. It was erected in 1963 on the Domain Baths' site, which had a grandstand for 1,700.*

Woolloomooloo Finger Wharf has been developed as a dynamic entertainment and residential complex.

LOCATOR MAP
See Street Finder, map 2

THE ROCKS AND CIRCULAR QUAY

BOTANIC GARDENS AND THE DOMAIN

CITY CENTRE

KINGS CROSS AND DARLINGHURST

Harry's Café de Wheels, *a snack van, has been a Sydney culinary institution for more than 50 years. Photographs of celebrity customers are pinned to the van, attesting to its fame.*

The Royal Botanic Gardens *display a profusion of both flowering and non-flowering plants. The first trees were planted by the newly arrived European colonists. Some of these plants survive today.*

Farm Cove *has long been a mooring place for visiting naval vessels. The land opposite, now the Botanic Gardens, has been continuously cultivated for over 200 years.*

Sydney Cove to Walsh Bay

It is estimated that over 70 km (43 miles) of harbour foreshore have been lost as a result of the massive land reclamation projects carried out since the 1840s. That the 13 islands existing when the First Fleet arrived in 1788 have now been reduced to just eight is a startling indication of rapid and profound geographical transformation.

Detail from railing at Circular Quay

Redevelopments around the Circular Quay and Walsh Bay area from the 1980s have opened up the waterfront for public use and enjoyment, acknowledging it as the city's greatest natural asset. Sydney's environmental and architectural aspirations recognize the need to integrate city and harbour.

Conservatorium of Music

1857 Man O'War Steps

The Sydney Opera House *was designed to take advantage of its spectacular setting. The roofs shine during the day and seem to glow at night. The building can appear as a visionary landscape to the pedestrian onlooker.*

Government House, a Gothic Revival building, was home to the state's governors until 1996.

Harbour cruises *regularly depart from Circular Quay, taking visitors out and about both during the day and in the evening. They are an incomparable way to see the city and its waterways.*

The Sydney Harbour Bridge *was also known as the "Iron Lung" at the time of its construction. During the Great Depression it provided on-site work for approximately 1,400, while many more were employed in the specialist workshops.*

| 0 metres | 250 |
| 0 yards | 250 |

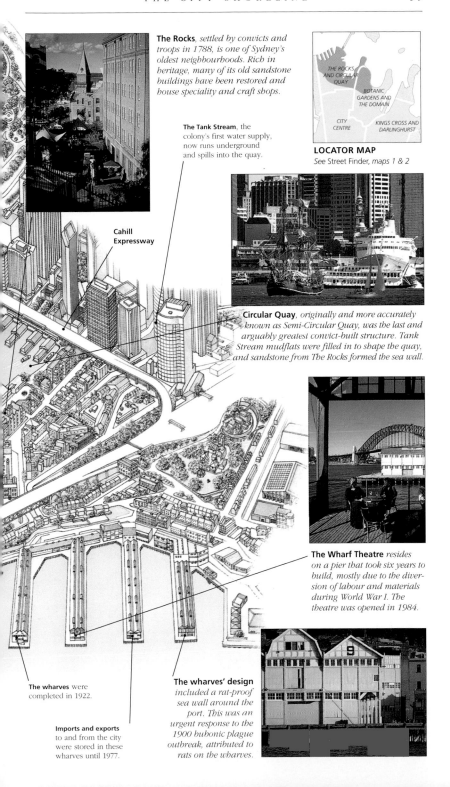

The Rocks, *settled by convicts and troops in 1788, is one of Sydney's oldest neighbourhoods. Rich in heritage, many of its old sandstone buildings have been restored and house speciality and craft shops.*

The Tank Stream, the colony's first water supply, now runs underground and spills into the quay.

LOCATOR MAP
See Street Finder, maps 1 & 2

THE ROCKS AND CIRCULAR QUAY

BOTANIC GARDENS AND THE DOMAIN

CITY CENTRE

KINGS CROSS AND DARLINGHURST

Cahill Expressway

Circular Quay, *originally and more accurately known as Semi-Circular Quay, was the last and arguably greatest convict-built structure. Tank Stream mudflats were filled in to shape the quay, and sandstone from The Rocks formed the sea wall.*

The Wharf Theatre *resides on a pier that took six years to build, mostly due to the diversion of labour and materials during World War I. The theatre was opened in 1984.*

The wharves were completed in 1922.

Imports and exports to and from the city were stored in these wharves until 1977.

The wharves' design *included a rat-proof sea wall around the port. This was an urgent response to the 1900 bubonic plague outbreak, attributed to rats on the wharves.*

SYDNEY AREA
BY AREA

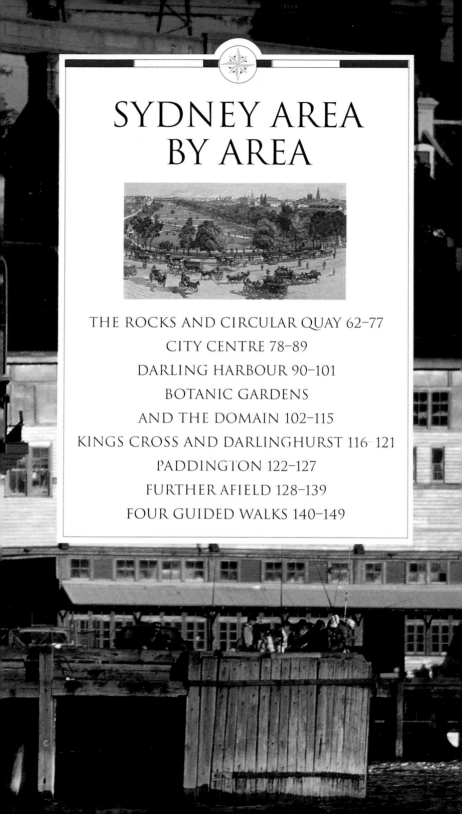

THE ROCKS AND CIRCULAR QUAY

Circular Quay, once known as Semi-Circular Quay, is often referred to as the "birth-place of Australia". It was here, in January 1788, that the First Fleet landed its human freight of convicts, soldiers and offi-cials, and the new British colony of New South Wales was declared. Sydney Cove became a rallying point whenever a ship arrived bringing much-needed supplies from "home". Crowds still gather here whenever there is some-thing to celebrate. The Quay and The

Sculpture on the AMP Building, Circular Quay

Rocks are focal points for New Year's Eve revels, and Circular Quay drew huge crowds when, in 1994, Syd-ney was awarded the year 2000 Olympic Games. The Rocks area offers visitors a taste of Sydney's past, but it is a far cry from the time, less than 100 years ago, when most inhabitants lived in rat-infested slums and gangs ruled its streets. Now scrubbed and polished, The Rocks forms part of the colourful promenade from the Sydney Harbour Bridge to the spectacular Opera House.

SIGHTS AT A GLANCE

Historic Streets and Buildings
Campbell's Storehouses **1**
George Street **2**
Cadman's Cottage **6**
Argyle Stores **8**
Sydney Observatory **10**
Hero of Waterloo **11**
Sydney Harbour Bridge pp70–71 **13**
Writers' Walk **15**

Customs House **17**
Macquarie Place **18**

Churches
Garrison Church **9**
St Philip's Church **21**

Theatres and Concert Halls
Wharf Theatre **12**
Sydney Opera House pp74–7 **14**

Museums and Galleries
The Rocks Discovery Museum **3**
Susannah Place **4**
Sailors' Home **5**
Westpac Museum **7**
Justice and Police Museum **16**
Museum of Contemporary Art **19**
National Trust Centre **20**

GETTING THERE
Circular Quay is the best stop for ferries and trains. Sydney Explorer and bus routes 431, 432, 433 and 434 run regularly to The Rocks, while most buses through the city go to the Quay.

KEY

Street-by-Street map
See pp64–5

CityRail station

Bus terminus

Ferry boarding point

JetCat/RiverCat boarding point

Railway line

0 metres 500
0 yards 500

◁ **The brilliant white walls of the Sailors' Home, parts of which date back to 1864**

Street-by-Street: The Rocks

Governor Arthur Phillip

Named for the rugged cliffs that were once its dominant feature, this area has played a vital role in Sydney's development. In 1788, the First Fleeters under Governor Phillip's command erected makeshift buildings here, with the convicts' hard labour used to establish more permanent structures in the form of rough-hewn streets. The Argyle Cut, a road carved through solid rock using just hammer and chisel, took 18 years to build, beginning in 1843. By 1900, The Rocks was overrun with disease; the street now known as Suez Canal was once Sewer's Canal. Today, the area is still rich in colonial history and colour.

Hero of Waterloo
Lying beneath this historic pub is a tunnel originally used for smuggling ⓫

★ Sydney Observatory
The first European structure on this prominent site was a windmill. The present museum holds some of the earliest astronomical instruments brought to Australia ⓾

Garrison Church
Columns in this church are decorated with the insignia of British troops stationed here until 1870. Australia's first prime minister was educated next door ⓽

★ Museum of Contemporary Art
The stripped Classical façade belies the avant-garde nature of the Australian and international art displayed in an ever-changing programme ⓳

Argyle Cut

Suez Canal

Walkway along Circular Quay West foreshore

The Rocks Discovery Museum
Key episodes in The Rocks' history are illustrated by this museum's collection of maritime images and other artefacts ❸

LOCATOR MAP
See Street Finder, map 1

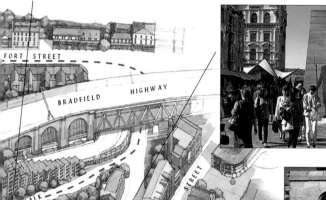

The Rocks Market
is a hive of activity every weekend, offering an eclectic range of craft items and jewellery utilizing Australian icons from gum leaves to koalas.

★ Cadman's Cottage
John Cadman, government coxswain, resided in what was known as the Coxswain's Barracks with his family. His wife Elizabeth was also a significant figure, believed to be the first woman to vote in New South Wales, a right she insisted on ❻

0 metres		100
0 yards		100

KEY

– – – Suggested route

STAR SIGHTS

★ Cadman's Cottage

★ Museum of Contemporary Art

★ Sydney Observatory

The Overseas Passenger Terminal
is where some of the world's luxury cruise liners, including the QEII, berth during their stay in Sydney.

Campbell's Storehouses ❶

7–27 Circular Quay West, The Rocks.
Map 1 B2. 🚌 *Sydney Explorer, 431,
432, 433, 434.* 📷 ♿

In 1798, the Scottish
merchant Robert Campbell
sailed into Sydney Cove and
soon established himself as a
founding father of commerce
for the new colony. With
trade links already established
in Calcutta, his business
blossomed. In 1839, Campbell
began constructing a private
wharf and stores to house the
tea, sugar, spirits and cloth he
imported from India. Twelve
sandstone bays had been
built by 1861 and a brick
upper storey was added in
about 1890. Part of the old
sea wall and 11 of the original
stores still remain. The area
soon took on the name of
Campbell's Cove, which it
retains to this day.

Today the bond stores
contain several harbourside
restaurants catering for a range
of tastes, from contemporary
to Chinese and Italian. It is a
delightful area in which to
relax with a meal and watch
the bustling boats in the
harbour go by. The pulleys
that were used to raise cargo
from the wharf can still be
seen on the outside, near the
top of the building.

George Street ❷

Map 1 B2. 🚌 *Sydney Explorer, 431,
432, 433, 434.*

Formerly the preserve of
wealthy merchants, sailors
and the city's working class,
George Street today is a
popular attraction with visitors
to Sydney, who are drawn to
its restaurants, art galleries,
museums, jewellery stores
and craft souvenir shops. For
one-stop memento and gift
shopping it is ideal, with little
of the mass-produced and
tacky, but a great deal in the
way of modern Australian
craft of a very high calibre,
with many unique pieces.

One of Sydney's original
thoroughfares – some say
Australia's first street – it ran
from the main water supply,
the Tank Stream, to the tiny
community in the Rocks, and
was known as Spring Street.
In 1810 it was renamed in
honour of George III. George
Street today runs all the way
from the Harbour Bridge to
the Central Railway Station
north of Chinatown.

Many 19th-century buildings
remain, such as the 1844
Counting House at No. 43,
the Old Police station at No.
127 (1882), and the Russell
Hotel at No. 143 (1887).

But it is The Rocks end that
most reflects what the early
colony must have looked like,
characterized by cobbled pave-
ments, narrow side streets,
warehouses, bond stores, pubs
and shop fronts that reflect the
area's maritime history. Even
the Museum of Contemporary
Art *(see p73)*, constructed
during the 1950s, began its life
as the Maritime Services
Board's administration offices.

In the early 1970s union
workers placed "green bans"
on the demolition of The
Rocks *(see p31)*. These streets
had been considered slum
areas by the government of
the day. However many of
the buildings in George Street
were restored and are now
listed by the National Trust.
The Rocks remains a vibrant
part of the city, with George
Street at its hub. A market is
held here every weekend,
when part of the street is
closed off to traffic *(see p203)*.

The Rocks Discovery Museum ❸

2–6 Kendall Lane, The Rocks. **Map** 1
B2. **Tel** 9251 9793. 🚆 *Circular
Quay.* 🚌 *Sydney Explorer, 431, 432,
433, 434.* ⏰ *10am–5:30pm daily.*

This museum, scheduled to
open in 2006, is in a restored
1850s coach house, and has

Umbrellas shade the terrace restaurants overlooking the waterfront at Campbell's Storehouses

Old-style Australian products at the corner shop, Susannah Place

Sailors' Home ❺

106 George St, The Rocks. **Map** 1 B2. *Tel* 9255 1788. 📟 *Sydney Explorer, 339, 340, 431, 432, 433, 434.* ⬤ *9am–6pm daily.* ⬤ *25 Dec.* 📷 ♿

Built in 1864 as lodgings for visiting sailors, the building is now used as an exhibition centre. The L-shaped wing that fronts onto George Street was added in 1926.

At the time it was built, the Sailors' Home was a welcome alternative to the many seedy inns and brothels in the area, saving sailors from the perils of "crimping". "Crimps" would tempt newly arrived men into lodgings and bars providing much-sought-after entertainment. While drunk, the sailors would be sold on to departing ships, waking miles out at sea and returning home in debt.

Sailors used the home until 1980, when it was adapted for use as a puppet theatre. From 1994 until 2005 it was used as a heritage centre and a tourist information and tour-booking facility.

Permanent exhibitions on the first and second levels outline the archaeological, architectural and social heritage of The Rocks. The third level hosts temporary exhibitions. On the same level, at the eastern end, a re-creation of a 19th-century sleeping cubicle gives visitors a good impression of the spartan nature of the original accommodation available to sailors.

exhibitions on the history of The Rocks, including displays on its first inhabitants, the Cadigal people, and Sydney's maritime history and traditions in the 18th and 19th centuries.

A unique collection of archaeological artifacts and historical images dating from the early establishment of the European colony to the postwar era helps visitors explore the eventful and colourful history of this neighbourhood. The displays are enhanced by interactive high-tech touch screens and audiovisual exhibits.

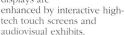

Billy Tea on sale at the Susannah Place shop

Susannah Place ❹

58–64 Gloucester St, The Rocks. **Map** 1 B2. *Tel* 9241 1893. 🚆 *Circular Quay, Wynyard.* 📟 *Sydney Explorer, 431, 432, 433, 434.* ⬤ *Jan: 10am– 5pm daily; Feb–Dec: 10am– 5pm Sat & Sun.* ⬤ *Good Fri, 25 Dec.* 📷 📷 🎥

This 1844 terrace of four brick and sandstone houses has a rare history of continuous domestic occupancy from the 1840s right through to 1990. The museum now housed here examines this working-class domestic history, evoking the living conditions of its inhabitants. Rather than re-creating a single period, the museum retains the many renovations made by successive tenants.

Built for Edward and Mary Riley, who arrived from Ireland with their niece Susannah in 1838, these solid houses have basement kitchens and backyard outhouses. Connections to piped water and sewerage had probably arrived by the mid-1850s. The museum surveys the houses' development over the years, from wood and coal to gas and electricity, which enables the visitor to gauge the gradual lightening of the burden of domestic labour.

The terrace, including a corner grocer's shop, escaped the wholesale demolitions that occurred after the outbreak of bubonic plague in 1900, as well as later clearings of land to make way for the Sydney Harbour Bridge and the Cahill Expressway. In the 1970s, it was saved once again when the Builders Labourers' Federation, under the leadership of activist Jack Mundey, imposed a conservation "green ban" on The Rocks (*see p31*), temporarily halting all demolition and redevelopment work.

Interior of the Sailors' Home, looking down to the shop

Façade of Cadman's Cottage, the oldest extant building in the city

Cadman's Cottage **6**

110 George St, The Rocks. **Map** 1
B2. *Tel* 9247 5033. ▣ *431, 432, 433
434.* ◯ *9:30am–4:30pm Mon–Fri;
10am–4:30pm Sat & Sun.* ◉ *Good
Fri, 25 Dec.* ◙

Dwarfed by the adjacent
Sailors' Home, of which it was
once part, this sandstone
cottage serves as the information centre for the Sydney
Harbour National Park and has
information about guided
harbour tours. Built in 1816 as
a barracks for the crews of the
governor's boats, it is Sydney's
oldest surviving dwelling.

The cottage is named after
John Cadman, a convict who
was transported in 1798 for
horse-stealing. By 1813, he was
coxswain of a timber boat and
the following year received an
unconditional pardon. In 1821,
he was granted a full pardon.
Six years later, he was made
boat superintendent of government craft and took up residence in the four-room cottage
that now bears his name.

Cadman married Elizabeth
Mortimer in 1830. She had also
arrived in Sydney as a convict,
sentenced to seven years transportation for the theft of one
hairbrush. The couple, along
with Elizabeth's two daughters,
lived in the cottage until 1846.

When Cadman's Cottage was
built it stood on the foreshore
of Sydney Harbour. At high
tide, the water used to lap just
2.5 m (8 ft) from the door.

Now, as a result of successive
land reclamations such as the
filling-in of Circular Quay in
the 1870s, it is set well back
from the waterfront.

Westpac Museum **7**

6–8 Playfair St, The Rocks.
Map 1 B2. *Tel* 9763 5670. ▣
Sydney Explorer, 431, 432, 433, 434.
◯ *10am–4pm Mon–Thu, 9am–5pm
Fri.* ◉ *public hols.*

From 1817, when the "holey"
dollar was in circulation and
Sydney's first bank opened, to
present-day plastic credit cards,
this museum, located on the
first floor, traces the history
of banking in Australia. It also
covers the Olympic history in
1956 and 2000 as Westpac
was a sponsor of both of
these games. There is a self-
guided tour with interactive
and holographic displays but
this small museum can be
seen in less than an hour.

Argyle Stores **8**

18–24 Argyle St, The Rocks.
Map 1 B2. ▣ *Sydney Explorer, 431,
432, 433, 434.* ◯ *10am–6pm daily.*
◉ *Good Fri, 25 Dec.* ◙ ♿

The Argyle Stores consists of
a number of warehouses
around a cobbled courtyard.
They have been converted
into a retail complex of
mostly fashion and
accessories shops that retains
its period character.

Built between 1826 and the
early 1880s, the stores held
imported goods such as spirits.
All goods forfeited for the
non-payment of duties were
auctioned in the courtyard.
The oldest store was built for
Captain John Piper, but it was
confiscated and sold after his
arrest for embezzlement.

Argyle Centre from the courtyard

Garrison Church **9**

Cnr Argyle and Lower Fort Sts, Millers
Point. **Map** 1 A2. *Tel* 9247 1268.
▣ *431, 433.* ◯ *9am–6pm daily.*
◙ ♿

Officially named the Holy
Trinity Church, this was
dubbed the Garrison Church
because it was the colony's
first military church. Officers
and men from various British

Bank of New South Wales one pound note from around 1830

regiments, stationed at Dawes Point fort, attended morning prayers here until 1870.

Henry Ginn designed the church and, in 1840, the foundation stone was laid. In 1855, the architect Edmund Blacket was engaged to enlarge the church to accommodate up to 600 people. These extensions, minus the spire that Blacket proposed, were completed in 1878. Regimental plaques hung along interior walls recall the church's military associations.

Other features to look out for are the brilliantly coloured east window and the carved red cedar pulpit. The window was donated by a devout parishioner, Dr James Mitchell, scion of a leading Sydney family. The church also houses a museum displaying early Australian military and historical items.

East window, Garrison Church

Sydney Observatory ❿

Watson Rd, Observatory Hill, The Rocks. **Map** 1 A2. *Tel* 9241 3767. 🚌 *Sydney Explorer, 343, 431, 432.* ⏲ *10am–5pm daily.* **Night viewings** *Call to book.* ⬤ *25 Dec.* 📷 ♿ ✔ **www.**sydneyobservatory.com.au

In 1982, this domed building, which had been a centre for astronomical observation and research for almost 125 years, became the city's astronomy museum. It has interactive equipment and games, along with night sky viewings; it is essential to book for these.

The building began life in the 1850s as a time-ball tower. At 1pm daily, the ball on top of the tower dropped to signal the correct time. A cannon was fired simultaneously at Fort Denison. This custom continues today *(see p107)*.

In the 1880s, some of the first astronomical photographs of the southern sky were taken here. From 1890–1962, the observatory mapped 750,000 stars as part of an international project that produced an atlas of the entire night sky.

Hero of Waterloo ⓫

81 Lower Fort St, The Rocks. **Map** 1 A2. *Tel* 9252 4553. 🚌 *431, 432, 433, 434.* ⏲ *10am–11pm Mon–Wed, 10am–11:30pm Thu–Sat, 10am–10pm Sun.* ⬤ *Good Fri, 25 Dec.* 📷 ♿ *ground floor only*

This picturesque old inn is welcoming in the winter, when its log fires and cosy ambience offer respite from the chill outside. Built in 1844 from sandstone excavated from the Argyle Cut, this was a favourite drinking place for the nearby garrison's soldiers. Unscrupulous sea captains were said to use the hotel to recruit. Patrons who drank themselves into a stupor were pushed into the cellars through a trapdoor. From here they were carried along underground tunnels to the wharves nearby and onto waiting ships.

The corner façade of the Hero of Waterloo hotel in Millers Point

Wharf Theatre ⓬

Pier 4, Hickson Rd, Walsh Bay. **Map** 1 A1. *Tel* 9250 1700. 🚌 *430, 431, 432, 433, 434.* **Box office** *Tel 9250 1777.* ⏲ *9am–8:30pm Mon–Sat;* 📷 ♿ *phone in advance. See* **Entertainment** *p210.*

The then recently formed Sydney Theatre Company took possession of this early 20th-century finger wharf at Walsh Bay in 1984. Pier 4/5 is

one of four finger wharves at Walsh Bay, reminders of the time when this was a busy part of the city's maritime industry.

Pier 4/5 fulfilled the Sydney Theatre Company's need for a base large enough to hold theatres, rehearsal rooms and administration offices. The ingenious conversion of the once-derelict heritage building into a modern theatre complex is recognized as an outstanding architectural achievement.

Since then, the main theatre, a small and intimate space, has been a venue for many of the company's productions. It has seen premieres of plays from leading Australian playwrights such as Michael Gow and David Williamson, as well as performances of new works from overseas and plays from the standard repertoire.

At the tip of the wharf, the bar area and Wharf Restaurant *(see p185)* command superb harbour views across to the Harbour Bridge *(see pp70–71)*.

The Wharf Theatre, a former finger wharf, jutting on to Walsh Bay

Sydney Harbour Bridge ⑬

Completed in 1932, the construction of the Sydney Harbour Bridge was an economic feat, given the depressed times, as well as an engineering triumph. Prior to this, the only links between the city centre on the south side of the harbour and the residential north side were by ferry or a circuitous 20-km (12½-mile) road route with five bridge crossings. Known as the "Coathanger", the single-span arch bridge was manufactured in sections and took eight years to build, including the railway line. Loans for the total cost of approximately 6.25 million Australian pounds were paid off in 1988. Intrepid visitors can make the vertiginous climb to its summit, with spectacular views as reward.

Ceremonial scissors

The 1932 Opening
The ceremony was disrupted when zealous royalist Francis de Groot rode forward and cut the ribbon, in honour, he claimed, of King and Empire.

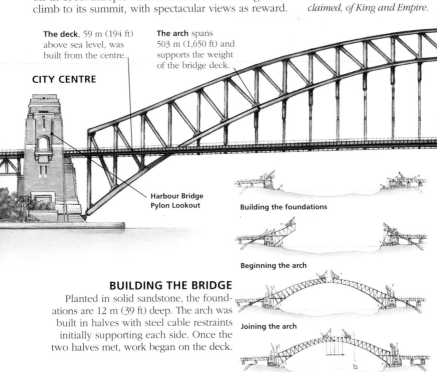

The deck, 59 m (194 ft) above sea level, was built from the centre.

The arch spans 503 m (1,650 ft) and supports the weight of the bridge deck.

CITY CENTRE

Harbour Bridge Pylon Lookout

Building the foundations

Beginning the arch

BUILDING THE BRIDGE

Planted in solid sandstone, the foundations are 12 m (39 ft) deep. The arch was built in halves with steel cable restraints initially supporting each side. Once the two halves met, work began on the deck.

Joining the arch

Deck under construction

Anchoring tunnels are 36 m (118 ft) long and dug into rock at each end.

Support cables were slackened over a 12-day period, enabling the two halves to join.

Temporary attachment plate

The Bridge Design

The steel arch of the bridge supports the deck, with hinges at either end bearing the bridge's full weight and spreading the load to the foundations. The hinges allow the structure to move as the steel expands and contracts in response to wind and extreme temperatures.

BridgeClimb
Thousands of people have enjoyed the spectacular bridge-top views after a 3.5-hour guided tour up ladders, catwalks and finally the upper arch of the bridge (see p53).

Over 150,000 vehicles cross the bridge each day, about 15 times as many as in 1932.

Bridge Workers
The bridge was built by 1,400 workers, 16 of whom were killed in accidents during construction.

NORTH SHORE

Maintenance
Painting the bridge has become a metaphor for an endless task. Approximately 30,000 litres (6,593 gal) of paint are required for each coat, enough to cover an area equivalent to 60 soccer pitches.

The vertical hangers support the slanting crossbeams which, in turn, carry the deck.

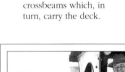

FATHER OF THE BRIDGE
Chief engineer Dr John Bradfield shakes the hand of the driver of the first train to cross the bridge. Over a 20-year period, Bradfield supervised all aspects of the bridge's design and construction At the opening ceremony, the highway linking the harbour's south side and northern suburbs was named in his honour.

Paying the Toll
The initial toll of sixpence helped pay off the construction loan. The toll is now used for maintenance and to pay for the 1992 Sydney Harbour Tunnel.

Strolling along a section of the Writers' Walk at Circular Quay

Sydney Opera House ⑭

See pp74–7.

Writers' Walk ⑮

Circular Quay. **Map** 1 C2.
🚌 Circular Quay routes.

This series of plaques is set in the pavement at regular intervals between East and West Circular Quay. It gives the visitor the chance to ponder the observations of famous Australian writers, both past and present, on their home country, as well as the musings of some noted literary visitors.

Each plaque is dedicated to a particular writer, with a quotation and a brief biographical note. Australian writers include novelists Miles Franklin and Peter Carey, poets Oodgeroo Noonuccal and Judith Wright, humorists Barry Humphries and Clive James, and the influential feminist writer Germaine Greer. Among visiting writers are Charles Darwin, Joseph Conrad and Mark Twain.

Justice and Police Museum ⑯

Cnr Albert & Phillip sts. **Map** 1 C3.
Tel 9252 1144. 🚌 Circular Quay routes. 🕙 10am–5pm Sat–Sun (daily in January). 🌑 Good Fri, 25 Dec.
📷 🎥 📷 ♿ restricted.

The museum's buildings were originally the Water Police Court, designed by Edmund Blacket in 1856; Water Police

Station, designed by Alexander Dawson in 1858; and Police Court designed by James Barnet in 1885. Here the rough-and-tumble underworld of quayside crime, from the petty to the violent, was dealt swift and, at times, harsh justice. The museum exhibits bear vivid testimony to that turbulent period, as they document and re-create legal and criminal history. Late-Victorian legal proceedings can be easily imagined in the fully restored courtroom.

Menacing implements from knuckledusters to bludgeons are displayed as the macabre relics of violent and notorious crimes. Other aspects of policing and justice are highlighted in regularly changing exhibitions. The bushranger exhibit, prison artefacts, and forensic display powerfully evoke the realities of the justice system in Australia.

Montage of criminal "mug shots", Justice and Police Museum

Customs House ⑰

31 Alfred St, Circular Quay. **Map** 1 B3.
Tel 9242 8595. 🚌 Circular Quay routes. 🕙 8am–7pm Mon–Fri, 10am–4pm Sat, noon–4pm Sun. 🌑 25 Dec, Good Fri. 📷 🖥 🍴 ♿

Colonial architect James Barnet designed this 1885 sandstone Classical Revival building on the site of an earlier Customs House. It recalls the days when trading ships loaded and unloaded their goods at the quay. Features include columns in polished granite, a sculpted coat of arms and a clock face, added in 1897, bearing a pair of tridents and dolphins.

Customs House reopened in 2005 after major refurbishment. Facilities include a City Library with a reading room and exhibition space, and an open lounge area with an international newspaper and magazine salon, internet access and bar. On the roof, Café Sydney offers great views.

Detail from Customs House

Macquarie Place ⑱

Map 1 B3. 🚌 Circular Quay routes.

In 1810, governor Lachlan Macquarie created this park on what was once part of the vegetable garden of the first Government House. The sandstone obelisk, designed by convict architect Francis Greenway (see p114), was erected in 1818 to mark the starting point for all roads in the colony. The gas lamps recall the fact that this was also the site of Sydney's first street lamp, installed in 1826.

Also in this little triangle of history are the remains of the bow anchor and cannon from HMS Sirius, flagship of the First Fleet. There is also a statue of Thomas Mort, a 19th-century industrialist whose vast business interests embraced gold, coal and copper mining, dairy and cotton farming, wool auctioning and ship repair. These days his statue is a marshalling place for the city's somewhat kamikaze bicycle couriers.

Façade of the Museum of Contemporary Art

Museum of Contemporary Art ⑲

Circular Quay West, The Rocks.
Map 1 B2. *Tel* 9245 2400. Sydney Explorer, 431, 432, 433 434. 10am–5pm daily. 25 Dec. book in advance. **www**.mca.com.au

Sydney's substantial collection of contemporary art has grown steadily, but largely out of public view, since 1943. This was the year John Power died, leaving his art collection and a financial bequest to the University of Sydney.

In 1991 the permanent collection, including works by Hockney, Warhol, Lichtenstein and Christo, was transferred to this 1950s Art Deco-style former Maritime Services Board Building. The museum also hosts temporary exhibitions of works by both Australian and International artists

At the front of the building the MCA Café *(see p195)* spills out onto a terrace with superb views across to the Sydney Opera House. The MCA Store sells distinctive gifts by Australian designers.

National Trust Centre ⑳

Observatory Hill, Watson Rd, The Rocks.
Map 1 A3. *Tel* 9258 0123. Sydney Explorer, 343, 431, 432, 433, 434. 9am–5pm Tue–Fri. **Gallery** 11am–5pm Tue–Sun. public hols.

The buildings that form the headquarters of the conservation organization, the National Trust of Australia, date from 1815, when Macquarie chose the site on Observatory Hill for a military hospital.

Today they house a café, a National Trust shop and the SH Ervin Gallery, containing works by prominent 19th- and 20th-century Australian artists such as Thea Proctor, Margaret Preston and Conrad Martens.

St Philip's Church ㉑

3 York St (enter from Jamison St).
Map 1 A3. *Tel* 9247 1071. George St routes. 9am–5pm Tue–Fri. 26 Jan. 1pm Wed, 8am, 10am, 6:15pm Sun.

Despite its elevated site, this Victorian Gothic church seems overshadowed in its modern setting. Yet, when it was first built, the tall square tower with its decorative pinnacles was a local landmark.

Begun in 1848, St Philip's is by Edmund Blacket, dubbed "the Christopher Wren of Australia" for the 58 churches he designed. In 1851, work was disrupted when its stonemasons left for the gold fields, but was completed by 1856.

A peal of bells was donated in 1858, with another added in 1888 to mark Sydney's centenary. These bells still announce the services each Sunday.

The interior and pipe organ of St Philip's Anglican church

The Founding of Australia by Algernon Talmage, which hangs in Parliament House *(see pp112–13)*

A FLAGPOLE ON THE MUDFLATS

It is easy to miss the modest flagpole in Loftus Street near Customs House. It flies a flag, the Union Jack, on the spot where Australia's first ceremonial flag-raising took place. On 26 January 1788, Captain Arthur Phillip came ashore to hoist the flag and declare the foundation of the colony. A toast to the King was drunk and a musket volley fired. On the same day, the rest of the First Fleet arrived from Botany Bay to join Phillip and his men. (On this date each year, the country marks Australia Day with a national holiday.) In 1788, the flagpole was on the edge of mudflats on Sydney Cove. Today, because of the large amount of land reclaimed to build Circular Quay, it is some distance from the water's edge.

Sydney Opera House ⑭

No building on earth looks like the Sydney Opera House. Popularly known as the "Opera House" long before the building was complete, it is, in fact, a complex of theatres and halls linked beneath its famous shells. Its birth was long and complicated. Many of the construction problems had not been faced before, resulting in an architectural adventure which lasted 14 years *(see p77)*. An appeal fund was set up, eventually raising $900,000, while the Opera House Lottery raised the balance of the $102 million final cost. As well as being the city's most popular tourist attraction, the Sydney Opera House is also one of the world's busiest performing arts centres.

★ Opera Theatre
Mainly used for opera and ballet, this 1,507-seat theatre is big enough to stage grand operas such as Verdi's Aida.

The Opera Theatre ceiling and walls are painted black to focus attention on the stage.

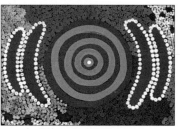

Detail of The Possum Dreaming *(1988)*
The mural in the Opera Theatre foyer is by Michael Tjakamarra Nelson, an artist from the central Australian desert.

Opera House Walkway
Extensive public walkways around the building offer the visitor views from many different vantage points.

Northern Foyers
With spectacular views over the harbour, the Reception Hall and the large northern foyers of the Opera Theatre and Concert Hall can be hired for conferences, lunches, parties and weddings.

STAR FEATURES

★ The Roofs

★ Concert Hall

★ Opera Theatre

★ **Concert Hall**
This is the largest hall, with seating for 2,679. It is used for symphony, choral, jazz, folk and pop concerts, chamber music, opera, dance and everything from body building to fashion parades.

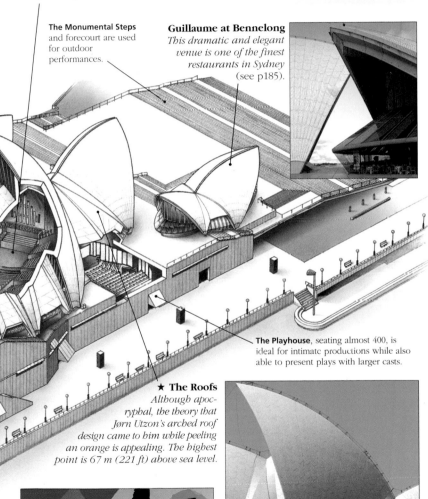

The Monumental Steps and forecourt are used for outdoor performances.

Guillaume at Bennelong
This dramatic and elegant venue is one of the finest restaurants in Sydney (see p185).

The Playhouse, seating almost 400, is ideal for intimate productions while also able to present plays with larger casts.

★ **The Roofs**
Although apocryphal, the theory that Jørn Utzon's arched roof design came to him while peeling an orange is appealing. The highest point is 67 m (221 ft) above sea level.

Detail of Utzon's Tapestry *(2004)*
Jørn Utzon's original design for this Gobelin-style tapestry, which hangs floor to ceiling in the remodelled Reception Hall, was inspired by the music of Carl Philipp Emanuel Bach.

Exploring Sydney Opera House

The Sydney Opera House covers almost 2 ha (4.5 acres), and is the fourth building to stand on this prominent site. Underneath the ten spectacular roofs of varying planes and textures lies a complex maze of more than 1,000 rooms of all shapes and sizes. It is constantly evolving: the newest space is The Studio, dedicated to innovative, contemporary performing arts.

Carl Vine
Choreography & set projection

GRAEME MURPHY

DRAMA THEATRE
SYDNEY OPERA HOUSE
JUNE 30 - JULY 8

Sydney Dance Company poster

Coppelia in the Opera Theatre

OPERA THEATRE

The relatively compact size of this venue is a bonus for patrons who savour intimacy. Stage designers continue to demonstrate the opera theatre's great versatility for both opera and dance. The proscenium opening is 12 m (39 ft) wide, and the stage extends back 25 m (82 ft), while the orchestra pit accommodates up to 70–80 musicians. It is rumoured that Box C plays host to a resident ghost.

CONCERT HALL

The rich concert acoustics under the vaulted ceiling of this venue are much admired. Sumptuous Australian wood panelling and the 18 acoustic rings above the stage clearly reflect back the sound. The 10,500 pipe Grand Organ was designed and built by Ronald Sharp from 1969–79.

DRAMA THEATRE AND PLAYHOUSE

The Drama Theatre was not in the original building plan, so jackhammers were brought in to hack it out of the concrete. Its stage is 15 m (160 ft) square, and can be clearly viewed from every seat in the auditorium. Refrigerated aluminium panels in the ceiling control the temperature.

The Playhouse is used for small cast plays, lectures and seminars, and is also a fully-equipped cinema. The Sydney Theatre Company (see p69) puts on at least one performance here every year.

BACKSTAGE

Artists performing at the Opera House have the use of five rehearsal studios, 60 dressing rooms and suites and a green room complete with restaurant, bar and lounge.

The scene-changing machinery works on very well-oiled wheels; most crucial in the Opera Theatre where there is regularly a nightly change of performance, with an average of 14 operas being performed in repertoire each year.

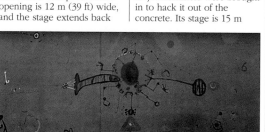

John Olsen's Salute to Five Bells (1973) in the Concert Hall foyer

TIMELINE

Roof in mid-construction

Old tram shed at Bennelong Point

1945	1950	1955	1960	1965	1970

1955 International design competition announced

1948 Sir Eugene Goossens lobbies government and Bennelong Point is chosen as opera house site

1957 Utzon's design wins and a lottery is established to finance the building

1963 Building of roof shells begins

1973 Opera House officially opened by Queen Elizabeth II

1959 Construction begins

1963 Utzon opens Sydney office

1966 Utzon resigns. Australian architects appointed to complete interior design

1967 Concrete roof shells completed

1973 Prokofiev's opera War and Peace is the first public performance in Opera House

The Design of the Opera House

In 1957, Jørn Utzon won the international competition to design the Sydney Opera House. He envisaged a living sculpture that could be viewed from any angle – land, air or sea – with the roofs as a "fifth façade". It was boldly conceived, posing architectural and engineering problems that Utzon's initial compendium of sketches did not begin to solve. When

Jørn Utzon

construction began in 1959, the intricate design proved impossible to execute and had to be greatly modified. The project remained so controversial that Utzon resigned in 1966 and an Australian design team completed the building's interior. In 1999 Sydney Opera House was delighted when Utzon agreed to be involved in guiding future changes to the building.

The Red Book, *as submitted for the 1957 design competition, contains Utzon's original concept sketches for the Sydney Opera House.*

Segmented globe　　**Segments separated**

Roof comes into view

Several pieces *cut out of a globe were used in an ingenious manner by architect Jørn Utzon to make up the now familiar shell roof structure.*

UTZON'S OPERA HOUSE MODEL

Shell membrane roof

The northern foyers overlook Sydney Harbour.

Utzon visualized a building that "floated" on water.

The construction materials remain clearly exposed.

Stepped base

Utzon's original interiors *and many of his design features now exist only in model form. The architect donated his models and plans to the State Library of NSW (see p112).*

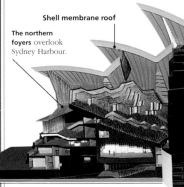

The pre-cast roof *has its inspiration in nature. The basic idea for the formwork of the roof was taken from the fanlike ribs of a palm. Realizing this deceptively simple idea took Utzon six years of design work.*

The roof tiles *were not fixed in place individually, but installed in panels to create the smooth and continuous roof surface.*

CITY CENTRE

Australia's first thorough-fare, George Street, was originally lined with clusters of mud and wattle huts. The gold rushes brought bustling prosperity, and by the 1880s shops and the archi-tecturally majestic edifices of banks dominated the area. The city's first skyscraper – Culwulla Chambers in Castlereagh Street – was completed in 1913, but the city council then imposed a 46-m (150-ft) height restriction which remained in place until 1956. Hyde Park, on the edge of the city centre, was first used as a race-

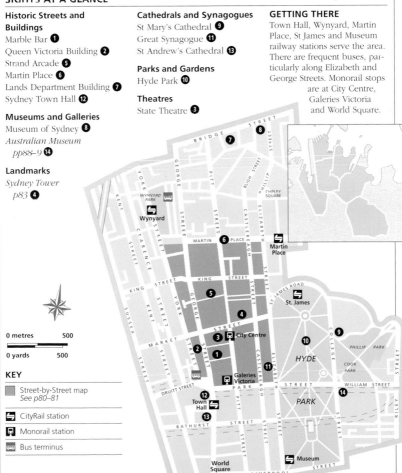

Mosaic floor detail, St Mary's Cathedral

course, attracting illegal betting and gambling taverns to Eliza-beth Street. The park later hosted other amusements: wrestling matches, circuses, public hangings and, from 1804 onwards, cricket matches between the army and the town. Today it provides a peaceful oasis, while the city's commercial centre is an area of glamorous boutiques, department stores, arcades and malls. Various exercise needs are also catered for: the Cook & Phillip Park Centre in College Street is a great pool and gym complex.

SIGHTS AT A GLANCE

Historic Streets and Buildings
Marble Bar **1**
Queen Victoria Building **2**
Strand Arcade **5**
Martin Place **6**
Lands Department Building **7**
Sydney Town Hall **12**

Museums and Galleries
Museum of Sydney **8**
Australian Museum pp88–9 **14**

Landmarks
Sydney Tower p83 **4**

Cathedrals and Synagogues
St Mary's Cathedral **9**
Great Synagogue **11**
St Andrew's Cathedral **13**

Parks and Gardens
Hyde Park **10**

Theatres
State Theatre **3**

GETTING THERE
Town Hall, Wynyard, Martin Place, St James and Museum railway stations serve the area. There are frequent buses, particularly along Elizabeth and George Streets. Monorail stops are at City Centre, Galeries Victoria and World Square.

0 metres 500
0 yards 500

KEY

Street-by-Street map
See p80–81

CityRail station

Monorail station

Bus terminus

◁ **Mythological figures in the Archibald Fountain, Hyde Park**

Street-by-Street: City Centre

Sculpture outside the MLC Centre

Although closely rivalled by Melbourne, this is the business and commercial capital of Australia. Vibrant by day, at night the streets are far less busy when office workers and shoppers have gone home. The comparatively small city centre of this sprawling metropolis seems to be almost jammed into a few city blocks. Because Sydney grew in such a haphazard fashion, with many of today's streets following tracks from the harbour originally made by bullocks, there was no allowance for the expansion of the burgeoning city into what has become a major international centre. A colourful night scene of cafés, restaurants and theatres is emerging, however, as more people return to the city centre to live.

★ **Queen Victoria Building**
Taking up an entire city block, this 1898 former produce market has been lovingly restored and is now a shopping mall **❷**

State Theatre
A gem from the era when the movies reigned, this glittering and richly decorated 1929 cinema was once hailed as "the Empire's greatest theatre" **❸**

To Sydney Town Hall

The Queen Victoria Statue was found after a worldwide search in 1983 ended in a small Irish village. It had lain forgotten and neglected since being removed from the front of the Irish Parliament in 1947.

STAR SIGHTS

- ★ Queen Victoria Building
- ★ Sydney Tower
- ★ Martin Place

YORK STREET

STREET

GEORGE

MARKET

PITT STREET

PARK STREET

CASTLEREAGH

ELIZABETH

| 0 metres | | 100 |
| 0 yards | | 100 |

KEY

– – – Suggested route

Marble Bar
Once a landmark bar in the 1893 Tattersalls hotel, it was dismantled and re-erected in the Sydney Hilton in 1973 **❶**

Strand Arcade
A reminder of the late 19th century Victorian era when Sydney was famed as a city of elegant shopping arcades, this faithfully restored example is said to have been the finest of them all **5**

LOCATOR MAP
See Street Finder, maps 1 & 4

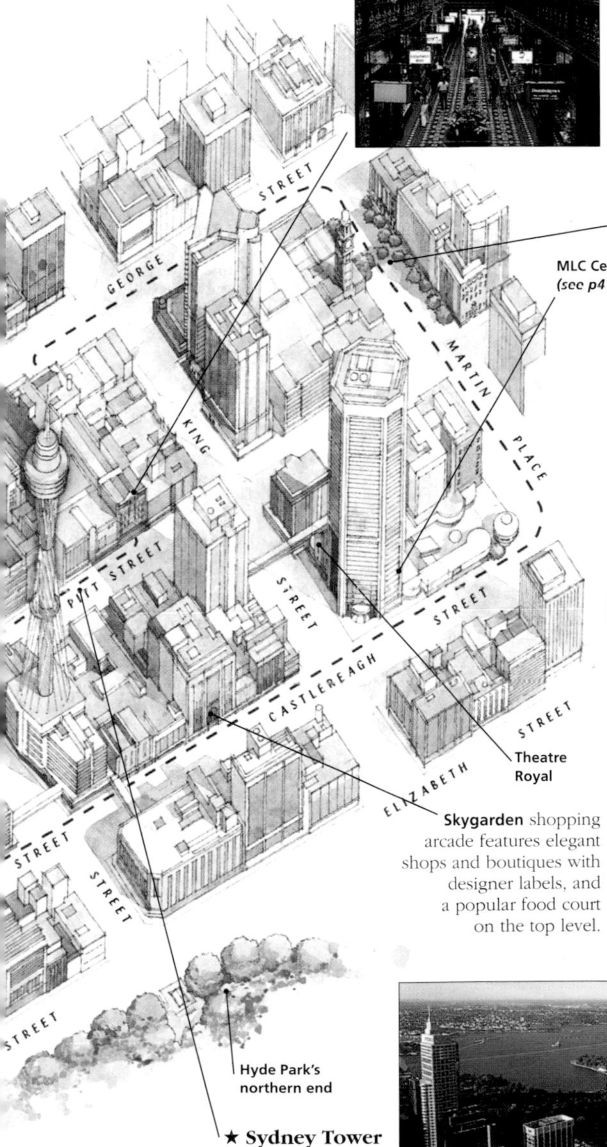

MLC Centre
(see p41)

★ **Martin Place**
Martin Place's 1929 Art Deco Cenotaph is the site of annual Anzac Day war remembrance services **6**

Theatre
Royal

Skygarden shopping arcade features elegant shops and boutiques with designer labels, and a popular food court on the top level.

Hyde Park's
northern end

★ **Sydney Tower**
The tower tops the city skyline, giving a bird's eye view of the whole of Sydney. It rises 305 m (1,000 ft) above the ground and can be seen from as far away as the Blue Mountains **4**

Entrance to the Marble Bar

The Marble Bar ❶

488 George St. **Map** 1 B5. **Tel** 9266 2000 🚌 George St routes. ⏰ 3pm–11pm Mon–Wed, 3pm–midnight Thu, 3pm–2am Fri, 5pm–2am Sat. 🍷 public hols. 📷 See **Restaurants, Cafés and Pubs** p197.

The Marble Bar, originally part of George Adams' Tattersalls Hotel built in 1893, is an inspired link with the Sydney of an earlier era. The bar, whose rich and decadent Italian Renaissance style had made it a local institution, was dismantled before the demolition of the hotel in 1969. Its colonnade entrance, fireplaces and counters were re-erected in the Sydney Hilton basement and reopened in 1973.

During the week, the bar attracts a broad range of city workers for after-work drinks. On Fridays and at weekends if a band is playing, the bar bustles with a younger crowd who come to hear the mostly jazz and rhythm and blues music.

Queen Victoria Building ❷

455 George St. **Map** 1 B5. **Tel** 9264 9209. 🚌 George St routes. ⏰ 9am–6pm Mon–Wed, 9am–9pm Thu, 9am–6pm Fri & Sat, 11am–5pm Sun & public hols. 📷 ♿ 🎫 See **Shops and Markets** pp198 and 200.

French Designer Pierre Cardin called the Queen Victoria Building "the most beautiful shopping centre in the world". Yet this spacious and ornate Romanesque building, better known as the QVB, began life as the Sydney produce market. The dust, flies, grime and shouts as horses struggled with heavy loads on the slippery ramps are now difficult to imagine. Completed to the design of City Architect George

Roof detail, Queen Victoria Building

McRae in 1898, the dominant features are the central dome, sheathed in copper, as are the 20 smaller domes, and the glass barrel vault roof which lets in a flood of natural light.

The market closed at the end of World War I and the building fell into disrepair. It had various roles during this time, including that of City Library. By the 1950s, after extensive remodelling and neglect, it was threatened with demolition.

Refurbished at a cost of over $75 million, the QVB reopened in 1986 as today's grand shopping gallery, housing over 190 shops and boutiques on four levels. At the Town Hall end a wishing well incorporates a

stone from Blarney Castle, Ireland and a sculpture of Islay, beloved dog of Queen Victoria. In 1983, a worldwide search began for a statue of the queen herself. One was finally found in the village of Daingean, Republic of Ireland, where it had lain forgotten since its removal from the front of the Irish Parliament in 1947.

Now fully restored, the Queen Victoria Statue stands near the wishing well. Inside the QVB, suspended from the ceiling, is the Royal Clock. Weighing more than 1 tonne and over 5 m (17 ft) tall, the clock was designed by Neil Glasser in 1982. The upper structure features part of Balmoral Castle above a copy of the four dials of Big Ben. At one minute to every hour, a fanfare is played and there follows a parade depicting six scenes from the lives of various kings and queens of England.

State Theatre ❸

49 Market St. **Map** 1 B5. **Tel** 9373 6852. 🚌 George St routes. **Box office** ⏰ 9am–5:30pm Mon–Fri. 🍷 Good Fri, 25 Dec. ♿ 🎫 bookings essential. www.statetheatre.com.au.

When it opened in 1929, this picture palace was hailed as the finest that local craftsmanship could achieve. The State Theatre is one of the best examples in Australia of the architectural fantasies used to entice people to the movies.

Its Cinema Baroque style is evident right from the Gothic foyer, with its vaulted ceiling, mosaic floor, richly decorated marble columns and statues. Inside the brass and bronze doors, the auditorium, which seats over 2,000 people, is lit by a 20,000-piece chandelier. The Wurlitzer organ (currently under repair) rises from below stage just before performances. Now one of Sydney's premier concert and theatre venues, it is also the main base for the Sydney Film Festival, held in June of each year (see p51).

The ornately decorated Gothic foyer of the State Theatre

Sydney Tower ❹

The highest observation deck in the southern hemisphere, the Sydney Tower was conceived as part of the 1970s Centrepoint shopping centre, but was not completed until 1981. About a million visitors a year appreciate the stunning views, often stretching for over 85 km (53 miles). A landmark in itself, it can be seen from almost anywhere in the city, and far beyond. Visitors can also take a 75-minute SkyWalk tour over the roof of the tower.

VISITORS' CHECKLIST

100 Market St. **Map** 1 B5. **Tel** 8251 7835. 🚌 Sydney Explorer, all city routes. 🚌 Darling Harbour. 🚃 St James, Town Hall. 🚆 City Centre. ⏰ 9am–10:30pm Mon–Fri & Sun, 9am–11:15pm Sat (last adm: 45 mins before closing). ⛔ 25 Dec. 📷 👍 📶 🍴 🛒 ♿
www.sydneytower.com.au

The 30-m (98-ft) spire completes the total 305 m (1,000 ft) of the tower's height.

The water tank holds 162,000 litres (35,500 gallons) and acts as an enormous stabilizer on very windy days.

Skywalk

Level 4: Observation

Level 3: Coffee shop

Level 2: Buffet restaurant

Level 1: A la carte restaurant

Observation Level
Views from Level 4 stretch to Pittwater in the north, Botany Bay to the south, westwards to the Blue Mountains, and along the harbour out to the open sea.

The turret's nine levels include two restaurants, a café, the Observation Level, and SkyTour, the largest simulated virtual ride in the southern hemisphere.

The windows comprise three layers. The outer has a gold dust coating. The frame design prevents panes falling outwards.

The 56 cables weigh seven tonnes each. If laid end to end, they would reach from New Zealand to Sydney.

The shaft is designed to withstand wind speeds expected only once in 500 years, as well as unprecedented earthquakes.

The stairs are two separate, fireproofed emergency escape routes. Each year in April or May Sydney's fittest race up the 1,504 stairs.

Construction of Turret
The nine turret levels were erected on the roof of the base building, then hoisted up the shaft using hydraulic jacks.

Double-decker lifts can carry up to 2,000 people per hour. At full speed, a lift takes only 40 seconds to ascend the 76 floors to the Observation Level.

New Year's Eve
Every year, fireworks are set off on top of the tower as part of the official public fireworks displays to mark the New Year.

Strand Arcade ❺

412–414 George St. **Map** 1 B5.
Tel 9232 4199. 🚌 *George St
routes.* ⏱ *9am–5:30pm Mon–Wed
& Fri, 9am–9pm Thu, 9am–4pm Sat,
11am–4pm Sun.* ⬤ *some public
hols, 25, 26 Dec.* ♿ 📷 *See Shops
and Markets pp198–201.*

Victorian Sydney was a city of
grand shopping arcades. The
Strand, joining George and Pitt
Streets and designed by
English architect John Spencer,
was the finest jewel in the city's
crown. The blaze of publicity
surrounding its opening in
April 1892 was equalled only
by the natural light pouring
through the glass roof and the
artificial glare from the chandeliers, each carrying 50 jets
of gas as well as 50 lamps.

The boutiques and shops in
the galleries make window
shopping a delight in this airy
building which, after a fire in
1976, was restored to its original splendour. Be sure to stop,
as shoppers have done since
opening day, for refreshments
at one of the beautiful coffee
shops in the arcade.

The Pitt Street entrance to the
majestic Strand Arcade

Martin Place ❻

Map 1 B4. 🚌 *George St & Elizabeth
St routes.* 🚊 *Martin Place.*

Running from George Street
across Pitt, Castlereagh and
Elizabeth Streets to Macquarie
Street, this plaza was opened
in 1891 and made a traffic-free
precinct in 1971. It is busiest at
lunchtime when city workers
enjoy their sandwiches while
watching free entertainment,

Interior of National Australia Bank, George Street end of Martin Place

sponsored by the Sydney City
Council, in a performance
space near Castlereagh Street.

Every Anzac Day, a national
day of war remembrance on
25 April, the focus moves to
the Cenotaph at the George
Street end. Thousands of past
and present servicemen and
women attend a dawn service
and wreath-laying ceremony,
followed by a march-past. The
shrine, with bronze statues of a
soldier and a sailor on a granite
base, by Bertram MacKennal,
was unveiled in 1929.

On the southern side of the
Cenotaph is the symmetrical
façade of the Renaissance-
style General Post Office,
considered to be the finest
building by James Barnet,
Colonial Architect. Con-
struction of the GPO, as
Sydneysiders call it, took
place between 1866 and
1874, with additions in
Pitt Street between 1881
and 1885. Most contro-
versial were the relief
figures executed by
Tomaso Sani. Although
Barnet declared that
the figures represented
Australians in realistic form,
they were labelled "grotesque".

A stainless steel sculpture
of upended cubes, the Dobell
Memorial Sculpture stands
above a waterfall which was

**Statue of explorer
Gregory Blaxland**

funded by public subscription
following a donation by artist
Lloyd Rees. The sculpture, a
tribute to the artist William
Dobell *(see p31)*, was created
by Bert Flugelman in 1979.

Lands Department
Building ❼

23 Bridge St. **Map** 1 B3. 🚌 *325,
George St routes.* ⏱ *only 2 weeks,
dates vary.* ♿

Designed by the Colonial
Architect James Barnet, the
three-storey Classical Revival
sandstone edifice was built
between 1877 and 1890.
As for the GPO building,
Pyrmont sandstone was
used for the exterior.
Decisions about the sub-
division of much of rural
eastern Australia were
made in offices within.
Statues of explorers and
legislators who "pro-
moted settlement" fill
23 of the façade's 48
niches; the remainder
are still empty. The
luminaries include the
explorers Hovell and Hume,
Sir Thomas Mitchell, Blaxland,
Lawson and Wentworth *(see
p136)*, Ludwig Leichhardt, Bass
and Matthew Flinders and the
botanist Sir Joseph Banks.

Museum of Sydney ❽

Cnr Bridge & Phillip Sts. **Map** 1 B3.
Tel 9251 5988. 🚌 *Circular Quay routes.* ⏰ *9:30am–5pm daily.* ⬤
Good Fri, 25 Dec. 🗓 💻 🍴 📷 📷
♿ **www**.museumofsydney.gov.au

Situated at the base of Governor Phillip Tower, the Museum of Sydney is on the site of the first Government House, the home, office and seat of authority for the first nine governors of NSW from 1788 until its demolition in 1846. The design assimilates a valuable archaeological site into a modern office block. The museum itself traces the city's turbulent history, from the 1788 arrival of the British colonists until the present day.

Indigenous Peoples

The museum sits on Cadigal land. A new gallery explores the culture, history, continuity and place of Sydney's original Aboriginal inhabitants, and the "turning point" of colonization/ invasion. Collectors' chests hold items of daily use such as flint and ochre, each piece painstakingly catalogued and evocatively interpreted.

There are two audio-visual exhibits which explore the history of indigenous peoples

The Lookout, Level 3, overlooking the piazza towards Circular Quay

from a contemporary perspective. In the square at the front of the complex, the acclaimed *Edge of the Trees* sculpture, a collection of 29 sandstone, steel and wooden pillars, symbolizes the first contact between the Aboriginal peoples and Europeans. Haunting voices in the Eora tongue fill the space. Inscribed in the wood are signatures of the First Fleeters and names of botanical species in both the indigenous language and Latin. Incisions made in the pillars are filled with organic materials such as ash, feathers, bone, shells and human hair.

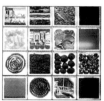

Display from Trade exhibition on Level 2

History of Sydney

Outside the museum, a paving pattern outlines the site of first Government House. Original foundations, lost under street level for many years, can be seen here through a window. Inside the entrance a viewing floor reveals more foundations. A segment of wall has been reconstructed using sandstone excavated during archaeological exploration of the site.

The Colony display on Level 2 focuses on Sydney during the critical decade of the 1840s when convict transportation ended, the town officially became a city and suffered an economic depression. There is also a set of scale models of the 11 First Fleet ships. The Museum presents stories of the Fleet's journey, arrival, first contacts with Indigenous people and the survival challenges faced by those on board.

On Level 3, 20th century Sydney is explored with panoramic images of the developing city providing a vivid backdrop. The Museum of Sydney has a changing exhibition program every four months.

Edge of the Trees **sculptural installation by Janet Laurence and Fiona Foley (1995)**

Terrazzo mosaic floor in the crypt of St Mary's Cathedral

St Mary's Cathedral ⓿

St. Mary's Rd. **Map** 1 C5. **Tel** 9220 0400. ▦ Elizabeth St routes. ◯ 6:30am–6pm Mon–Fri, 6:30am–7pm Sat–Sun. ♿ with advance notice. ✉ noon Sun. **www**.sydney.catholic.org.au

Although Catholics arrived with the First Fleet, the celebration of Mass was at first prohibited in case the priests provoked civil strife among the colony's large Irish Catholic population. The first priests were appointed in 1820 and services allowed. In 1821, Governor Macquarie laid the

foundation stone for St Mary's Chapel on the site of today's cathedral, the first land granted to the Catholic Church in Australia.

The initial section of the Gothic Revival style cathedral was opened in 1882. In 1928, the building was completed, but without the twin southern spires proposed by the architect, William Wardell. By the entrance steps are statues of Australia's first cardinal, Moran, and Archbishop Kelly who laid the stone for the final stage in 1913. They were

sculpted by Bertram MacKennal, also responsible for the Martin Place Cenotaph (see p84) and the Shakespeare group outside the State Library (see p112). The crypt's Celtic-inspired terrazzo mosaic floor took 15 years to complete.

Great Synagogue ⓫

187 Elizabeth St, entrance on 166 Castlereagh St. **Map** 1 B5. **Tel** 9267 2477. ▦ 394, 396, 380, 382. ◯ for services and tours. ● public & Jewish hols. ♿ advance notice ✉ ✉ **www**.greatsynagogue.org.au

Candelabra from the Great Synagogue

The longest established Jewish Orthodox congregation in Australia assembles in this synagogue, consecrated in 1878. Although Jews had arrived with the First Fleet, worship did not begin until the 1820s. With its carved entrance columns and magnificent stained-glass windows, the synagogue is perhaps the finest work of Thomas Rowe, the architect of Sydney Hospital (see p113). The panelled ceiling is decorated with hundreds of tiny gold leaf stars.

Hyde Park ⓾

Map 1 B5. ▦ Elizabeth St routes.

Fenced and named after its London equivalent by Governor Macquarie in 1810, Hyde Park marked the outskirts of the township. It was a popular exercise field for garrison troops and later incorporated a racecourse and a cricket pitch. Though much smaller today than the original park, it still provides a peaceful haven in the middle of the bustling city centre.

Anzac Memorial
The 30-m (98-ft) high Art Deco memorial, reflected in the poplar-lined Pool of Remembrance, commemorates those Australians who were killed at war in the service of their country. Opened in 1934, the Anzac Memorial now includes a photographic and military artifact exhibition downstairs.

Sandringham Garden
In spring, the pergola in this sunken garden is a cascade of mauve-flowering wisteria. The garden, a memorial to the English kings George V and George VI, was opened by Queen Elizabeth II in 1954.

Tomb of the Unknown Soldier in the Art Deco Anzac Memorial

Diana, goddess of purity and the chase, Archibald Fountain

Archibald Fountain
This bronze and granite fountain commemorates the French and Australian World War I alliance. It was completed by François Sicard in 1932 and donated by JF Archibald, one of the founders of the Bulletin, a popular literary magazine which encouraged the work of Henry Lawson and "Banjo" Paterson, among many others. It was Archibald's bequest that established the Archibald Prize for portraiture (see p50).

The Grand Organ in Sydney Town Hall's Centennial Hall

Sydney Town Hall ⓬

483 George St. **Map** 4 E2.
Tel 9265 9333. 🚌 *George St routes.* ⭕ *8:30am–6pm Mon–Fri.* ⬤ *public hols.* ♿ 🎫

The steps of this sandstone building, central to George Street's Victorian architecture, have been a favourite Sydney meeting place since it opened in 1869. Walled burial grounds had originally covered the site.

It is a fine example of high Victorian architecture, even though the plans of the original architect, JH Wilson, proved

beyond the builders' capabilities. A rapid succession of designers was brought in. The vestibule – an elegant salon with intricate plasterwork, lavish stained glass and a crystal chandelier – is the work of Albert Bond. The Bradbridge brothers completed the clock tower in 1884. From 1888–9, other architects were used for the Centennial Hall, with its coffered zinc ceiling and the imposing 19th-century Grand Organ with over 8,500 pipes.

On the façade, you will see numerous carved lion heads. Just to the north of the main entrance, facing George Street, a lion has been carved with one eye shut. This oddity appeared because of the head stonemason's habit of checking the line of the stonework by closing one eye. The sly joke was not found until work was finished.

Some people have concluded that Sydney Town Hall became the city's most elaborate building by accident, as each architect strove to outdo his predecessors. Today, it makes a magnificent venue for concerts, dances and balls.

St Andrew's Cathedral ⓭

Sydney Square, Cnr George & Bathurst Sts. **Map** 4 E3. *Tel 9265 1661.* 🚌 *George St routes.* ⭕ *Contact the cathedral for opening hours and tour times.* 📷 ♿ 🎫

While the foundation stone of the country's oldest cathedral was laid in 1819, almost 50 years elapsed before the building was consecrated in 1868. The Gothic Revival design is by Edmund Blacket, whose ashes are interred here. Inspired by York Minster in England, the twin towers were completed in 1874. In 1949, the main entrance was moved to the eastern end near George Street.

The Great Bible, St Andrew's Cathedral

Inside are memorials to Sydney pioneers, including Thomas Mort *(see p72)*. A 1539 bible and beads collected in the Holy Land are among the religious memorabilia.

The southern wall incorporates stones from London's St Paul's Cathedral, Westminster Abbey and the House of Lords.

Obelisk
This monument was dubbed "Thornton's Scent Bottle" after the mayor of Sydney who had it erected in 1857. The mock-Egyptian edifice is in fact a ventilator for a sewer.

Emden Gun
Standing at the corner of College and Liverpool Streets, this monument commemorates a World War I naval action. HMAS *Sydney* destroyed the German raider *Emden* off the Cocos Islands on 9 November 1914, and 180 crew members were taken prisoner.

City Circle Railway
The park we see today bears very little resemblance to the Hyde Park of old. In fact, the dictates of city railway tunnels have largely created its present landscape. Tunnels were excavated through an open cut that

ran through the park, and after the rail system was opened in 1926 the entire area had to be remodelled and replanted.

Busby's Bore Fountain
This is a reminder of Busby's Bore, the city's first piped water supply opened in 1837.

John Busby, a civil engineer, conceived and supervised the construction of the 4.4-km (2¾-mile) tunnel. It carried water from bores on Lachlan Swamp, now within Centennial Park *(see p127)*, to horse-drawn water carriers on the corner of Elizabeth and Park Streets.

Game in progress on the giant chessboard, near Busby's Bore Fountain

Australian Museum ⑭

**Model head of
*Tyrannosaurus rex***

The Australian Museum, the nation's leading natural science museum, founded in 1827, was the first museum established and remains the premier showcase of Australian natural history. The main building, an impressive sandstone structure with a marble staircase, faces Hyde Park. Architect Mortimer Lewis was forced to resign his position when building costs began to far exceed the budget. Construction was completed in the 1860s by James Barnet. The collection provides a journey across Australia and the near Pacific, covering prehistory, biology, botany, environment and cultural heritage. Australian Aboriginal traditions are celebrated in a community access space also used for dance and other performances.

Museum Entrance
The façade features massive Corinthian square pillars or piers.

Rhodochrosite   Cuprite

Mesolite with green apophyllite

Planet of Minerals
This section features a walk-through re-creation of an underground mine with a display of gems and minerals.

Education Centre

Indigenous Australians
From the Dreaming to the struggle for self-determination and land rights, this exhibit tells the stories of Australia's first peoples.

Ground floor

Main entrance

The Skeletons Gallery, on the ground floor, provides a different perspective on natural history.

MUSEUM GUIDE

The Indigenous Australians Gallery is on the ground floor, as is the skeleton gallery. Mineral and rock exhibits are in two galleries on level 1. On level 2 are Birds and Insects, Human Evolution, Kids' Island, Biodiversity, Search and Discover and More than Dinosaurs.

STAR EXHIBITS

★ More than Dinosaurs

★ Kids' Island

★ Search & Discover

★ Search & Discover
Sydneysiders bring bugs, rocks and bones to this area for identification. The public can also access CD-Roms for research.

Level 2

VISITORS' CHECKLIST

6 College St. **Map** 4 F3.
Tel *9320 6000.* 🚌 *Sydney Explorer, 323, 324, 325, 327, 389.* 🚆 *Museum, Town Hall.*
🕒 *9:30am–5pm daily.* ⬤ *25 Dec.* ♿ 📷 ♿ 📋 🍴 🛍 📷
www.amonline.net.au

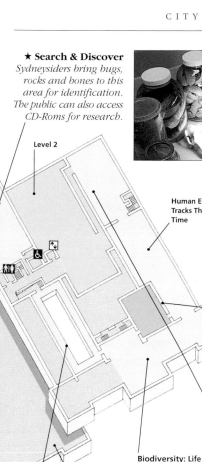

Human Evolution:
Tracks Through
Time

★ Kids' Island
Displays designed especially for children aged five and under are heartily enjoyed both by kids and their families.

Biodiversity: Life
Supporting
Life shows how plants, animals and ecosystems work together.

Level 1

★ More than Dinosaurs
Discover Australia's ancient megafauna in this exhibition that features a time line beginning 4,600 million years ago, and includes some impressive dinosaur skeletons looming alongside the giant prehistoric relatives of Australia's marsupials.

Birds and Insects
Australia's most poisonous spider, the male of the funnel-web species, dwells exclusively in the Greater Sydney region.

KEY TO FLOORPLAN

- ☐ Australian Environments
- ☐ Kids' Island
- ☐ More than Dinosaurs
- ☐ Indigenous Australians
- ☐ Temporary exhibition space
- ☐ Non-exhibition space

"WELCOME STRANGER" GOLD NUGGET
In 1869, the largest gold nugget ever found in Australia was discovered in Victoria. It weighed 71.06 kg (156 lb). The museum holds a cast of the original in a display examining the impact of the gold rush, when the Australian population doubled in ten years.

◄──── 67.5 cm (26½ in) wide ────►

DARLING HARBOUR

amed in honour of the seventh governor of New South Wales, Ralph Darling, this area was originally called Cockle Bay because of the molluscs early European settlers collected here. Darling Harbour was an unsavoury place in the late 19th century, known for its thieves' dens and bawdy houses. Its docks, backed by a railway yard, were an embarkation point for wool and other exports. The country's industrial age began here in 1815 with the opening of a steam mill. Darling

Horatio Nelson, National Maritime Museum

Harbour continued as, first, a grimy workplace and, later, with the industrial decline of Sydney Harbour, an obsolete and run-down backwater. In the 1980s, it was decided to make this prime city site a focal point of the 1988 Bicentenary. The project was the largest urban redevelopment ever carried out in Australia. Today Darling Harbour is an extension of the city centre with a mixture of fine museums, shopping and open space. It has become a popular and lively area of Sydney.

SIGHTS AT A GLANCE

Historic Districts and Buildings
Pyrmont Bridge ❸
Chinatown ❼
King Street Wharf ❹

Museums and Galleries
National Maritime Museum pp94–5 ❶
Powerhouse Museum pp100–101 ❿

Parks and Gardens
Chinese Garden ❻

Entertainment
Sydney Aquarium pp96–7 ❷
Convention and Exhibition Centre ❺

Theatres
Capitol Theatre ❽

Markets
Paddy's Markets ❾

GETTING THERE
Harbourside, Convention and Paddy's Markets monorail stations are convenient. Ferries run to Darling Harbour wharf, while the most useful buses are the Sydney Explorer, 456 and 501.

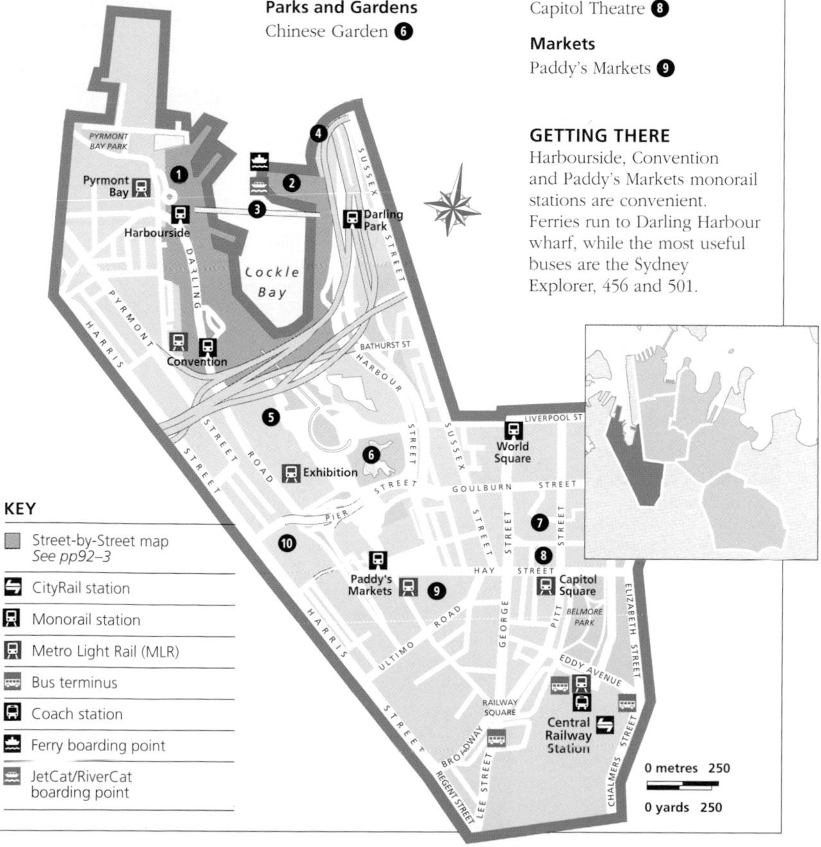

KEY

Street-by-Street map
See pp92–3

CityRail station

Monorail station

Metro Light Rail (MLR)

Bus terminus

Coach station

Ferry boarding point

JetCat/RiverCat boarding point

0 metres 250
0 yards 250

◁ View from Harbourside Shopping Centre looking east towards the city

Street-by-Street: Darling Harbour

Carpentaria lightship, National Maritime Museum

Darling Harbour was New South Wales' bicentennial gift to itself. This imaginative urban redevelopment, in the heart of Sydney, covers a 54-ha (133-acre) site that was once a busy industrial centre and international shipping terminal catering for the developing local wool, grain, timber and coal trades. In 1984 the Darling Harbour Authority was formed to examine the area's commercial options. The resulting complex opened in 1988, complete with the Australian National Maritime Museum and Sydney Aquarium, two of the city's tourist highlights. Free outdoor entertainment, for children in particular, is a regular feature, and there are many shops, cafés and restaurants, as well as several major hotels overlooking the bay.

Harbourside Complex offers restaurants and cafés with superb views over the water to the city skyline. There is also a wide range of speciality shops, selling unusual gifts and other items.

Convention and Exhibition Centre
This complex presents an alternating range of trade shows displaying everything from home decorating suggestions to bridal wear ❺

DARLING DRIVE

WESTERN DISTRIBUTOR

WESTERN DISTRIBUTOR

The Tidal Cascades sunken fountain was designed by Robert Woodward, also responsible for the El Alamein Fountain *(see p120)*. The double spiral of water and paths replicates the circular shape of the Convention Centre.

IMAX large-screen cinema

Chinese Garden of Friendship ✗

The Chinese Garden of Friendship is a haven of peace and tranquillity in the heart of Sydney. Its landscaping, with winding pathways, waterfalls, lakes and pavilions, offers an insight into the rich culture of China.

STAR SIGHTS

★ Sydney Aquarium

★ Australian National Maritime Museum

Pyrmont Bridge
The swingspan bridge opens for vessels up to 14 m (46 ft) tall. The monorail track running above the walkway also opens up to allow access for even taller boats ❸

LOCATOR MAP
See Street Finder, maps 3 & 4

Swingspan supports for Pyrmont Bridge are sunk 10 m (33 ft) below the harbour floor.

Star City Casino

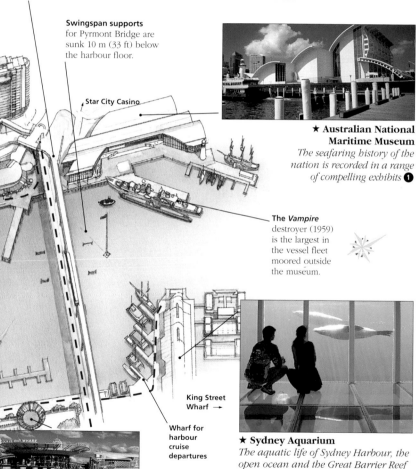

★ **Australian National Maritime Museum**
The seafaring history of the nation is recorded in a range of compelling exhibits ❶

The *Vampire* destroyer (1959) is the largest in the vessel fleet moored outside the museum.

King Street Wharf →

Wharf for harbour cruise departures

★ **Sydney Aquarium**
The aquatic life of Sydney Harbour, the open ocean and the Great Barrier Reef is displayed in massive tanks which can be seen from underwater walkways ❷

0 metres   100

0 yards   100

KEY

– – – Suggested route

Cockle Bay Wharf is vibrant and colourful, and an exciting food and entertainment precinct.

Australian National Maritime Museum ❶

1602 Willem Blaeu Celestial Globe

Bounded as it is by the sea, Australia's history is inextricably linked to maritime traditions. The museum displays material in a broad range of permanent and temporary thematic exhibits, many with interactive elements. As well as artifacts relating to the enduring Aboriginal maritime cultures, the exhibits survey the history of European exploratory voyages in the Pacific, the arrival of convict ships, successive waves of migration, water sports and recreation, and naval life. Historic vessels on show at the wharf include a flimsy Vietnamese refugee boat, sailing, fishing and pearling boats, a navy patrol boat and a World War II commando raider.

Museum Façade
The billowing steel roof design by Philip Cox suggests both the surging sea and the sails of a ship.

Merana Eora Nora – First People traces the seafaring traditions of Aboriginal peoples and Torres Strait Islanders.

The Tasman Light was used in a Tasmanian lighthouse.

Passengers
The model of the Orcades reflects the grace of 1950s liners. This display also charts harrowing sea voyages made by migrants and refugees.

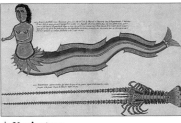

The *Sirius* anchor is from a 1790 wreck off Norfolk Island.

Main entrance (sea level)

★ Navigators
This 1754 engraving of an East Indian sea creature is a European vision of the uncharted, exotic "great south".

The Navy exhibit examines naval life in war and peace, as well as the history of colonial navies.

Linked by the Sea honours enduring links between the US and Australia. American traders stopped off in Australia on their way to China.

KEY TO FLOORPLAN

- ☐ Navigators and Merana Eora Nora
- ☐ Passengers
- ☐ Commerce
- ☐ Watermarks
- ☐ Navy
- ☐ Linked by the Sea: USA Gallery
- ☐ Temporary exhibitions
- ☐ Non-exhibition space

STAR EXHIBITS

★ Navigators and Merana Eora Nora

★ Watermarks

★ Vampire

Commerce
This 1903 Painters' and Dockers' Union banner was carried by waterfront workers in marches. It shows the Niagara *entering the dry dock at Cockatoo Island* (see p106).

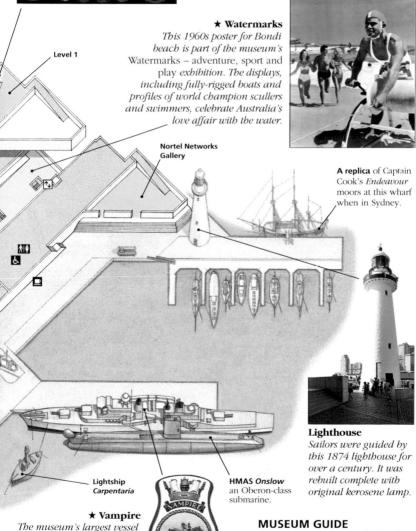

★ Watermarks
This 1960s poster for Bondi beach is part of the museum's Watermarks – adventure, sport and play *exhibition. The displays, including fully-rigged boats and profiles of world champion scullers and swimmers, celebrate Australia's love affair with the water.*

Level 1

Nortel Networks Gallery

A replica of Captain Cook's *Endeavour* moors at this wharf when in Sydney.

Lighthouse
Sailors were guided by this 1874 lighthouse for over a century. It was rebuilt complete with original kerosene lamp.

Lightship *Carpentaria*

HMAS *Onslow* an Oberon-class submarine.

★ Vampire
The museum's largest vessel is the 1959 Royal Australian Navy destroyer, whose insignia is shown here. Tours of "The Bat" are accompanied by simu-lated battle action sounds.

MUSEUM GUIDE

The Leisure, Navy and Linked by the Sea: USA Gallery exhibits are located on the main entrance level (sea level). The First Australians, Discovery, Passengers and Commerce sections are found on the first level. There is access to the fleet from both levels.

Sydney Aquarium ❷

Tropical
sea star

Sydney Aquarium contains the largest, most comprehensive collection of Australian aquatic wildlife, with over 11,500 animals from 650 species. Both freshwater and marine exhibits simulate the animals' natural environments. For many visitors, the highlight is a walk "on the ocean floor" through the floating oceanarium with 145 m (480 ft) of acrylic underwater tunnels. Here you can watch huge sharks and rays passing overhead, just inches away. Seals may also be viewed above and below water in the special seal sanctuary. Other highlights include the platypus exhibit, the fairy or little penguins, and the interactive touch pool.

Saltwater Crocodiles
The largest and most dangerous species of crocodile, "salties" live in the swamps and estuaries of Australia's north.

Platypus
Exhibit

Entrance

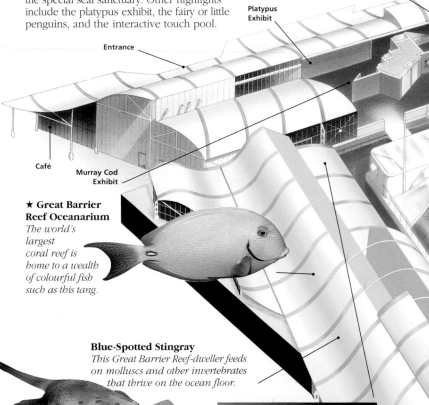

Café

Murray Cod
Exhibit

★ Great Barrier Reef Oceanarium
The world's largest coral reef is home to a wealth of colourful fish such as this tang.

Blue-Spotted Stingray
This Great Barrier Reef-dweller feeds on molluscs and other invertebrates that thrive on the ocean floor.

Touch Pool
This area, resembling a rock pool, gives the visitor a rare chance to touch, with care, marine invertebrates found along the coastline. They include sea urchins, tubeworms, crabs and sea stars.

VISITORS' CHECKLIST

Aquarium Pier, Darling Harbour.
Map 4 D2. **Tel** 8251 7800. 🚇
Sydney Explorer. 🚌 Darling Harbour. 🚆 Town Hall. 🅿 Darling
Park. 🕐 9am–10pm daily (last
adm 9pm). 🎦 📷 ♿ 🍴 🛍
www.sydneyaquarium.com.au

Aquarium Building and Pier
*The stark white design of the aquarium is Structuralist
(see p41), a common architectural style in this area.*

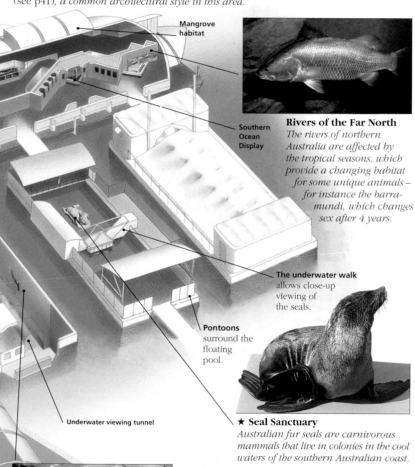

Mangrove
habitat

Southern
Ocean
Display

Rivers of the Far North
*The rivers of northern
Australia are affected by
the tropical seasons, which
provide a changing habitat
for some unique animals –
for instance the barra-
mundi, which changes
sex after 4 years.*

The underwater walk
allows close-up
viewing of
the seals.

Pontoons
surround the
floating
pool.

Underwater viewing tunnel

★ Seal Sanctuary
*Australian fur seals are carnivorous
mammals that live in colonies in the cool
waters of the southern Australian coast.*

★ The Open Ocean
*Take a walk through
the viewing tunnel
and be surrounded
by large sharks and
fish at close range.
Giant stingrays are
also a feature.*

STAR EXHIBITS

★ Great Barrier Reef
  Oceanarium

★ Seal Sanctuary

★ The Open Ocean

Pyrmont Bridge ❸

Darling Harbour. **Map** 1 A5.
🚉 *Darling Park, Harbourside.*
📷 ♿ 🛒

Pyrmont Bridge opened in 1902. The world's oldest electrically operated swingspan bridge, it was fully functional before Sydney's streets were lit by electricity. It was the second Pyrmont Bridge and provided access to what, at the time, was a busy international shipping terminal with warehouses and wool stores. Electricity for the new bridge came from the Ultimo power station, the building that now houses the city's Powerhouse Museum *(see pp100–101).*

Percy Allan, the bridge's designer, achieved overseas recognition for his two central steel swingspans and went on to design 583 more bridges in the course of his career. JJ Bradfield, the designer of the Sydney Harbour Bridge *(see pp70–71),* was also involved in construction of this bridge.

The 369-m (1,200-ft) long Pyrmont Bridge has 14 spans, with only the two central swingspans being made of steel. The remaining spans are made of ironbark, an Australian hardwood timber. The bridge was permanently closed to road traffic in 1981, but reopened to pedestrians when the Darling Harbour complex opened in 1988. A portion of the monorail route travels along the bridge. The

The view from Pyrmont Bridge looking up towards the city centre

The architectural geometry of the Convention and Exhibition Centre

central steel swingspans are still driven by their original motor. The bridge is opened regularly to allow boats access to and from Cockle Bay.

Night lights at King Street Wharf, Darling Harbour

King Street Wharf ❹

Lime St, between King and Erskine sts. **Map** 4 D1. 🚉 *Darling Park.* 🚆
🍴 📷 📱 ♿ **www.**ksw.com.au

Journalists from nearby newspaper offices and city workers flock to this harbourside venue, which combines an aggressively modern glass and steel shrine to café society with a working wharf. Passengers arrive and depart in style on ferries, water taxis and rivercats.

The complex is flush with bars that vie for the best views, and restaurants including Thai, Japanese, Italian and Modern Australian. Midway along the wharf is a boutique brewery that caters for those who revere the best kind of cleansing ales. This is not just a party circuit, there are residents here as well in low-rise apartments set back from the water on the city side.

Convention and Exhibition Centre ❺

Darling Drive, Darling Harbour. **Map** 3 C3. **Tel** 9282 5000. 🚉 *Convention.* ⏱ *daily (check in advance).* 📷 📱 ♿ **www.**darlingharbour.com

This purpose-built facility was completed in 1988. Major international and local conventions are held in the main auditorium. For trade shows and exhibitions, the Exhibition Centre's five halls can be combined to form a column-free area the size of five sports fields. The roof is supported by a system of sail-like masts and rigging, which reflects the maritime history of Darling Harbour. Works of art by such noted Australian artists as Brett Whiteley and John Olsen hang within.

Chinese Garden ❻

Darling Harbour. **Map** 4 D3. **Tel** 9281 6863. 🚉 *Paddy's Markets.* ⏱ *9:30am–5pm daily.* ⏺ *25 Dec.* 🎫 📷 📱 ♿

Known as the Garden of Friendship, the Chinese Garden was built in 1984. It is a tranquil refuge from the city streets. The garden's design was a gift to Sydney from its Chinese sister city of Guangdong. The Dragon Wall is in the lower section beside the lake. It has glazed carvings of two dragons, one representing Guangdong province and the other the state of New South Wales. In the centre of the wall, a carved pearl, symbolizing prosperity, is lifted by the waves. The lake is covered with lotus and water lilies for much of the year and a rock monster guards against evil. On the other side of the lake is the Twin Pavilion. Waratahs (New South Wales's floral symbol) and flowering apricots are carved into its woodwork, and also grow at its base.

A tea house, found at the top of the stairs in the Tea House Courtyard, serves traditional Chinese tea and cakes.

Chinatown ❼

Dixon St Plaza, Sydney. **Map** 4 D4.
🚇 Paddy's Markets.

Originally concentrated around Dixon and Hay Streets, Chinatown is expanding to fill Sydney's Haymarket area, stretching west to Harris Street, south to Broadway and east to Castlereagh Street. It is close to the Sydney Entertainment Centre, where some of the world's best-known rock and pop stars perform and indoor sporting events are held.

For years, Chinatown was a run-down district at the edge of the city's produce markets where many Chinese migrants worked. Today Dixon Street, its main thoroughfare, has been

Chinatown entrance, Dixon Street

spruced up, with street lanterns and archways, and a new wave of Asian migrants fills the now up-market restaurants.

Chinatown is a distinctive area with greengrocers, traditional herbalists and butchers' shops with wind-dried ducks hanging in their windows. Jewellers, clothing shops and confectioners fill the arcades. There are also two Chinese-language cinema complexes.

Capitol Theatre ❽

13 Campbell St, Haymarket. **Map** 4 E4.
Tel 9320 5000. 🚌 George St routes.
◐ performances only. **Box office**
◐ 9am–5pm Mon–Fri, 9am–8pm
during performances. ♿

In the mid-1800s a cattle and corn market was situated here. It became Paddy's Market Bazaar with sideshows and an outdoor theatre, which were

in turn replaced by a circus with a floodable ring. The present building was erected in the 1920s as a luxurious picture palace. In the mid-1990s, the cinema was restored, in keeping with the original theme of a Florentine Garden.

The Capitol reopened as a lyric theatre with productions of *West Side Story* and *Miss Saigon* being staged beneath its Mediterranean-blue ceiling studded with twinkling stars reflecting the southern sky.

The lavishly renovated Capitol Theatre in Chinatown

Paddy's Markets ❾

Cnr Thomas & Hay sts, Haymarket.
Map 4 D4. **Tel** 1300 361 589. 🚇
Paddy's Markets. ◐ 9am–5pm Thu–Sun & public hols. ● 25 Apr, 25 Dec.
📷 ♿ See also **Shops and Markets**
p203. **www**.paddysmarkets.com.au

Haymarket, in Chinatown, is home to Paddy's Markets, Sydney's oldest market. It has been in this area, on a number of sites, since 1869 (with only one five-year absence). The name's origin is uncertain, but is believed to have come from either the Chinese who originally supplied much of its produce, or the Irish, their main customers.

Once the shopping centre for the inner-city poor, Paddy's Markets is now an integral part of an ambitious development including residential apartments and the Market City Shopping Centre, with fashion outlet stores, an Asian food court and a cinema complex. However, the familiar clamour and chaotic bargain-hunting atmosphere of the original marketplace remain. Every weekend the market has up to 800 stalls selling everything from fresh produce to chickens, puppies, electrical products and leather goods.

Pavilion in the grounds of the Chinese Garden

Powerhouse Museum

This former Power Station, completed in 1902 to provide power for Sydney's tramway system, was redesigned to cater for the needs of a modern, hands-on museum. Revamped, the Powerhouse opened in 1988. The early collection was held in the Garden Palace hosting the 1879 international exhibition of invention and industry from around the world *(see pp26–7)*. Few exhibits survived the devastating 1882 fire, and today's huge and ever-expanding holdings were gathered after this disaster. The buildings' monumental scale provides an ideal context for the epic sweep of ideas encompassed within: everything from the realm of space and technology to the decorative and domestic arts. The museum emphasizes Australian innovations and achievements, celebrating both the extraordinary and the everyday.

Silver cricket trophy

Cyberworlds: Computers and Connections
This display explores the past, present and future of computers. Pictured here is a Japanese tin toy robot.

Soviet Organic Satellite Model
Replica spacecraft and a "habitation module", complete with kitchenette and sleeping area, detail the past and future of space exploration.

Level 3

Bayagul: Contemporary Indigenous Australian Communication
This handtufted rug, designed by Jimmy Pike, is displayed in an exhibit showcasing Aboriginal and Torres Strait Island cultures.

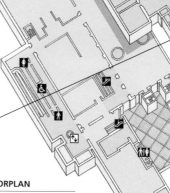

Level 2

MUSEUM GUIDE

The museum is two buildings: the former powerhouse and the Neville Wran building. There are over 20 exhibitions on four levels, descending from Level 5, the restaurant level. The shop, entrance and main exhibits are on Level 4. Level 3 has thematic exhibits and a Design Gallery. Level 2 has experiments and displays on space, computers and transport.

KEY TO FLOORPLAN

☐ Level 5: Asian Gallery

☐ Level 4: Decorative Arts, Innovation & Temp. Exhibitions

☐ Level 3: Social History & Design

☐ Level 2: Science & Technology

☐ Non-exhibition spa

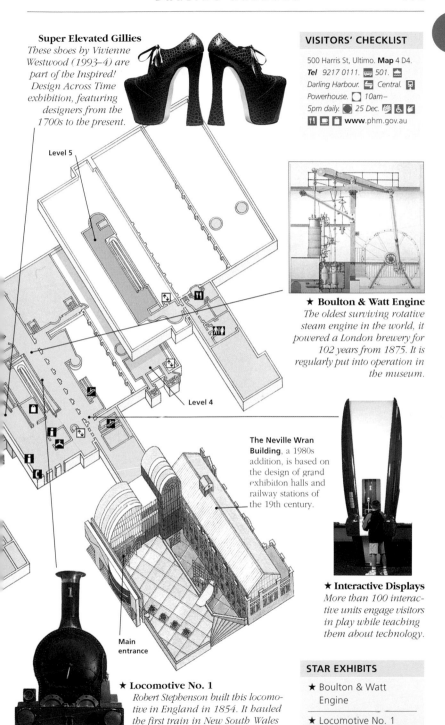

Super Elevated Gillies
*These shoes by Vivienne
Westwood (1993–4) are
part of the Inspired!
Design Across Time
exhibition, featuring
designers from the
1700s to the present.*

Level 5

★ **Boulton & Watt Engine**
*The oldest surviving rotative
steam engine in the world, it
powered a London brewery for
102 years from 1875. It is
regularly put into operation in
the museum.*

Level 4

**The Neville Wran
Building**, a 1980s
addition, is based on
the design of grand
exhibition halls and
railway stations of
the 19th century.

★ **Interactive Displays**
*More than 100 interac-
tive units engage visitors
in play while teaching
them about technology.*

Main
entrance

★ **Locomotive No. 1**
*Robert Stephenson built this locomo-
tive in England in 1854. It hauled
the first train in New South Wales
in 1855. Using models and voices,
the display re-creates a 19th-century
day trip for a group of Sydneysiders.*

STAR EXHIBITS

★ Boulton & Watt
  Engine

★ Locomotive No. 1

★ Interactive Displays

BOTANIC GARDENS AND THE DOMAIN

This tranquil part of Sydney can seem a world away from the bustle of the city centre. It is rich in the remnants of Sydney's convict and colonial past: the site of the first farm, and the boulevard-like Macquarie Street where the barracks, hospital, church and mint – bastions of civic power – are among the oldest surviving public buildings in Australia. This street continues to assert its dominance today as the home of the state government of New South Wales. The Domain, an open, grassy space, was originally set aside by the colony's first governor for his private use. Today it is a democratic place with joggers and touch footballers sidestepping picnickers. In January, during the Festival of Sydney, it hosts outdoor concerts with thousands of people enjoying fine music. The Botanic Gardens, which with The Domain was the site of Australia's first park, is a haven where visitors can stroll around and enjoy the extensive collection of native and exotic flora.

Wooden angel, St James Church

SIGHTS AT A GLANCE

Historic Streets and Buildings
Conservatorium of Music **2**
Government House **3**
Woolloomooloo Finger
  Wharf **6**
State Library of NSW **9**
Parliament House **10**
Sydney Hospital **11**
The Mint **12**
Hyde Park Barracks **13**

Museums and Galleries
*Art Gallery of New South
  Wales pp108–11* **7**

Churches
St James Church **14**

Islands
Fort Denison **5**

Monuments
Mrs Macquaries Chair **4**

Parks and Gardens
*Royal Botanic Gardens
  pp104–5* **1**
The Domain **8**

GETTING THERE
Visit on foot, if possible. St James and Martin Place train stations are close to most of the sights. The 311 bus from Circular Quay runs near the Art Gallery of NSW and past the Woolloomooloo Finger Wharf. The Sydney Explorer also stops at several sights.

0 metres	500
0 yards	500

KEY

Royal Botanic Gardens
See pp104–5

CityRail station

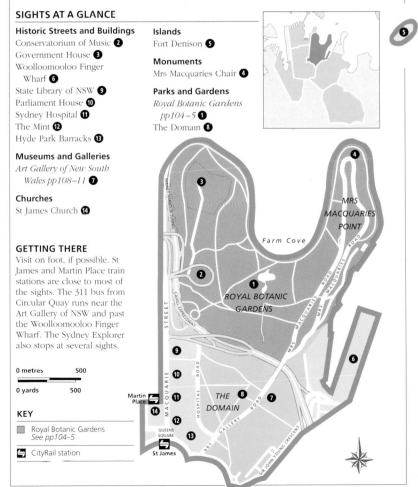

◁ Succulents and cacti from the Succulent Garden in the Royal Botanic Gardens

Royal Botanic Gardens ❶

Statue in the Botanic Gardens

The Royal Botanic Gardens, an oasis of 30 ha (74 acres) in the heart of the city, occupy a superb position, wrapped around Farm Cove at the harbour's edge. Established in 1816 as a series of pathways through shrubbery, they are the oldest scientific institution in the country and house an outstanding collection of plants from Australia and overseas. A living museum, the gardens are also the site of the first farm in the fledgling colony. Fountains, statues and monuments are today scattered throughout. Plant specimens collected by Joseph Banks on Captain James Cook's epic voyage along the east coast of Australia in 1770 are displayed in the National Herbarium of New South Wales, an important centre for research on Australian plants.

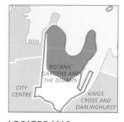

LOCATOR MAP
See Street Finder, maps 1 & 2

Government House (1897)

★ **Palm Grove**
Begun in 1862, this cool summer haven is one of the world's finest outdoor collections of palms. There are about 180 species. Borders planted with kaffir lilies make a colourful display in springtime.

★ **Herb Garden**
Herbs from around the world used for a wide variety of purposes – culinary, medicinal and aromatic – are on display here. A sensory fountain and a sundial modelled on the celestial sphere are also features.

★ **Sydney Tropical Centre**
Two glasshouses contain tropical ecosystems in miniature. Native vegetation is displayed in the Pyramid, while the Arc holds plants not found locally, commonly known as exotics.

| 0 metres | 200 |
| 0 yards | 200 |

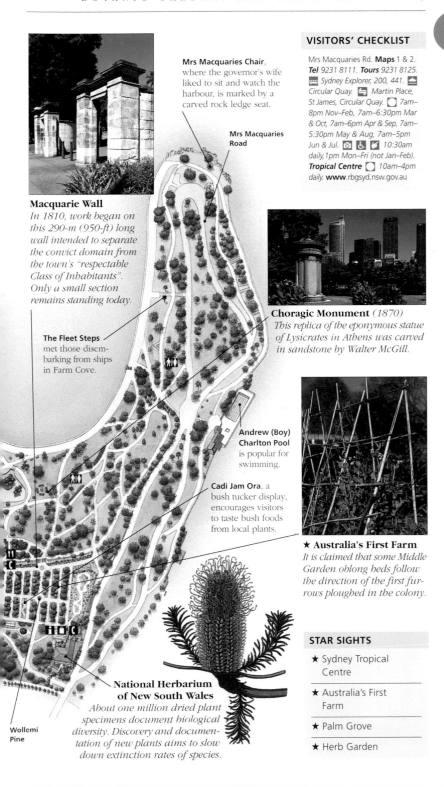

Mrs Macquaries Chair, where the governor's wife liked to sit and watch the harbour, is marked by a carved rock ledge seat.

Mrs Macquaries Road

Macquarie Wall
In 1810, work began on this 290-m (950-ft) long wall intended to separate the convict domain from the town's "respectable Class of Inhabitants". Only a small section remains standing today.

The Fleet Steps met those disembarking from ships in Farm Cove.

Choragic Monument *(1870)*
This replica of the eponymous statue of Lysicrates in Athens was carved in sandstone by Walter McGill.

Andrew (Boy) Charlton Pool is popular for swimming.

Cadi Jam Ora, a bush tucker display, encourages visitors to taste bush foods from local plants.

★ Australia's First Farm
It is claimed that some Middle Garden oblong beds follow the direction of the first furrows ploughed in the colony.

National Herbarium of New South Wales
About one million dried plant specimens document biological diversity. Discovery and documentation of new plants aims to slow down extinction rates of species.

Wollemi Pine

STAR SIGHTS

★ Sydney Tropical Centre

★ Australia's First Farm

★ Palm Grove

★ Herb Garden

Conservatorium of Music ❷

Macquarie St. **Map** 1 C3. **Tel** 9351 1222. 🚌 Sydney Explorer, Circular Quay routes. ⬜ 9am–5pm Mon–Fri, 9am–4pm Sat (public areas only). ⬤ public hols, Easter Sat, 24 Dec–2 Jan. 📷 ♿ 🎫 by appointment (phone 9351 1296 for details).

When it was finished in 821, this striking castellated Colonial Gothic building was meant to be stables and servants' quarters for Government House, but construction of the latter was delayed for almost 25 years. That stables should be built in so grand a style, and at such great cost, brought forth cries of outrage and led to bitter arguments between the architect, Francis Greenway (see p114), and Governor Macquarie – and a decree that all future building plans be submitted to London.

Between 1908 and 1915, "Greenway's folly" underwent a dramatic transformation. A concert hall, roofed in grey slate, was built on the central courtyard and the building in its entirety was converted for the use of the new Sydney Conservatorium of Music.

Recently added facilities include a café which holds regular lunchtime concerts during the school term and an upper level with great harbour views. "The Con" continues to be a training ground for future musicians as well as being a great place to visit.

The Conservatorium of Music at the edge of the Royal Botanic Gardens

---

THE HISTORY OF COCKATOO ISLAND

HMS *Orlando* in dry dock at Cockatoo Island in the 1890s

Now deserted, the largest of the 12 Sydney Harbour islands was used to store grain from the 1830s. It was a penal establishment from the 1840s to 1908, with prisoners being put to work constructing dock facilities. The infamous bushranger "Captain Thunderbolt" made his escape from Cockatoo in 1863 by swimming across to the mainland. From the 1870s to the 1960s, Cockatoo Island was a thriving naval dockyard and shipyard, the hub of Australian industry.

Government House ❸

Macquarie St. **Map** 1 C2. **Tel** 9931 5222. 🚌 Sydney Explorer, Circular Quay routes. **House** ⬜ 10am–3pm Fri–Sun. ⬤ Good Fri, 25 Dec. **Garden** ⬜ 10am–4pm daily. 📷 ♿ 🎫 every 30 mins. **www**.hht.net.au

What used to be the official residence of the governor of New South Wales overlooks the harbour from within the Royal Botanic Gardens, but the grandiose, somewhat sombre, turreted Gothic Revival edifice seems curiously out of place in its beautiful park setting.

It was built of local sandstone and cedar between 1837 and 1845. A fine collection of 19th- and early 20th-century furnishings and decoration is housed within.

Resting on the carved stone seat of Mrs Macquaries Chair

Mrs Macquaries Chair ❹

Mrs Macquaries Rd. **Map** 2 E2. 🚌 Sydney Explorer, 888. ♿

The scenic Mrs Macquaries Road winds alongside much of what is now the city's Royal Botanic Gardens, from Farm Cove to Woolloomooloo Bay and back again. The road was built in 1816 at the instigation of Elizabeth Macquarie, wife of the Governor. In the same year, a stone bench, inscribed with details of the new road, was carved into the rock at the point where Mrs Macquarie would stop to admire the view on her daily constitutional.

Although today the outlook from this famous landmark is much changed, it is just as arresting, taking in the broad sweep of the harbour and foreshore with all its landmarks.

Historic Woolloomooloo Finger Wharf redevelopment, including apartments, restaurants and a hotel

Fort Denison **5**

Sydney Harbour. **Map** 2 E1. **Tel** *9247 5033.* from Circular Quay. 25 Dec. cadman. cottage@environment.nsw.gov.au

First named Rock Island, this prominent, rocky outcrop in Sydney Harbour was very quickly dubbed "Pinchgut". This was probably because of the meagre rations given to convicts who were confined there as punishment. It had a grim history of incarceration in the early years of the colony.

In 1796, con-victed murderer Francis Morgan was hanged on the island in chains. His body was left to rot on the gallows for three years as a grisly warning to the other convicts.

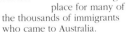

Fort Denison in 1907

Between 1855 and 1857, the Martello tower (the only one in Australia), gun battery and barracks that now occupy the island were built as part of Sydney's defences and the site was renamed after the gover-nor of the time. The gun, still fired at 1pm each day, was an important aid for navigation, allowing mariners to set their ships' chronometers.

Today the island is a popu-lar tourist spot, commanding spectacular views of Sydney

Harbour, the Opera House and Kirribilli. To explore Fort Denison, book a boat tour from Cadman Cottage.

Woolloomooloo Finger Wharf **6**

Cowper Wharf Roadway, Woolloomooloo. **Map** 2 E4. Sydney Explorer, 311.

This is the largest of several finger wharves that jut out into the harbour. The wharf, completed in 1914, was one of the points of embarkation for soldiers bound for both world wars. Following World War II, it was a landing place for many of the thousands of immigrants who came to Australia.

The wharf was the subject of public controversy in the late 1980s and early 1990s, when demolition plans were thwart-ed by conservation groups. Since then, this National-Trust-listed maritime site has been redeveloped to include a hotel, lively restaurants and bars, and apartments.

Art Gallery of New South Wales **7**

See pp108–11.

The Domain **8**

Art Gallery Rd. **Map** 1 C4. Sydney Explorer, 111, 411.

People who swarm to the January concerts and other Festival of Sydney events in The Domain (see p49) are part of a long-standing tradition.

This extensive public space has long been a rallying point for crowds of Sydneysiders whenever emotive issues of public importance have arisen, such as the attempt in 1916 to introduce military conscription or the dismissal of the elected federal government by the then governor-general in 1975.

From the 1890s, part of The Domain was also used as the Sydney version of "Speakers' Corner". Today, you are more likely to see joggers or office workers playing touch foot-ball in their lunch hours, or simply enjoying the shade.

A dramatic view of Sydney Opera House from Mrs Macquaries Chair

Art Gallery of New South Wales ❼

Established in 1874, the art gallery has occupied its present imposing building since 1897. Designed by the Colonial Architect WL Vernon, the gallery doubled in size following 1988 building extensions. Two equestrian bronzes – *The Offerings of Peace* and *The Offerings of War* – greet the visitor on entry. The gallery itself houses some of the finest works of art in Australia. It has sections devoted to Australian, Asian, European, photographic and contemporary and photographic works, along with a strong collection of prints and drawings. The Yiribana Gallery, the largest in the world to exclusively exhibit Aboriginal and Torres Strait Islander art and culture, was opened in 1994.

Cycladic figure (c.2,500 BC)

Lower Level 3

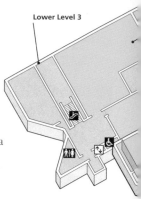

Sofala *(1947)*
Russell Drysdale's visions of Australia show "ghost" towns laid waste by devastating natural forces such as drought.

Sunbaker *(1937)*
Max Dupain's iconic, almost abstract, Australian photograph of hedonism and sun worship uses clean lines, strong light, and geometric form. The image's power lies in its simplicity.

Madonna and Child with Infant St John the Baptist
This oil on wood (c.1541) is the work of Siena Mannerist artist Domenico Beccafumi.

STAR EXHIBITS

★ The Golden Fleece – Shearing at Newstead by Tom Roberts

★ Pukumani Grave Posts

GALLERY GUIDE

There are five levels. The Upper Level has the Rudy Komon Gallery for temporary exhibitions, which are also held on Lower Level 1. The Ground Level has European and Australian works, 20th-century European prints are on Lower Level 2 and the Yiribana Aboriginal Gallery is on Lower Level 3.

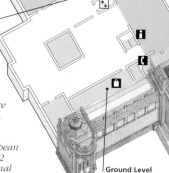

Ground Level

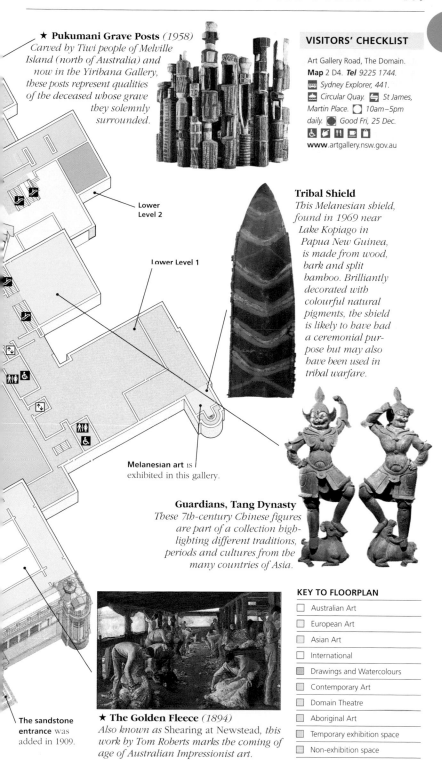

★ **Pukumani Grave Posts** (1958)
Carved by Tiwi people of Melville Island (north of Australia) and now in the Yiribana Gallery, these posts represent qualities of the deceased whose grave they solemnly surrounded.

VISITORS' CHECKLIST

Art Gallery Road, The Domain.
Map 2 D4. **Tel** 9225 1744.
Sydney Explorer, 441.
Circular Quay. St James,
Martin Place. 10am–5pm
daily. Good Fri, 25 Dec.
www.artgallery.nsw.gov.au

Lower
Level 2

Lower Level 1

Tribal Shield
This Melanesian shield, found in 1969 near Lake Kopiago in Papua New Guinea, is made from wood, bark and split bamboo. Brilliantly decorated with colourful natural pigments, the shield is likely to have had a ceremonial purpose but may also have been used in tribal warfare.

Melanesian art is exhibited in this gallery.

Guardians, Tang Dynasty
These 7th-century Chinese figures are part of a collection highlighting different traditions, periods and cultures from the many countries of Asia.

KEY TO FLOORPLAN

- [ ] Australian Art
- [ ] European Art
- [ ] Asian Art
- [ ] International
- [ ] Drawings and Watercolours
- [ ] Contemporary Art
- [ ] Domain Theatre
- [ ] Aboriginal Art
- [ ] Temporary exhibition space
- [ ] Non-exhibition space

The sandstone entrance was added in 1909.

★ **The Golden Fleece** (1894)
Also known as Shearing at Newstead, *this work by Tom Roberts marks the coming of age of Australian Impressionist art.*

Exploring the Art Gallery's Collection

Although local works had been collected since 1875 the gallery did not seriously begin seeking Australian and non-British art until the 1920s, and not until the 1940s did it begin acquiring Aboriginal and Torres Strait Islander paintings. These contrasting collections are now its great strength. Major temporary exhibitions are also regularly staged, with the annual Archibald, Wynne and Sulman prizes being most controversial and highly entertaining.

Study for Self Portrait, a Francis Bacon painting from 1976

Grace Cossington Smith's 1955 *Interior with wardrobe mirror*

AUSTRALIAN ART

Among the most important colonial works is John Glover's *Natives on the Ouse River, Van Diemen's Land* (1838), an image of doomed Tasmanian Aborigines.

The old wing holds paintings from the Heidelberg school of Australian Impressionism. Charles Conder's *Departure of the Orient – Circular Quay* (1888) and Tom Robert's *The Golden Fleece – Shearing at Newstead* (1894) hang alongside fine works by Frederick McCubbin and Arthur Streeton. Rupert Bunny's sensuous *Summer Time* (c.1907) and *A Summer Morning* (c.1908), and

George Lambert's heroic *Across the black soil plains* (1899), impress with their huge size and complex compositions.

Australia was slow to take up Modernism. *Implement blue* (1927) and *Western Australian Gum Blossom* (1928), both by Margaret Preston, are her most assertive of the 1920s. Sidney Nolan's works range from *Boy in Township* (1943) to *Burke* (c.1962), exploiting myths of early Australian history. There are fine holdings of William Dobell and Russell Drysdale, as well as important collections of Arthur Boyd, Fred Williams, Grace Cossington Smith and Brett Whiteley *(see p130).*

EUROPEAN ART

The scope of the scattered European collection ranges from the medieval to the modern. British art from the late 19th to the early 20th centuries forms an outstanding component.

Among the Old Masters are some significant Italian works that reflect Caravaggio's influence. There are also several notable works from the Renaissance in Sienese and Florentine styles.

Henry Moore's *Reclining Figure: Angles* (1980)

Hogarth, Turner and Joshua Reynolds are represented, as are Neo-Classical works. *The Visit of the Queen of Sheba to King Solomon* (1884–90) by Edward Poynter has been on display since 1892. Ford Madox Brown's *Chaucer at the Court of Edward III* (1845–51) is the most commanding work in the Pre-Raphaelite collection.

The Impressionists and Post-Impressionists, represented by late-1880s Pissarro and Monet, are housed in the new gallery wing. Bonnard, Kandinsky, Braque and many other well-known European artists are also here. *Old Woman in Ermine* (1946) by Max Beckmann and *Three Bathers* (1913) by Ernst Kirchner are strong examples of German Expressionism. The gallery's first Picasso, *Nude in a Rocking Chair* (1956), was purchased in 1981. Among distinguished sculptures is Henry Moore's *Reclining Figure: Angles* (1980), found resting by the side of the entrance.

PHOTOGRAPHY

Australian photography from 1975 to today, represented in all its various forms, is a major part of the collection. In recent years, however, the emphasis has been on building up a body of 19th-century Australian work in a range of early mediums. Nearly 3,000

Brett Whiteley's vivid *The Balcony (2)* from 1975

prints constitute this collection with pieces by Charles Kerry, Charles Bayliss and Harold Cazneaux, the latter a major figure of early 20th-century Pictorialism. Such international photographers as Muybridge, Robert Mapplethorpe and Man Ray are also represented here.

ASIAN ART

This collection is one of the finest in Australia. Chinese art is represented by a chronological presentation of works from the pre-Shang dynasty (c.1600–1027 BC) to the 20th century. The Ming porcelains, earthenware funerary pieces *(mingqi)* and the sculptures deserve close attention.

The Japanese painting collection contains fine examples by major artists of the Edo period (1615–1867). The Indian and Southeast Asian holdings consist of lacquer, ceramics and sculptures, with painting displays changing regularly.

PRINTS AND DRAWINGS

As so many of the works in this collection are fragile, the exhibitions are changed frequently. The collection represents the European tradition from the High Renaissance to the 19th and 20th centuries, with work by Rembrandt, Constable, William Blake and Edvard Munch. A strong bias towards Sydney artists from the past 100 years has resulted in a fine gathering of work by Thea Proctor, Norman and Lionel Lindsay and Lloyd Rees.

Egon Schiele's *Poster for the Vienna Secession* (1918)

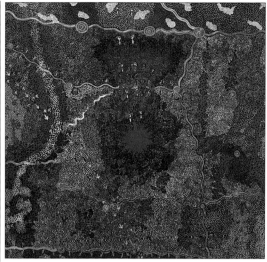

Warlugulong by Clifford Possum Tjapaltjarri and Tim Leura Tjapaltjarri

CONTEMPORARY ART

The significance of the art of our time is reflected in the collection of recent work by international and Australian artists, only a fraction of which can be displayed at any time. The collection highlights the artistic themes that have been central to art practice of the last three decades. Works by Australian artists, such as *Pataphysical Man* (Imants Tillers, 1984) and *Suspended Stone Circle II* (Ken Unsworth, 1988), are on display alongside pieces by notable international artists of the calibre of Cindy Sherman, Yves Klein, Philip Guston and Anselm Kiefer. The gallery also has a contemporary project space that features temporary experimental installations.

YIRIBANA GALLERY

Devoted to the exhibition of Aboriginal and Torres Strait Islander artworks bought since the 1940s, traditional bark paintings hang alongside innovative works from both desert and urban areas, including stone and wood carvings, ceramics and weavings. The ability of contemporary artists to apply traditional ceremonial body and sand painting styles to new media forms, and the endurance of "Aboriginality", are repeatedly demonstrated. The significant early purchases are mainly natural pigment paintings on bark and card, often containing a simple, figurative motif of everyday life. Also of interest are two sandstone carvings by Queenslanders Linda Craigie and Nora Nathan, the only women artists in the collection until 1985. Topographical, geographical and cultural mapping of the land is displayed in a number of intricate landscapes. The qualities and forms of the natural world, and the actions and tracks of Ancestral Beings, are coded within the images. These paintings are maps of Ancestral journeys and events. The bark painting *Three Mimis Dancing* (1964) by Samuel Wagbara examines the habitation of the land by Spirits and the recurrence of the Creation Cycles.

Pukumani Grave Posts Melville Island (1958) is a solemn ceremonial work dealing with death, while the eminent Emily Kame Kngwarreye honours the land from which she comes. The canvases of her intricate dot paintings, created using new tools and technology, appear to move and shimmer, telling stories of the animals and food to be found there.

Mosaic replica of the Tasman Map in the State Library of NSW

The newest section, a modern structure facing Macquarie St, houses the State Reference Library and a gourmet café.

Outside the library, also facing Macquarie Street, is a statue of explorer Matthew Flinders. Behind him on the windowsill is a statue of his co-voyager, his faithful cat, Trim.

Parliament House ❿

Macquarie St. **Map** 4 F1. **Tel** 9230 2111. 🚌 Sydney Explorer, Elizabeth St routes. ⬛ Martin Place. 📋 book in advance 9230 3444. ⬜ 9:30am–4:30pm Mon–Fri. ⬤ most public hols. ♿ www.parliament.nsw.gov.au

The central section of this building, which houses the State Parliament, is part of the original Sydney Hospital built from 1811–16. It has been a seat of government since 1829 when the newly appointed Legislative Council first held meetings here. The building was extended twice during the 19th century and again during the 1970s and 1980s. The current building contains the chambers for both houses of state parliament, as well as parliamentary offices.

Malby's celestial globe, Parliament House

State Library of NSW ❾

Macquarie St. **Map** 4 F1. **Tel** 9273 1414. 🚌 Sydney Explorer, Elizabeth St routes. ⬜ 9am–9pm Mon–Fri, 11am–5pm Sat & Sun. ⬤ some public hols. Mitchell Library closed Sun. 🔲 ♿ 📷 www.sl.nsw.gov.au

The State Library is housed in two separate buildings connected by a passageway and a glass bridge. The older building, the Mitchell Library wing (1906), is a majestic sandstone edifice facing the Royal Botanic Gardens. Huge stone columns supporting a vaulted

ceiling frame the impressive vestibule. On the vestibule floor is a mosaic replica of an old map illustrating the two voyages made to Australia by Dutch navigator Abel Tasman in the 1640s. The original Tasman Map is held in the Mitchell Library as part of its large collection of historic Australian paintings, books, documents and pictorial records.

The Mitchell wing's vast reading room, with its huge skylight and oak panelling, is just beyond the main vestibule.

MACQUARIE STREET

Described in the 1860s as one of the gloomiest streets in Sydney, this could now claim to be the most elegant. Open on the northeastern side to the harbour breezes and the greenery of The Domain, a leisurely walk down this tree-lined street is one of the most pleasurable ways to view the architectural heritage of Sydney.

The new wing *of the library was built in 1988 and connected to the old section by a glass walkway.*

The Mitchell Library wing's portico (1906) has Ionic columns.

The Legislative Assembly, *the lower house of state parliament, is furnished in the traditional green of the British House of Commons.*

Parliament House was once the convict-built Rum Hospital's northern wing.

STATE LIBRARY OF NSW *(1906–41)*   **PARLIAMENT HOUSE** *(1811–16*

Parliamentary memorabilia is on view in the Jubilee Room, as are displays showing Parliament House's development and the legislative history of New South Wales.

The corrugated iron building with a cast-iron façade tacked on at the southern end was a pre-fabricated kit from England. It was originally intended as a chapel for the gold fields, but was diverted from this purpose and sent to Sydney. In 1856, this dismantled kit became the chamber for the new Legislative Council. Its packing cases were used to line this chamber; the rough timber is still on view inside.

Stained glass at Sydney Hospital

the Rum Hospital because the builders were paid by being allowed to import rum for resale. Both the north and south wings of the Rum Hospital survive as Parliament House and the Sydney Mint. The central wing, which was in danger of collapsing, was demolished in 1879 and the new hospital, which still functions today, was completed in 1894. The Classical Revival building boasts a Baroque staircase and elegant floral stained-glass windows in its entrance hall.

Florence Nightingale approved the design of the 1867 nurses' wing. In the inner courtyard, there is a brightly coloured Art Deco fountain (1907).

At the front of the hospital sits *Il Porcellino*, a brass boar. It is a copy of a 17th-century fountain in Florence's Mercato Nuovo. Donated in 1968 by an Italian woman whose relatives had worked at the hospital, the statue is an enduring symbol of the close friendship between Italy and Australia.

Like his Florentine counterpart, *Il Porcellino* is supposed to bring good luck to all those who rub his snout. All coins tossed in the shallow pool at his feet for luck and fortune are collected for the hospital.

Sydney Hospital ⓫

Macquarie St. **Map** 1 C4.
Tel *9382 7111.* 🚌 *Sydney Explorer, Elizabeth St routes.* ⭕ *daily.* 📷 *for tours.* 📷 ♿ 🎫 *must be booked in advance by telephone.*

This imposing collection of Victorian sandstone buildings stands on the site of what was once the central section of the original convict-built Sydney Hospital – known as

Il Porcellino, the brass boar in front of Sydney Hospital

The lamps *hanging over the gateways of Parliament House are reproductions of the 19th-century gas lamps that used to stand here.*

The Little Shop, *a tiny corner store, currently resides in one of two domed former gatehouses.*

The entrance stairs *of Pyrmont sandstone have set the tone for all renovations. The stone, quarried in colonial times, must be matched exactly.*

Corrugated iron and cast-iron façade

Arched sandstone bridges

Arcaded stone verandas with ornate balustrading

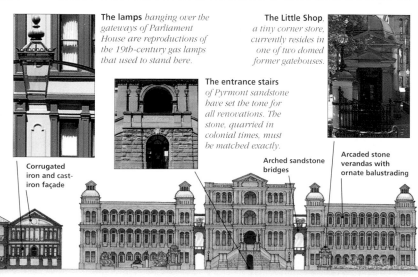

SYDNEY HOSPITAL *(1868–94)*

The Mint

10 Macquarie St. **Map** 1 C5.
Tel 8239 2288. 🚌 *Sydney Explorer,
Elizabeth St routes.* 🕐 *9am–5pm
Mon–Fri.* ⬤ *Good Fri, 25 Dec.*
Box Office *Tel* 8239 2211.
🅿 📷 ♿ *ground floor only*
www.hht.net.au/museums

The gold rushes of the mid-
19th century transformed
colonial Australia. The Sydney
Mint opened in the 1816 Rum
Hospital's south wing in 1854
to turn recently discovered
gold into bullion and currency.
    It was the first branch of the
Royal Mint to be established
outside London. The Mint

was closed in 1927 as it was
no longer competitive with the
Melbourne and Perth Mints.
The Georgian building went
into its own decline after it was
converted into government
offices. In the 1950s, the front
courtyard was even used as a
car park. In 1982, it opened as
a branch of the Powerhouse
Museum *(see pp100–101)*, but
the collection moved to the
main museum in Harris Street.
    This building is now the
head office of the Historic
Houses Trust of NSW and you
can wander through the front
of the building, or view the
small historical display near
the entrance.

**Replica convict hammocks on the
third floor of Hyde Park Barracks**

FRANCIS GREENWAY, CONVICT ARCHITECT

Until recently, Australian $10 notes bore
the portrait of the early colonial architect
Francis Greenway, the only currency in
the world to pay tribute to a convicted
forger. Greenway was transported to
Sydney in 1814 to serve 14 years for
his crime. Under the patronage of
Governor Macquarie, who appointed him
Civil Architect in 1816, Greenway
designed more than 40 buildings,
of which only 11 remain today.
He received a full pardon in 1819,
but soon fell out of favour as he
persisted in charging large fees
while still on a government salary.
Greenway died in poverty in 1837.

**Francis Greenway
(1777–1837)**

Hyde Park Barracks Museum ⑬

Queens Square, Macquarie St. **Map**
1 C5. *Tel 8239 2311.* 🚆 *St James,
Martin Place.* 🕐 *9:30am–5pm daily.*
⬤ *Good Fri, 25 Dec.* 🎫 📷 🅿 ♿
level one only. 🎧 *on request.*
www.hht.net.au/museums

Described by Governor
Macquarie as "spacious" and
"well-aired", the beautifully
proportioned barracks are the
work of Francis Greenway and
are considered his masterpiece.
They were completed in 1819

MACQUARIE STREET

Fine examples of Francis Greenway's Georgian
style are within an easy walk of one another at
the Hyde Park end of Macquarie Street. The
brick and sandstone of Hyde Park Barracks, St
James Church and the Old Supreme Court
Building form a harmonious group on the site
the governor envisaged as the city's civic centre.

The Mint,
*like its twin, Parliament
House, has an unusual
double-colonnaded,
two-storeyed veranda.*

The roof *of The Mint
has now been com-
pletely restored to
replicate the original
wooden shingles in
casuarina (she-oak).*

The stone wall
*of Hyde Park Barracks' north-
west pavilion still bears the
marks of the convicts' chisels.*

**Hyde Park
Barracks Café**

THE MINT *(1816)*

by convict labour and designed to house 600 convicts who had previously been forced to find their own lodgings after their day's work. Subsequently, the building housed Irish orphans and then single female immigrants, before becoming courts and legal offices. Refurbished in 1990, it reopened as a museum with exhibits covering the the site and its occupants over the years.

The displays include a room reconstructed as convict quarters of the 1820s, as well as pictures, models and artifacts relating to this period of Australian history. Many of the objects recovered during archaeological digs at the site and now on display had been dragged away by rats to their nests; the scavenging rodents are acknowledged as valuable agents of preservation.

The Greenway Gallery on the first floor holds temporary exhibitions on history, ideas and culture. From the Barracks Café, which incorporates the original confinement cell area, the visitor can enjoy refreshment, gazing out over the now serene courtyard, once the scene of brutal convict floggings.

Detail from the Children's Chapel mural in the St James' Church crypt

St James Church ⑭

173 King St. **Map** 1 B5. **Tel** 9232 3022. 🚇 St James, Martin Place. ⬜ 8am–5pm Mon–Fri, 8am–4pm Sat, 7:30am–4pm Sun. **Free concerts** Wed 1:15pm.

This fine Georgian building, constructed with convict-made bricks, was designed as a courthouse in 1819. The architect, Francis Greenway, was forced to convert it into a church in 1820, when plans to build a grand cathedral on George Street were abandoned.

Greenway unhappy about the change, designed a simple yet elegant church. Consecrated in 1824 by Samuel Marsden, the infamous "flogging parson", it is Sydney's oldest church. Many additions have been carried out, including designs by John Verge in which the pulpit faced towards high-rent pews, while convicts and the military sat behind the preacher where the service would have been inaudible. A Children's Chapel was added in 1930.

Prominent members of early 19th-century society, many of whom died violently, are commemorated in marble tablets. These tell the full and bloody stories of luckless explorers, the governor's wife dashed to her death from her carriage, and shipwreck victims.

This clock, *dating from 1817 and one of Sydney's oldest, is on the Hyde Park Barracks façade.*

The Land Titles Office, *a WL Vernon building from 1908, has a Classical form with some fine Tudor Gothic detailing.*

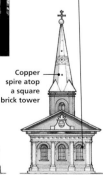

The stained-glass windows *in St James Church are mostly 20th century, and represent the union formed by air, earth, fire and water.*

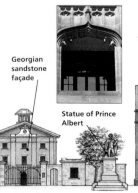

Georgian sandstone façade

Statue of Prince Albert

DE PARK BARRACKS (1817–19)

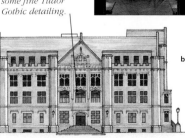

LAND TITLES OFFICE (1908–13)

Copper spire atop a square brick tower

ST JAMES (1820)

KINGS CROSS AND DARLINGHURST

DEL RIO
22-24

Façade detail, Del Rio *(see p119)*

Situated on the eastern fringe of the city, Kings Cross, known as "The Cross", and Darlinghurst are a couple of Sydney celebrities. Their allure is tarnished – or enhanced, perhaps – by trails of scandal and corruption. Kings Cross, particularly, is still regarded as a hotbed of vice; both areas still bear the taint of 1920s gangland associations. In fact, both are now cosmopolitan areas – among the most densely populated parts of Sydney, famed as much for their street life and thriving café culture as for their unsavoury features. Kings Cross exudes a welcome breath of bohemia, in spite of the sleaze of Darlinghurst Road and the flaunting of its red light district. Darlinghurst comes brilliantly into its own every March, when the flamboyant Gay and Lesbian Mardi Gras parade, supported by huge crowds of spectators, makes its triumphant way along Oxford Street.

SIGHTS AT A GLANCE

Historic Streets and Buildings
Victoria Street 2
Elizabeth Bay House 3
Old Gaol, Darlinghurst 6
Darlinghurst Court House 7

Parks and Gardens
Beare Park 4

Monuments
El Alamein Fountain 1

Museums and Galleries
Sydney Jewish Museum 5

GETTING THERE

Kings Cross railway station serves the area. Bus number 311 travels through Kings Cross and Darlinghurst, while the 324, 325 and 389 are also useful. Buses 378, 380 and 382 travel along Oxford Street.

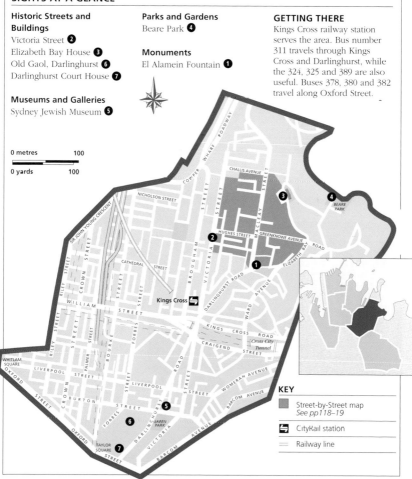

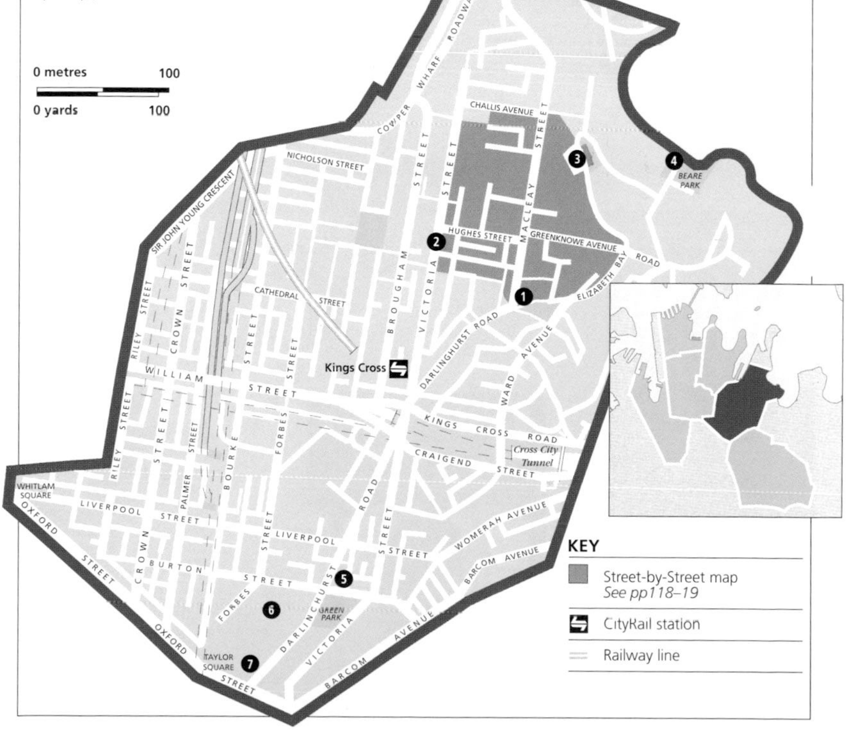
0 metres 100
0 yards 100
COWPER WHARF ROADWAY
CHALLIS AVENUE
NICHOLSON STREET
MACLEAY STREET
BEARE PARK
HUGHES STREET
GREENKNOWE AVENUE
ELIZABETH BAY ROAD
SIR JOHN YOUNG CRESCENT
CATHEDRAL STREET
BROUGHAM
VICTORIA
DARLINGHURST ROAD
WARD AVENUE
Kings Cross
WILLIAM STREET
RILEY STREET
CROWN STREET
BOURKE
FORBES
PALMER STREET
KINGS CROSS ROAD
CRAIGEND STREET
Cross City Tunnel
WHITLAM SQUARE
LIVERPOOL STREET
OXFORD STREET
BURTON STREET
WOMERAH AVENUE
BARCOM AVENUE
GREEN PARK
TAYLOR SQUARE
KEY
Street-by-Street map See pp118–19
CityRail station
Railway line

The large neon sign at the top of William Street marking the entrance to Kings Cross

Street-by-Street: Potts Point

Beare Park fountain detail

The substantial Victorian houses filling the streets of this old suburb are excellent examples of the 19th-century concern with architectural harmony. New building projects were designed to enhance rather than contradict the surrounding buildings and general streetscape. Monumental structures and fine details of moulded stuccoed parapets, cornices and friezes, even the spandrels in herringbone pattern, are all integral parts of a grand suburban plan. (This plan included an 1831 order that all houses cost at least £1,000.) Cool and dark verandas extend the street's green canopy of shade, leaving an impression of cool drinks enjoyed on hot summer days in fine Victorian style.

The McElhone Stairs were preceded by a wooden ladder that linked Woolloomooloo Hill, as Kings Cross was known, to the estate far below.

Horderns Stairs

These villas, from the Georgian and Victorian eras, can be broadly labelled as Classical Revival and are fronted by leafy gardens.

Kings Cross Station

★ Victoria Street
In 1972–4, residents of this historic street fought a sometimes violent battle against developers wanting to build high-rise office towers, motels and blocks of flats **2**

Werrington, a mostly serious and streamlined building, also has flamboyant Art Deco detailing which is now subdued under brown paint.

STAR SIGHTS

★ Victoria Street

★ Elizabeth Bay House

Tusculum Villa was just one of a number of 1830s houses subject to "villa conditions". All had to face Government House, be of a high monetary value and be built within three years.

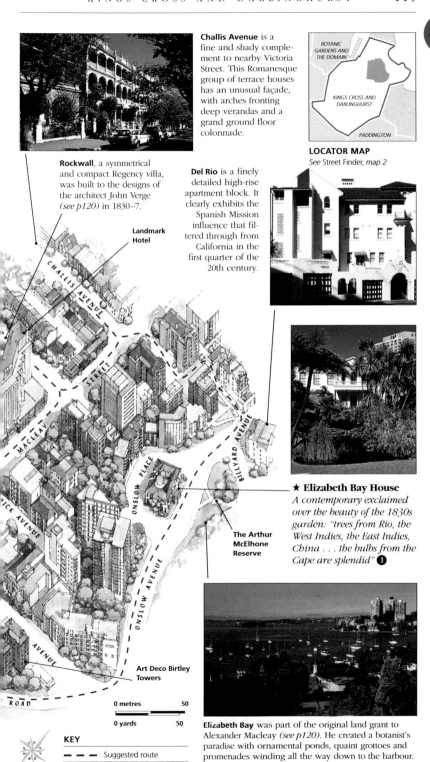

Challis Avenue is a fine and shady complement to nearby Victoria Street. This Romanesque group of terrace houses has an unusual façade, with arches fronting deep verandas and a grand ground floor colonnade.

LOCATOR MAP
See Street Finder, map 2

Rockwall, a symmetrical and compact Regency villa, was built to the designs of the architect John Verge *(see p120)* in 1830–7.

Del Rio is a finely detailed high-rise apartment block. It clearly exhibits the Spanish Mission influence that filtered through from California in the first quarter of the 20th century.

Landmark Hotel

★ **Elizabeth Bay House**
A contemporary exclaimed over the beauty of the 1830s garden: "trees from Rio, the West Indies, the East Indies, China . . . the bulbs from the Cape are splendid" ❸

The Arthur McElhone Reserve

Art Deco Birtley Towers

0 metres   50

0 yards   50

KEY

– – – Suggested route

Elizabeth Bay was part of the original land grant to Alexander Macleay *(see p120)*. He created a botanist's paradise with ornamental ponds, quaint grottoes and promenades winding all the way down to the harbour.

El Alamein Fountain, commemorating the World War II battle

El Alamein Fountain ❶

Fitzroy Gardens, Macleay St, Potts Point. **Map** 2 E5. 🚌 *311.*

This dandelion of a fountain in the heart of the Kings Cross district has a reputation for working so spasmodically that passers-by often murmur facetiously, "He loves me, he loves me not." Built in 1961, it commemorates the Australian army's role in the siege of Tobruk, Libya, and the battle of El Alamein in Egypt during World War II. At night, when it is brilliantly lit, the fountain looks surprisingly ethereal.

Victoria Street ❷

Potts Point. **Map** 5 B2. 🚌 *311, 324, 325.*

At the Potts Point End, this street of 19th-century terrace houses, interspersed with a few incongruous-looking high-rise blocks, is, by inner-city standards, almost a boulevard. This gracious street was once at the centre of a bitter conservation struggle, one which almost certainly cost a prominent heritage campaigner's life.

In the early 1970s, many residents, backed by the "green bans" *(see p31)* put in place by the Builders' Labourers' Federation of New South Wales, fought to prevent demolition of old buildings for high-rise

development. Juanita Nielsen, publisher of a local newspaper and heiress, vigorously took up the conservation battle. On 4 July 1975, she disappeared without trace. A subsequent inquest into her disappearance returned an open verdict.

As a result of the actions of the union and residents, most of Victoria Street's superb old buildings still stand. Ironically, they are now occupied not by the low-income residents who fought to save them, but by the well-off professionals who eventually displaced them.

Elizabeth Bay House ❸

7 Onslow Ave, Elizabeth Bay. **Map** 2 F5. **Tel** 9356 3022. 🚌 *Sydney Explorer, 311.* 🕙 *10am–4:30pm Tue–Sun.* ⬤ *Good Fri, 25 Dec.* 📷 🅰 **www**.hht.net.au/museums

Elizabeth Bay House *(see pp24–5)* contains the finest colonial interior on display in Australia. It is a potent expression of how the 1840s depression cut short the 1830s' prosperous optimism. Designed in the fashionable Greek Revival style by John Verge, it was built for Colonial Secretary Alexander Macleay, from 1835–9. The domed oval saloon with its cantilevered staircase is recognized as Verge's masterpiece. The exterior is less satisfactory, as the intended colonnade and portico were not finished owing to a crisis in Macleay's finan-

Juanita Nielsen

cial affairs. The present portico dates from 1893. The interior is furnished to reflect Macleay's occupancy from 1839–45, and is based on inventories drawn up in 1845 for the transfer of the house to Macleay's son, William Sharp. He took the house in return for payment of his father's debts, leading to a rift never to be resolved.

Macleay's original 22-hectare (54-acre) land grant was subdivided for flats and villas from the 1880s to 1927. In the 1940s, the house itself was divided into 15 flats. In 1942, the artist Donald Friend, while standing on the balcony of his flat – the former morning room – saw the ferry *Kuttabul* hit by a torpedo from a Japanese midget submarine.

The house was restored and opened as a museum in 1977.

The sweeping staircase under the oval dome, Elizabeth Bay House

Beare Park ❹

Ithaca Rd, Elizabeth Bay. **Map** 2 F5. 🚌 *311, 350.*

Originally a part of the Macleay Estate, Beare Park is now encircled by a jumble of apartment blocks. A refuge from hectic Kings Cross, it is one of only a handful of parks serving a densely populated area. In the shape of a natural amphitheatre, the park puts Elizabeth Bay on glorious view.

The family home of JC Williamson, a famous theatrical entrepreneur who came to Australia from America in the 1870s, formerly stood at the eastern extremity of the park.

Star of David in the lobby of the Sydney Jewish Museum

Sydney Jewish Museum [5]

148 Darlinghurst Rd, Darlinghurst. **Map** 5 B2. ***Tel*** *9360 7999.* 🚌 *Sydney Explorer, Bondi & Bay Explorer, 311, 389.* 🕒 *10am–4pm Sun–Thu, 10am–2pm Fri.* ⛔ *Sat, Jewish hols.* 👋 ♿ 👉 🛍 **www**.sydneyjewishmuseum.com.au

Sixteen Jewish convicts were on the First Fleet and many more were to be transported before the end of the convict era. As with other convicts, most would endure and some would thrive, seizing all the opportunities the colony had to offer for those wishing to make something of themselves.

The Sydney Jewish Museum relates stories of Australian Jewry within the context of the Holocaust. The ground floor display explores present-day Jewish traditions and culture within Australia. Ascending the stairs to mezzanine levels 1–6, the visitor passes through chronological and thematic exhibitions which unravel the history of the Holocaust.

From Hitler's rise to power and *Kristallnacht,* through the evacuation of the ghettos and the Final Solution, to the ultimate liberation of the infamous death camps and Nuremberg Trials, the harrowing events are graphically documented. This horrific period is recalled using photographs and relics, some exhumed from mass graves, as well as audiovisual exhibits and oral testimonies.

Holocaust survivors act as volunteer guides. Their presence, bearing witness to the recorded events, lends considerable power and moving authenticity to the exhibits.

Old Gaol, Darlinghurst [6]

Cnr Burton & Forbes Sts, Darlinghurst. **Map** 5 A2. ***Tel*** *9339 8744.* 🚌 *378, 380, 382, 389* 🕒 *9am–5pm Mon–Fri.* ⛔ *public hols.* 📷 ♿

Originally known as the Woolloomooloo Stockade and later as Darlinghurst Gaol, this complex is now part the National Art School. It was constructed over a 20-year period from 1822.

Surrounded by walls almost 7 m (23 ft) high, the cell blocks radiate from a central roundhouse. The jail is built of stone quarried on the site by convicts which was then chiselled by them into blocks.

No fewer than 67 people were executed here between 1841 and 1908. Perhaps the most notorious hangman was Alexander "The Strangler" Green, after whom Green Park, outside the jail, is thought to have been named. Green lived near the park until public hostility forced him to live in relative safety inside the jail.

Some of Australia's most noted artists, including Frank Hodgkinson, Jon Molvig and William Dobell, trained or taught at the art school which was established here in 1921.

The former Governor's house, Old Gaol, Darlinghurst

Darlinghurst Court House [7]

Forbes St, Darlinghurst. **Map** 5 A2. ***Tel*** *9368 2947.* 🚌 *378, 380, 382.* 🕒 *Feb–Dec: 10am–4pm Mon–Fri.* ⛔ *mid-Dec–Jan, public hols.* ♿ 👉

Abutting the grim old jail, to which it is connected by underground passages, and facing tawdry Taylors Square, this unlikely gem of Greek Revival architecture was begun in 1835 by Colonial Architect Mortimer Lewis. He was only responsible for the central block of the main building with its splendid six-columned Doric portico with fine Greek embellishments. The balancing side wings were not added until the 1880s.

The court house is still used by the state's Supreme Court mainly for criminal cases, and these are open to the public.

Beare Park, a quiet inner-city park with harbour views

PADDINGTON

Paddington is justly celebrated for its handsome terraces, but this "village in the city", as it is often dubbed, is also famed for its interesting speciality shops full of oddities and collectables, fine restaurants, small hotels, fashionable art galleries and antique dealers' shops. Paddington boasts a lively street culture, especially on Saturdays when people from far and wide flock to the famous weekly Paddington Bazaar, spilling out into the streets, pubs and cafés of the surrounding area. Stretching from the Victoria Barracks at its western end, along Oxford Street to the green haven of Centennial Park, Paddington slopes away from this bustling central thoroughfare into the narrow lanes and elegant, leafy streets. The suburb has undergone a series of quite radical transformations. The first Paddington was built in the 1830s as a Georgian weekend retreat for the moneyed class. These gracious homes had a short life, before being knocked down and subdivided. The terraces succeeding them fell into ruin by the 1920s, but are now admired as finely restored Victorian homes with their distinctive wrought-iron "lace" verandas. The glimpses of harbour found in the quiet streets make Paddington one of Sydney's most sought-after residential areas.

Clock tower on Paddington Town Hall

SIGHTS AT A GLANCE

Historic Streets and Buildings

Paddington Street ❶
Fox Studios Entertainment
  Quarter ❷
Five Ways ❹
Juniper Hall ❺
Paddington Town
  Hall ❻
Paddington
  Village ❼
Victoria
  Barracks ❽

Parks and Gardens

Centennial Park ❾

Markets

Paddington Markets ❸

GETTING THERE

The best way to travel to and around this area is by bus. Buses 378, 380 and 382 run along Oxford Street on their way between the city and beach suburbs, while bus 389 cuts through the back streets.

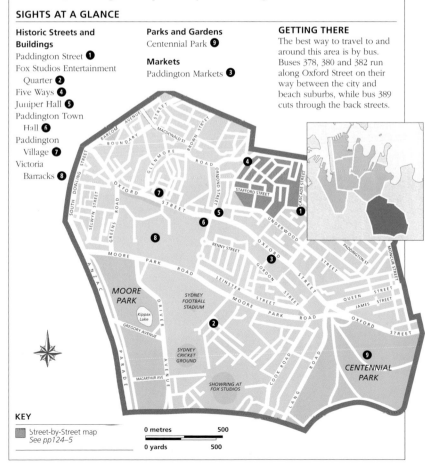

KEY

Street-by-Street map
See pp124–5

0 metres   500
0 yards   500

◁ **The front entrance to a lovingly restored Victorian terrace house in Paddington**

Street-by-Street: Paddington

Paddington began to flourish in the 1840s, when the decision was made to build the Victoria Barracks. At the time much of it was "the most wild looking place . . . barren sand-hills with patches of scrub, hills and hollows galore". The area began to fill rapidly, as owner builders bought into the area and built short rows of terrace houses, many extremely narrow because of the lack of building regulations.

Victorian finial in Union Street

After the Depression, most of Paddington was threatened with demolition, but was saved and restored by the large influx of postwar migrants.

★ Five Ways
This shopping hub was established in the late 19th century on the busy Glenmore roadway trodden out by bullocks ❹

Duxford Street's terrace houses in toning pale shades constitute an ideal of town planning: the Victorians preferred houses in a row to have a pleasingly uniform aspect.

"Gingerbread" houses can be seen in Broughton and Union Streets. With their steeply pitched gables and fretwork barge-boards, they are typical of the rustic Gothic Picturesque architectural style.

The London Tavern opened for business in 1875, making it the suburb's oldest pub. Like many of the pubs and delicatessens in this well-serviced suburb, it stands at the end of a row of terraces.

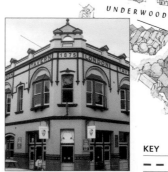

STAR SIGHTS

★ Paddington Street

★ Five Ways

KEY

- - - Suggested route

The Sherman Gallery is housed in a strikingly modern building. It is designed to hold Australian and international contemporary sculpture and paintings. Suitable access gates and a special in-house crane enable the movement of large-scale artworks, including textiles.

Paddington streets are a treasure chest of galleries, bars and restaurants.

LOCATOR MAP
See Street Finder, *maps 5 & 6*

Warwick, built in the 1860s, is a minor castle lying at the end of a row of humble terraces. Its turrets, battlements and assorted decorations, in a style somewhat fancifully described as "King Arthur", even adorn the garages at the rear.

Windsor Street's terrace houses are, in some cases, a mere 4.5 m (15 ft) wide.

Street-making in Paddington's early days was often an expensive and complicated business. A cascade of water was dammed to build Cascade Street.

★ **Paddington Street**
Under the established plane trees, some of Paddington's finest Victorian terraces exemplify the building boom of 1860–90. Over 30 years, 3,800 houses were built in the suburb ①

0 metres 50

0 yards 50

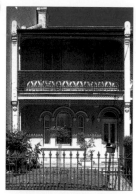

Paddington Street terrace house

Paddington Street ❶

Map 6 D3. 🚌 *378, 380, 382.*

With its huge plane trees shading the road and fine two-, three- and four-storey terrace houses on each side, Paddington Street is one of the oldest, loveliest, and at the same time most typical of the suburb's streets.

Paddington grew rapidly as a commuter suburb in the late 19th century and most of the terraces were built for renting to the city's artisans. They were cheaply decorated with iron lace (some of which had arrived in ships as ballast), as well as Grecian-style friezes, worked parapets, swagged urns, lions rampant, cornices, pilasters, scrolls and other fancy plastering. By the 1900s, these terraces had become unfashionable but in the 1960s, tastes changed again and Paddington experienced a renaissance.

Paddington Street now has a chic atmosphere where small art galleries operate out of quaint and grand shopfronts.

Fox Studios Entertainment Quarter ❷

Lang Rd, Moore Park. *Tel 9383 4333.* **Map** 5 C5. 🚌 *339, 355.* ⬜ *Many retail shops open 10am–10pm.* **www**.foxstudios.com.au

There's a vibrant atmosphere at the Fox Studio complex, which is located next door to the

working studios that produced such well-known films as *The Matrix* and *Moulin Rouge.*

There are 16 cinema screens where you can watch the latest movies, and at the La Premiere cinema you can enjoy your movie with wine and cheese, sitting on comfortable sofas. There are four live-entertainment venues which regularly feature the latest local and international acts. You can also enjoy a game of miniature golf, bungy trampolining, bowling or seasonal ice-skating, and children love the three, well-designed playgrounds.

In addition to shops there are plenty of restaurants, cafés and bars offering a range of meals, drinks and snacks.

Every Wednesday and Saturday you can sample fresh produce at the Farmers Market or try a gourmet delicacy from one of the 40 stallholders. Many of the stalls offer free tastings – from pickled garlic to chilli sauce. There is an International Food Market on Friday nights, and Sunday's market focuses on merchandise rather than food.

Shops are open until late, and there is a good selection – offering fashion, books and homewares. There is plenty of undercover parking and the Studios are a pleasant stroll away from Oxford Street.

Paddington Markets ❸

395 Oxford St. **Map** 6 D4. *Tel 9331 2923.* 🚌 *378, 380, 382.* ⬜ *10am–4pm (5pm daylight saving) Sat.* ⬤ *25 Dec.* 📷 ♿ *See Shops and Markets p203.*

This market, which began in 1973, takes place every Saturday, come rain or shine, in the grounds of Paddington Village Uniting Church and its neighbouring school. It is a place to meet and be seen as much as it is to shop. Stall-holders come from all over the world, and many young designers, hoping to launch their careers, display their wares. Among the offerings are jewellery, pottery new and secondhand clothing and an array of other arts and crafts.

Whatever you are looking for, you are likely to find it here, from designer bags and clothes or a tarot reading, to Oriental massages, bonsai trees and handmade soaps.

Five Ways ❹

Cnr Glenmore Rd & Heeley St. **Map** 5 C3. 🚌 *389.*

At this picturesque junction, a busy shopping hub developed by the tramline that once ran to Bondi Beach. On the five corners stand Victorian and early 20th-century shops, one now a restaurant.

On another corner is the impressive Royal Hotel (see p197), built in 1888. This mixed Victorian and Classical Revival building has a characteristic intricate cast-iron "lace" screen balcony offering stunning harbour views.

Juniper Hall ❺

250 Oxford St. **Map** 5 C3. *Tel 9258 0123.* 🚌 *378, 380, 382.* ⬤ *to public.*

The emancipist gin distiller Robert Cooper built this superb example of Colonial Georgian architecture for his third wife, Sarah. He named it after the main ingredient of the gin that made his fortune.

Completed in 1824, it is the oldest building in Paddington still standing. It is probably also the largest and most extravagant. It had to be: he already had 14 children when he declared that Sarah would have the finest house in Sydney.

Juniper Hall was saved from demolition in the mid-1980s and restored in fine style. Now part of the National Trust, it is used as private office space.

Balcony of the Royal Hotel in the heart of Paddington

Paddington Town Hall ❻

Cnr Oxford St & Oatley Rd. **Map** 5 C3.
🚌 378, 380, 382. ⬜ 10am–4pm
Mon–Fri. 🌑 public hols. 📷

The Paddington Town Hall
was completed in 1891. An
international competition
which, in a spirit of Victorian
self-confidence, was intended
to produce the state's finest
town hall was won by local
architect JE Kemp. His
Classical Revival building, to
which a clock tower was later
added, still dominates the
surrounding area, although it
is no longer a centre of local
government.

The building now houses
Chauvel Cinema, managed
by the Australian Film
Institute, Paddington Library
and a large ballroom that is
available for hire.

Paddington Town Hall

Paddington Village ❼

Cnr Gipps & Shadforth Sts. **Map** 5
C3. 🚌 378, 380, 382.

Paddington began its life as
a working-class suburb. The
community comprised the
carpenters, quarrymen and
stonemasons who supervised
the convict gangs that built
Victoria Barracks in the 1840s.

The artisans and their families occupied a tight huddle of
spartan houses, a few of which
still remain, crowded into the
narrow streets nearby. Like
the barracks, these dwellings
and surrounding shops and
hotels were built mainly of
locally quarried stone.

The lush green expanse of Centennial Park

Victoria Barracks ❽

Oxford St. **Map** 5 B3. **Tel** 9339 3330.
🚌 378, 380, 382. **Museum** ⬜ 10am–
12:30pm Thu, 10am–3:45pm Sun. 🌑
25-26 Dec, 1 Jan. 📷 ♿ 🅿 **Parade
& tour:** 10am Thu.

Victoria Barracks is the largest
and best-preserved group of
late Georgian architecture in
Australia, covering almost
12 ha (29 acres). It is widely
considered to be one of the
best examples of a military
barracks in the world.

Designed by the Colonial
Engineer, Lieutenant Colonel
George Barney, the barracks
were built between 1841 and
1848 using local sandstone
quarried by mainly convict
labour. Originally intended to
house 800 men, it has been in
continuous military use ever
since, and still operates as a
centre of military planning,
administration and command.

The main block is 225 m
(740 ft) long and has symmetrical two-storey wings with
cast-iron verandas flanking a
central archway. The perimeter
walls, which are designed to

**The archway at the Oxford Street
entrance to Victoria Barracks**

repel surprise attacks, have
foundations 10 m (40 ft) deep
in places. In a former jail
block, a museum traces New
South Wales' military heritage.

Centennial Park ❾

Map 6 E5. **Tel** 9339 6699. 🚌 Clovelly,
Coogee, Maroubra, Randwick, Bronte,
City, Bondi Beach & Bondi Junction
routes. ⬜ Mar–Apr: 6am–6pm daily,
May–Aug: 6:30am–5:30pm daily,
Sep–Oct: 6am–6pm daily, Nov–Feb
5:45am–8pm daily. 🅿 🍽 ♿ 🅿 on
request. **www**.cp.nsw.gov.au

Entering this 220-ha (544 acre)
park through one of its sandstone and wrought-iron gates,
the visitor may wonder how
such an extensive and idyllic
place has survived so close to
the centre of the city.

Formerly a common, it was
dedicated "to the enjoyment
of the people of New South
Wales forever" on 26 January
1888, the centenary of the
foundation of the colony. On
1 January 1901, more than
100,000 people gathered here
to witness the Commonwealth
of Australia come into being,
when Australia's first federal
ministry was sworn in by the
first governor-general.

Today picnickers, painters,
runners, and those on horses,
bikes and in-line skates (all of
which can be hired nearby)
use this vast recreation area.

Once the source of Sydney's
water supply, the swamps are
now home to many waterbirds.
Within the park are ornamental ponds, cultivated gardens,
an Avenue of Palms, a sports
ground and a café (see p194).

FURTHER AFIELD

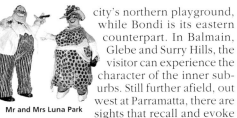

Mr and Mrs Luna Park

Beyond the inner city, numerous places vie for the visitor's attention. Around the harbour foreshores are picturesque suburbs, secluded beaches, scenic outlooks and cultural and historic sights. Taronga Zoo is worth a visit as much for its incomparable setting as for its birds and animals. Manly, stretching between harbour and ocean, is the city's northern playground, while Bondi is its eastern counterpart. In Balmain, Glebe and Surry Hills, the visitor can experience the character of the inner suburbs. Still further afield, out west at Parramatta, there are sights that recall and evoke the first days of European settlement and the colony's initially unsteady steps towards agricultural self-sufficiency.

SIGHTS AT A GLANCE

Historic Districts and Buildings
University of Sydney **3**
Balmain **6**
Kirribilli Point **8**
North Head **12**
Vaucluse House **13**
Watsons Bay **15**
Macquarie Lighthouse **16**
Captain Cook's Landing Place **18**
Elizabeth Farm **20**
Hambledon Cottage **21**
Experiment Farm Cottage **22**
Old Government House **24**

16 km = 10 miles

Parks and Gardens
Nielsen Park **14**

Museums and Galleries
Brett Whiteley Studio **1**
Nutcote **9**

Entertainment
Luna Park **7**
Taronga Zoo pp134–5 **10**
Sydney Olympic Park **19**

Beaches
Manly **11**
Bondi Beach **17**

Restaurants and Pubs
Surry Hills **2**
Glebe **4**

Markets
Sydney Fish Market **5**

Cemeteries
St John's Cemetery **23**

KEY

▢	Main sightseeing areas
▫	Park or reserve
✈	Airport
③	Metroad route
▬	Freeway or motorway
▬	Major road
▭	Minor road

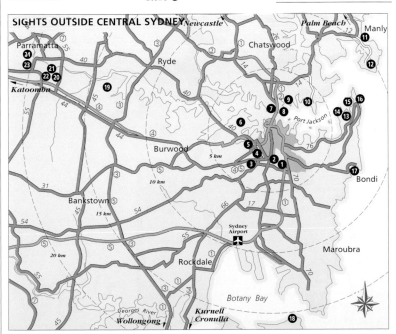

SIGHTS OUTSIDE CENTRAL SYDNEY

Newcastle
Palm Beach
Manly
Parramatta
Chatswood
Ryde
Katoomba
Port Jackson
Burwood
Bondi
Bankstown
Maroubra
Sydney Airport
Rockdale
Botany Bay
Georges River
Kurnell
Cronulla
Wollongong

◁ **The majestic clock tower rising above the main quadrangle at the University of Sydney**

Brett Whiteley Studio ❶

2 Raper St, Surry Hills. **Map** 5 A4.
Tel 9225 1881. 🚌 343, 372, 393.
🕐 10am–4pm Sat & Sun, or by
appointment on Thu & Fri. ⬤ Easter
Sun, 25 Dec. 📷 ♿ partial access.

In June 1992, Brett Whiteley,
enfant terrible of Australian
contemporary art, died unex-
pectedly at the age of 53. An
internationally acclaimed and
prolific artist, he produced
some of the most sumptuous
images of Sydney and its distinctive harbour ever painted.
    In 1985, Whiteley bought a
former factory and converted
it into a studio and residence.
The studio is now a public
museum and art gallery. It
features the work of Whiteley
and other artists. Visitors gain
an insight into Whiteley's life
and work through changing
exhibitions and displays of his
effects and memorabilia. The
studio is under the administration of the Art Gallery of New
South Wales *(see pp108–11).*

Surry Hills ❷

Map 5 A3. 🚌 301, 302, 303, 304,
339. See **Shops and Markets**
pp200–201.

This was once one of the
more depressed areas of the
inner city. In the 1920s, Surry
Hills was a haunt of the razor
gangs that terrorized inner-
city Sydney. The 1940s slums
were vividly described in Ruth
Park's celebrated novels *Poor
Man's Orange* and *The Harp*

Shop in Crown Street, Surry Hills

in the South. In the postwar
years, the low property and
rental prices attracted a large
number of new migrants to
the already-hectic district.
    In recent decades, young
professionals have moved into
the area, lured by the charm
of its Victorian terraces and
closeness to the city. Many
of the suburb's traditional
inhabitants have since
been displaced.
    Today Surry Hills
is a curious mixture
of fashion and seedi-
ness. Newly renovated
houses stand alongside
dilapidated dwellings,
while streets of elegant
Victorian terraces abut
modern high-rise flats and
factory warehouses.
    For the visitor, the
suburb offers a wide
range of ethnic cuisines, often
at bargain prices. It is famed
for the Lebanese and Turkish
restaurants that cluster near
the intersection of Cleveland
and Elizabeth Streets. You will
also find Indian, Chinese, Thai,

French and numerous Italian
eateries scattered around the
suburb, along with smart and
casual cafés and stylish pubs.
    Once the centre of Sydney's
garment trade, it still has factory outlets where clothing,
lingerie and haberdashery can
be purchased at below retail
prices. Alternative fashion and
retro clothing shops are found
at the Oxford Street end of
Crown Street. These boutiques
attract the street-smart crowd.

University of Sydney ❸

Parramatta Rd, Camperdown.
Map 3 B5. **Tel** 9351 2222. 🚌 343,
Parramatta Rd & City Rd routes.
🕐 daily. 📷 ♿ 📱 phone 9351
2274 (book one week in advance).

Inaugurated in 1850, this is
Australia's oldest university.
The campus is a sprawling
hotchpotch of buildings
from different eras, of
often dubious architec-
tural merit. However,
the original Victorian
Gothic main building
still stands on its ele-
vated site, dominating
its surroundings. The
work of the Colonial
Architect Edmund
Blacket, it is scrupulously
modelled on the
architecture of Cam-
bridge and Oxford.
It features intricate stone
tracery, a clock tower with
carved pinnacles, gargoyles
(one, in the quadrangle, represents a crocodile) and a
cloistered main quadrangle.
    The gem of the complex,
and probably Blacket's finest
work, is the Great Hall at the
main building's northern end.
This grandly sombre hall, with
its carved cedar ceiling and
stained-glass windows depicting famous philosophers and
scientists, is often used for
public concerts as well as for
university ceremonies.
    The Nicholson Museum of
antiquities, the natural history
Macleay Museum and the War
Memorial Art Gallery, which
houses the university's art
collection, are all within the
grounds. They are open to the
public on most weekdays.

**Statue of Hermes,
Nicholson Museum**

Brett Whiteley Studio: former artist's studio, now a museum

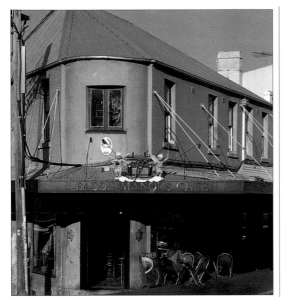

Corner view of Badde Manors Café on Glebe Point Road, Glebe

Glebe ❹

Map 3 A4. 🚌 *431, 433. See Shops and Markets p203.*

The word "Glebe" means land assigned to a clergyman as part of his benefice. In 1789, Governor Phillip granted 162 ha (400 acres) to Richard Johnson, the First Fleet chaplain, and his wife Mary. Almost all of the present suburb was once part of that Glebe Estate. Many of its streets wind down to the working harbour and contain terrace houses with Sydney wrought-iron "lace" in varying states of repair.

The once-grand residences of the 19th-century élite were mostly towards the harbour end of Glebe Point Road, with workers' cottages clustered nearer Parramatta Road. Glebe is still partly a gentrified member of the café society, although its proximity to the Broadway shopping mall and its popularity with students from the nearby University of Sydney have given it a more bustling atmosphere.

It is densely populated and lively, with many restaurants and cafés in all price ranges, traditional and trendy pubs, good bookshops, an art-house cinema and shops selling every-thing from antique clocks to New Age goods and chattels. Glebe Market, held every Saturday, sells jewellery, second-hand clothing and bric-a-brac.

Sydney Fish Market ❺

Cnr Pyrmont Bridge Rd & Bank St, Pyrmont. **Map** 3 B2. **Tel** 9004 1100. 🚌 *443, 501.* 🕐 *7am–4pm daily.* ⬤ *25 Dec.* 📷 ♿ 🅿 *Call for details.* **www**.sydneyfishmarket.com.au *See Shops and Markets pp202–3.*

Every weekday, about 200 seafood retailers and dealers arrive at this cooperative fish market to bid for the previous day's catch. It is sold by Dutch auction, with prices starting high and decreasing, which halves the sale time. The volume and variety of the catch, including fish and seafood makes this the most diverse fish market after Tokyo.

A fair amount of this catch ends up, later in the morning, in the fish market's six large retail outlets which, for the general public, are its main attraction. As well as fresh fish, these retailers sell smoked salmon and roe, sushi, marinated baby octopus and many other ready-to-eat delicacies.

Visitors watch the experts as they tenderize octopus and squid in concrete mixers. As well as fishmongers, there are a number of fresh food shops, several restaurants and a seafood school – cost includes tuition, seafood and wine.

Balmain ❻

🚌 *433, 434, 442. See Shops and Markets p203 and Four Guided Walks pp142–3.*

Balmain was once one of Sydney's most staunchly working-class areas, with shipyards, a dry dock and repair yards, a coal mine, numerous rough-and-ready pubs and an intimidating criminal element. Its late 19th-century town hall, post office, court house and fire station in Darling Street reflect the civic pride of the suburb in the Victorian era.

In recent years, the many stone and timber cottages of what had become a slum have transformed into a charming, bustling suburb that still retains its village character, with interesting shops, galleries, cafés, restaurants and pubs.

The quietness of the Balmain peninsula, its proximity to the city and its bohemian ambience may explain why many prominent writers – including novelist Kate Grenville and playwright David Williamson – have lived and worked here.

The Saturday market, held at St Andrews Congregational Church in Darling Street, is one of Sydney's best. Antiques, estate jewellery and ingenious art and craft items are on sale.

Imposing entrance to Balmain court house on Darling Street

THE COLOURFUL FACES OF LUNA PARK

The gateway to Luna Park is the gaping mouth of a huge laughing face, flanked by two 36-m (129-ft) Art Deco towers. Between 1935 and 1945, four successive canvas, wire and plaster faces fell to the ravages of time. Built in the 1950s, the fifth face was replaced in 1973 with one designed by the Sydney artist Martin Sharp. The seventh, made in 1982, is now at the Powerhouse Museum *(see pp100–101)*. Today's face (1994) is made of polyurethane and fibreglass.

The present Luna Park face, crossing the harbour by barge

The Big Dipper at Luna Park

Luna Park ❼

1 Olympic Drive, Milsons Point. **Tel** 9922 6644. ☐ 11am–7:30pm Sun–Thu, 11am–midnight Fri, 10am–midnight Sat. ⛴ Milsons Point. ♿ **www**.lunaparksydney.com.au

This famous fun fair, built on the site of former Harbour Bridge construction workshops, was modelled on Luna Park at Coney Island, New York. Built in South Australia, Sydney's Luna Park was dismantled and re-erected on its present site in 1935. For the next 43 years it was one of the most conspicuous landmarks on the harbour foreshores. Except during the compulsory blackouts of World War II, its brilliant illuminations were a feature of the city's night scene.

In 1979, seven people were killed in a ghost train fire, a tragedy that led to the park's eventual closure in April 1988.

The park is now open again, and entry is free so you can just enjoy the atmosphere or buy a ticket and catch the views from the Ferris Wheel. Las Vegas glitz and 1940s Futurism are just two of the styles at one of Sydney's most treasured icons. The old-style fun house Coney Island, Crystal Palace and the gateway face are all heritage listed. The Big Top, a 2,000-seat venue, hosts music, dance and comedy acts.

Kirribilli Point ❽

Kirribilli Ave, Kirribilli. ⛴ Kirribilli North Sydney.

The two houses occupying this prominent headland, in their delightful garden settings, are typical of the magnificent homes in sprawling grounds that once ringed the harbour. Most have been demolished now and the land subdivided for apartment living. Kirribilli, meaning "place for fishing", is the most densely populated suburb in Australia.

The larger, more dominant of the two houses is Admiralty House, built as a single-storey residence in 1843. Between 1885 and 1913 it served as the residence of the commanding officer of Britain's Royal Navy Pacific Squadron, which was based in Sydney. Fortifications on the shoreline recall its military history. Now the official Sydney home of Australia's governor-general, it is said that even its shed could be considered the city's best address.

In 1855, the charming Gothic Kirribilli House, with its steep gables and decorative fretwork, was built in the grounds of Admiralty House. Today it is the official Sydney residence of Australia's prime minister.

Nutcote ❾

5 Wallaringa Ave, Neutral Bay. **Tel** 9953 4453. ⛴ Kurraba Point, Neutral Bay. ☐ 11am–3pm Wed–Sun. ● some public hols. 🎟 📷 ♿

One of the classics of Australian children's literature, *Snugglepot and Cuddlepie*, was published in 1918. Since then, these two characters – known as the "gumnut" babies along with the cartoon creatures Bib and Bub – have been loved by countless young Australians.

Nutcote was, for 44 years, the home of their creator, illustrator and author May Gibbs. Saved from demolition then

Admiralty House and Kirribilli House, near Sydney Harbour Bridge

Shop façades featuring decorative gables along Manly's Corso

pines. Nearby is a monument to a local newspaper proprietor who, in 1902, defied bans on daytime bathing and was promptly arrested.

Every October Manly hosts a great jazz festival *(see p48)*.

North Head ⓬

Tel 9247 5033. ⚓ *Manly.*
Quarantine Station ⏰ *1:10pm Fri–Mon, Wed. Bookings essential.* **Ghost tours** *Wed, Fri–Sun. Bookings essential (starting times vary).* ⬤ *Good Friday, 25 Dec.* 🎫 📷 ♿ *partial access in Quarantine Station.* 🚩 *See* **Parks and Reserves** *pp44–7.*

The majestic cliffs of North Head afford the finest views in Sydney Harbour National Park, providing vistas along the coastline, across to Middle Harbour and towards the city. North Head is also the ideal place for observing the movements of harbour and seagoing craft and especially for seeing off the yachts at the start of the annual Sydney to Hobart race *(see p49)*.

The Quarantine Station nestles just above Spring Cove within the national park. Here, between 1832 and the 1960s, many ships, with their crews and passengers, were quarantined to protect Sydneysiders from the spread of epidemic diseases. More than 500 people died here, leading some people to believe the area is haunted.

Countless migrants spent their first months in Australia in this place of splendid isolation. Many of its internees left poignant messages and poems carved in the sandstone.

restored and refurbished in the style of the 1930s, it opened in 1994 as an historic house museum. Visitors can view the author's painstakingly kept notebooks and other memorabilia (including the table at which she worked), as well as original editions of her books. There is a garden tea room, with views across the harbour and a shop that sells a range of May Gibbs' souvenirs.

May Gibbs' studio at Nutcote

Taronga Zoo ❿

See pp134–5.

Manly ⓫

⚓ *Manly.* **Oceanworld Manly** *West Esplanade.* **Tel** *8251 7877.* ⏰ *10am–5:30pm daily.* ⬤ *25 Dec.* 🎫 📷 🚩 *See* **Four Guided Walks** *pp146–7.* **www**.oceanworld.com.au

Long after Australia's conversion to the metric system, the slogan "seven miles from Sydney and a thousand miles from care" is still current. It refers to Manly and the 7-mile (11-km) journey from Circular Quay by harbour ferry. If asked

to suggest a single excursion to enjoy during your time in the city, most Sydneysiders would nominate a ferry ride to Manly. This narrow stretch of land lying between the harbour and ocean was named by Governor Phillip, even before the township of Sydney got its name, for the impressive bearing of the Aboriginal men.

As the ferry pulls in to Manly wharf you will notice on the right many shops, restaurants and bars and on the left, the tranquil harbourside beach known as Manly Cove.

At the far end of Manly Cove is Oceanworld Manly, where visitors can see reptiles, sharks and giant stingrays in an underwater viewing tunnel. You can also dive with sharks, and details of Shark Xtreme are on Oceanworld's website.

The Corso is a lively pedestrian thoroughfare of souvenir shops and fast food outlets, with a market held there on Sundays. The Corso leads to Manly's ocean beach, with its promenade lined by towering

First-class quarters at the Quarantine Station, North Head

Taronga Zoo ⑩

Red kangaroo

This famous harbourside zoo is home to almost 2,000 animals, with a special emphasis on unique Australian wildlife. Conspicuous iron bars and fences are absent, with moats used to separate the wandering public from the curious animal onlookers contained in environments closely resembling their natural habitat. The zoo is involved in the breeding of endangered animals, and readily donates or exchanges animals to capitalize on the worldwide "gene pool".

Fishing Cat
These cats have especially long claws and close-set eyes, making it easy for them to focus on and catch fish and reptiles underwater. Two cubs were born at Taronga Zoo in 2002.

Backyard to Bush

Athol Wharf Road

Bradleys Head Road

Lower entrance

0 metres 100
0 yards 100

The platypus is one of only three species of egg-laying mammals.

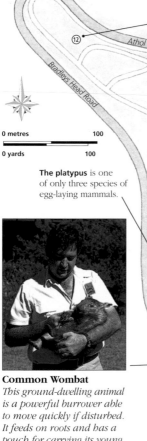

Common Wombat
This ground-dwelling animal is a powerful burrower able to move quickly if disturbed. It feeds on roots and has a pouch for carrying its young.

Bradleys Head Road

Sky Safari Cable Car

Upper entrance

Capral seal theatre

STAR DISPLAYS

★ Free Flight Bird Show

★ Orang-utan Rainforest

★ Koala Walkabout

Upper Entrance
This edifice has greeted visitors since the opening in 1916. By 1917, more than half of Sydney's population had paid a visit.

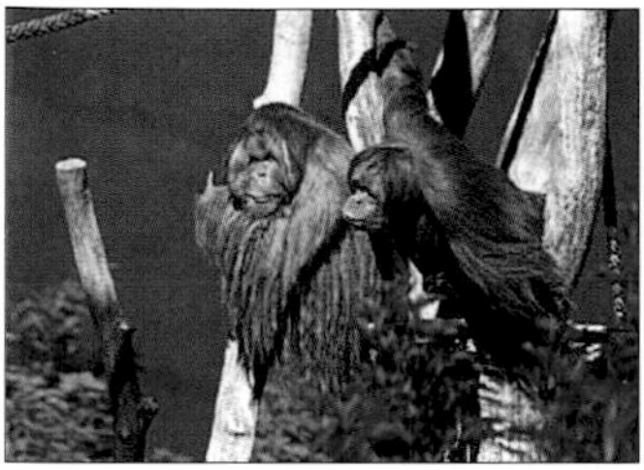

★ Orang-utan Rainforest
Threatened by widespread destruction of their natural habitat in the Sumatran and Borneo rainforests, these primates are on the world's endangered species list.

VISITORS' CHECKLIST

Bradleys Head Rd, Mosman. ***Tel*** *9969 2777.* 🚌 *238, 247, 250.* ⛴ *Taronga Zoo.* 🕒 *9am–5pm daily (last adm 4:30pm).*
www.zoo.nsw.gov.au

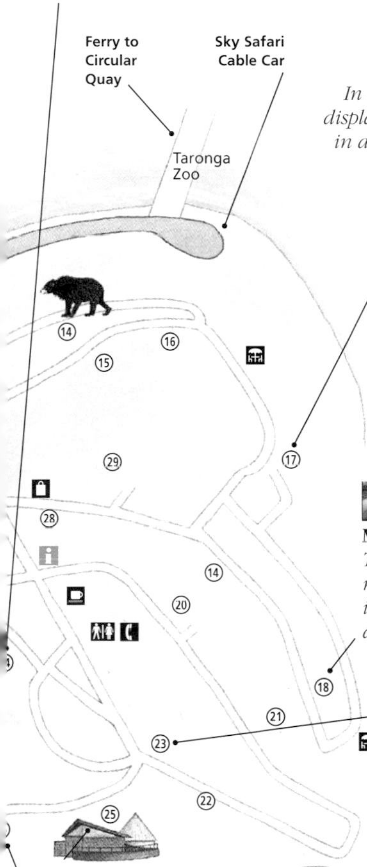
Ferry to Circular Quay
Sky Safari Cable Car
Taronga Zoo
14
16
15
29
17
28
14
20
18
21
23
22
25

★ Free Flight Bird Show
In this spectacular display, birds fly free in an amphitheatre overlooking the harbour.

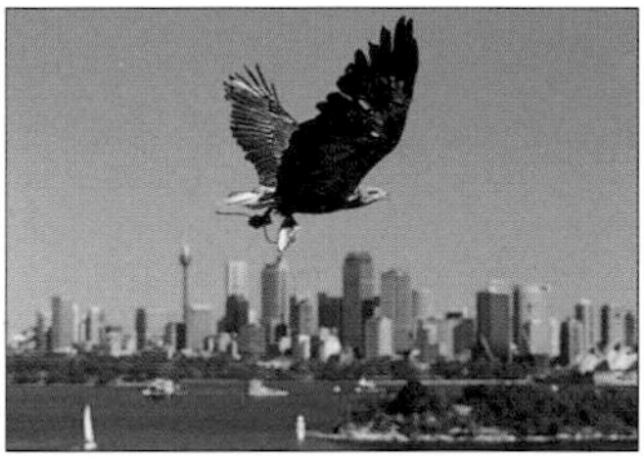

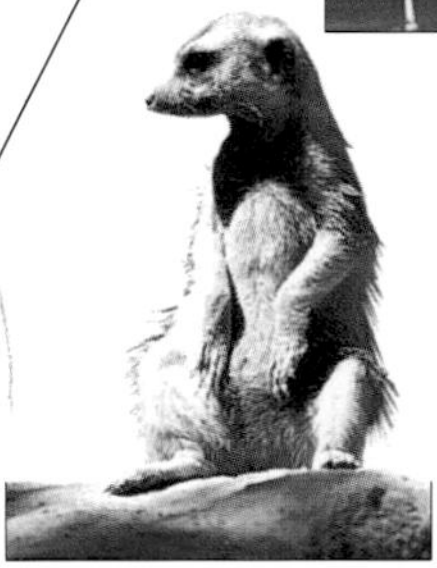

Meerkat
This southern African mongoose always forages in groups, with a guard alert for signs of danger.

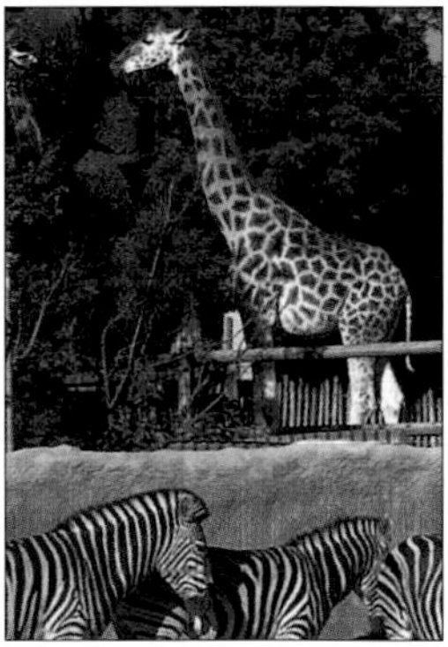

African Waterhole
Savannah waterholes attract many species. The zoo recreates that environment for giraffes, zebras and pygmi hippopotami.

The Serpentaria has amphibians, invertebrates and reptiles.

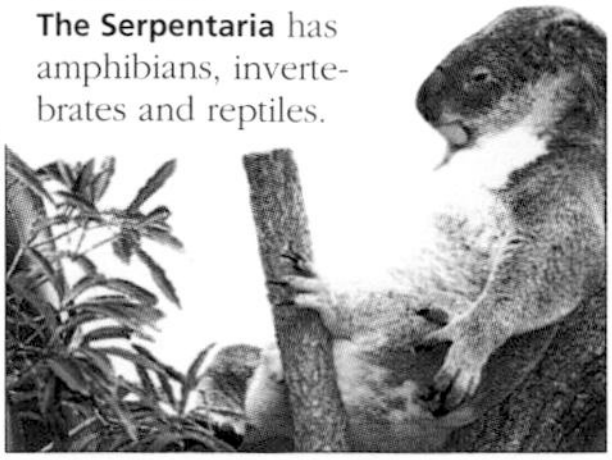

★ Koala Walkabout
Visitors can see the koalas in their eucalypt habitat at tree level. The spiral ramp allows you to get close to feeding and sleeping animals.

KEY TO ANIMAL ENCLOSURES

African Waterhole 23
Australian Walkabout 3
Australia's Night Life 5
Backyard to Bush 12
Bear 14
Chimpanzee Park 22
Creatures of the Wollemi 19
Dingo & Tasmanian devil 7
Echidna & platypus 4
Free Flight Bird Show 17
Gorilla 27
Jungle Cats 11
Koala Walkabout 26
Lion 20
Meerkat 18
Orang-utan Rainforest 24
Otter 15
Penguin 8
Rainforest Aviary 6
Red panda 16
Saltwater crocodile 9
Seals and sea-lions 13
Serpentaria 25
Snow leopard 21
Taronga International Food Market 28
Wetlands 1
Wild Asia 29
Wombat 2
Yellow-footed rock wallaby 10

Façade of Vaucluse House, with its garden and fountain

Vaucluse House ⓭

Wentworth Rd, Vaucluse.
Tel 9388 7922. 📟 325. ⭕ 10am–
4:30pm Tue–Sun. 🌑 Good Fri,
25 Dec. 🎫 📷 ♿ limited. 📷

Tradition has it that the most
riotous party colonial Sydney
ever saw took place on the
Vaucluse House lawns in
1831. WC Wentworth and
4,000 of his political cronies
gathered there to celebrate the
recall to England of Governor
Ralph Darling, the arch-enemy.
WC Wentworth was a major
figure in the colony, being one
of the first three Europeans to
cross the Blue Mountains *(see
pp160–61)*. He was the son of
a female convict and a physi-
cian forced to "volunteer" his
services to the new colony in
order to avoid conviction on
a highway robbery charge.
The younger Wentworth
became an author, barrister and
statesman who stood for the
Australian-born "currency" lads
and lasses against the "sterling"
English-born. He lived here
with his family from 1829–53,
during which time he drafted
the Constitution Bill, giving
self-government to the state.
Vaucluse House was begun
in 1803 by Sir Henry Browne
Hayes, a knight of the realm
transported for kidnapping a
Quaker heiress. Sitting comfortably in 11 ha (27 acres) of
parkland, natural bush and
cultivated gardens, this Gothic
Revival house, with its many
idiosyncratic additions, has
been compared to a West
Indian plantation house. The
interior and grounds have been
restored to 1840s style and the

house contains some furniture
that originally belonged to the
Wentworth family. A popular
tea house is in the grounds.

Greycliffe House, in the tranquil
grounds of Nielsen Park

Nielsen Park ⓮

📟 325. ⭕ Sunrise–10pm daily.

Part of the Sydney Harbour
National Park, Nielsen Park,
with its grassy expanses, sandy
beach and netted swimming
pool, is the perfect spot for a
family picnic. Here visitors can

savour the unusual peace that
descends on many harbour
beaches on an endless sunny
day. It is also an ideal vantage
point from which to enjoy a
spectacular summer sunset or
simply to observe the coming
and going of ferries and the
meandering harbour traffic.
In the midst of this tranquil
setting, enhancing its charm,
stands Greycliffe House with
its decorative gables and ornate
chimney stacks. This Victorian
Gothic mansion was completed
in 1852 for WC Wentworth's
daughter and now offers local
national park information.

Watsons Bay ⓯

📟 324, 325. 🚢 Watsons Bay.
See **Four Guided Walks** pp148–9.

As the base for the boats
that take the pilots out to
arriving ships, this pretty bay
has long been a vital part of
the working harbour. It is also
the home of Doyle's famous
waterfront seafood restaurant,
long a magnet for Sydneysiders
and visitors alike.
Just up the hill and almost
opposite the bay on the ocean
side is The Gap, a spectacular
cliff with tragic associations.
Many troubled people have
taken a suicidal leap from this
rugged cliff on to the wave-
lashed rocks below.
It was here that the ill-fated
ship *Dunbar* was wrecked in
1857, with the loss of all but
one of its 122 passengers and
crew. Treacherous conditions
had led to miscalculation of
the ship's distance from the
Heads. All hands were ordered

View over Watsons Bay, looking southwest towards the city

The crescent-shaped Bondi Beach, Sydney's most famous beach, looking towards North Bondi

on deck as The Gap's rock walls loomed. The recovered anchor is now set into the cliff near the shipwreck site.

The 1883 Macquarie Lighthouse overlooking the Pacific Ocean

Macquarie Lighthouse **16**

🚌 324, 325. 📷 ♿

This is the second lighthouse on this windswept site that is attributed to the convict architect Francis Greenway *(see p114).* He supervised the construction of the first tower, which was completed in 1818 and described by Governor Macquarie as a "noble magnificent edifice". The colony's first lighthouse, it replaced the previous system of bonfires lit up along the headland and earned Greenway a conditional pardon. When the sandstone

eventually crumbled away, the present lighthouse was built. Although designed by Colonial Architect James Barnet, it was based on Greenway's original and was illuminated for the first time in 1883.

Bondi Beach **17**

🚌 380, 381, 382. See **Four Guided Walks** *pp144–5.*

This long crescent of golden sand, so close to the city, has long been a mecca for the sun and surf set *(see pp54–5).* Throughout the year, surfing enthusiasts visit from far and

wide in search of the perfect wave, and inline skaters hone their skills on the promenade. Despite a growing awareness of the dangers of sun exposure *(see p223)* and an expansion of other cultural preoccupations, beach life still defines the lives of many Australians, who regard it as healthier than ever.

People seek out Bondi for its trendy seafront cafés and cosmopolitan milieu as much as for the beach. The pavilion, built in 1928 as changing rooms, has been a community centre since the 1970s. It is now a busy venue for festivals, plays, films and craft displays.

BONDI SURF BATHERS' LIFE SAVING CLUB

The founding of the surf lifesaving club at Bondi Beach in 1906 gave impetus to the formation of other local clubs, and ultimately to a global movement. An early club member demonstrated his new lifesaving reel, designed using hair pins and a cotton reel. Now updated, it is standard equipment on beaches worldwide. In 1938, Australia's largest surf rescue was mounted at Bondi, when more than 200 people were washed out to sea by freak waves. Five died, but lifesavers rescued more than 180, establishing their highly dependable reputation.

Bondi surf lifesaving team at the Bondi Surf Carnival, 1937

Captain Cook's Landing Place ⑱

Captain Cook Drive, Botany Bay
National Park, Kurnell. *Tel* 9668
9111. 🚌 987. **Toll Gate** ⭕ *7am–
7pm daily.* **Discovery Centre** ⭕
*11am–3pm Mon–Fri, 10am–4:30pm
Sat & Sun.* ⬤ *25 Dec.* 📷 ♿
www.nationalparks.nsw.gov.au

Although difficult to get to,
visitors will find this place
worth the effort. It is, after all,
one of Australia's most important European historic sites.
Here James Cook, botanists
Daniel Solander and Joseph
Banks and the crew of HMS
Endeavour landed on 29 April
1770. Aboriginal peoples with
spears were shot at. One, hit
in the legs, returned with a
shield to defend himself.

Nowadays people can cast
a fishing line from the rock
where the Europeans stepped
ashore. Nearby are the site of

**Cook's Obelisk, overlooking Botany
Bay, Captain Cook's Landing Place**

a well where, Cook recorded,
a shore party "found fresh
water sufficient to water the
ship" and a monument which
marks the first recorded European burial in Australia.

There are also monuments
to Solander, Banks and Cook,
but it is the peaceful ambience
that is most impressive. Now
part of Botany Bay National
Park, Captain Cook's Landing
Place has lovely walks, some
accessible to wheelchairs,
where visitors may roam and
observe the flora which led to
the naming of Botany Bay.

The Discovery Centre in the
park focuses on a number of
themes: the bay's wetlands and

Pampas grass and banana plants in the garden at Elizabeth Farm

the importance of their conservation; an interesting exhibition detailing Cook's
exploration of the area; and
an introduction to Aboriginal
customs and culture.

Sydney Olympic Park ⑲

Homebush Bay. *Tel* 9714 7958/
7888. 🚆 *Olympic Park. Visitors
Centre (1 Showground Rd).* ⭕ *9am–
5pm daily.* ⬤ *Good Fri, 25 Dec, 26
Dec, 1 Jan.* ♿ 🖥 🚻 **www**.
sydneyolympicpark.nsw.gov.au

Once host to the 27th Summer
Olympic Games and Paralym-
pic Games, Sydney Olympic
Park is situated at Homebush
Bay, 14 km (8.5 miles) west
of the city centre. Visitors can
follow a self-guided walk or
buy a ticket for a guided tour
to access venues such as the
Showground and the Super-
Dome. The interactive "Explore, Telstra Stadium Tour"
gives a taste of some of the
stadium's best-loved sporting
moments. For nature lovers,
there is a tour of the five wetlands of the Bicentennial
Park. You can buy tickets for
tours at the Visitor's Centre.

Other facilities at the park
include the Aquatic Centre,
with a kids waterpark, and
the Tennis Centre, where you
can play in the footsteps of
such greats as Lleyton Hewitt.
There are picnic areas and
cafés throughout the park and
on the fourth Sunday of every
month you can sample fresh
produce and gourmet food at
the Boulevard Market.

Elizabeth Farm ⑳

70 Alice St, Rosehill. *Tel* 9635 9488.
🚆 *Parramatta.* 🚌 *Parramatta or
Granville.* ⭕ *10am–5pm daily.* ⬤
Good Fri, 25 Dec. 📷 ♿ 🖥 📷

The discovery of fertile land
at Parramatta, and the harves-
ting of its first successful grain
crop in 1790, helped save the
fledgling colony from starvation and led to the rapid
development of the area.

This zone was the location
of several of Australia's first
colonial land grants. In 1793,
John Macarthur, who became
a wealthy farmer and sheep
breeder, was granted 40 ha
(100 acres) of land at
Parramatta. He named the
property after his wife and
this was to be Elizabeth's
home for the rest of her life.
Macarthur was often absent
from the farm as the centre of
his wool operations had
moved to Camden.

Part of the house, a simple
stone cottage built in 1793, still
remains and it is the oldest
European building in Australia.
As it was added to over the

John Macarthur, 1766–1834

next 50 years, it developed into a substantial home with many features of a typical Australian homestead. Simply furnished to the period of 1820–50, with reproductions of paintings and other possessions, the house is now a museum that strongly evokes the original inhabitants' life and times.

The kitchen, Hambledon Cottage

Hambledon Cottage ㉑

63 Hassall St, Parramatta. **Tel** 9635 6924. ▤ Parramatta. ⬭ 11am–4pm Wed, Thu, Sat, Sun & public hols. ⬤ Good Fri, 25, 26 Dec. 🎫 ♿ 📷

This delightful cottage, with its walls of rendered and painted sandstock, was built in 1824 as the retirement home for Penelope Lucas, governess to the Macarthur daughters. It is set in a park containing trees brought to Australia in 1817 by John Macarthur.

Visitors can wander through rooms that have been restored to the period 1820–50. An 1830 Broadwood piano is one of the furniture exhibits. The kitchen has walls of convict-made bricks. It contains such original appliances and utensils as a handmill for grinding wheat and a bread oven.

Experiment Farm Cottage ㉒

9 Ruse St, Parramatta. **Tel** 9635 5655. ▤ Harris Park. ⬭ 10:30am–3:30pm Tue–Fri, 11am–4pm Sun & public hols. ⬤ Good Fri, 18–31 Dec. 🎫 📷 ♿ 📷 (Groups must book in advance)

When his sentence expired in 1789, convict farmer James Ruse was given 0.6 ha (1½ acres) of land at Parramatta on which to start a farm, along with a hut, grain for sowing, vital farming tools, two sows and six hens. He successfully planted and harvested a substantial wheat crop with his wife Elizabeth's help. She was the first female convict to be emancipated in New South Wales. In 1791, they were rewarded with a grant of 12 ha (30 acres), the colony's first land grant. Arthur Phillip, governor of the day, called it Experiment Farm.

In 1793, Ruse sold this farm to surgeon John Harris for £40. The date of the cottage is not certain, but it is believed to be early 1830s. The woodwork is Australian red cedar and the cottage is furnished according to an 1838 inventory.

Medicine chest (c.1810), Experiment Farm

St John's Cemetery ㉓

O'Connell St, Parramatta. **Tel** 9635 5904. ▤ Parramatta. 📷 ♿

This walled cemetery – the oldest European cemetery in Australia – houses the graves of many convicts and settlers who arrived on the First Fleet in 1788. The oldest grave that can be identified is the flat sandstone slab simply inscribed, "H.E. Dodd 1791". Henry Edward Dodd, known to be Governor Phillip's butler, was the tenth person buried in the cemetery, but the location of the other nine graves is unknown. The first recorded burial was of a child on 31 January 1790. One prominent grave is that of churchman Samuel Marsden, who earned the title of the "flog-ging parson" during his time as magistrate general because of his harsh judgments.

The merchant Robert Campbell (see p66) and the father of explorer William Charles Wentworth (see p136), D'Arcy Wentworth, are also buried here.

Old Government House ㉔

Parramatta Park (entry by Macquarie St gates), Parramatta. **Tel** 9635 8149. ▤ Parramatta. ⬭ 10am–4pm Mon–Fri, 10:30am–4pm Sat, Sun & most public hols. ⬤ Good Fri, 25 Dec. 🎫 ♿ limited. 📷

The central block of Old Government House is the oldest intact public building in Australia. This elegant brick structure, plastered to resemble stone, was built by Governor Hunter in 1799 on the site of a cottage constructed in 1790 for Governor Phillip. Wings to the side and rear were added between 1812 and 1818. The Doric porch, added in 1816, has been attributed to Francis Greenway (see p114).

Australia's finest collection of early 19th-century furniture is now housed inside. A structure on the site has been identified as an early worker's cottage.

The drawing room of Old Government House, Parramatta

FOUR GUIDED WALKS

Sydney's temperate climate and natural beauty make it an ideal city for walking. The following walks have been chosen for their distinct character; they all capture a view of the essential Sydney. You can follow the paths that trace the headlands and inlets around Watsons Bay; enjoy an invigorating clifftop walk at Bondi; catch glimpses of the original landscape in Manly's unspoilt bushland; or explore the narrow streets of historic Balmain. Three of the walks incorporate ocean or harbourside beaches, so be prepared in warmer weather by packing a swimsuit, towel

Mural on a Manly surf shop

and hat and wearing a reliable sunscreen. In Sydney's national parks and bushland all the indigenous flora and fauna is protected; the best sign of appreciation is to leave the bush as you found it. The *Tips for Walkers* provide practical information about each walk, listing accessibility by bus, train or ferry and estimated distance of the walk, along with scenic rest areas, picnic spots, cafés and restaurants en route. Tourism NSW's Information Line *(see p218)* and www.sydneywalkingtours.com.au give details of the many accompanied walking tours available throughout Sydney.

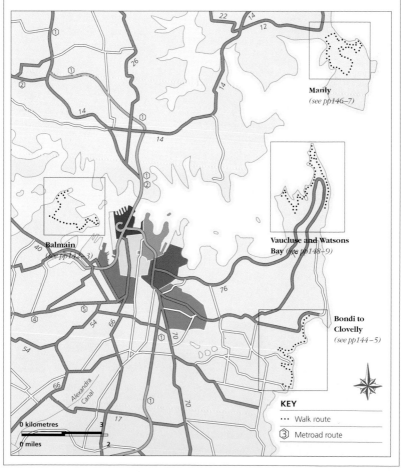

Manly
(see pp146–7)

Balmain
(see pp142–3)

Vaucluse and Watsons Bay *(see pp148–9)*

Bondi to Clovelly
(see pp144–5)

Alexandra Canal

0 kilometres 3

0 miles 2

KEY

··· Walk route

③ Metroad route

◁ A lookout rising high above the treacherous waters of the Pacific Ocean at The Gap *(see p148)*

A Two-Hour Walk Around Balmain

Historic Balmain village was named after William Balmain, a ship's surgeon on the First Fleet. In 1800, he was granted rights to 223 ha (550 acres) of the peninsula, which he later sold for a paltry 5 shillings in a dubious business transaction. From the mid-1800s, much of the land was subdivided for housing to support the then flourishing mining and maritime industries. Today, grand colonial and Victorian buildings stand side by side with tiny workers' cottages, adding variety to every street.

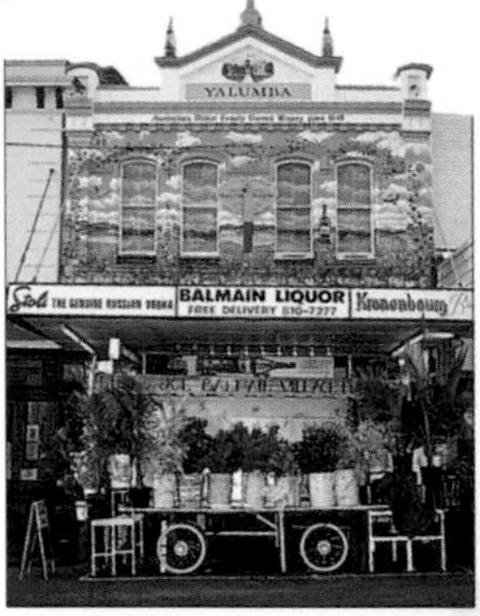

Colourful shopfront on Darling Street, Balmain

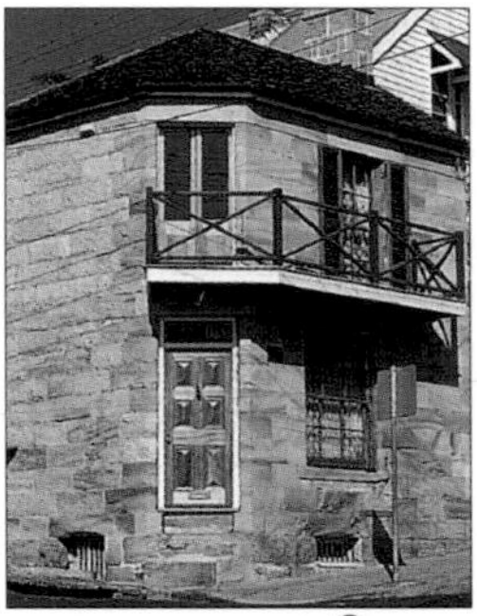
The Waterman's Cottage ③

East Balmain

Begin from the Darling Street Wharf ①. By the 1840s, when the ferry service began, shipyards dotted these foreshores. The sandstone building at No. 10 Darling Street ②, once the Dolphin Hotel then the Shipwright's Arms, was a watering hole for sailors and ferrymen. On the opposite corner is The Waterman's Cottage (1841) ③, home to Henry McKenzie, whose boat ferried residents to and from Sydney Town.

Turn left into Weston Street and walk through the Illoura Reserve for views of the city and Darling Harbour. Leave the park via William and Johnston Streets, stopping in the latter to view Onkaparinga ④, the colonial residence at No. 12. When building started in 1860, mussel shells from Aboriginal feasts stood in mounds upon the harbour foreshore beyond.

Turn left onto Darling Street then right into Duke Street. Gilchrist Place then leads down to Mort Bay Reserve ⑤. Ship's propellers stand as monuments to the area's working past. A path leads up to The Avenue's timber workers' cottages.

Back on Darling Street, turn left down Killeen Street. Take the path across Ewenton Park to Ewenton ⑥ (c.1854). Past the park, Hampton Villa ⑦ at 12B Grafton Street was home to state premier Henry Parkes.

Turn right into Ewenton Street and then left into Wallace Street, with its variety of early Australian architecture. The rough stone home at No. 1 is called the Railway Station as its narrow frontage makes it resemble one. The charming Clontarf ⑧ is at No. 4, while Maitland House ⑨ has a symmetry worth a second glance. Return to Darling Street.

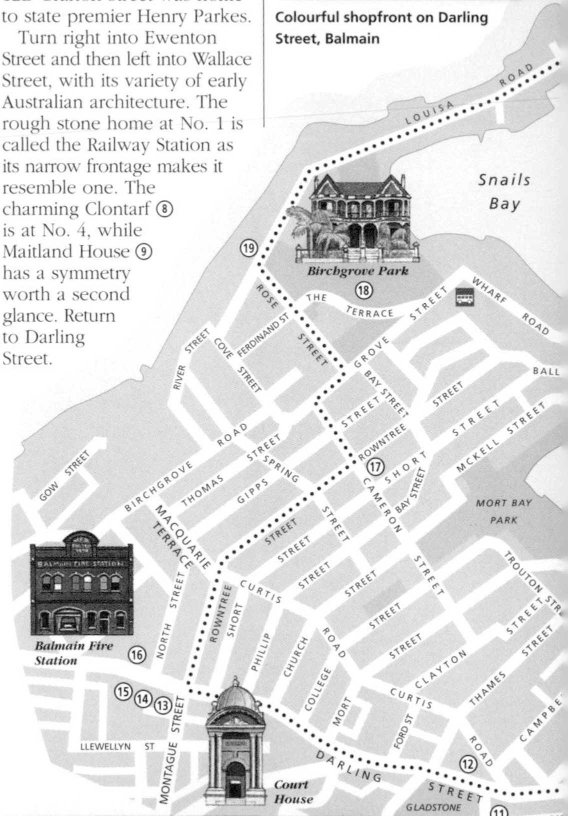

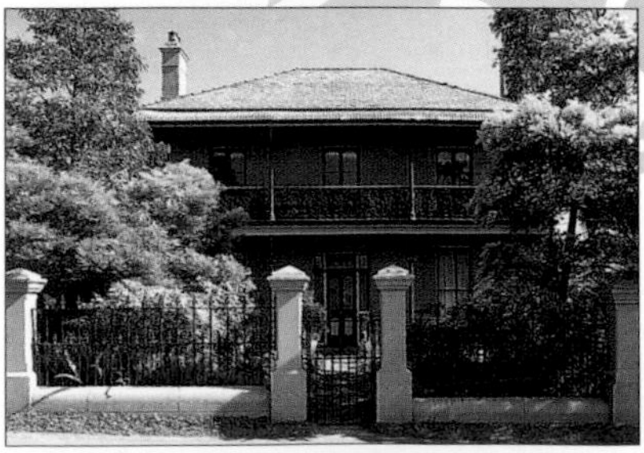
The domestic grandeur of Louisa Road

Historic Links

Sydney's oldest extant lock-up, The Watch House (1854) ⑩ at No. 179 Darling Street, has been restored, but a ghostly female form remains. Further along, enjoy a drink at The London Hotel (1870) ⑪, where the balcony stools are made of old-fashioned tractor seats.

After the roundabout, visit St Andrew's Church ⑫ before losing yourself to the bookshops, cafés and delicatessens of Balmain. Every Saturday, Balmain Market fills the churchyard *(see p203)*. At the shops' far end, the Victorian Post Office (1887) ⑬ and neighbouring Court House ⑭ reflect 1880s Sydney's prosperity. The Town Hall ⑮ dome was removed during World War II for fear of air raids. Across the street is the Fire Station ⑯ (1894). Set on the crest of a hill, its horse-drawn vehicles always travelled downhill on their outward journey.

Distant views of the city and Sydney Harbour Bridge from Snails Bay

Balmain to Birchgrove

Retrace your steps to Rowntree Street. Turn left and wander down to Birchgrove (about 10 minutes' walk). From Birchgrove shops ⑰, take Cameron Street left and Grove Street right, to Birchgrove Park ⑱ and Snails Bay. Walk down Rose Street to Louisa Road. Two of the most notable homes are Nos. 12 and 14, Keba (1878) and Vidette (1876) ⑲, where deep verandas and iron-lace balconies hint at colonial opulence. A poem in praise of the nearby park is inscribed on a plaque at Keba's entrance. Amid Vidette's formal greenery, a deep well is still fed by a natural spring.

Balmain War Memorial

There is a wealth of interest in the homes that follow: a tiny porch, Victorian entrance tiles, ornate iron lace – plus occasional glimpses of water frontage and private moorings. At the road's end, the reserve at Yurulbin Point ⑳ marks the mouth of Parramatta River. A fishing nook on its eastern corner is a perfect vantage point for taking in the city skyline and passing harbour traffic.

Shops nestled in the quiet Birchgrove village ⑰

TIPS FOR WALKERS

Starting point: *Darling Street Wharf.*
Length: *5.5 km (3 1/2 miles).*
Getting there: *Ferries regularly leave Circular Quay for Darling Street Wharf. The 442 bus from the Queen Victoria Building stops in Darling Street. To return, there is a 15-minute ferry ride at hourly intervals from Birchgrove (pick up a schedule at Circular Quay). Alternatively, take Bus 441 from Grove Street (Snails Bay) back to the city (weekdays only).*
Stopping-off points: *Darling Street, in particular, has many good delicatessens, patisseries, restaurants and cafés. Places to picnic include Mort Bay Reserve, Gladstone Park, Birchgrove Park and Yurulbin Point.*

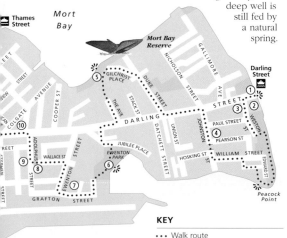

KEY

- ••• Walk route
- 🌱 Viewpoint
- 🚌 Bus stop
- ⚓ Ferry boarding point

0 metres	250
0 yards	250

A Two-Hour Walk from Bondi Beach to Clovelly

This invigorating oceanside and clifftop walk explores the beautiful shoreline and surfing beaches of eastern Sydney. The local colour along this scenic trail is at its most vibrant at weekends, when people flock to the cafés and beaches. The Victorian cemetery at the walk's end bears witness to Sydney's multicultural heritage.

Pool at North Bondi Beach

A Seaside Community

Walk north along Campbell Parade [1], passing a colourful array of hotels, beachwear shops and lively cafés that give the street a raffish atmosphere. The stylish Gelato Bar at No. 140 makes an indulgent pit-stop. Keep walking until the Hotel Bondi [2], the parade's most significant building and easily spotted by its pretty clock tower. Opened as a first-class hotel in 1920, it initially stood quite alone by what was then a bush-fringed beach. Turn right, crossing the road in front of the hotel, and walk down to Queen Elizabeth Drive leaving the traffic and noise of Campbell Parade behind as you reach Sydney's most famous beach, Bondi.

Statue of lifesaver near Bondi Pavilion

Bondi's popularity dates back to the 1880s. Although daylight bathing was banned at the time, the beach was considered a fashionable place to stroll. Bondi trams came into use shortly after and, by the time bathing restrictions were lifted in 1902, the red and white trams were filled with beach-goers. Just ahead you will see Bondi Pavilion [3]. Built in 1928 to replace a modest timber building, it was designed on a grand scale and originally housed a ballroom, gymnasium, restaurant, café, Turkish baths and open-air theatre. Although decidedly less glamorous today, the complex is still a thriving local community centre hosting cultural events. Photographs inside recall the romance of Bondi Beach in earlier times.

Next to the Pavilion is the home of arguably Australia's oldest surf life saving club, the Bondi Surf Bathers [4] *(see p137)*. Follow the sweep of the beach to its southern end.

Climb a flight of steps to continue on Notts Avenue, above Bondi Baths [5] and alongside the Bondi Icebergs clubhouse. Prospective members must swim every Sunday, regardless of weather, 50 weeks of the year for four years to join.

TIPS FOR WALKERS

Starting point: *Campbell Parade, southern end.*
Length: *4 km (21/2 miles).*
Getting there: *Take the train to Bondi Junction, then Bus 380 to Bondi Beach. Bus 339 runs from Clovelly Beach to Circular Quay. Waverley Cemetery is open from 8am to dusk every day.*
Stopping-off points: *Public toilets, showers and food and refreshments are available at Bondi, Tamarama and Bronte Beaches. Take-away cuisine can be bought along Bondi's Campbell Parade as the walk begins. Tamarama's beach café serves refreshing drinks. In warm weather, make the most of four of Sydney's best beaches by packing your swimming gear.*

Tamarama Surf Life Saving Club, at the beach's northern end

Bronte's swimming baths

Bondi to Bronte

Veer left off Notts Avenue as the path drops down and skirts sharp rock formations, the result of years of erosion. Take the steep steps to Mackenzies Point lookout [6] on the headland. The magnificent view stretches for 180 degrees from Ben Buckler in the north to Malabar in the distant south.

KEY

- ••• Walk route
- Viewpoint
- Bus stop
- [P] Parking

Bondi Hotel

Bondi Pavilion

Bondi Bay

Mackenzies Bay

Nelson Bay

Waverley Cemetery

Clovelly Bay

0 metres   500

0 yards   500

Bronte to Waverley

Continue down Bronte Road towards the southern end of Bronte Beach. After passing Bronte's cafés, walk through the car park and follow the road uphill, through a cutaway originally dug for trams. As the road winds through the cutting and veers right, take the steps through Calga Reserve. Walk down Trafalgar Street to the Waverley Cemetery ⑪.

In grand displays of Edwardian and Victorian monumental masonry, English, Italian and Irish residents have been laid to rest. Among notable Australians buried here are writers Henry Lawson and Dorothea Mackellar; Fanny Durack, the

Irish Memorial, Waverley Cemetery

first woman to win an Olympic gold medal (in 1912), and do the Australian crawl swimming stroke; and aeronautical pioneer Lawrence Hargrave.

The Irish Memorial honours the 1798 Irish Rebellion and its leader Michael Dwyer, who was transported to Australia for his part in the uprising.

Leave the cemetery at the southern end. Walk through Burrows Park, hugging the coast, to Eastbourne Avenue, which leads to the walk's end at Clovelly Beach ⑫.

Resume your walk, passing through Marks Park into rocky Mackenzies Bay and over the next headland and down to Tamarama Bay ⑦. In 1906–11, this beach was the unlikely home of Wonderland City – a rowdy fun fair, boasting a roller coaster.

Across the beach and park, climb the steps to Tamarama Marine Drive. Follow the road around to the slopes of Bronte Park ⑧, once part of Bronte Estate. To explore Bronte Gully ⑨, and glimpse Bronte House ⑩, continue away from the beach. Take the track that follows the creek into a valley, passing beneath a canopy of fig and flame trees. The waterfall was once a natural feature of the ornamental gardens designed for Bronte Estate.

The steps on your left lead to Bronte Road and Bronte House. The mixture of Gothic and Swiss styling was the inspiration of the original owner, architect Mortimer Lewis (*see p121*). Today it is owned by the municipal council and is leased as a private residence.

Lookout at Mackenzies Point, a popular spot for watching surfers ⑥

A Three-Hour Walk Around Manly

This walk takes in the holiday atmosphere of downtown Manly and its splendid surf beach, before passing along quieter shorelines and clifftop streets, and through unspoilt bushland replete with native flora and fauna. It features marvellous views, the commanding architecture of the historic building that was formerly St Patrick's Seminary, and the charm of Collins Beach and Fairy Bower.

Brass band plays in The Corso

From Harbour to Ocean

Start at Manly Wharf ①. This suburb was little more than a cosy fishing village until 1852, when entrepreneur Henry Gilbert Smith's vision of a resort similar to fashionable Brighton in his native England started to take shape. The ferry service began in 1855, operating from the same spot in use today.

Leaving Manly Cove, cross The Esplanade and walk down The Corso, a pedestrian mall. At the end of The Corso, to the left, stands the New Brighton Hotel ② in striking Egyptian Classical Revival Style. In 1926, it replaced the original New Brighton, built in 1880 as the resort's first attraction.

Head towards the rolling surf and sweeping sands of Manly Beach ③ then continue south along the promenade. From the 1950s-style Surf Pavilion, follow Marine Parade walkway around to Cabbage Tree Bay. The pretty area around the rock pool was named Fairy Bower ④ for the delicate wildflowers and maidenhair ferns that once grew on the hillside. Beyond the rock pool, continue on the pathway around to Shelly Beach ⑤, a secluded scuba diving and snorkelling spot, which is also ideal for child swimmers. The 1920s beach kiosk has now been stylishly restored and converted into the smart Le Kiosk restaurant.

Detail on the New Brighton Hotel

TIPS FOR WALKERS

Starting point: *Manly Wharf*
Length: *7.5 km (41/2 miles).*
Getting there: *Regular ferry and JetCat services depart from Wharf 2 at Circular Quay.*
Stopping-off points: *The wide range of fresh food counters at Manly Pier make it an ideal place to stock up on picnic fare. Restaurants and cafés line The Corso and Manly Beach Promenade. Le Kiosk at Shelly Beach offers the choice of a smart restaurant, barbecue or snack bar. In warm weather, come prepared with a swimsuit, hat, towel and sunscreen.*

Shelly Beach to the former St Patrick's Seminary

Across the park, take the steps to your left to Shelly Beach Headland. A path further left loops around the headland. Viewing platforms ⑥ overlook the vast South Pacific Ocean.

Take the carpark exit into Bower Street. Follow the road as it rounds high above Fairy Bower, passing by homes of diverse architectural styles, from Spanish Mission to Neo-Georgian. Turn left into College Street, then right into Reddall Street, and left again

Houses rising above Fairy Bower

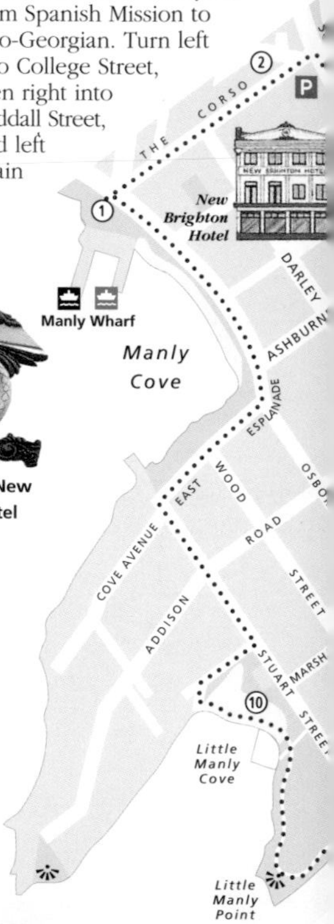

The clear waters of sheltered Shelly Beach ⑤

into Addison Road. Opposite the Victorian buildings at Nos. 97–99 and 95, a lane into Fairy Bower Road leads to views of the former St Patrick's Seminary, now the International College of Tourism and Hotel Management ⑦. Both Romanesque and Neo-Gothic architecture are in evidence in this 1885 edifice, built only after much deliberation by an essentially Protestant government.

Leave Fairy Bower Road by Vivian Street to turn left into Darley Road and arrive at the seminary building. Just opposite, the site of the former Archbishop's House, once known as the Cardinal's Palace, is being redeveloped.

The former St Patrick's Seminary, now the International College of Tourism ⑦

North Head Reserve
At the top of Darley Road, turn right beneath the Parkhill Sandstone Arch 8 into North Head

Reserve. Follow the right-hand fork (leading to the Institute of Police Management) onto Collins Beach Road down through bushland alive with bird calls and native lizards. Paperbarks, smooth-barked apple trees and banksias are some of the native flora growing in abundance.

At the road's end, follow the track to your right across two footbridges, then down steps to Collins Beach ⑨. A stone cairn between the second footbridge and the beach marks where Governor Arthur Phillip was speared by the Aboriginal Wil-ee-ma-rin after a misunderstanding. The quiet waterfall and dense bushland make it possible to imagine this beach in pre-colonial days.

Leave via a small set of stone steps at the right-hand end of the beach which lead to a footpath, then out into Stuart Street.

Back to the Present
For memorable harbour views, follow the direction of Stuart Street through Little Manly Point Reserve, passing by the baths of Little Manly Cove ⑩. If you are reluctant to end this charming walk, turn left and proceed to the end of Addison Road. Manly Point Peace Park offers a quiet place to take in a panorama of the distant city.

Return down Addison Road, making your way back to the wharf via Stuart Street and the East Esplanade. With its boat sheds and bleached timber yacht clubs, the East Esplanade Park has a nautical amosphere and is a relaxing place to meander. Continue past the attractions of the amusement pier to Manly Wharf, which was your starting point.

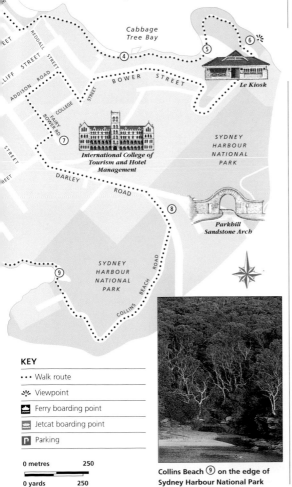

Cabbage Tree Bay

Le Kiosk

BOWER STREET

ADDISON ROAD

COLLEGE

FAIRY BOWER RD

⑦ **International College of Tourism and Hotel Management**

DARLEY ROAD

SYDNEY HARBOUR NATIONAL PARK

⑧ *Parkhill Sandstone Arch*

⑨ **SYDNEY HARBOUR NATIONAL PARK**

COLLINS BEACH ROAD

KEY
∙∙∙ Walk route

⚡ Viewpoint

🚢 Ferry boarding point

🚤 Jetcat boarding point

🅿 Parking

| 0 metres | 250 |
| 0 yards | 250 |

Collins Beach ⑨ on the edge of Sydney Harbour National Park

A Three-Hour Walk in Watsons Bay and Vaucluse

Tracing the perimeters of spectacular South Head, this walk touches on the area's colonial connections and takes in a variety of ocean and harbourside terrain, from headlands with sweeping views and crashing waves, to secluded coves, white sandy beaches and the streets of one of Sydney's most desirable neighbourhoods.

Signal Station ② at Dunbar Head

Macquarie Lighthouse to Camp Cove

The start of this walk is majestic Macquarie Lighthouse (1883) ①. A copy of the country's first lighthouse built in 1818 *(see p137)*, it stands on the same site.

Take the walk northwards, passing by the Signal Station ② following Old South Head Road. Before the station was built in 1848, a flag was hoisted to warn the colony of ships entering the harbour.

Continue along the footpath, where a plaque marks the location of Australia's worst maritime disaster. It was here that the migrant ship *Dunbar* crashed onto the rocks in a gale in 1857 *(see pp136–7)*. The only survivor was hauled to safety up the treacherous cleft in the cliff face known as Jacob's Ladder ③. From here, follow the descending path, arriving at the turbulent seas and jutting stony ledges of The Gap ④. The *Dunbar's* anchor is here set into concrete, while salvaged personal effects are displayed at the National Maritime Museum *(see pp94–5)*.

Taking the steps down from The Gap, bear right into the entrance of Sydney Harbour National Park. This single-lane roadway leads through natural bushland into HMAS *Watson* Military Reserve. Follow the road up to visit the Naval Memorial Chapel ⑤. A large clear window inside the chapel offers spectacular views of North Head and the Pacific Ocean. Resume your walk by taking the road out of the reserve, and then turn right into Cliff Street. Passing a row of weatherboard cottages on your left, follow the street to its end and onto Camp Cove Beach ⑥. It was here in 1788 that Captain Arthur Phillip first stepped ashore after leaving Botany Bay to explore the coastline.

Bust, Macquarie Lighthouse ①

Camp Cove to Watsons Bay

Take the wooden steps at the northern end of the cove to make the 40-minute return walk to South

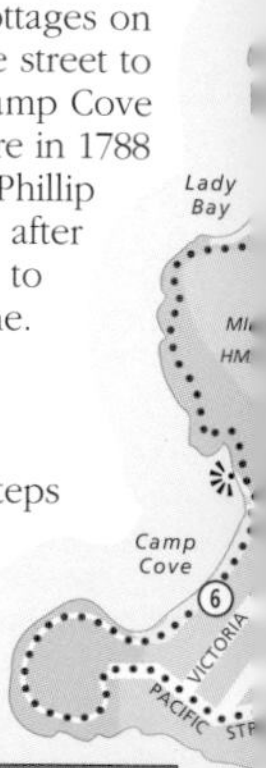

Lady Bay
HM
Camp Cove
VICTORIA
PACIFIC

Nudist Lady Bay Beach

Shark Bay
NIELSEN PARK
SYDNEY HARBOUR
NATIONAL PARK
GREYCLIFFE AVE
COOLONG ROAD
Vaucluse Bay
Parsley Bay
THE CRESCENT
SASSAFRAS LANE
FITZWILLIAM RD
WENTWORTH ROAD
PARSLEY ROAD
BOAMBILLEE AVE
FITZWILLIAM ROAD
Vaucluse House
OLOLA AVENUE
VAUCLUSE PARK
SERPENTINE PAR
SAMUEL PARK
HOPETOUN AVENUE
VAUCLUSE ROAD
CARRARA ROAD
WENTWORTH ROAD
FISHER AVENUE
GILLIVER AVENUE
NEW SOUTH H
KEY
Walk route
Viewpoint
Bus stop
Ferry boarding point

Doyle's well-known restaurant at Watsons Bay ⑧

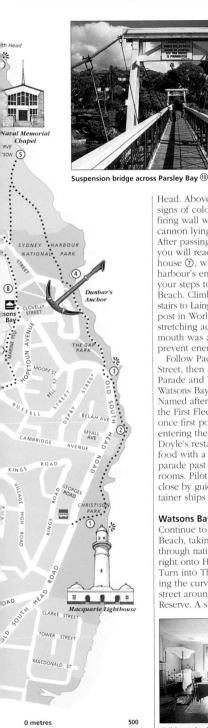

Macquarie Lighthouse

0 metres   500

0 yards   500

Children's bedroom, one of the exhibits at Vaucluse House ⑪

Suspension bridge across Parsley Bay ⑩

Head. Above the steps are signs of colonial defences: a firing wall with rifle slots; a cannon lying further along. After passing Lady Bay Beach, you will reach Hornby Light-house ⑦, which marks the harbour's entrance. Retrace your steps to Camp Cove Beach. Climb the western-end stairs to Laings Point, a defence post in World War II. A net stretching across the harbour mouth was anchored here to prevent enemy ships entering.

Follow Pacific Street to Cove Street, then along to Marine Parade and Wharf Beach in Watsons Bay ⑧ *(see pp136–7)*. Named after Robert Watson of the First Fleet's *Sirius*, this was once first port of call for ships entering the harbour. Nearby, Doyle's restaurant offers seafood with a view. Follow the parade past the baths and tea rooms. Pilot boats ⑨ moored close by guide cruise and container ships into the harbour.

Watsons Bay to Vaucluse

Continue to secluded Gibsons Beach, taking the footpath left through native shrubbery, then right onto Hopetoun Avenue. Turn into The Crescent, tracing the curve of this exclusive street around to Parsley Bay Reserve. A short descent opens

onto a suspension bridge hung across the waters of tranquil Parsley Bay ⑩. Crossing the bridge, follow the pathway between two houses to arrive on Fitzwilliam Road. Continue right along Fitzwilliam Road, turning left into Wentworth Road to reach the extravagant Vaucluse House ⑪, surrounded by exotic gardens *(see p136)*.

To finish your walk, make your way along Coolong Road to Nielsen Park *(see p136)* and Shark Bay ⑫. Protected from its namesake by a netted enclosure, the natural setting and safe waters of this beach make it a favourite for picnics.

Dramatic rock cleft known as Jacob's Ladder ③ near The Gap

TIPS FOR WALKERS

Starting point: *Macquarie Lighthouse.*
Length: *8 km (5 miles).*
Getting there: *Take Bus 324 from Circular Quay, or Bus 387 from Bondi Junction. Return by Bus 325 from Nielsen Park.*
Stopping-off points: *There are public toilets and showers at Camp Cove, Watsons Bay, Parsley Bay and Nielsen Park. Food and refreshments are available throughout the walk at Watsons Bay, Parsley Bay, Vaucluse and Nielsen Park. The tea rooms at Vaucluse House offer views of the gardens, and the café at Nielsen Park sells homemade fare in generous portions. The walk covers several harbour beaches where you can swim safely. In warm weather, bring a swimsuit, towel, hat and sunscreen, and allow time for swimming, sunbathing and picnicking.*

BEYOND SYDNEY

Exploring Beyond Sydney

To the east, Sydney is bounded by the Pacific Ocean; to the west, by the Great Dividing Range. To the north and south, within easy distance of the city, are superb beaches and stretches of coastal scenery, while inland, you will encounter waterfalls, deep valleys and fascinating flora and wildlife. On the Hawkesbury River, to the north and west of the city, are settlements of historical as well as scenic interest while, further north, the Hunter River meanders through sloping vineyards. The excursions on pages 154–65 offer the visitor the chance to sample the rich variety of Sydney landscapes from the exhilarating to the tranquil.

Cable car ride over
the Blue Mountains

Façade of Rothbury Estate in the Hunter Valley

SIGHTS AT A GLANCE

Blue Mountains **4**
Hawkesbury Tour **2**
Hunter Valley **3**
Pittwater and Ku-ring-gai Chase
   National Park **1**
Royal National Park **6**
Southern Highlands Tour **5**

GETTING AROUND

All the areas covered in these excursions can be easily reached by road from Sydney. Freeways and motorways take travellers part of the way to the Southern Highlands, Blue Mountains and Hunter Valley, while the other areas are accessible on sealed, well-signposted major roads. A number of tour operators offer guided one-day, or longer, tours to the Blue Mountains, Hunter Valley, Southern Highlands and South Coast, and parts of the Hawkesbury region. CityRail has regular train services to the Blue Mountains, Royal National Park and to parts of the area covered by the Southern Highlands Tour. Ferries offer access to some parts of the Hawkesbury River.

0 kilometres   50

0 miles   25

Grand old house in Kiama, near
the Southern Highlands

Mudgee
Glen Davis
86
Cullen Bullen
Portland
Bathurst
Meadow Flats
Orange   Walang   32   Lithgow   Zig Zag Railway
Dubbo   Tarana   Berambing
Mount Victoria
Hampton   Blackheath   **4**
Oberon   BLUE
MOUNTAIN
Katoomb
Black Springs   Jenolan Caves
Porters Retreat
Natt
Richlands   Bullio
Taralga
Myrtleville   Bowra
Chatsbury   Moss Vale
Tarlo   Brayton   SOUTHER
31
Canberra
Bungonia   Morton
National
Park
Nerriga   Sassafra
Conjola
Bega

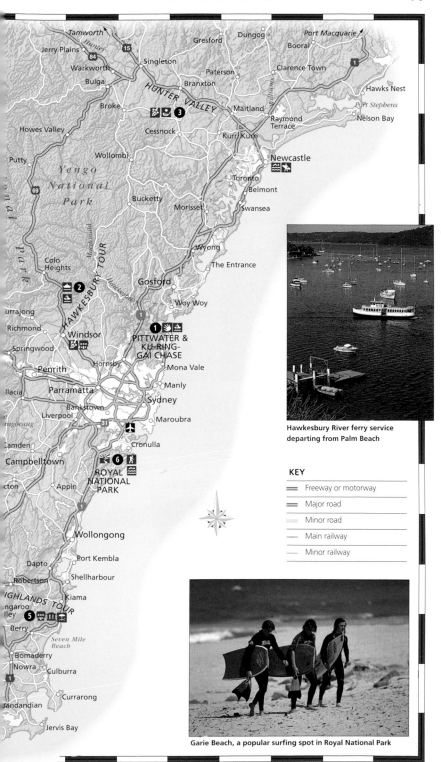

Tamworth
Jerry Plains
Warkworth
Bulga
Broke
Howes Valley
Putty
Gresford
Dungog
Singleton
Paterson
Branxton
Cessnock
Maitland
Kurri Kurri
Port Macquarie
Booral
Clarence Town
Raymond Terrace
Hawks Nest
Port Stephens
Nelson Bay
Newcastle
Toronto
Belmont
Swansea

Yengo National Park

Wollombi
Bucketty
Morisset
Colo Heights
Wyong
The Entrance
Gosford
Woy Woy
Richmond
Windsor
Springwood
Penrith
Parramatta
Bankstown
Liverpool
Camden
Campbelltown
Appin
Hornsby
PITTWATER & KU-RING-GAI CHASE
Mona Vale
Manly
Sydney
Maroubra
Cronulla
ROYAL NATIONAL PARK
Wollongong
Dapto
Port Kembla
Shellharbour
Kiama
Robertson
Berry
Bomaderry
Nowra
Culburra
Currarong
Jervis Bay

Seven Mile Beach

HAWKESBURY TOUR
HIGHLANDS TOUR

Hawkesbury River ferry service departing from Palm Beach

KEY

	Freeway or motorway
	Major road
	Minor road
	Main railway
	Minor railway

Garie Beach, a popular surfing spot in Royal National Park

Pittwater and Ku-ring-gai Chase ●

Pittwater and the adjacent Ku-ring-gai Chase National Park lie on Sydney's northernmost outskirts. They are bounded to the north by Broken Bay, at the mouth of the Hawkesbury River *(see pp156–7)*. Sparkling waterways and golden beaches are set against the unspoiled backdrop of the national park.

Barrenjoey Lighthouse Picnicking, bushwalking, surfing, boating, sailing and windsurfing are popular pastimes with visitors. The Hawkesbury River system curls around an ancient sandstone landscape rich in Aboriginal rock art, and flora and fauna.

Coal and Candle Creek
The pretty inlet is typical of eroded valleys formed during the last Ice Age. Water melted from the ice caps flooded the valleys to form the bays and creeks of Broken Bay.

Akuna Bay
The isolated marina, general store and café serve the Hawkesbury River boating fraternity.

ABORIGINAL ART IN KU-RING-GAI CHASE

Ku-ring-gai Chase has literally hundreds of Aboriginal rock art sites, providing an insight into one of the world's oldest cultures. The most common are rock engravings, generally made in groups with as many as 100 individual figures. They include whales up to 8 m (26 ft) long, fish, sharks, wallabies, echidnas and Ancestral Spirits such as Daramulan, who created the land, its people and animals.

Aboriginal rock art near the Basin, Ku-ring-gai Chase

KEY

▬	Major road
▭	Secondary road
─	Minor road
□	National Park
- - -	Ferry route
- - -	Walk route
⚓	Boat hire
◪	Aboriginal rock art
✳	Viewpoint

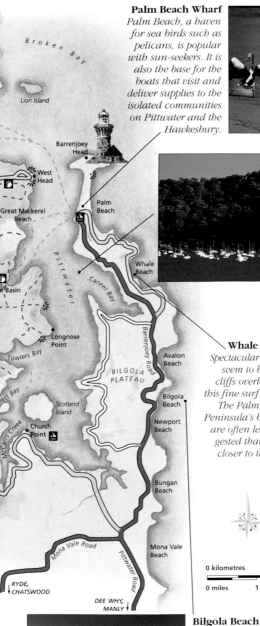

Palm Beach Wharf

Palm Beach, a haven for sea birds such as pelicans, is popular with sun-seekers. It is also the base for the boats that visit and deliver supplies to the isolated communities on Pittwater and the Hawkesbury.

Pittwater

This graceful finger of water separates Palm Beach from Ku-ring-gai Chase. Pittwater boasts secluded beaches, picnic areas and several hamlets that can only be reached by water.

Whale Beach

Spectacular houses seem to hug the cliffs overlooking this fine surf beach. The Palm Beach Peninsula's beaches are often less congested than those closer to the city.

TIPS FOR TRAVELLERS

Distance from Sydney: *About 30 km (19 miles).* **Duration of journey:** *About 45 minutes to Mona Vale Beach.* **Getting there:** *Take Military Rd on the city's North Shore and cross the Spit Bridge. Follow Pittwater Rd to Mona Vale Beach.* **When to go:** *The Christmas Holiday period is the peak season and beaches can be crowded. Ku-ring-gai Chase offers everything from shoreline to bushwalks and can be enjoyed year round.* **Where to stay and eat:** *Contact the visitors' information centre for full details of facilities.* **Tourist information:** *NPWS N. Region Info Centre.* **Tel** *9472 9300.* ☐ *10am–4pm Mon–Fri, 10am–5pm Sat–Sun.* **www**.npws.nsw.gov.au

Bilgola Beach

A small community of residents backs this patrolled surf beach set against a pretty rainforested valley. Wooden steps lead down from the ridge above through coastal heathland.

0 kilometres 2

0 miles 1

Hawkesbury Tour [2]

Australia's longest eastward-flowing river, the Hawkesbury–Nepean, forms Sydney's northern and western boundaries. It was at first thought to be two separate rivers until further exploration revealed that they were in fact one. The section known as the Hawkesbury runs from the Colo River Valley to Broken Bay in the north *(see pp154–5)*.

Settled in 1794, by 1799 the Hawkesbury Valley's small farms produced three-quarters of the colony's grain. Its riverscape is little changed since then and much of the area remains a quiet backwater. It is an area rich in relics of the early colonial period, including towns and villages established during the Macquarie era of 1810–19 *(see p24)*. It is also a place of great scenic grandeur, with magnificent vistas of one of Australia's most beautiful rivers.

Tizzana Winery [5]
A touch of Tuscany on the banks of the Hawkesbury, this sandstone winery was built in 1887 by Dr Thomas Fiaschi. It is open to visitors on weekends and public holidays.

Ebenezer Uniting Church [4]
Built in 1809, the church and its 1817 schoolhouse have been superbly restored. The tree under which services were first held still stands.

Portland Reach [6]
On the river, pleasure craft have replaced the grain barges of the past, but the area's farming community survives.

Colo River Drive [3]
This pretty route travels along the Putty Road to Colo, then follows the river to Lower Portland.

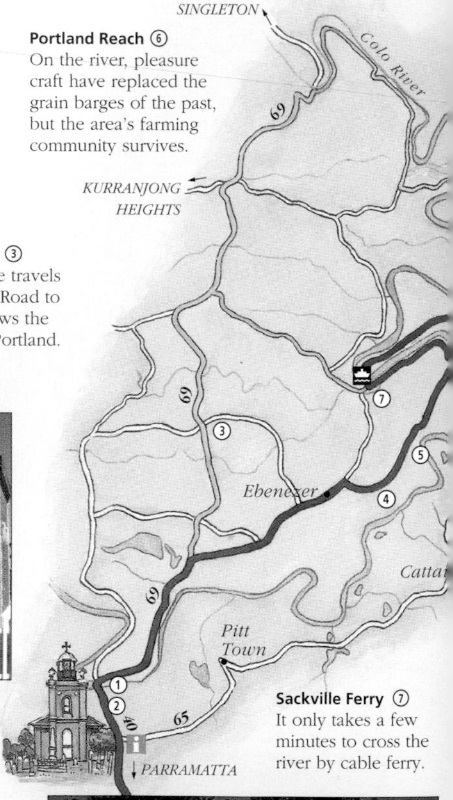
SINGLETON
Colo River
69
KURRANJONG HEIGHTS
69
3
7
5
Ebenezer
4
Catta
69
Pitt Town
1
2
40
65
PARRAMATTA

Tebbutts Observatory [2]
John Tebbutt (1834–1916), an early amateur astronomer, built this observatory in Windsor in 1854, where he studied the solar system and discovered a comet in 1861.

Sackville Ferry [7]
It only takes a few minutes to cross the river by cable ferry.

Windsor [1]
Built in 1815, the Macquarie Arms Hotel is just one of Windsor's fine early colonial buildings. Many others, including several by architect Francis Greenway *(see p114)*, remain from the town laid out in 1810.

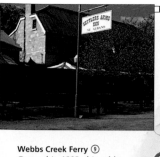

Settlers Arms Inn ⑩
Once an overnight stop for stage coaches to the Hunter Valley *(see pp158–9)*, this atmospheric 1836 hotel is in the largely unchanged village of St Albans.

Webbs Creek Ferry ⑨
Opened in 1908, this cable ferry gives access to the western bank of the Hawkesbury for the drive beside the Macdonald River.

Old General Cemetery ⑪
A stark reminder of the hardships and tragedies of early settlement, this is the resting place of six First Fleeters *(see p22)*.

Portland Ferry ⑧
If taking the Colo River Drive, cross the river here by ferry for the River Road to Wisemans Ferry.

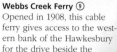

GOSFORD

Old Great North Road ⑫
The convict-built road with its massive buttresses was completed in 1828. Part of it still remains.

Maroota

Cornelia

HORNSBY

Wisemans Ferry ⑬
This small village on a bend in the Hawkesbury River is where ex-convict Solomon Wiseman started his ferry service, Australia's oldest, in 1827.

TIPS FOR DRIVERS

Distance from Sydney: 55 km (35 miles) to Windsor.
Duration of tour: About 3½ hours, excluding stops.
Getting there and back: Follow M4 to James Ruse Drive (53) just before Parramatta, then Windsor Rd (40). To return from Wisemans Ferry, take the Old Northern Rd (36) to Middle Dural, then Galston Rd to Hornsby. From here, follow Pacific Hwy south.
When to go: Peak season is from December to February. The river, national parks and small towns can be enjoyed year round.
Where to stay and eat: Cafés, restaurants and accommodation can be found at Windsor and Wisemans Ferry. The Settlers Arms Inn at St Albans has a few rooms, and a bar and restaurant.
Tourist information:
Hawkesbury Valley Information Centre. *Tel* 4588 5895.
www.hawkesburyvalley.com

KEY

█ Tour route

═ Scenic route

═ Other road

⛴ Cable ferry

ℹ Tourist information

※ Viewpoint

0 kilometres   5

0 miles   3

Hunter Valley ➌

Cheese made by local producer

Some of the earliest vineyards to be planted in Australia were on the fertile flats of the Hunter River in the 1830s, developing a thriving industry in fortified wine. Since the 1970s, it has evolved into a premium wine district *(see pp182–3)*. With some 90 wineries the area is a popular weekend trip from Sydney. Hot air ballooning, golf, horse riding and events of the Harvest Festival (March to May) supplement vineyard visits. The Jazz in the Vines festival takes place in October. Many wineries open daily but it is best to phone ahead and check.

Brokenwood
Under the ownership of Ben Riggs, this medium-sized winery has produced some of the region's finest Shiraz from the Graveyard vineyard, as well as an excellent Semillon.

Lindemans
In 1842, Dr Henry John Lindeman resigned his naval commission to establish a vineyard in the Hunter Valley. His company has been a major producer in the Australian wine industry ever since.

PERSONALITIES OF THE HUNTER VALLEY

The wine industry seems to attract or create larger-than-life characters. Among the current living legends is Len Evans, writer, wine judge, *bon vivant* and founder of the ambitious Rothbury Estate and Evans Family Wines (his new venture is Tower Estate). His contemporaries include Max Lake, a Sydney surgeon who started Lake's Folly as a weekend winery, and the late Murray Tyrrell, patriarch of a wine-making family that produced its first Hunter vintage in 1864 and proudly retains its independence.

Len Evans checking grape vines

Map labels:

SINGLETON, UPPER HUNTER

Sweetwater Creek

TERRACE RANGE

Old North Road

Hermitage Road

Rothbury Creek

Hunter Estate

Marsh Estate

Deaseys Road

Suther

ROSEMOUNT ESTATE, UPPER HUNTER

Mary Anne's Creek

Broke Road

Brian
McGuigan

Tyrell's Wines

Brokenwood

Tambu

Tulle

Pokolbin

Debeyers Road

Hungerford Hill

Drayton

Drayton Family Estate

Oakey

McWilliam's

Marrowb

BROKEN BACK RANGE

Petersons

Rothbury Estate
Founded by Len Evans, this winery is dedicated to wine excellence and education. Dinners and concerts held in the winery's cask hall are popular events.

Pepper's Convent
A restored 1909 convent is now an elegantly appointed guesthouse, with the Pepper Tree vineyard and winery and Robert's Restaurant only a short walk away.

Lake's Folly
Australian growers stopped planting Cabernet Sauvignon vines in the 19th century. But in the 1960s, former owner Max Lake reintroduced the variety.

Golden Grape Estate
A popular coach stop, the winery has a vine gallery showing grape varieties found around the world. There is also a museum which features early wine-making equipment.

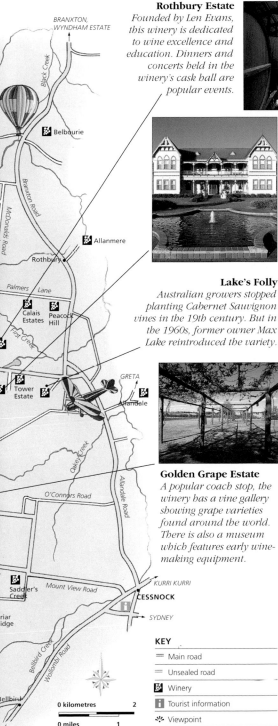

Map labels:
BRANXTON, WYNDHAM ESTATE
Black Creek
Belbourie
Branxton Road
McDonalds Road
Allanmere
Rothbury
Palmers Lane
Calais Estates
Peacock Hill
Frost Creek
Tower Estate
GRETA
Allandale
Oakey Creek
Allandale Road
O'Connors Road
Saddler's Creek
Mount View Road
Briar Ridge
KURRI KURRI
CESSNOCK
SYDNEY
Bellbird Creek
Wollombi Road
Bellbird
WOLLOMBI, SYDNEY

KEY

=	Main road
=	Unsealed road
🍷	Winery
ℹ	Tourist information
❋	Viewpoint

0 kilometres   2
0 miles   1

TIPS FOR TRAVELLERS

Distance from Sydney: 160 km (100 miles).
Duration of journey: About 2 hours from the centre of Sydney.
Getting there and back: Take the Sydney–Newcastle F3 freeway north of Sydney and follow the signs to Cessnock. Another route is through the picturesque Wollombi Valley. Allow about 3 hours as there are unsealed roads.
When to go: Year round. Vintage is Jan–Mar.
Where to stay and eat: There is a wide variety of motels, guest-houses, self-catering cottages and cabins, cafés and restaurants.
Visitor information: Hunter Valley Wine Country Tourism, 455 Wine Country Drive, Pokolbin. **Tel** 4990 0900. **www**.winecountry.com.au
Further afield: The Upper Hunter vineyardn ns are about 40 minutes by car northwest of Pokolbin.

Blue Mountains **4**

The Blue Mountains, designated a World Heritage area in 2000, prevented westward expansion of the European colony until 1813, when explorers Gregory Blaxland, William Lawson and William Charles Wentworth found a way across. The magnificent scenery, characterized by rugged cliffs and rock formations, ravines and waterfalls, is best appreciated on the bushwalks that wind along cliff tops and through valleys. The restaurants, cafés and antique shops will tempt the less energetic. The mountains are named for the perennial blue haze, caused by light striking eucalyptus oil particles in the air.

Zig Zag Railway
A steam train travels through cuttings and tunnels, and over three impressive viaducts built from 1866–9.

The Grose River
flows between the two roads crossing the mountains.

Victoria Falls

Mount York

Grose Valley from Govetts Leap
Considered by many to be the most imposing view in the Blue Mountains, a great panorama with a series of ridges stretches into the far distance.

Three Sisters
This giant rock formation near Echo Point takes its name from an Aboriginal legend. The story tells of three sisters turned to stone by their witchdoctor father to keep them safe from an evil bunyip or monster.

JENOLAN CAVES

About 55 km (34 miles) southwest of Mount Victoria is a magical series of spectacular underground limestone caves with icy blue rivers and fleecy limestone formations. They are surrounded by an extensive wildlife reserve. People have been making the trek here since the caves were discovered in 1838, staying originally in the Grand Arch cave and later in the Edwardian splendour of Jenolan Caves House, which still operates today.

The vividly coloured Pool of Cerberus at Jenolan Caves

KEY

▬▬	Major road
	Other road
•••	Suggested walk
🚶	Starting points for other walks
Ⓐ	Campsite
🎪	Picnic area
ℹ️	Tourist information
☀	Viewpoint

Mount Wilson
A picturesque village with cultivated gardens and exotic trees, it has been called a "little corner of the northern hemisphere". Some gardens are open to the public in spring and autumn.

The Cathedral of Ferns is a remnant of the temperate rainforest that once covered this area.

Mount Tomah Botanic Gardens
This superbly landscaped garden, specializing in cool-climate plants, has sweeping views over the Grose Valley.

RICHMOND

Mount Banks

Yester Grange
The beautifully restored Victorian country house at Wentworth Falls has tea rooms and a restaurant, as well as a collection of antiques and crafts.

Kings Tableland

Jamison Valley

Leura village is classified by the National Trust. Nearby are Leura Cascades, floodlit at night and one of the prettiest sights in the mountains.

Wentworth Falls
An impressive double waterfall is the starting point for the National Pass track, a challenging four-hour return walk to the next valley.

0 kilometres   5

0 miles   3

TIPS FOR TRAVELLERS

Distance from Sydney: About 105 km (65 miles).
Duration of journey: About 90 minutes to Wentworth Falls.
Getting there and back: Follow Metroad route 4 and the Great Western Highway. Return by Bells Line of Road to Windsor. State Rail has regular services to the area. An Explorer Bus runs from Katoomba train station at 9:30am on weekends and public holidays.
When to go: Year round. Always be prepared for the cold, especially when hiking, as the weather can change rapidly in all seasons.
Where to stay and eat: Contact the visitor information centre.
Tourist information: Blue Mountains Visitors' Information Centre, Echo Point, Katoomba. *Tel* 1300 653 408. **www.** bluemountainstourism.org.au

Southern Highlands Tour 5

Common wombat

This easily accessible area to the south of Sydney is often said to be more typical of Great Britain than Australia. It is actually a delightful combination of both: Australian high country and coastal hinterland with many European qualities. It is a land of abrupt hills and valleys, waterfalls and streams; of quaint villages, cosy restaurants, antique shops and elegant places to stay. The tour takes in spectacular Seven Mile Beach and the pretty town of Berry before heading to Kangaroo Valley, sleepy Bundanoon and the antique shops and newly emerging wineries of Berrima and Bowral. An exhilarating adjunct to the tour is nearby Minnamurra Falls with its boardwalk through rainforest.

Bowral ⑧
This highlands town holds a famous spring tulip festival every year and is home to cricket's Bradman Museum.

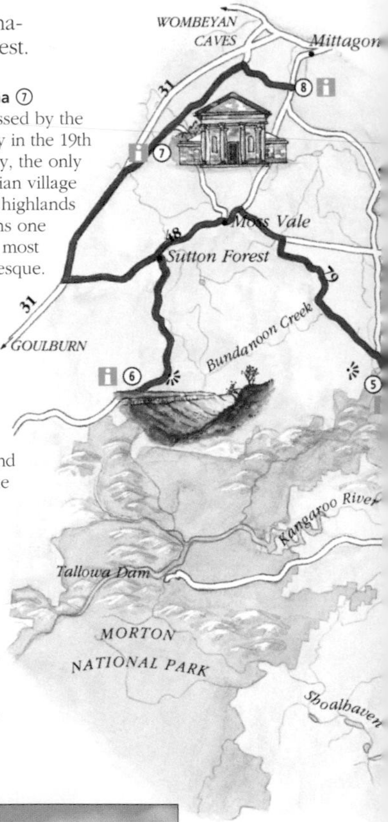

WOMBEYAN CAVES
Mittagong
31
⑧
⑦
Moss Vale
48
Sutton Forest
79
31
GOULBURN
Bundanoon Creek
⑥
⑤
Kangaroo River
Tallowa Dam
MORTON NATIONAL PARK
Shoalhaven

Berrima ⑦
By-passed by the railway in the 19th century, the only Georgian village in the highlands remains one of the most picturesque.

Bundanoon ⑥
Romantic guesthouses and a glow-worm cave make this town a popular weekend destination.

Fitzroy Falls ⑤
Part of Morton National Park, the falls plunge 80 m (262 ft) into the subtropical rainforest below. The falls lookout has access for the disabled and walking trails with stunning views.

0 kilometres 10

0 miles 5

KEY

- Tour route
- Scenic route (alternative)
- Other roads
- ℹ Tourist information
- ☼ Viewpoint

Kangaroo Valley ④
Hampden Bridge, a castellated suspension bridge, crosses the Kangaroo River at this small village. The river is an idyllic place for canoeing.

BERRIMA GAOL

Completed in 1839 by convict labour, this Georgian sandstone jail is featured in Rolf Boldrewood's classic 1888 bushranging novel, *Robbery Under Arms*. The fictitious character Captain Starlight, who escapes from Berrima, describes it as "the largest, most severe, the most dreaded of all prisons in New South Wales".

Kiama ①

The historic town began life in the 1820s as a port for shipping cedar. Its blowhole can spurt water as high as 60 m (200 ft).

Seven Mile Beach ②

Part of a national park and best seen from Gerroa's Black Head, the beach is flanked by dunes and hardy coastal vegetation, including forest and swamp. It is a great fishing, swimming and picnicking spot.

Berry ③

This town, surrounded by lush dairy country, is well known for its main street lined with shady trees, antique and craft shops, tea rooms and historic buildings. The Berry Museum, built in 1886, is in a former bank.

TIPS FOR DRIVERS

Distance from Sydney: 120 km (75 miles).
Duration of tour: About 3½ hours, excluding stops.
Getting there and back: Take Metroad route 1, then follow the F3 freeway and Princes Hwy (1) to Kiama. Return via the F5 freeway (31) from Mittagong, then Metroad route 5 into the city.
When to go: Year round. The beaches are best in summer, the gardens in spring and autumn. History buffs, antique-lovers and country-style aficionados will enjoy many of these little towns.
Where to stay and eat: Eating places, hotels and guesthouses are found all over the area.
Tourist information: Kiama Visitors Centre, Blowhole Point, Kiama. **Tel** 4232 3322. **www.** kiama.com.au Southern Highlands Visitors Information Centre, 62–70 Main St, Mittagong. **Tel** 4871 28 88. **www.**highlandsnsw.com.au

Royal National Park ❻

Designated as a national park in 1879, the "Royal" is the oldest national park in Australia. It covers 16,000 ha (37,100 acres) of landscape typical of the Sydney Basin sandstone. To the east, waves from the Pacific Ocean have undercut the sandstone and produced majestic coastal cliffs broken occasionally by small creeks and some spectacular beaches. Streams flowing north and east have incised deep river valleys. Heath vegetation on the plateaux merges with woodlands on the upper slopes. The park is ideal for bushwalking, picnicking, camping, swimming and birdwatching.

Waratah

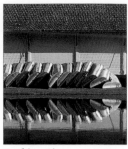

Hacking River
Boating, fishing and canoeing are common water sports.

Audley
A popular picnic area since the Edwardian era, it has a pavilion that was built in 1901. Look out for the 1920s dance hall also in the park.

Heathcote

Lady Carrington Drive
Named after a governor's wife and now closed to vehicles, the road is crossed by 15 creeks and is delightful to walk or cycle. It also leads to the track to Palona Cave.

KEY

━━	Main road
	Walking track
🚆	CityRail station
⛴	Ferry boarding point
🎪	Picnic area
🅰	Campsite
🏊	Swimming
🅿	Parking
☀	Viewpoint

The Forest Path follows a circular route, passing through subtropical rainforest.

Garie Beach is a popular surf beach accessible by road.

Werrong Naturist Beach

0 kilometres　　　4
0 miles　　　2

Figure Eight Pool

Bundeena

Enclosed by national park on three sides, the small settlement at the mouth of the Hacking River may be reached by ferry from Cronulla or by road through the national park.

Cronulla

Jibbon Head

Guided tours of the Jibbon Head Aboriginal rock engravings site may be arranged.

Jibbon Lagoon

Deer Pool

One of many fresh-water pools in the park, this sheltered spot is on the track from Bundeena Drive to Marley and Little Marley.

Little Marley Beach

Wattamolla Lagoon

This pretty picnic spot has a lagoon with a waterfall at its edge and a protected ocean beach.

Curracurrang

This rock formation is about halfway along the two-day Coast Walk. Sea eagles and terns nest in caves at the base of this rocky cove which also has a secluded swimming hole and waterfall.

TIPS FOR TRAVELLERS

Distance from Sydney: *34 km (21 miles).*

Duration of journey: *About 1 hour from the centre of Sydney.*

Getting there: *Follow Metroad route 1 south to Sutherland, then follow the signs to Heathcote and Wollongong. The turn-off to Farnell Avenue and the park entrance is shortly after Sutherland and well signposted.*

When to go: *Year round, but conditions for walking in summer can be hot so allow for this. If bushwalking, carry fresh water at all times and check on the fire danger at the Visitors' Centre before setting off.*

Where to stay and eat: *There are kiosks at Audley, Garie Beach and Wattamolla, but it is best to bring your own food. Camping information can be obtained at the Visitors' Centre.*

Tourist information: *Royal National Park Visitors' Centre, Farnell Ave, Audley.* **Tel** *9542 0648.* **www**.*npws.nsw.gov.au*

TRAVELLERS' NEEDS

WHERE TO STAY

With Australia's recent emergence as a major tourist destination, the urgent need for more high-quality and good-value accommodation became apparent. Previously, most Sydney hotels and guesthouses had been regarded as expensive and of varying standard. There has since been an enormous improvement in both quality and value, and there are excellent choices for visitors ranging from five-star luxury to the homeliness of a small, unpretentious hotel. In addition to hotels, Sydney has

Observatory Hotel doorman (p172)

self-catering apartments, homestay accommodation and budget and backpacker hostels for those travelling on a budget. Information on these alternatives is given below. From a survey of various types of accommodation in different areas and varying price brackets, we have selected those offering good value for money. Detailed descriptions of each hotel can be found on pages 172–7. Included with each hotel review is a list of symbols indicating the full range of facilities on offer there.

New façade of the refurbished Hilton Sydney Hotel (see p174)

WHERE TO LOOK

Most of the expensive hotels are in or near the city centre, but it is possible to find accommodation within most price ranges throughout Sydney. The city centre has the advantage of having many of the larger theatres, galleries and shops at hand, as well as easy transport access to more distant sights and attractions.

Cheaper accommodation can be found in the vibrant Kings Cross district. Choices here range from backpacker hostels to the small "boutique" hotels where the emphasis is on quality and personal service.

In The Rocks area, with its beautifully restored colonial buildings, you can choose from bed and breakfast in a traditional Sydney pub or the opulence of a five-star luxury hotel with good views of the Sydney Opera House.

The hotels around Darling Harbour and Chinatown offer good value for shoppers and are also within easy reach of

the city centre. Paddington has smaller hotels and self-catering apartments, while to the east are the up-market hotels of Double Bay. On the other side of Sydney Harbour Bridge, the leafy North Shore provides a more relaxed look at Sydney, and you can travel to and from the city centre by ferry.

The popular beachside suburbs of Bondi and Manly are a little way out of the centre of Sydney, but some visitors may like the opportunity to be close to superb beaches and yet still be reasonably near to the city.

You should also remember that in Australia a hotel can be a pub or a place to drink (see pp196–7). Pubs do not always provide accommodation.

HOW TO BOOK

It is advisable to book well in advance, especially for the Christmas school holidays in December and January, the Gay and Lesbian Mardi Gras

Festival in February and Mardi Gras Parade in early March, the Easter holidays and July and September school holidays.

Bookings can be made by letter, phone, fax, e-mail or through your local international travel agent. A credit card number or bank cheque in Australian dollars is usually required to secure your booking. Check cancellation requirements and reconfirm before you arrive in Sydney.

The **Sydney Visitors Centre** books certain hotels and will send a brochure pack. **Australian Accommodation Services** does not charge for bookings. If you belong to a motoring association, ask your travel agent to check which NRMA-(National Roads and Motorists' Association-) affiliated hotels offer a discount. **Countrylink** agencies at major railway stations offer a comprehensive service and AFTA travel agencies will book most hotels. Some travel

Indoor pool at the Observatory Hotel in The Rocks (see p172)

Curvilinear shape of the Four Points By Sheraton *(see p174)*

agencies specialize in specific areas. Tourist information centres can also offer valuable advice about where to stay in Sydney.

DISCOUNT RATES

With fewer visitors staying in Sydney from April to October (except during the school holiday periods), some of the more expensive hotels may be willing to negotiate a better rate. This is particularly so if they think you will look elsewhere for accommodation. It is always worth asking for the corporate rate at which hotels give discounts for group or company bookings. Most hotels give these without question.

At the weekend there are fewer business clients around, so this is the time when prices are frequently cheaper in the top hotels. Money can also be saved by booking for a week at a time. Asking for a room without a harbour or ocean view is another good way of reducing the costs.

The **Travellers Information Service** in the city can often arrange up to 50 per cent off the price of regular hotel accommodation rates (this does not normally apply to budget hotels) for those who book in person on the day a room is required.

Stained glass at Simpsons hotel *(see p176)*

HIDDEN EXTRAS

Breakfast is usually charged on top of the room rate in the more expensive hotels. It is best to avoid consuming any of the contents of the mini-bar until you have checked the price. Alcohol is usually much more expensive here than in shops. Also, be wary of the telephone charges. There will almost certainly be a considerable mark-up on any calls you make from your room. In general, tipping is not widespread, but it is expected in the more expensive hotels. You should make a note of the check-out time when you arrive, or negotiate a late check-out, as a surcharge may be incurred if you stay late.

SPECIAL OFFERS

Hotels often cooperate with airlines, rail services, bus companies, theatres and entertainment promoters to provide package deals that include discounted accommodation. Booking agencies will have brochures with details of these seasonal offers, or ask the hotel for information on any special deals.

"Special occasion" packages (such as for anniversaries or honeymoons) are available at the top end of the market.

DISABLED TRAVELLERS

The information regarding wheelchair access that is given on pages 172–7 relies very much on each hotel's own assessment of its facilities.

Spinal Cord Injuries Australia supplies a booklet called *Access Sydney* for people with mobility problems. It details accessible locations around Sydney and is available from their office in Little Bay, or it can be delivered by post. Their website is also worth visiting.

TRAVELLING WITH CHILDREN

It is worth inquiring about special rates or deals that allow children to stay in their parents' room for no extra cost. Most hotels in Sydney welcome children, although you should ask about special facilities before booking.

SELF-CATERING FLATS

Accommodation including full kitchen and laundry facilities offers the traveller greater independence. Such self-catering apartments are the latest accommodation trend in Australia. In addition to comfort, they also provide good value because the living space is larger than standard hotel rooms and the prices are competitive: although rates can vary, they are generally on a par with the major chain hotels.

The choice ranges from one- to three-bedroom luxury apartments in the inner city to basic flats at the beach. Some apartments cater for business travellers, complete with fax and other communications amenities. They are also ideal for families, especially those with young children, who appreciate not only the greater amount of space but also the flexibility provided by self-catering.

All the "apartment" hotels in the listings on pages 172–7 offer self-catering facilities. In addition, Sydney has several agencies that can help visitors to arrange self-catering accommodation *(see p170)*.

A luxurious room at the Regents Court hotel in Potts Point *(see p175)*

PRIVATE HOMES

European-style bed-and-breakfast accommodation in a private home can be an ideal way to experience a city. It is fast becoming a popular alternative to more impersonal hotel rooms for many people who choose to visit Sydney.

People from all walks of life offer rooms in a wide variety of house styles and locations. Agencies such as **Bed and** Breakfast Sydney Central and the **Homestay Network** make every effort to match the host and guest if possible, so ring to discuss any preferences before making a reservation.

BUDGET ACCOMMODATION

As a favoured destination for many young travellers, Sydney has a large number of hostels that cater specifically for their needs. Despite fierce competition, standards vary widely. At their best, hostels offer excellent value.

While it is necessary to book in advance at some hostels, others do not take bookings and beds are on a first come, first served basis. Apartments,

DIRECTORY

DISCOUNT AGENCIES

Travellers Information Service
Sydney Coach Terminal, Eddy Ave, Sydney NSW 2000. **Map** 4 E5. *Tel 9281 9366.*
Fax 9281 0123.

USEFUL BOOKING ADDRESSES

Australian Accommodation Services
Tel 9974 4884 / 8354 1602.
Fax 9974 1692.
www.tourist.net

Countrylink
Central Railway Station.
Map 4 E5. *Tel 132 232.*

Sydney Visitors Centre
Cnr Argyle & Playfair sts, The Rocks NSW 2000.
Map 1 A4.
Tel 9255 1788.

DISABLED ASSISTANCE

Ideas Incorporated
PO Box 786, Tumut NSW 2720.
Tel 6947 3377.
Fax 6947 3723.
www.ideas.org.au

Spinal Cord Injuries Australia
I Jennifer St, Little Bay NSW 2036.
Tel 9661 8855.
Postal Address
P.O Box 397 Matraville NSW 2036.
www.scia.org.au

SELF-CATERING AGENCIES

Medina
359 Crown St, Surry Hills NSW 2010. **Map** 5 A3.
Tel 1300 300 232.
www.medina apartments.com.au
Also at 15 other locations.

Pacific International Hotels
Sydney and Parramatta.
Tel 1800 224 584.
www.pacificinthotels.com

HOMESTAY AGENCIES

Bed and Breakfast Australia
29 Burlington Rd, Homebush NSW 2140.
Tel 9763 5833. **www.**
bedandbreakfast.com.au

Bed and Breakfast Sydney Central
139 Commonwealth St, Sydney NSW 2000.
Tel 9211 9920.
www.bedandbreakfast sydney.com.au

Homestay Network
5 Locksley St, Killara NSW 2071. *Tel 9498 4400.*
Fax 9498 8324.
www.homestay network.com.au

HOSTELS

Forbes Terrace
153 Forbes St, Woolloomooloo NSW 2011. **Map** 5 B1. *Tel 9358 4327.*

Pink House
6-8 Barncleuth Sq, Kings Cross NSW 2011. **Map** 5 C1. *Tel 1800 806 385.*

Sydney Central YHA
Cnr Pitt St & Rawson Pl, Sydney NSW 2000.
Tel 9281 9111

University of Sydney
International House
Tel 9950 9800.
St John's College
Tel 9394 5200.
Sancta Sophia
Tel 9577 2100.
Wesley College
Tel 9565 3333.
Women's College
Tel 9517 5000.

Wattle House Travellers' Accommodation
44 Hereford St, Glebe NSW 2037.
Tel 9552 4997.
www.wattlehouse.com.au

Wake Up!
509 Pitt St (opposite Central Station). **Map** 4 E5. *Tel 9288 7888.*
www.wakeup.com.au

World Youth Hostel
477 Kent St, Sydney NSW 2000. *Tel 9261 1551.*

YHA Australia
422 Kent St, Sydney NSW 2000. **Map** 4 D3. *Tel 9261 1111.* www.yha.com.au

GAY AND LESBIAN ACCOMMODATION

Downunder Destination
709/105 Campbell St, Surry Hills. *Tel 9281 1450.*

IGLTA
PO Box 1397, Rozelle NSW 2039. *Tel 9818 6669.* www.iglta.org

CAMPING

Blue Mountains National Park
Tel 1 300 653 408.

Jenolan Caravan Park
Tel 6336 0344.

Ku-ring-gai Chase National Park
Tel 9472 8949.

Royal National Park
Tel 9542 0648.

Interior of boutique hotel Medusa, Darlinghurst *(see p175)*

rooms and dormitories are all available, but dormitories are often mixed sex; check before arriving. The backpacker scene changes quickly, so ask other travellers for the latest developments. Kings Cross and Glebe have the largest concentration of cheap accommodation.

Wake Up! backpacker hostel is one of the best of the bunch, with clean, modern facilities, including a bistro, café, bar and internet connection. It is also well located right next to Central Railway Station and offers a free orientation morning to all guests. If required, staff can also provide a list of suitable employment agencies for those who would like to work during their stay in Sydney.

Forbes Terrace and **Pink House** are smaller hostels offering good facilities in restored buildings close to Kings Cross. Pink House also provides plenty of help if you need to find work in Sydney.

Sydney Central combines modern facilities, such as a swimming pool, sauna and 24-hour security access, with old-world charm and is very conveniently situated right opposite Sydney Central Railway Station.

Wattle House Travellers' Accommodation in Glebe is a restored Victorian residence, offering quiet, budget-priced rooms for adults only. They are also a good source of recommendations for other budget places to stay further afield in New South Wales and throughout Australia.

YHA Australia is a useful source of information when planning your trip, offering advice about travel deals as well as helping you decide on your itinerary and find places to stay. Two other useful online sources that provide lists of budget hostels in Sydney are **hostels.com** and **hostelworld.com**.

HALLS OF RESIDENCE

Student rooms, with shared bathroom facilities, are available at the University of Sydney over the summer break from December to February. The university is conveniently close to the city and to public transport, and the moderate price includes breakfast.

GAY AND LESBIAN ACCOMMODATION

Lesbian and gay visitors are welcome in all of Sydney's hotels. In fact, quite a number of places cater primarily, if not exclusively, for same-sex couples. Many of the small hotels in the inner city areas of Darlinghurst, Paddington, Newtown and Surry Hills are geared specifically towards gay and lesbian visitors, although most of them also welcome heterosexual guests.

At the **IGLTA** (International Gay and Lesbian Travel Association) website you can search for gay or gay-friendly travel-related businesses, including hotels, guesthouses and tours.

Some travel agencies, such as **Downunder Destination**, specialise in holidays and accommodation for gay and lesbian travellers.

CAMPING

Although not an option in the city itself, camping is available in several national parks close to Sydney. This can be a cheap and idyllic way of enjoying the natural beauty and wildlife of the bushland.

The **Royal National Park** *(see pp164–5)* has a campsite with facilities at Bonnie Vale, just outside Bundeena. Advance booking is required all year round. Free bush or "walk-in" camping is allowed in several other places, but first ring the park to obtain the necessary camping permit.

At The Basin in **Ku-ring-gai Chase National Park** *(see pp154–5)*, bookings should be made and all fees paid before your stay or on arrival. There are toilets, cold showers, barbecue facilities and a phone.

There are basic campsites near Glenbrook, Woodford, Blackheath and Wentworth Falls in the **Blue Mountains National Park** *(see pp160–61)*. **Jenolan Caravan Park** in Oberon has cabins and caravans for hire as well as camping pitches with and without electric hook-ups. You will need to book if you want to camp at the Euroka Clearing near Glenbrook, but this is not necessary for the other sites. Bush camping is also permitted in the park, but there are some restrictions. Contact the national park for more details before you visit.

Manly Pacific Parkroyal *(see p177)*, overlooking Manly's ocean beach

Choosing a Hotel

These hotels have been selected across a wide price range for their good value, excellent facilities and location. This chart lists the hotels by area in the same order as the rest of the guide. Entries are listed alphabetically within each price category, from the least to the most expensive. Restaurant listings are on pages 184–193.

PRICE CATEGORIES
For a standard double room per night including service (prices in Australian dollars)

$ under $120
$$ $120–$200
$$$ $200–$280
$$$$ $280–$380
$$$$$ over $380

THE ROCKS AND CIRCULAR QUAY

Mercantile Hotel
🍴 $

25 George St, The Rocks **Tel** *9247 3570* **Fax** *9247 7047* **Rooms** *15* **Map** *1 B2*

Its George Street location means that all of the Rocks attractions are nearby, including the Argyle Cut and Garrison Church. The hotel boasts spacious rooms containing period fittings and marble fireplaces. Some even have jacuzzis. The basic rate is for a room with a shared bathroom; en suites cost a little more. Breakfast is included.

Lord Nelson Brewery Hotel
🍴🛏 $$

19 Kent St, The Rocks **Tel** *9251 4044* **Fax** *9251 1532* **Rooms** *10* **Map** *1 A2*

The top floor of the celebrated pub, famous for its home brews, offers cosy bedrooms with stonewalls and rustic furnishings. Basic rooms have shared bathrooms, for those not on a tight budget rooms are available. Breakfast is included in the price. Located close to the trains, buses and ferries of Circular Quay. **www.lordnelson.com.au**

The Russell
🍴 $$

143A George St, The Rocks **Tel** *9241 3543* **Fax** *9252 1652* **Rooms** *29* **Map** *1 B2*

This lovely old-fashioned hotel sits above a historic 19th-century pub, the Fortune of War. The Russell offers free breakfast, a quaint sitting room, well-stocked library and sunny rooftop garden overlooking the busy Quay. The interior is decorated with country-style antiques. Some rooms have shared bathrooms. **www.therussell.com.au**

Rendezvous Stafford
📺🅿🍴♨🛏👤 $$$

75 Harrington St, The Rocks **Tel** *9251 6711* **Fax** *9251 3458* **Rooms** *61* **Map** *1 B2*

There really is something for everyone at this unusual boutique hotel. Most rooms are studio and one-bedroom apartments but suites are available in the seven charmingly restored 1870s terrace houses nearby. Excellent business services, a spa and sauna and Continental breakfasts are available. **www.rendezvoushotels.com**

Old Sydney Holiday Inn
📺🅿🍴♨🛏👤 $$$$

55 George St, The Rocks **Tel** *9252 0524* **Fax** *9251 2093* **Rooms** *175* **Map** *1 B2*

Big enough to offer all the facilities of a grand establishment, this hotel is also small enough to provide personal attention. Great location within the historic Rocks area and close to Circular Quay and the Sydney Opera House. The view from the sparkling blue rooftop pool is spectacular. There is also a sauna and a whirlpool. **www.holiday-inn.com**

The Observatory Hotel
📺🅿🍴♨🛏👤 $$$$$

89–113 Kent St, Millers Point **Tel** *9256 2222* **Fax** *9256 2233* **Rooms** *99* **Map** *1 A2*

Although its rack rate makes this absolute luxury hotel one of Sydney's most expensive, there are often great internet deals to be found on the hotel's website. It is elegantly furnished, with original antiques and fine artwork. There are excellent facilities for business travellers as well. **www.observatoryhotel.com.au**

Park Hyatt Sydney
📺🅿🍴♨🛏👤 $$$$$

7 Hickson Rd, The Rocks **Tel** *9241 1234* **Fax** *9256 1555* **Rooms** *158* **Map** *1 B1*

Many rooms in this six-star hotel have Opera House views, as does the rooftop swimming pool. Walking up the road for a few minutes takes you to the small park beneath the Harbour Bridge, a few minutes in the other direction to Circular Quay. Well-equipped for business travellers and offers high-speed internet. **sydney.park.hyatt.com**

Shangri-La
📺🅿🍴♨🛏👤 $$$$$

176 Cumberland St, The Rocks **Tel** *9250 6000* **Fax** *9250 6250* **Rooms** *563* **Map** *1 A3*

This hotel has just spent A$31 million on a complete refurbishment and it shows. The spacious rooms are now decorated in neutral tones with rich gold brocade highlights, and all offer lovely views of the harbour. On the top floor, Altitude restaurant and the Blu Horizon bar are popular dining and nightspots. **www.shangri-la.com**

Quay Grand
📺🅿🍴♨🛏 $$$$$

61–69 Macquarie St **Tel** *9256 4000* **Fax** *9256 4040* **Rooms** *68* **Map** *1 C3*

Next door to the Opera House at one of Sydney's premiere addresses, the hotels' bedroom apartments are tastefully furnished. Features include spa baths, kitchen and laundry facilities, televisions and stereos. There is grocery service available, or try Quadrant Restaurant or ECQ, the hotel's dress-circle bar. **www.mirvachotels.com.au**

Key to Symbols *see back cover flap*

WALSH BAY The Sebel Pier One ⇅ [P] 🍴 🍸 🏋 $$$$$

11 Hickson Rd, Walsh Bay ***Tel*** *8298 9999* ***Fax*** *8298 9777* ***Rooms*** *161* ***Map*** *1 A2*

This is Sydney's first over-the-water hotel, built on a 1912 finger wharf in the Walsh Bay World Heritage precinct, beside the Harbour Bridge. The hotel's luxurious rooms combine original features with contemporary design. An extensive room service menu is available, and all the rooms have internet access. **www.mirvachotels.com.au**

CITY CENTRE

Railway Square YHA 🍴 🏊 ♿ $

8–10 Lee St ***Tel*** *9281 9666* ***Fax*** *9281 9688* ***Rooms*** *64* ***Map*** *4 E5*

Located in a historic 1904 building, this YHA hostel adjoins Central Station's Platform Zero. Some rooms are inside converted railway carriages, while others are in the main building. Features modern design and a timber deck for sunbathing beside the over-sized spa pool. There is an internet cafe and a tour desk. **www.yha.org.au**

Y Hotel ⇅ [P] 🍴 🏋 ♿ $

5–11 Wentworth Ave ***Tel*** *9264 2451* ***Fax*** *9285 6288* ***Rooms*** *121* ***Map*** *4 F3*

Expect less of the party crowd at this peaceful backpacker spot, since all dorm rooms have just four single beds and are single-sex. Standard double rooms are basic but clean and have shared toilets. Rooms with en suites and more luxurious amenities are reasonably priced. Coffee, tea and breakfast included in the price. **www.yhotel.com.au**

Castlereagh Boutique Hotel ⇅ 🍴 🏋 ♿ $$

169–171 Castlereagh St ***Tel*** *9284 1000* ***Fax*** *9284 1045* ***Rooms*** *82* ***Map*** *1 B5*

Full of character, this hotel has a plush old-fashioned dining room, decorated with chandeliers and elaborate paint and plasterwork. The rooms, furnished with period pieces and patterned upholstery, offer essentials such as TVs, bars, fridges and tea and coffee facilities. Continental breakfast is included in few deals. **www.thecastlereagh.net.au**

Central Park Hotel ⇅ [P] 🏋 $$

185 Castlereagh St ***Tel*** *9283 5000* ***Fax*** *9283 2710* ***Rooms*** *36* ***Map*** *1 B4*

Their "hip on a budget" slogan is a great description of this boutique hotel. Its studio rooms and light-and-airy New York-style loft suites are complemented by neutral colours and clean-lined furniture. All rooms have cable TV, while some have CD players and large granite bathrooms. Parking is available nearby. **www.centralpark.com.au**

Hotel Pensione ⇅ $$

631–635 George St ***Tel*** *9265 8888* ***Fax*** *9211 9825* ***Rooms*** *68* ***Map*** *4 E4*

Many features of this heritage building survived its transformation into a hotel, including an old staircase and wood-panelled elevator. All rooms have stylish mosaic-tiled en suites, phones, dataports, cable TV and air conditioning. Quad rooms are fabulous value. Breakfast boxes are also available. **www.pensione.com.au**

Blacket Hotel ⇅ [P] 🍴 $$$

70 King St ***Tel*** *9279 3030* ***Fax*** *9279 3020* ***Rooms*** *42* ***Map*** *1 A4*

Opened in June 2001, the Blacket is housed in the refurbished 1850s ANZ bank site designed by 19th-century architect Edmond Samuel Blacket. There are five two-storey lofts with large bedrooms, kitchenettes and spa baths. Ask about deals that include dinner at Minc restaurant, and you also get free breakfast. **www.blackethotel.com.au**

Meriton World Tower ⇅ [P] 🍴 🏊 🍸 🏋 ♿ $$$

95 Liverpool St ***Tel*** *8263 7500* ***Fax*** *9261 5722* ***Rooms*** *114* ***Map*** *4 E3*

Some serviced apartments are available short term in this brand new vertical village, the tallest residential building in Sydney. Spacious two-bedroom apartments can sleep up to five. Everything guests might need is just a short stroll away. Facilities include a child-minding centre, DVD players and much more. **www.meritonapartments.com.au**

Sheraton on the Park ⇅ [P] 🍴 🏊 🍸 🏋 ♿ $$$

161 Elizabeth St ***Tel*** *9286 6000* ***Fax*** *9286 6686* ***Rooms*** *557* ***Map*** *1 B5*

Arriving at this hotel's very grand entrance, guests can expect all the complete luxuries of a five-star hotel. Amenities include marble bathrooms, stylish furnishings, dataports, 24-hour room service, helpful concierges, baby-sitting services and lounges. Many rooms have views over the trees of Hyde Park. **www.sheraton.com**

wake up! ⇅ 🍴 ♿ $$$

509 Pitt St ***Tel*** *9288 7888* ***Fax*** *9288 7889* ***Beds*** *500* ***Map*** *4 E5*

If your plan for Sydney is all action, this is the place for you. It is a party hostel, and here large mixed dorms are more popular than the smaller, single-sex ones. Some hotel-style double rooms with en suites are available. Offers laundry and kitchen facilities, a lounge room with TV and a video library. **www.wakeup.com.au**

The York ⇅ [P] 🍴 🏊 🍸 🏋 ♿ $$$

5 York St ***Tel*** *9210 5000* ***Fax*** *9290 1487* ***Rooms*** *120 apartments* ***Map*** *1 A3*

There is an understated elegance throughout this centrally-located hotel. Each of its apartments is individually designed and has a balcony, fully-equipped kitchen and large bathroom. Apartments vary in size from studios to executive two bedroom penthouses. Close to The Rocks and Circular Quay. **www.theyorkapartments.com.au**

Avillion Hotel   ⓢⓢⓢⓢ

Cnr Pitt & Liverpool Sts **Tel** *8268 1888* **Fax** *9283 5899* **Rooms** *445*   **Map** *4 E3*

Close to Town Hall station and the monorail stop at World Square, this hotel offers comfortable, reasonably priced rooms. The hotel's gallery includes work by Australian luminaries such as Peter Kingston and John Coburn, as well as important indigenous art. There is live jazz in the bar on Thursday and Friday nights. **www.avillion.com.au**

Establishment Hotel   ⓢⓢⓢⓢ

5 Bridge Lane **Tel** *9240 3100* **Fax** *9240 3101* **Rooms** *35*   **Map** *1 B3*

This is one of the most fashionable and desirable places in town. The rooms offer a choice of lively or tranquil colour schemes, marble or stone bathrooms with separate baths and showers. Although there are bars, restaurants and a nightclub in the building, soundproofing ensures a peaceful stay. Limited parking. **www.establishmenthotel.com**

Hotel Mercure Sydney   ⓢⓢⓢⓢ

818–820 George St, PO Box 7082 **Tel** *9217 6666* **Fax** *9217 6888* **Rooms** *517*   **Map** *4 D5*

Close to trains and buses that depart from Central Station and Railway Square, this hotel is also a comfortable walking distance from Darling Harbour and Chinatown. A popular choice for families because two children are able to stay for free in their parents' room. All rooms have dataports and cable TV. **www.accorhotels.com.au**

Waldorf Apartment Hotel   ⓢⓢⓢⓢ

57 Liverpool St **Tel** *9261 5355* **Fax** *9261 3753* **Rooms** *48*   **Map** *4 E3*

This hotel is a short stroll away from the city shopping centres and cinemas and a slightly longer one to Darling Harbour attractions, such as Tumbalong Park, the Chinese Gardens and IMAX Theatre. The apartments are spacious, with balconies overlooking the city. Has a rooftop pool and free in-house movies. **www.waldorf.com.au**

The Grace   ⓢⓢⓢⓢⓢ

77 York St **Tel** *9272 6888* **Fax** *9299 8189* **Rooms** *382*   **Map** *1 A4*

You could not be closer to the action than at The Grace as General Douglas Macarthur used the building as a base during WWII. The hotel dates from the 1930s and its restoration has retained the building's original Art Deco style. Rooms are well equipped and there is a beauty salon, a health club and a wine bar. **www.gracehotel.com.au**

Hilton Sydney   ⓢⓢⓢⓢⓢ

488 George St **Tel** *9266 2000* **Rooms** *577*   **Map** *1 B5*

An enormous renovation was carried out on this hotel, with the aim of setting new standards in luxury. The slick new design is immediately apparent and upgraded features include stylish interiors, quality furniture, LCD TVs and avant-garde Internet Protocol technology phones. Guests have access to the health clubs. **www.hiltonsydney.com.au**

Sofitel Wentworth   ⓢⓢⓢⓢⓢ

61–101 Phillip St **Tel** *9230 0700* **Fax** *9228 9133* **Rooms** *436*   **Map** *1 B4*

The Sofitel Wentworth building is a Sydney classic because of its curved, copper-clad façade. Inside, modern chandeliers feature hundreds of glass teardrops, and throughout the hotel, pale wood and rich, dark fabrics are used to maximum effect. They also offer live jazz and a DJ in the bar. **www.accorhotels.com.au**

DARLING HARBOUR

Carlton Crest Hotel Sydney   ⓢⓢⓢⓢ

169–179 Thomas St, Haymarket **Tel** *9281 6888* **Fax** *9281 6688* **Rooms** *251*   **Map** *4 D5*

Located near Paddy's Market in Chinatown, this hotel is close to many city attractions. Part of the Crest is made up of the original 1902 Infants' Hospital Building. All rooms and suites are large and guest facilities include a rooftop pool, barbeque area and garden. The hotel specializes in arranging theatre tickets. **www.carltoncrest-sydney.com.au**

Four Points By Sheraton   ⓢⓢⓢⓢ

161 Sussex St **Tel** *9290 4000* **Fax** *9290 4040* **Rooms** *630*   **Map** *4 D2*

With 630 rooms, the contemporary Four Points is Sydney's largest hotel. Located on the CBD side of Darling Harbour, it is close to the restaurant and entertainment precincts including King Street and Cockle Bay wharfs. The hotel is also an easy walk from the Queen Victoria Building and Town Hall station. **www.fourpoints.com**

Holiday Inn Darling Harbour   ⓢⓢⓢⓢ

68 Harbour St, Darling Harbour **Tel** *9281 0400* **Fax** *9281 1212* **Rooms** *304*   **Map** *4 D3*

The location is great and so is the heritage-listed wool store that houses this hotel. The Holiday Inn has good facilities for business travellers with special executive suites. The restaurant offers à la carte and casual dining plus a breakfast buffet. Children eat for free. **www.holidayinndarlingharbour.com.au**

Star City   ⓢⓢⓢⓢ

80 Pyrmont St, Pyrmont **Tel** *9777 9000* **Fax** *9657 8345* **Rooms** *480*   **Map** *3 B1*

You might think of it as casino tacky, but the hotel is first-rate, with stylish rooms and an endless list of facilities. Draw cards include king-size beds in the standard rooms, 13 restaurants and bars, 24-hour entertainment, a health club and 24-hour butler service. Choose between hotel and apartment-style accommodation. **www.starcity.com.au**

Key to Price Guide *see p172* **Key to Symbols** *see back cover flap*

Novotel Darling Harbour
100 Murray St, Pyrmont **Tel** *9934 0000* **Fax** *9934 0099* **Rooms** *525*   **Map** *3 C2*

These superstructure towers above the Harbourside centre at Darling Harbour are close to the Powerhouse and Maritime Museums. The four-star quality rooms are available in many different ranges and have views across the city. In cooler weather, guests avoid the unheated pool and play tennis instead. **www.accorhotels.com.au**

BOTANIC GARDENS AND THE DOMAIN

Hotel InterContinental
117 Macquarie St **Tel** *9253 9000* **Fax** *9240 1240* **Rooms** *509*   **Map** *1 C3*

The foyer and lower stories of this luxurious hotel are made up of part of the old 1851 Treasury Building. Small music ensembles frequently perform in the lobby, where guests and visitors indulge in high tea, served on tiered cake stands. Well-equipped rooms have window seats, chaise lounges and fine views. **www.sydney.intercontinental.com**

Sir Stamford Circular Quay
93 Macquarie St **Tel** *9252 4600* **Fax** *9252 4286* **Rooms** *105*   **Map** *1 C3*

There is a refined but relaxed air in this intimate hotel. The decor is built around the hotel's collection of 18th-century antiques, and fine art. Paying a little extra per night allows guests access to the Quay Lounge, and with it a host of benefits including complimentary breakfast, tea/coffee, drinks and faxes, plus limos. **www.stamford.com.au**

KINGS CROSS AND DARLINGHURST

Formule 1
191–201 William St **Tel** *9326 0300* **Fax** *9326 0155* **Rooms** *115*   **Map** *5 B1*

You can count on rooms being spick and span at this reliable budget motel chain. Located just down the hill from the famous Coke sign at the top of Kings Cross, it is close to the action. Rooms can accommodate two, three or four people for the flat room rate. Do not expect much here, they only have TV. Limited parking. **www.formule1.com.au**

Hotel Altamont
207 Darlinghurst Rd **Tel** *9360 6000* **Fax** *9360 7096* **Rooms** *14*   **Map** *5 A2*

At this fun budget hotel, all rooms have king- or queen-sized beds and solid, comfy wooden furniture. There are discounted weekly rates and a few good quality backpacker rooms: they fill up quickly so book early. Formerly a Georgian mansion, the hotel now boasts a private lounge bar, the Diamante Lounge. **www.altamont.com.au**

The Chelsea
49 Womerah Ave, Darlinghurst **Tel** *9380 5994* **Fax** *9332 2491* **Rooms** *13*   **Map** *5 C1*

At this beautiful guesthouse, decorated in French Provincial and contemporary styles, your stay is made tranquil by attentive hosts and a quiet street. Particularly popular with businesswomen, the property is gay and lesbian friendly. On-street parking is available nearby. Breakfast included in the price. **www.chelsea.citysearch.com.au**

L'otel
114 Darlinghurst Rd **Tel** *9360 6868* **Fax** *9331 4536* **Rooms** *16*   **Map** *5 A2*

This large terrace house has been converted into a designer hotel, with small but lovely rooms decorated in white French-Provincial style with painted furniture and art pieces. There is a hip bar and restaurant downstairs, and the hotel is close to Oxford Street's cafés and bars. The concierge can arrange tours. **www.lotel.com.au**

Regents Court
18 Springfield Ave, Potts Point **Tel** *9358 1533* **Fax** *9358 1833* **Rooms** *30*   **Map** *2 E5*

An innovative team transformed this Art Deco gentlemen's chambers into a stylish boutique hotel, favoured by artists, actors and writers. Spacious and well-equipped, all studios have queen beds. A rooftop garden has lush plants and great views of the city. Cots and child-minding available. **www.regentscourt.com.au**

Medusa
267 Darlinghurst Rd, Darlinghurst **Tel** *9331 1000* **Fax** *9380 6901* **Rooms** *18*   **Map** *5 B1*

Medusa makes its own rules as only a boutique hotel can. An old Victorian row house has been transformed into a brightly-coloured miracle of modernism, with inspiration from Caravaggio's *Medusa*. Lindt chocolates and Aveda toiletries are complimentary, as is use of a neighbouring gym. **www.medusa.com.au**

Morgan's
304 Victoria St, Darlinghurst **Tel** *9360 7955* **Fax** *9360 9217* **Rooms** *26*   **Map** *2 E5*

This boutique Art Deco hotel is set in a leafy location in the café district. A garden courtyard and fountain add to the hotel's charm. Rooms have cable TV and fully-equipped kitchens, and some can accommodate a third person for an extra charge. It also has a restaurant serving breakfast, lunch and dinner. **www.morganshotel.com.au**

Simpsons of Potts Point   P 🍴 $$$

8 Challis Ave, Potts Point **Tel** *9356 2199* **Fax** *9356 4476* **Rooms** *14*   **Map** *2 E4*

A charming B&B at the "Paris" end of Potts Point, where the complimentary breakfast is served in a glass-roofed conservatory. Built in 1892 as a family residence, the hotel has been exquisitely restored and boasts elegantly designed rooms. Guests staying in the romantic Cloud Suite enjoy a private spa bath. **www.simpsonshotel.com.au**

W Sydney   P 🍴 ≋ 📺 👚 & $$$$$

6 Cowper Wharf Rd, Woolloomooloo **Tel** *9331 9000* **Fax** *9331 9031* **Rooms** *100*   **Map** *2 D5*

This hotel's glamour and reputation as the coolest in Sydney makes up for the far from spacious rooms. Guests enjoy luxury robes and Aveda bath products, a fabulous cocktail bar and a row of great restaurants below on the finger wharf. All rooms are equipped with cutting-edge business technology and 27-inch TV screens. **www.whotels.com**

PADDINGTON

Hughenden Hotel   P 🍴 $$

14 Queen St, Woollahra **Tel** *9363 4863* **Fax** *9362 0398* **Rooms** *35*   **Map** *6 E4*

This rambling old building, once a 19th-century family home, is restored to its original grandeur with beautifully carved staircases and marble fireplaces. Rooms are comfortably furnished and the restaurant is very good. Writers groups meet and artists exhibit their work here. Breakfast included in the price. **www.hughendenhotel.com.au**

Sullivans   P 🍴 ≋ 📺 $$

21 Oxford St, Paddington **Tel** *9361 0211* **Fax** *9360 3735* **Rooms** *64*   **Map** *5 B3*

Standard rooms at this friendly, family-owned hotel face the bustle of Oxford Street. It is worth paying a tiny bit more for a garden room that overlooks the courtyard and swimming pool. Guests can use the gym and bicycles. The restaurant, with its windows looking out onto the street, is great for people-watching. **www.sullivans.com.au**

FURTHER AFIELD

Dive $$

234 Arden St, Coogee **Tel** *9665 5538* **Fax** *9665 4347* **Rooms** *14*

A stylish hotel featured in design magazines, with rooms that feature polished floorboards, high ceilings and designer bathrooms. This is a great sanctuary from the backpacker madness of Coogee Beach. Complimentary breakfast and unlimited tea and coffee are available. No air conditioning but there are ceiling fans. **www.divehotel.com.au**

Hotel Unilodge   ≋ 📺 & $$

Cnr of Broadway & Bay St, Broadway **Tel** *9338 5000* **Fax** *9338 5111* **Rooms** *100*   **Map** *3 C5*

This three-and-a-half star hotel is superbly located and good value. While not plush, it offers a heated lap pool, spa, gym and a rooftop barbeque area, as well as a proximity to Chinatown, Central Station and the western side of Darling Harbour. Convenient for nearby Sydney and UTS universities. **www.unilodge.com.au**

Periwinkle Manly Cove   P $$

18–19 East Esplanade, Manly **Tel** *9977 4668* **Fax** *9977 6308* **Rooms** *18*

A striking Federation-era mansion has been converted into a B&B, with antique furniture and colour schemes. Rooms with a view attract only a small premium. Features high ceilings, wrought-iron verandahs and a leafy courtyard. Also has private outdoor areas. Breakfast included in the price. **www.periwinklemanlycove.com.au**

Ravesi's   🍴 $$

Cnr Campbell Parade & Hall Sts, Bondi Beach **Tel** *9365 4422* **Fax** *9365 1481* **Rooms** *16*

This lovely boutique hotel has been recently refurbished and epitomizes the relaxed style of beach life at Bondi. Split-level suites cost more but are gorgeous, opening onto private terraces with ocean views. Ravesi's has a restaurant downstairs and popular bar, which is packed with a mix of tourists and funky locals. **www.ravesis.com.au**

Rydges Camperdown   P 🍴 ≋ 📺 & & $$

9 Missenden Rd, Camperdown **Tel** *9516 1522* **Rooms** *143*

One of the few hotels in the gay and lesbian enclaves of Newtown and Camperdown. The hotel is close to Parramatta Road where buses leave for the city and Leichhardt. Relax in the pool, sauna or games room. Rooms feature all the usual basics. The bar has a daily happy hour from 5:30 to 6:30pm. **www.rydges.com/camperdown**

The Tiffany Apartments   P ≋ 📺 $$$

95–97 Grafton St, Bondi Junction **Tel** *9388 9700* **Fax** *9388 0391* **Rooms** *140*

Built above the Bondi Junction bus and train interchange, the two-bedroom apartments have views of Sydney Harbour and the ocean. Great features include full-sized kitchens and laundries, tennis and basketball courts and virtual golf. Close to a giant, luxury shopping centre and cinema complex. **www.meritonapartments.com.au**

Key to Price Guide *see p172* **Key to Symbols** *see back cover flap*

Manly Pacific

🛗 P ⅱ ♒ ⅱ ⅱ $$$$

*55 N Steyne, Manly **Tel** 9977 7666 **Fax** 9977 7822 **Rooms** 218*

Manly's ocean beach is one of Sydney's most famous. It plays host to iron man competitions and triathlons, along with herds of surfers, tourists and locals just after a suntan. Situated right on the beach, this hotel has unbeatable views of sand and surf. All rooms are light and spacious. Balconies offer an ideal spot for relaxing. **www.accorhotels.com**

Medina on Crown

🛗 P ⅱ ♒ ⅱ ⅱ ⅱ $$$$

*359 Crown St, Surry Hills **Tel** 8302 1000 **Fax** 9361 5965 **Rooms** 85*   **Map** 5 A1

Close to the groovy Crown Street shops and restaurants, SCG and the Fox Studios, this hotel is a favourite with visiting rock bands. It is also right above the restaurants bills 2, Marque and Billy Kwong. Charge-to-the-room facilities are established at all three. Apartments are spacious and have full kitchens. **www.medinaapartments.com.au**

Sir Stamford Plaza

🛗 P ⅱ ♒ ⅱ ⅱ ⅱ $$$$

*83 Cross St, Double Bay **Tel** 9362 4455 **Fax** 9362 4744 **Rooms** 140*   **Map** 6 F1

Guests can live in old-world style at this luxurious hotel. The lounge and dining areas are magnificent. The rooms are large and traditionally decorated, and the hotel's proximity to the classiest shopping precinct in Sydney is unbeatable. The central courtyard is in the style of a Mediterranean villa garden. **www.stamford.com.au**

Swiss Grand

🛗 P ⅱ ♒ ⅱ ⅱ ⅱ $$$$

*Cnr Campbell Parade & Beach Rd, Bondi Beach **Tel** 9365 5666 **Fax** 9365 5330 **Rooms** 202*

This luxurious all-suite hotel is a kitsch take on the style of the French Riviera. Its exterior of terraces and creamy decorative balustrades looks a little like a giant wedding cake. Inside, marble adorns the lobby's surface. The hotel's beachfront location is unbeatable, with full facilities, a rooftop pool and restaurants. **www.swissgrand.com.au**

BEYOND SYDNEY

BOWRAL, SOUTHERN HIGHLANDS Berida Manor

P ⅱ ♒ ⅱ ⅱ $$

*6 David St, Bowral **Tel** 4861 1177 **Fax** 4861 1219 **Rooms** 59*

Adjacent to the Royal Bowral Golf Course, this restored manor house is walking distance from the cafés and antique stores of Bowral town. Equally good for romantic weekends or families, there is plenty to keep children occupied, including tennis, billiards and bikes. Expensive on weekends. Includes breakfast. **www.beridamanor.com.au**

COLLAROY, NORTHERN BEACHES Sydney Beach House YHA

P ♒ ⅱ $

*4 Collaroy St, Collaroy **Tel** 9981 1177 **Fax** 9981 1114 **Rooms** 56*

Those after a true Aussie holiday of sun, surf and sand head to Sydney's Northern Beaches. This friendly hostel is close to shops and a bus stop from where services run to the CBD. Amenities include a guest lounge, kitchen, barbeque, games room and bikes. Non-YHA members pay an extra charge. **www.sydneybeachouse.com.au**

CRONULLA, ROYAL NATIONAL PARK Rydges Cronulla Beach

🛗 P ⅱ ♒ ⅱ ⅱ $$$

*20–26 The Kingsway, Cronulla **Tel** 9527 3100 **Fax** 9523 9541 **Rooms** 84*

An excellent base from which to explore the Royal National Park, Cronulla is less than an hour's drive or train trip from the CBD in Sydney's southern suburbs. This smart hotel has views over Cronulla's long surf beach, made famous by the movie, *Puberty Blues*. There are dozens of cafés and restaurants nearby. **www.rydges.com**

KATOOMBA, BLUE MOUNTAINS Carrington Hotel

🛗 P ⅱ ⅱ ⅱ ⅱ $$

*15–47 Katoomba St, Katoomba **Tel** 4782 1111 **Fax** 4782 7033 **Rooms** 66*

A popular weekend retreat, this hotel offers old-world charm in the heart of Katoomba. The basic rate is for a budget room with shared bathroom, en suite rooms are more. The Yindi Day Spa specializes in hydrotherapy and various facial, massage and body treatments. Breakfast included in the price. **www.thecarrington.com.au**

KATOOMBA, BLUE MOUNTAINS Lilianfels

🛗 ⅱ ♒ ⅱ ⅱ ⅱ $$$$$

*Lilianfels Ave, Katoomba **Tel** 4780 1200 **Fax** 4780 1300 **Rooms** 85*

Overlooking the Jamison Valley and a short walk from the Three Sisters in the Blue Mountains, this hotel is listed among the Small Luxury Hotels of the World. It boasts a cosy lounge, first-class indoor and outdoor heated pools, open fires and a library. Staff can arrange personal tours and gourmet picnic baskets. **www.lilianfels.com.au**

POLKOBIN, HUNTER VALLEY Peppers Guest House

P ⅱ ♒ ⅱ $$$$$

*Ekerts Rd, Pokolbin **Tel** 4993 8999 **Fax** 4998 7739 **Rooms** 48*

In the heart of the Hunter Valley wine district, Peppers is a luxury lodge with lovely gardens and excellent facilities. There is also a swimming pool, spa, sauna, tennis court and *boules*. Friendly staff can arrange trips to nearby wineries or a leisurely tour of the area. Breakfast included in the price. **www.peppers.com.au**

WHALE BEACH, PITTWATER Jonah's

P ⅱ ♒ $$$$$

*69 Bynya Rd, Palm Beach **Tel** 9974 5599 **Fax** 9974 1212 **Rooms** 7*

Originally built in 1929 as a roadhouse, Jonah's has been one of Sydney's most desirable destinations for many years. The rooms have been refurbished with king-size beds, hand-crafted furniture and limestone bathrooms featuring spa baths. The restaurant is acclaimed and the suites share its amazing views of the ocean. Breakfast is included. **www.jonahs.com.au**

RESTAURANTS, CAFES AND PUBS

Sydneysiders are justifiably proud of their dining scene. Australia's largest city has been populated by successive waves of migrants, all of whom have added something of their home countries to the communal table. These influences have spilled over into contemporary cuisine, which is often called "Modern Australian". This term covers just about any ethnic style the chef may fancy, loosely based on French cuisine. The result is that, in terms of ethnic diversity, Sydney is

Fresh seafood, Chinese style

able to offer many dining options. From a survey of different types of restaurant in varying price brackets, we have selected those offering good value for money. Detailed descriptions of each restaurant can be found in the listings on pages 184–93. Casual eating places, where you can often enjoy food that is as good as at a restaurant but cheaper, are featured on pages 194–7; here you will also find mention of pubs that have recommended bistros and dining areas.

WHERE TO EAT

Circular Quay, The Rocks, Darlinghurst, Potts Point and Paddington are the areas where you will find the widest choice of places to eat. Just outside the city centre, and not covered in depth in these listings, are the inner-city "eat streets" of Glebe Point Road, Glebe (see p131), and King Street, Newtown.

On the lower North Shore is Military Road, which extends from Neutral Bay to Mosman. It would be difficult to walk along any of these streets and not find a café or restaurant to suit your taste and budget.

All of the major hotels have at least one restaurant and a few of these, such as the Galileo Restaurant at the Observatory Hotel (see p172), offer beautiful surroundings, too. To enjoy a spectacular view while you dine, start with drinks at the Horizon Blu bar at the Shangri-La Hotel (see

p172), followed by any of the restaurants at the Opera Quays or at one of Sydney's best restaurants, Quay (see p185), at the Overseas Passenger Terminal.

Many restaurants at Darling Harbour, Cockle Bay and King Street Wharf have outside tables, so diners can enjoy the atmosphere of the lights, the water and the boats.

HOW MUCH TO PAY

Compared with other major world capitals, dining out in Sydney is relatively inexpensive. The cost of a three-course meal in an average restaurant is probably 25 per cent lower than its equivalent in, say, New York or London. The cost is further reduced if you choose a BYO restaurant where you can avoid paying the marked-up price of restaurant wine by taking your own alcohol. However, there will usually be a "corkage" cost per drinker.

Doyle's On The Beach, Watsons Bay (see p191)

The restaurant in Ravesi's boutique hotel at Bondi Beach (see p193)

OPENING TIMES

Most restaurants serve lunch from noon to 3pm and dinner from 6pm to about 11pm, though last orders are often at 10:30pm. Cheap and cheerful ethnic kitchens may close earlier, around 9:30pm, but this largely depends on demand. Many restaurants close on some, if not all, public holidays (see p51). This is particularly true of Christmas Day, Boxing Day and Good Friday.

RESERVATIONS

Booking is recommended in most places – earlier in the day is usually adequate. If, you want to be sure of a table for Friday or Saturday in a spot that is currently fashionable, however, you may need to make a reservation up to one month in advance. If a restaurant says it's full, it is worth asking about an early table, around 6pm, or whenever the place opens. Many casual brasseries and bistros are open all through the day and, as they aren't the sort of place where people linger over their meal, they do not take bookings. You may have to wait a few minutes for a table if you arrive at a busy time.

LICENSING LAWS

Sydney restaurants must be licensed to sell food, but when a place is described as licensed, this usually refers to its licence to sell alcohol. BYO (bring your own) restaurants are not licensed to sell liquor and you will need to buy it beforehand if you want to drink alcohol with your meal. A small amount will probably be charged for "corkage".

BYO restaurants not only reduce the cost of dining out, but also allow wine buffs to choose exactly the wines they wish to drink with their meal. At up-market establishments such as Claude's *(see p191)*, it is a good idea to inquire about the day's menu, so you can choose your wine accordingly.

Bondi Icebergs Dining Room and Bar *(see p193)*

Relaxing in a café at the top end of Oxford Street, Paddington

DRESS CODES AND SMOKING

Dress standards in Sydney restaurants are really quite relaxed, even in the more up-market establishments. Most restaurants will draw the line, however, at patrons in beach-wear and flip flops.

Neat and tidy is the general rule. Smart casual dress is the safest option when considering what to wear. Jackets and ties are a rare sight unless the wearer has come straight from the office or is conducting a business meeting over a meal.

In line with recent trends with regard to smoking, many restaurants in Sydney now have a no smoking policy, although some restaurants still allow smoking in designated areas.

TAX AND TIPPING

In Australia, a GST tax is sometimes added to your bill. Some places include it in its prices but will indicate this on the menu. While tipping is not compulsory, 10 to 15 per cent of the total bill is customary as a reward for good service. You can leave a cash tip after you have paid or add it to the total if paying your bill by credit card.

EATING WITH CHILDREN

Most restaurants accept children who can sit still throughout a meal, although you may feel more comfortable in either Chinese restaurants or the cheap pasta eateries in East Sydney, where children are always welcome. Harry's Café de Wheels *(see p194)* is a roadside pie shop next to the Finger Wharf that is a cheap and cheerful lunch option. Eat outdoors beside the harbour where kids can make as much noise as they want.

The Harbourside food court in Darling Harbour is another inexpensive option. Here, there is a variety of eating places in one complex, including Mexican and Chinese food outlets, pasta and salad bars, all with a central seating area for convenience. For families who prefer to dine out rather than snack, chains such as Pizza Hut and the Black Stump steakhouses offer special menus for children but they also serve alcohol for the adults.

Perhaps the best locations to dine out with children are those where they can play safely outside after they have eaten. The Bathers Pavilion *(see p193)* is right on Balmoral Beach *(see pp54–5)*, a sheltered harbour beach which has a netted swimming pool. Centennial Park Café *(see p194)* is also a great place for families being within supervisory range of grassy lawns and a children's playground.

CREDIT CARDS

Many restaurants will accept credit cards, but you should ask if in doubt. Visa, Master-card, Japanese Credit Bureau and Bankcard are widely accepted; Amex and Diners Club are less commonly accepted, so always check before ordering a meal. Some restaurants also now offer EFTPOS transactions (electronic money transfers direct from your bank account) as an alternative method of payment, which may be more convenient.

The Flavours of Sydney

The city of Sydney surrounds its famous harbour, and countless bars, restaurants and cafés have views of sparkling sunlit water. Taking advantage of the mild climate, outdoor eating – from morning coffee to dinner – is the norm. The cutting-edge food scene is often categorized with New York, London and Paris, and Sydney's top-class chefs are admired the world over. Sydney is cosmopolitan, multicultural and vibrant, with the laid-back atmosphere of the beach always nearby. Sydneysiders are passionate about socializing and, whether eating out or cooking at home, food is always central to a good time.

Wattleseed, pepperberry and lemon myrtle

Fresh seafood dishes at one of the city's many upmarket restaurants

NATIVE INGREDIENTS

There are many native foods in Australia that have been used by aborigines for thousands of years, and which are now becoming widely popular. Fruits and vegetables with distinctive colours, flavours and textures include quandong, munthari, bush tomato, wild limes, warrigal greens and rosellas. All of them are still primarily wild-harvested by aboriginal communities. Although native Australians never used seasonings in their campfire cooking, modern Australians have discovered the exciting flavours of such indigenous herbs and spices as lemon myrtle, wattleseed, mountain pepperleaf, pepperberry, forest berry and akudjura. Native meats such as kangaroo and emu are also being used more frequently, although don't expect to see witchity grubs on many menus. These native meats sit alongside a vast and impressive array of beef, lamb and of course, seafood. Fish native to Australia include barramundi, trevalla and blue eye cod. The popular native shellfish, yabbies and moreton bay bugs, are similar to, but smaller than, lobster. Also worth a mention are the lovely fragrant honeys that are produced out of native Australian forests.

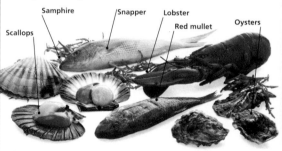

Scallops | Samphire | Snapper | Lobster | Red mullet | Oysters

Selection of seafood available in Sydney's restaurants and food shops

LOCAL DISHES AND SPECIALITIES

There's nowhere better in the world to enjoy fish and chips than sitting on a Sydney beach. As well as the standard choice of hake fillets, you may find more unusual fish on offer, such as wild barramundi or John Dory.

Alongside traditional Asian restaurants serving yum cha, dim sum curries and noodles, there is plenty of modern cuisine, fusing Asian flavours with local produce, such as a Thai-style salad of kangaroo with peanuts and lime. And you can rest assured that just about every other cuisine in the world will be represented in Sydney in some way.

Sandwiches and burgers are often made with Sydney's favourite "Turkish" bread – light and fluffy, and great toasted with Vegemite or for dipping in olive oil.

Anzac biscuits

Kangaroo pizza *This Italian classic is given a modern Australian spin with the addition of seared lean fillet.*

Diners enjoying an outdoor meal on the harbour at Circular Quay

THE WORLD ON A PLATE

Having one of the most eclectic populations on earth means great things for food (or "tucker"). Australians are happy with olive oil in one hand and fresh chilies in the other, so no rules apply – you can be sure of great flavours using the best produce.

Farming plays a very important role in Australia, the world's largest producer of beef. The lush pastures on the coast are particularly good for farming, and milk-fed lamb from New South Wales is as wonderful as the brie produced in South Australia. King Island, off the coast of Victoria, is dedicated to dairy produce, selling their amazing cheeses and creams all around the country. Alongside the rapidly growing wine industry is olive oil and balsamic vinegar production, examples of which you are likely to find at the cellar door of many vineyards.

Australia has one of the most diverse marine faunas in the world, due to its range

Fresh fruit on sale at Paddy's Market in Chinatown

of habitats, from the warm tropical northern waters to the sub-Antarctic Tasman sea, as well as its geographical isolation. A total of 600 marine and freshwater species are caught in Australian waters, providing chefs with plenty of inspiration *(see p202)*.

Every kind of fruit and vegetable is grown in Australia. Pineapples and mangoes are widely grown in Queensland, apples in Victoria, strawberries in New South Wales and rambutans in the Northern Territory. Exotic and notoriously hard to farm, truffles have recently been cultivated in Tasmania, highlighting just how versatile Australia's land is.

FOOD ON THE RUN

Sushi Major cities are dotted with tiny counters offering fresh sushi to grab on the go.

Juice bars This booming industry is found on most city streets, serving delicious, cool blends of fruits.

Milk bars As well as milk-shakes, ice creams and salads, these sell a wide range of deep-fried foods.

Coffee & cake Little cafés everywhere also sell Italian-style cakes and pastries.

Pubs Most pubs serve a decent steak sandwich.

Pies An Aussie institution, pies are readily available. Look out for gourmet versions.

Grilled barramundi *Served on ginger and bok choy risotto, this is a great mix of local seafood and Asian flavours.*

Prawn Laksa *This spicy coconut noodle soup can be found all over the country in noodle bars, cafés and pubs.*

Lamingtons *These little Victoria sponge cakes are coated in chocolate icing and shredded coconut.*

What to Drink in Sydney

Semillon Chardonnay

Australia has one of the world's finest cuisines and part of its enjoyment is the marriage of the country's wine with great food. Australians have a very relaxed attitude to food and wine mixes, so red wine with fish and a cold, dry Riesling as an aperitif can easily be the order of the day. Also, many of the restuarants in the wine regions offer exclusive brands, or offer rare wines so these are worth seeking out. Australians also enjoy some of the best good-value wine in the world. It is estimated that there are 10,000 different Australian wines on the market at any one time. Australians do love their beer, and it remains a popular drink, with a wide range of choices available. While the health-conscious can choose from a variety of bottled waters and select-your-own, freshly-squeezed fruit juices. Imported wines, beers and spirits are also readily available.

SPARKLING WINE

Domaine Chandon in the Yarra Valley produces high-quality sparkling wines

Australia is justly famous for its sparkling wines, from Yalumba's Angas Brut to Seppelts Salinger. Most recently, Tasmania has showed considerable promise in producing some high quality sparkling wines, particularly Pirie from Pipers Brook. However, the real hidden gems are the sparkling red wines – the best are made using the French *Méthode Champenois*, matured over a number of years and helped by a small drop of vintage port. The best producers of red sparkling wines are Rockford and Seppelts. These sparkling wines are available throughout Sydney from "bottle shops", which sell alcohol.

Angus Brut premium

WHITE WINE

Rhine Riesling   Botrytis Semillon

The revolution in wine making in the 1970s firmly established dry wines made from international grape varieties on the Australian table. Chardonnay, Sauvignon Blanc and, more recently, Viognier and Pinot Gris are all popular. However, in recent years there has also been a renaissance and growing appreciation for Riesling, Marsanne and Semillon, which age very gracefully. Australia's other great wines are their fortified and dessert wines. Australian winemakers use *botrytis cinera*, or noble rot, to make luscious dessert wines such as Muscats and Tokays.

Some of the vines in Australia are the oldest in the world.

GRAPE TYPE	STATE	BEST REGIONS	BEST PRODUCERS
Chardonnay	VIC	Geelong, Beechworth	Bannockburn, Giaconda, Stoniers
	NSW	Hunter Valley	Lakes Folly, Rosemount, Tyrrell's
	WA	Margaret River	Leeuwin Estate, Pierro, Cullen
	SA	Barossa Valley, Eden Valley	Penfolds, Mountadam
Semillon	NSW	Hunter Valley	Brokenwood, McWilliams, Tyrrell
	SA	Barossa Valley	Peter Lehmann, Willows, Penfolds
	WA	Margaret River	Moss Wood, Voyager, Evans & Tate
Riesling	SA	Clare Valley and Adelaide Hills	Grosset, Pikes, Petaluma, Mitchells
	SA	Barossa Valley	Richmond Grove, Leo Buring, Yalumba
	TAS	Tasmania	Piper's Brook
Marsanne	VIC	Goulburn Valley	Chateau Iahbilk, Mitchelton

Vineyards of Leeuwin Estate, Margaret River

RED WINE

Australia's benchmark red is Grange Hermitage, the creation of the late vintner Max Schubert in the 1950s and 1960s. Due to his work, Shiraz has established itself as Australia's premium red variety. However, there is also plenty of diversity with the acknowledged quality of Cabernet Sauvignon produced in the Coonawarra. Recently, there has also been a re-appraisal of traditional "old vine" Grenache and Mourvedre varieties in the Barossa Valley and McLaren Vale.

Shiraz   **Pinot Noir**

GRAPE TYPE	BEST REGIONS	BEST PRODUCERS
Shiraz	Hunter Valley (NSW)	Brokenwood, Lindmans, Tyrrells
	Great Western, Sunbury (VIC)	Bests, Seppelts, Craiglee
	Barossa Valley (SA)	Henschke, Penfolds, Rockford, Torbreck
	McLaren Vale (SA)	Hardys, Coriole, Chapel Hill
	Margaret River, Great Southern(WA)	Cape Mentelle, Plantagenet
Cabernet Sauvignon	Margaret River (WA)	Cape Mentelle, Cullen, Moss Wood
	Coonawarra (SA)	Wynns, Lindemans, Bowen Estate
	Barossa, Adelaide Hills (SA)	Penfolds, Henschke, Petaluma
	Yarra Valley, Great Western (VIC)	Yarra Yering, Yerinberg, Bests
Merlot	Yarra Valley, Great Western (VIC)	Bests, Yara Yering
	Adelaide Hills, Clare Valley (SA)	Petaluma, Pikes
Pinot Noir	Yarra Valley (VIC)	Coldstream Hills, Tarrawarra
	Gippsland, Geelong (VIC)	Bass Philip, Bannockburn, Shadowfax

BEER

Most Australian beer is vat fermented, or lager, and consumed chilled. Full-strength beer has an alcohol content of about 4.8 per cent, mid-strength beers have around 3.5 per cent while "light" beers have less than 3 per cent. Traditionally heat sterilized, cold filtration is now popular. Fans of real ale should seek out one of the city's pub breweries. Beer is ordered by glass size and brand: a schooner is a 426 ml (15 fl oz) glass and a middy is 284 ml (10 fl oz).

Tooheys Red Bitter   **Cascade Premium Lager**

Middy   **Schooner**

FRUIT JUICES

With the fabulous fresh fruit at their disposal year round, cafés concoct an astonishing array of fruit-based non-alcoholic drinks. They include frappés of fruit pulp and juice blended with crushed ice; smoothies of fruit blended with milk or yoghurt; and pure juices, extracted from everything from carrots to watermelons.

Pear and kiwi frappé   **Banana smoothie**   **Strawberry juice**

COFFEE

Sydney's passion for coffee means that short black, macchiato, caffe latte, cappuccino and flat white (with milk) are now available at every neighbourhood café.

Flat white coffee

OTHER DRINKS

Tap water in Sydney is fresh and clean, but local and imported bottled water is fashionable. The cola generation has graduated to alcoholic soft drinks and soda drinks. One brand, Two Dogs alcoholic lemonade, was born when a glut of lemons flooded the fruit market.

Alcoholic soda

Caffe latte

Choosing a Restaurant

The restaurants in this section have been selected for their exceptional food and good value. Within each area, entries are listed alphabetically within each price category, from the least to the most expensive. Details of *Light Meals and Snacks* are on pages 194-5 and for Sydney's best *Pubs and Bars* see pages 196-7.

PRICE CATEGORIES
For a three-course meal for one person including service and cover charge (prices in Australian dollars):

$ under $35
$$ $35–$60
$$$ $60–$85
$$$$ $85–$110
$$$$$ over $110

THE ROCKS AND CIRCULAR QUAY

Latte Brothers on the Rocks Café — $

Shop R2, Nurses Walk, The Rocks **Tel** *9252 2055* **Map** *1 B2*

Tucked away in a little cobble-stoned courtyard, in the earliest-settled part of Sydney, this sweet diner is a great place for a quick lunch or afternoon pit stop. Pierce Brosnan and Princess Anne were both spotted here when in town, though it is unknown whether they were dining on sandwiches or Devonshire tea. Big all-day breakfasts too.

The Australian Hotel — $$

100 Cumberland St, The Rocks **Tel** *9247 2229* **Map** *1 B2*

This pub specialises in topping pizzas with surprising combinations, including kangaroo, emu and crocodile meat. They also offer an all-day breakfast pizza, salads and pies. During lunch it is packed with office workers jostling for a table so it is best to take an early or late lunch or for an evening meal.

Amo Roma Ristorante — $$$

135 George St, The Rocks **Tel** *9247 1920* **Map** *1 B2*

This bustling, modern restaurant occupies three floors of a converted bank that was built in 1886. It is a great choice for kids or fussy eaters, with a wide range of classic dishes, including veal escalope, chicken fettuccini, gnocchi, pizzas and salads. Open from noon till late, it does a brisk lunch trade. Ideal for large groups.

East Chinese — $$$

Shop 8, 1 Macquarie St, East Circular Quay **Tel** *9252 6868* **Map** *1 C2*

There is no secret Chinese menu at this busy restaurant, just a range of dishes from the familiar to the adventurous. Native Australian meats, including kangaroo, emu and crocodile, are on the menu, as well as a bevy of seafood treats, fresh from the tank. It's the best Chinese restaurant for people-watching.

Heritage Belgian Beer Café — $$$

135 Harrington St, The Rocks **Tel** *9241 1775* **Map** *1 A3*

There are other options listed on the menu but for anyone in the know, mussels provide the only authentic Belgian experience, cooked one of eight ways and served in a pot. Other entrées include duck salads, oysters and a selection of Belgian Ardennes charcuterie. Of course, there are Belgian beers on tap and an amazing range of artisan brews.

MCA Café — $$$

Museum of Contemporary Art, 140 George St, The Rocks **Tel** *9241 4253* **Map** *1 B2*

The menu is full of Sydney favourites such as pan-fried kingfish, risotto and twice-baked cheese soufflé, and its fabulous location on the Circular Quay side of the MCA building, makes this restaurant a good choice *(see p195)*. After satisfying your sweet teeth with *crème brûlée*, diners head upstairs to the galleries to absorb the art.

Opera Bar — $$$

Lower Concourse Level, Sydney Opera House, Bennelong Point **Tel** *9247 1666* **Map** *1 C2*

This is a great place for a refreshing pit stop on the way to or from the Opera House and an excellent destination in its own right. Bar food is available from noon until 11pm, with good-value tasting plates. There are also pre-theatre, lunch and dinner menus. Nightly entertainment sees DJs and jazz, soul and funk bands.

Sailor's Thai — $$$

106 George St, The Rocks **Tel** *9251 2466* **Map** *1 B3*

Located at the historic Sailor's Home, chef and Thai food expert David Thompson continues to oversee the menu at this restaurant. Highly recommended are the crispy fish and green papaya salad, and braised beef ribs spiked with chilli. The cheaper Canteen, upstairs, is open for lunch and dinner too.

Aqua Luna — $$$$

5–7 Macquarie Street East Circular Quay **Tel** *9251 0311* **Map** *1 C2*

The menu at this sophisticated place changes daily, making the best use of the freshest produce. The hearty fare might include grain-fed eye fillet of beef with lentils and baby fennel. There is a 20-minute wait for risotto cooked to order and it is definitely worth it. The glowing-blue bar, downstairs, serves great cocktails and pizzas.

Key to Symbols *see back cover flap*

Café Sydney   🛗🎏Ⓥ $$$$

Level 5, Customs House, 31 Alfred St, Circular Quay Tel 9251 8683   **Map** *1 B3*

This buzzing restaurant, on the top floor of historic Customs House, has sweeping views. The terrace is delightful; in winter, gas heaters keep diners warm and special resin lamps make each table glow. The kitchen's tandoor oven, wood-fired grill, wok and rotisserie turn out a great variety of food. There is live jazz on Sunday afternoons.

The Wharf Restaurant   🛗🎏Ⓥ $$$$

Sydney Theatre Company, Harbour end of Pier 4, Hickson Rd, Walsh Bay Tel 9250 1761   **Map** *1 A1*

A wonderful setting in a restored wharf offering an unusual view of the Harbour Bridge. Directly opposite, Luna Park provides an glittering backdrop of night-lights. In the winter, special dishes such as truffle-infused Brie are added to the menu. Plan to dine after 8pm to avoid the theatre crowd. Disabled access should be arranged in advance.

Altitude   🛗 $$$$$

Level 36, Shangri-La Hotel Sydney, 176 Cumberland St, The Rocks Tel 9250 6123   **Map** *1 A3*

One of the few places in Sydney that requires guests to look smart, anything less would clash with the super-slick decor. Those who arrive early might sip on one of a great range of apéritif cocktails in the blu horizon bar before supper. Altitude serves modern Australian cuisine inspired by European influences.

Aria   🛗Ⓥ $$$$$

1 Macquarie St, East Circular Quay Tel 9252 2555   **Map** *1 C2*

There are many options here, from a seven-course *dégustation* to a set price one, two- or three-course lunch, pre-theatre meal or supper. Fish and seafood star in many dishes, such as the pumpkin ravioli and baked scampi with lemon butter and muscatels, and the ocean trout and salmon terrine with a dill dressing and grilled sourdough.

Guillaume at Bennelong $$$$$

Sydney Opera House, Bennelong Point Tel 9241 1999   **Map** *1 C2*

You cannot beat the excitement of dining in the Opera House, especially in such a romantic, elegant space. An emphasis on seafood produces dishes such as the signature basil-infused tuna with mustard seed and soy vinaigrette. A cheaper way to taste chef Guillaume Brahimi's food is by ordering tapas-style served from the cocktail bar.

harbour kitchen & bar   🎏🛗 $$$$$

Park Hyatt Sydney, 7 Hickson Rd, The Rocks Tel 9256 1661   **Map** *1 B1*

Especially lovely by day, when the bustle of Circular Quay can be fully appreciated and ferries pass close by the wall of windows. Good-value lunch and pre-theatre deals allow chef Danny Drinkwater's signature duck and beetroot tart to be tasted for less. Modern high tea is served in the more casual kitchen, which is a better choice for children.

Quay   🛗🎏Ⓥ $$$$$

Upper Level, Overseas Passenger Terminal, West Circular Quay Tel 9251 5600   **Map** *1 B2*

Another spectacular view, and food to match, with star chef Peter Gilmore making magic out of the best and freshest produce and combining ingredients in suprising ways. Try the crisp pressed cinnamon spiced duck, white turnips, sea scallops, spring onion and chive flowers. The famous five-textured chocolate cake is to die for.

Rockpool $$$$$

107 George St, The Rocks Tel 9252 1888   **Map** *1 B3*

Neil Perry opened his Sydney fine-dining institution in 1989 and invented modern Australian cuisine with his fusion of European and Asian flavours. The blue-swimmer crab omelette is mouth-watering. Recent renovations spruced the place up and added a seafood bar. For complete indulgence, book the tasting menu. Bookings recommended.

Wildfire   🛗🎏 $$$$$

Ground Level, Overseas Passenger Terminal, West Circular Quay Tel 8273 1222   **Map** *1 B2*

This glamorous restaurant has views of the Opera House when there is no cruise ship in port. Great for a big night out or a snack after a show. Enjoy a range of offerings from the wood-fired Brazilian *churrasco* grill or pull up a seat at the Sea Bar. Mixologists create some of Sydney's best cocktails at the intimate bar, Ember.

Yoshii $$$$$

115 Harrington St, The Rocks Tel 9247 2566   **Map** *1 A3*

Ryuichi Yoshii is one of Sydney's top sushi chefs and the author of a sushi cookbook. His restaurant serves dinner in the *kaiseki* style, a series of unique small dishes that gradually warm the stomach like a small stone (a Japanese precursor to the hot water bottle). Though pricey, this is excellent value. Lunchtime bento boxes are cheaper.

CITY CENTRE

Bodhi in the Park   🎏🛗🎏Ⓥ $

Cook & Phillip Park, 2–4 College St Tel 9360 2523   **Map** *1 C5*

This is a wonderful place to come for lunch on a sunny day, or for dinner on a summer's night, when you can sit outside. You will be amazed by the realistic vegan versions of fish and chicken. The *sang choy bau* (not-pork) is excellent, as is the signature dish, a skin-and-all vegan Peking duck. There is also a good wine and cocktail list.

Mother Chu's Vegetarian Kitchen   ♿ Ⓥ   Ⓢ

367 Pitt St **Tel** *9283 2828*   **Map** *4 E3*

A cheap and cheerful restaurant that offers big servings of hearty food by blending the flavours of Taiwan, China and Japan. It's often full of students and arty types enjoying the warm Buddhist hospitality. They offer delicious stir-fries and curries you can trust are really vegetarian. Do not be put off by the canteen decor.

Diethnes   ♿ 🚻 Ⓥ   ⓈⓈ

336 Pitt St **Tel** *9267 8956*   **Map** *1 B5*

A Sydney institution, Diethnes has been in the same basement spot for 35 years, and you can tell. But get past the kitsch decor, and you will find huge portions of hearty meals. With dozens of meat dishes, pastas, rice, salads and traditional Greek fare such as *tzaziki* and *spanakopita*, there is something for everyone.

Encasa   🚻 ♿   ⓈⓈ

423 Pitt St **Tel** *9211 4257*   **Map** *4 E4*

Near Central Station, this casual Spanish restaurant is one of Sydney's best. If you intend to try their signature dish, Romesco de Peix, a Catalan seafood stew, it is best to let them know in advance. Served in an earthenware bowl, the prawns, squid and fish swim in a traditional, hazelnut sauce. Their standards of tapas, paella and sangria are great.

GPO Woodfired Pizza   🚻 ♿ Ⓥ   ⓈⓈ

Lower Ground Floor, GPO, 1 Martin Place   **Map** *1 B4*

Serving a regular pizza for $15 makes this city diner fabulous value, meaning you can dine in the restored GPO building for a fraction of the cost of neighbours Prime and Post. The pizzas have crispy bases and the freshest toppings. Try a salame piccante with classic toppings of tomato, mozzarella, salami and olives.

Slip Inn   ♿ 🍴 Ⓥ   ⓈⓈ

111 Sussex St **Tel** *8295 9999*   **Map** *1 A4*

This is the gentrified pub where Australia's Mary Donaldson met her husband, Crown Prince Frederik of Denmark. During the day, two menus offer modern Australian and Thai fare, best devoured in the sunny courtyard. At night, a short and sweet selection of pizzas keeps the customers happy.

Post Seafood Brasserie   ♿ Ⓥ   ⓈⓈⓈ

Lower Ground Floor, GPO, 1 Martin Place **Tel** *9229 7744*   **Map** *1 B4*

Every fish that comes through the Post kitchen has been spiked, in the *ikijimi* method. This means that even dishes such as chargrilled tuna or roasted blue eye trevalla are made with sashimi quality fish. There are plenty of non-fishy options on the menu too, including vegetarian pumpkin ravioli, braised lamb shanks and duck confit.

Sky Phoenix   🚻 ♿ Ⓥ   ⓈⓈⓈ

Attic, Level 3, Skygarden, 77 Castlereagh St **Tel** *9223 8822*   **Map** *1 B5*

Yum cha means to drink tea, and while green or jasmine tea will accompany your lunch, the real attractions are the trolleys laden with dumplings. These include *gow gee*, dim sum and steamed buns, which might be filled with pork, green vegetables or prawns. The staff will be happy to explain the ordering system and each dish's content.

Sushi e   ♿   ⓈⓈⓈ

Level 4, Establishment, 252 George St **Tel** *9240 3041*   **Map** *1 B3*

Located inside the exclusive Hemmesphere Bar, there are so many magnificent sushi and sashimi dishes on offer here; it is impossible to list them. Ordering the set of little Asian spoons, each with a different delicious morsel, is a good idea. You might follow this with a nigiri sushi set or test your taste buds with a chilli-loaded dynamite sushi roll.

Glass Brasserie   ♿   ⓈⓈⓈⓈ

Hilton Sydney, Level 2, 488 George St **Tel** *9265 6068*   **Map** *1 B5*

When the Hilton completed its renovations in mid-2005 it became the snazziest hotel in Sydney. This restaurant aims to find a happy medium between the comfort and familiarity of a hotel bistro and the quality and excitement of chef Luke Mangan's previous restaurant, Salt. The menu is filled with classics such as steak tartare and duck *à l'orange*.

Industrie – South of France   Ⓥ   ⓈⓈⓈⓈ

107 Pitt St **Tel** *9221 8001*   **Map** *1 B4*

This is not just a restaurant but a café, bar and club too. It's anything you want it to be. There's breakfast, dinner, drinks and dancing, and it's all infused with the flavour and spirit of the French Riviera. Vodka appreciation courses are held on Tuesday and Wednesday nights, and there are DJs from Wednesday to Saturday.

Bécasse   ⓈⓈⓈⓈ

204 Clarence St **Tel** *9283 3440*   **Map** *1 A5*

Once a tiny bistro, Bécasse recently moved into this swanky city space. Chef Justin North does wonderful things with less popular cuts of meat, as well as luxe updates of classics such as smoked haddock soup with quail egg and oscietra caviar. Luckily, the very rich food is served in small portions. Diners are offered several complimentary nibbles.

est.   ♿   ⓈⓈⓈⓈⓈ

Level 1, Establishment, 252 George St **Tel** *9240 3010*   **Map** *1 B3*

The Establishment complex houses a lively ground level bar and a more restrained lounge above. In between, this dining room provides the setting for a luxurious meal. There are no views but the food shines as bright as the city lights. Don't miss the blood orange soufflé with blood orange sorbet. Booking is recommended.

Key to Price Guide *see p184* **Key to Symbols** *see back cover flap*

Forty One ♿ [V] $$$$$

Level 42, Chifley Tower, 2 Chifley Square ***Tel*** *9221 2500* **Map** *1 B4*

The old Sydney favourite offers impressive views of the city and the harbour. Chef Dietmar Sawyere's blend of European and Asian flavours is a winning combination. Specialities include roast wild hare with Israeli cous cous, chorizo and Medjool dates and Armagnac veloute. A vegetarian menu is also available.

Omega $$$$$

161 King St ***Tel*** *9223 0242* **Map** *1 B5*

The menu at this snazzy modern Greek fine diner reads like a recipe for exotica. Mains include duck pie with celeriac *skordalia* and black olive sauce; and herb-crusted whiting in *kataifi* pastry with crab, cavolo nero and savoro sauce. For dessert, a baked nougat tart is served with orange blossom custard, candied sour cherries and Iranian fairy floss.

Prime ♿ [V] $$$$$

Lower Ground Floor, GPO, 1 Martin Place ***Tel*** *9229 7777* **Map** *1 B4*

There are plenty of non-meaty options on the menu at this stylish steakhouse but really, everyone comes for the steak. Your pick of cuts can be grilled as little or as much as you wish and is served with a tomato confit, potato purée or gratin and a jus or sauce. They also have a separate menu for *wagyu*, the highest graded beef.

Tetsuya's ♿ [V] $$$$$

529 Kent St ***Tel*** *9267 2900* **Map** *4 E3*

Internationally revered and widely considered Australia's best restaurant, Tetsuya's serene space puts the emphasis on the food and wine. The *dégustation* menus fuse Japanese flavours with French technique. Wines can be matched to each course and vegetarian *dégustations* are available on request. Ask to meet the chef for a tour.

DARLING HARBOUR

Pasteur 💳 🪜 🚸 $

709 George St, Haymarket ***Tel*** *9212 5622* **Map** *4 E4*

Finish your $9 bowl of beef and rice noodle soup and you may not need dinner. *Pho* is a Vietnamese speciality, which may come with chicken or beef. These float in fragrant broth, served with a pile of mint and basil leaves, chilli and fish sauce. Fresh spring rolls are another delicious snack, filled with pork and prawns, which you can order here.

BBQ King 🚸 $$

18–20 Goulburn St ***Tel*** *9267 2586* **Map** *4 E4*

A large eatery with abrupt service and non-existent decor. Despite this it has long held cult status. To understand why, try dining late at the end of a big night and you will discover just how welcome this hearty food can be. Almost everyone orders the same thing, barbequed duck and Chinese beer. Open until 2am on weekends.

Chinta Ria: The Temple of Love ♿ 🍴 [V] $$

The Roof Terrace, Cockle Bay Wharf, 201 Sussex St, Darling Harbour ***Tel*** *9264 3211* **Map** *4 D2*

Feelings of happiness are brought into this lively restaurant by the giant Buddha that takes centre stage. Its reasonable prices and fun atmosphere make it popular with a young crowd. The fresh and spicy Malaysian food is great for sharing and may be an aphrodisiac. Bookings are not taken for dinner, so expect long queues.

Regal 🚸 🍴 [V] $$

347–353 Sussex St ***Tel*** *9261 8988* **Map** *4 E3*

Away from the bustle of Dixon and Hay Streets, the Regal is decked out with glittering chandeliers and private rooms. Waiters pushing dim sum-laden trolleys make it reminiscent of the *yum cha* places of Hong Kong. Cantonese seafood is popular, as well as roast suckling pig, steamed fish chosen from the tank and Peking duck.

Wagamama 🚸 ♿ 🍴 [V] $$

49 Lime St, King St Wharf, Darling Harbour ***Tel*** *9299 6944* **Map** *4 D1*

Sometimes when a restaurant is part of a multinational chain it is a good thing; especially if like Wagamama, the brand focuses on bringing diners healthy, cheap food. This outlet has the same big bowls of filling noodles and refreshing juices, plus those Darling Harbour views. There are also restaurants on Crown and Bridge streets.

Zaaffran 🚸 ♿ 🍴 [V] $$

Level 2, 345 Harbourside Shopping Centre, Darling Harbour ***Tel*** *9211 8900* **Map** *3 C2*

The pick of Darling Harbour's eateries, this Indian restaurant is heaven for vegetarians. The food goes beyond the standards, to offer eggplant and okra with coconut and tamarind. Carnivores will be satisfied by an aromatic lamb shank stew, chicken biryani or the excellent tandoori prawns. There are also good value set menus.

Golden Century 🚸 [V] $$$

393–399 Sussex St ***Tel*** *9212 3901* **Map** *4 E4*

The menu is huge, the staff are friendly and the selection of live seafood, including crab, abalone, lobster, parrot fish, barramundi and coral trout, is enormous. But what is truly amazing about this restaurant is that its kitchen stays open until 4am. It is not unusual to find the place full of other chefs relaxing after work.

Jordan's Seafood Restaurant
Map 3 C2

197 Harbourside, Darling Harbour **Tel** *9281 3711*

Jordan's Seafood Restaurant overlooks Darling Harbour and offers quality fresh seafood. Sushi, sashimi, char-grilled baby octopus, salmon, deep-fried snapper and calamari are all available. Splurging on a deluxe platter for two, you will be served a hot-and-cold selection of the market's best catch, including lobster. Excellent cocktails.

Kingsley's Steakhouse
Map 4 D1

17 Lime St, King St Wharf, Darling Harbour **Tel** *9279 2225*

This is one of three restaurants of the same name in the CBD. Each has a relaxed atmosphere and a bevy of good quality steaks to choose from, as well as a sprinkling of fish dishes and plenty of shellfish. All three also offer a cheap "biz" lunch on weekdays. The King Street Wharf venue has one extra: fantastic views of Darling Harbour.

Kobe Jones
Map 4 D1

29 Lime St, King St Wharf, Darling Harbour **Tel** *9299 5290*

Decorated in stylish black and red, this modern Japanese restaurant avoids being too touristy, despite front-row views of Darling Harbour. The large menu includes signature dishes such as a trio of oyster shooters, each with a distinctive flavour, and seared smoked salmon marinated in green tea with wasabi mash and nori cream. Great cocktails too.

Marigold
Map 4 D4

Levels 4 & 5, 683–689 George St **Tel** *9281 3388*

A truly enormous restaurant, Marigold takes up two floors atop a shopping arcade. Long considered Sydney's best *yum cha*, a meal of dumplings served with tea at lunchtime. At dinner, groups of six or more can choose from banquet menus, which offer excellent value dishes such as king prawns with vegetables and crispy-skinned chicken.

Nick's Seafood Restaurant
Map 4 D2

The Promenade, Cockle Bay Wharf, Darling Harbour **Tel** *9264 1212*

Nick's offers a menu full of crowd-pleasers and a fabulous spot to bask in Sydney's sunshine. At night, Darling Harbour's lights sparkle on the water. There is a cheap kids' menu of fish, calamari or chicken with chips, followed by vanilla ice cream. Grown-ups might try char-grilled tuna or octopus, served with chips and salad.

Coast
Map 4 D2

The Roof Terrace, Cockle Bay Wharf, 201 Sussex St **Tel** *9267 6700*

Eating fresh local seafood by the water is a quintessential Sydney experience. Business lunches by day and big groups at night pack this popular spot on the city side of Darling Harbour. The Italian-leaning menu focuses on seafood, with live lobsters available from the tank and a selection of shellfish offered as antipasti.

BOTANIC GARDENS AND THE DOMAIN

Pavilion on the Park
Map 2 D4

1 Art Gallery Rd, The Domain **Tel** *9232 1322*

Good versions of café standards including baguettes with Brie and quince paste or chicken, bacon and avocado, soups, salads and cakes. There is also Shepherd's pie, pastas, plenty of yummy cakes and a comprehensive breakfast menu. Outdoor tables look out over the Domain, where office workers play soccer at lunchtime.

Botanic Gardens Restaurant
Map 2 D4

Royal Botanic Gardens, Mrs Macquaries Rd **Tel** *9241 2419*

Set among the lush greenery, this excellent value lunch venue opens on to a terrace, letting in the sounds of the gardens, even the squawks of the famous bats. Serious gourmets might try the delicious grilled beef tenderloin with caramelized tomato tart. Weekend brunch is lovely too, and there is a café next door.

The Art Gallery Restaurant
Map 2 D4

The Art Gallery of New South Wales, Art Gallery Rd, The Domain **Tel** *9225 1819*

Open only for lunch daily and also for brunch on weekends, this restaurant provides a sophisticated place to discuss the latest exhibition. The menu is small but should please most. There is also a more casual café on the lower level, which is great for kids, offering little cardboard boxes with sandwiches, a drink and a chocolate.

KINGS CROSS AND DARLINGHURST

Bill and Toni's
Map 5 A1

74 Stanley St, East Sydney **Tel** *9360 4702*

A Sydney stalwart loved for its strong coffee, old-fashioned feel and checked tablecloths. Upstairs you will find basic but delicious home-style Italian fare, such as spaghetti Bolognese and *bistecca*, and fast, friendly service. Afterwards, head downstairs for *macchiato* and *gelato*. An excellent place to bring kids, with pinball and racing games.

Key to Price Guide *see p184* **Key to Symbols** *see back cover flap*

Govinda's 🖬 V Ⓢ

112 Darlinghurst Road, Darlinghurst **Tel** *9380 5155* **Map** 5 B1

Dining at this Indian vegetarian restaurant means piling up a plate of delicious curries, breads and salads from the all-you-can-eat buffet. Many of the dishes are Indian, but pastas and casseroles are available too. For a little extra you can see a film in the upstairs movie room, and it is best to eat afterwards to avoid drifting off in the comfy couches.

Dishy ⚓🚶🖬 V Ⓢ Ⓢ

68 Stanley St, East Sydney **Tel** *8354 0322* **Map** 5 A1

Widely recommended as a great place to take children, this café is in the fun Stanley Street strip. The kids' menu is reasonably priced and includes fish and chips, spaghetti Bolognese, chicken schnitzel, kids' brekkie and more. There is plenty on the menu for mums and dads too, from café classics to Asian-fusion dishes.

Fu Manchu ⚓ V Ⓢ Ⓢ

249 Victoria St, Darlinghurst **Tel** *9360 9424* **Map** 5 B2

A small, hip Chinese noodle bar, serving Northern Chinese and Southeast Asian hawker-style, home-cooked dishes. This is a fun place for a quick dinner at a communal table. The menu offers fresh and tasty dumplings, soups and stir-fries. Recently renovated it now features the Suzy Wong Banquet Rooms, which accepts credit cards. Dinner only.

Oh! Calcutta! V Ⓢ Ⓢ

251 Victoria St, Darlinghurst **Tel** *9360 3650* **Map** 5 B2

Serving modern Indian food with remarkable complexity of flavour, this small, stylish restaurant manages to offer the cuisine of a fine diner at almost café prices. The tasting menu is good value, allowing you to try three entrées and three mains, plus rice, accompaniments and bread. There are also pre-theatre deals. Booking is recommended.

Bayswater Brasserie 🖬 V Ⓢ Ⓢ Ⓢ

32 Bayswater Rd, suburb of Kings Cross **Tel** *9357 2177* **Map** 5 B1

This veteran of Kings Cross is famous for its freshly shucked oysters and friendly service. The modern Australian menu changes with the availability of the best produce, which may include blue swimmer crab lasagne with tomato *beurre blanc* or rhubarb *crème brûlée*. Everything is handmade here, such as bread, pasta, ice cream and pastries.

Fishface ⚓🖬 Ⓢ Ⓢ Ⓢ

132 Darlinghurst Rd, Darlinghurst **Tel** *9332 4803* **Map** 5 B2

In a tiny space which seats just 26, this restaurant offers the best value fish in town. The beer-battered fish and hand-cut chips are famous, and there is also a sushi bar. The menu is full of appealing choices, including the signature dish of blue-eye trevalla topped with thin rounds of potato shaped into scales. No bookings after 7pm.

Jimmy Liks 🖬 V Ⓢ Ⓢ Ⓢ

188 Victoria St, Potts Point **Tel** *8354 1400* **Map** 2 E5

The no-bookings policy at this buzzing, modern Asian joint means you can count on a lengthy wait for a seat at the communal table. Those who stick it out, dine on Southeast Asian treats such as betel leaves with chicken and smoked eggplant and good-sized mains. The adjoining bar offers 21 Asian-inspired and award-winning cocktails.

Lotus 🖬 Ⓢ Ⓢ Ⓢ

22 Challis Ave, Potts Point **Tel** *9326 9000* **Map** 2 E4

Chef Genevieve Copland has been behind many of Sydney's best restaurants, and here she cooks simple and hearty food. The small blackboard menu might include roasted lamb rump with beans, tomatoes and olive sauce or warm salad of duck livers with globe artichoke, crispy bacon and walnuts. A smart little bar is hidden out the back.

Mahjong Room V Ⓢ Ⓢ Ⓢ

312 Crown St, Surry Hills **Tel** *9361 3985* **Map** 5 A2

This modern Chinese restaurant, packed with a young crowd, is very different from the big Chinatown diners. Dishes such as bang bang chicken with century eggs and stir-fried prawns and snow peas are served at mahjong tables in a series of small rooms. Double the experience by sharing the reasonably priced dishes.

Tilbury Hotel ♿🖬 V Ⓢ Ⓢ Ⓢ

12–18 Nicholson St, Woolloomooloo **Tel** *9368 1041* **Map** 2 D5

The Tilbury Hotel was refurbished recently, resulting in its transformation into one of the trendiest pubs in Sydney. The restaurant offers excellent Italian fare, and the daily menu might include gnocchi with chicken, sausage, borlotti beans and fennel. Also has a café serving wraps, bagels and coffees. Jazz on Sunday afternoons in the bar.

Yellow Bistro 🚶🖬 V Ⓢ Ⓢ Ⓢ

57 Macleay St, Potts Point **Tel** *9357 3400* **Map** 2 E4

Van Gogh yellow walls make this, one of the most famous buildings in the Cross, stand out. In the 1970s it was an artists' commune, which housed Brett Whiteley. Today creative genius is obvious in the food. The brunch menu is lovely but nothing beats the celebrated date tart created by pastry chef, Lorraine Godsmark. It also has a food store.

Manta ♿🖬 Ⓢ Ⓢ Ⓢ Ⓢ

Wharf 9, 6 Cowper Wharf Rd, Woolloomooloo **Tel** *9332 3822* **Map** 2 D4

In a great pairing, chef Stefano Manfredi creates Italian flavours from Australian seafood. Diners don bibs to devour lobster and mud crab cooked straight from the tank, or order the signature roasted Murray cod. As many as five types of oyster may be available, including, in season, the superb native Angasis. Fantastic Italian desserts too.

Otto ♿ ⛱ [V] $$$$

Area 8, The Wharf, 6 Cowper Wharf Rd, Woolloomooloo ***Tel*** *9368 7488* ***Map*** *2 D4*

Otto is a piece of Melbourne brought to Sydney's waterfront and is so appreciated that it often draws celebrities, from footballers to Kylie Minogue, to its dark and handsome surrounds. Italian fare is jazzed up with local ingredients, such as fillet of Mandagery Creek venison with celeriac parsnip purée, pancetta, green beans and juniper jus.

Pello ⛱ [V] $$$$

71–73 Stanley St, East Sydney ***Tel*** *9360 4640* ***Map*** *5 A1*

This is a hip restaurant, with tables on the terrace or in a small courtyard, as well as in the dining room. There is also a great little bar, where you can drink without dining (rare in Sydney). London trained chef, Thomas Johns, uses the freshest ingredients to serve vegetables such as celeriac, salsify and Jerusalem artichoke in fabulous combinations.

PADDINGTON

Phamish 🍷 👶 ⛱ [V] $

354 Liverpool St, Darlinghurst ***Tel*** *9357 2688* ***Map*** *5 B2*

Its no-fuss attitude means Phamish offers no wine, desserts, lunches, bookings or website. Never mind, hordes of diners still flock here for the excellent, cheap food. You can bring your own wine, devour the large servings of fresh and spicy modern Vietnamese food and then walk up the hill to Victoria Street for a mouth-cooling *gelato*.

Paddington Inn ♿ [V] $$

338 Oxford St, Paddington ***Tel*** *9380 5913* ***Map*** *6 D4*

This perennially popular pub in the heart of the Paddington strip is especially busy on weekend afternoons, when hip locals meet over beers and tapas-style plates. Pub classics such as bangers and mash and fish and chips are given a restaurant touch. There are also plenty of lighter meals, such as salads and chicken on couscous. Great for lunch.

Bistro Moore 👶 $$$

Olympic Hotel, 308 Moore Park Rd, Paddington ***Tel*** *9361 6315* ***Map*** *5 C4*

Across the road from the Aussie Stadium and the Sydney Cricket Ground, this bistro serves excellent modern Italian food. There are just four or five entrées, pastas, mains and desserts on the seasonal menu, but you will feel spoilt for choice because each dish is so appealing. The pasta is handmade, the coffee spot on, and puddings delicious.

Buzo 👶 $$$

3 Jersey Rd, Woollahra ***Tel*** *9328 1600* ***Map*** *6 D4*

Buzo is another piece of evidence showing that bistro food is booming in Sydney. Bookings are essential at this restaurant, just off Oxford Street. Carnivores will delight in the meaty menu, offering roast lamb, char-grilled steak and even various offal dishes. You will need to order some side dishes to accompany your main.

Four In Hand [V] $$$

Sutherland Hotel, 105 Sutherland St, Paddington ***Tel*** *9362 1999* ***Map*** *6 E3*

Acclaimed chef Mark Best owns the fine diner Marque, which consistently takes top honours in Sydney restaurant awards. He oversees this pub dining room, inside Sutherland Hotel, allowing those on a budget to have a taste of his superb dishes. These might include a tomato and goat's cheese soufflé or brasserie classics such as boudin blanc.

Local 👶 ♿ ⛱ [V] $$$

211 Glenmore Rd, Paddington ***Tel*** *9332 1577* ***Map*** *5 C3*

This bar and restaurant is not called Local for nothing. It is the kind of place everyone wants to live next door to, open daily for snacks, wine and coffee. The please-everyone menu is designed so that most of the entrées can be eaten as main course and vice versa and offers dishes of Spanish, Italian, French and Moroccan flavours.

Bistro LuLu 👶 ♿ ⛱ [V] $$$$

257 Oxford St, Paddington ***Tel*** *9380 6888* ***Map*** *5 C3*

Located in the heart of the Oxford Street shopping strip, this charming French-influenced, neo-bistro serves specialities including duck confit with aligot, caramelized pear and hazelnut salad and sirloin steak served with café de Paris butter and pommes frites. Oysters can be dressed three ways, most impressively with a Bloody Mary granita.

Bistro Moncur ⛱ $$$$

The Woollahra Hotel, 116 Queen St, Woollahra ***Tel*** *9363 2519* ***Map*** *6 E4*

A stroll down Queen Street from the main strip, Bistro Moncur has been an eastern suburbs favourite for more than a decade. The menu lists such French classics as sirloin café de Paris, French onion soufflé gratin and pork sausages. No bookings, so arrive early or to start with a drink in the bar, where top jazz bands play on Sunday evenings.

Buon Ricordo $$$$$

108 Boundary St, Paddington ***Tel*** *9360 6729* ***Map*** *5 C2*

Ask a Sydney chef where he goes on nights off and the answer is likely to be this small restaurant. The decor is old-fashioned and the food is often Old World. So is the service, which sees the signature dish of fettuccine with Parmesan, cream and truffled egg tossed at table. Dishes here are said to be better than at most places in Italy.

Key to Price Guide *see p184* **Key to Symbols** *see back cover flap*

Claude's
$$$$$

10 Oxford St, Woollahra **Tel** *9331 2325*   **Map** *6 D4*

A Sydney icon for nearly thirty years, this intimate restaurant in a converted terrace house seats just 40 people. In season, the set-price menu features fresh Tasmanian truffles. Dishes sound simple on paper but are actually as close to works of art as food can get. Bookings recommended. Ring the doorbell when you arrive.

Lucio's
$$$$$

47 Windsor St, Paddington **Tel** *9380 5996*   **Map** *6 D3*

Lucio's is right in the middle of the area of Sydney's art galleries and the walls of the restaurant display a collection of contemporary Australian artists such as John Olsen, John Coburn, Gary Shead and Tim Storrier. There is art on the plate too, the expertly cooked Italian food varies according to what is in season.

FURTHER AFIELD

Burgerman
$

249 Bondi Rd, Bondi **Tel** *9130 4888*

This gourmet burger joint has long been one of the eastern suburb's favourite fast food outlets. There are no fatty, processed offerings here, instead you will find lean meat, home-made lemonade, loads of fresh vegetables and even an excellent vegetarian burger. The fit out and logo are cute and retro, and the portions are nothing short of gigantic.

Il Baretto
$

496 Bourke St, Surry Hills **Tel** *9361 6163*

Diners wishing to sup at this crammed café often face the longest waits in Sydney, so it is lucky the pasta is so good, and that there is a pub across the road. Very basic pastas, such as a penne arrabiata, laced with enough chillies to make your tongue tingle, start at $9. The duck ragu and hand-rolled gnocchi are loved by many.

Café Mint
$

579 Crown St, Surry Hills **Tel** *9319 0848*

Mint's precursor, Fez, was a top breakfast venue, often with long queues. This café is tiny and can seem equally crammed. The coffee is excellent and food is fabulous value, particularly at lunch. For a rainbow of dips and pickles, try the large meze plate, which easily fills two. The Lebanese *fattoush* salad with garlicky, crunchy pitta bread is great.

Maya Masala
$

470 Cleveland St, Surry Hills **Tel** *9699 8663*

Even almost broke vegetarians in board shorts and thongs do well at this sweet and chaat house, popular with a diverse crowd, including students, hippies, Indian taxi drivers and foodies. Authentic treats such as thali plates of assorted curries and breads and the famous masala dosai are promptly delivered. Finish off with some Indian fudge.

Rowda-Ya Habibi
$

101 King St, Newtown **Tel** *9557 5368*

Many Sydneysiders rely on Lebanese restaurants for consistently good, healthy, fresh food. Though some of the delicacies here are deep-fried, there are more than enough salads and vegetables to make up for that bit of oil. Servings are large and feel even bigger if you have filled up on dips and pitta first. Belly dancing on weekend nights.

Sushi Suma
$

421 Cleveland St, Surry Hills **Tel** *9698 8873*

The number of Japanese crammed around tables in this slightly grotty neighbourhood restaurant tells you how authentic the food is. The servings here are enormous so many people leave with doggy bags. When it is busy, and that is most of the time, orders are taken from the queue and food arrives as guests are seated. Great tempura too.

Mohr Fish
$$

202 Devonshire St, Surry Hills **Tel** *9318 1326*

The many devotees of this classy fish and chip shop cram into its tiny space. Those who cannot find a table wait in the neighbouring pub, the Shakespeare Hotel, or thanks to the amiable relations between the two establishments order their fish to take away and eat next door. The legendary chips are wide, hand cut and golden. No bookings.

Doyles on the Beach
$$

11 Marine Parade, Watson's Bay **Tel** *9337 2007*

Five generations on, the Doyles are still serving great fish and chips. Eat at a table outside and admire the stunning view of the CBD across the harbour. The menu offers an array of fish and seafood dishes, including wild barramundi fillets and live lobster mornay. Open daily. There are two branches at Watson's Bay wharf and Circular Quay.

Red Lantern
$$

545 Crown St, Surry Hills **Tel** *9698 4355*

A relaxed atmosphere and fiery red interior add to the enjoyment in this converted terrace. Most people, however, visit Red Lantern because they have heard of its high standards of fresh and spicy Southern Vietnamese food. For extra fun, order one of the "at the table" dishes you assemble yourself from rice paper or crepes. Bookings essential.

Uchi Lounge   V $$

15 Brisbane St, Darlinghurst **Tel** *9261 3524*   **Map** *4 F4*

A small bar that specialises in *saketinis*, and a long room with warm but minimal design, provide excellent environs for French-Japanese fusion food. The menu offers many small courses, including the chrysanthemum sushi and beef with wasabi mash dishes. The fusion of flavours is evident in vegetables with miso pesto.

3 Weeds Restaurant   V $$$

197 Evans St, Rozelle **Tel** *9818 7832*

The new Sydney bistro burst onto the inner West scene recently when this refurbished pub dining room opened. Off Rozelle and Balmain's main drag of Darling Street, the vibe is casual and comfortable. The food, whether bar snacks or a three-course meal, is excellent. The three weeds are the rose, shamrock and thistle.

Alhambra   V $$$

1/54 West Esplanade Manly **Tel** *9976 2975*

Hugely popular on Friday and Saturday nights, when flamenco dancers add to the din, this casual restaurant has views of the Manly Wharf. The Moroccan chef cooks Moorish and Spanish food. A meal might begin with tapas followed by a Moroccan tagine of chicken and preserved lemon or lamb and date.

Alio   V $$$

5 Baptist St, East Redfern **Tel** *8394 9368*

Alio is just off the main drags of Crown and Cleveland Streets and worth seeking out, particularly because of the warm room, good service and excellent food. Home-made breadsticks are a good start and mains are rich and filling. The chef here is a good friend of Jamie Oliver's, who dines (and sometime cooks) here when in town.

Billy Kwong   V $$$

355 Crown St, Surry Hills **Tel** *9332 3300*   **Map** *5 A3*

If the long queues are not a dead giveaway then the smell when you walk in the door will tell you that this place is special. Run by Kylie Kwong, Sydney's latest celebrity chef, it specializes in traditional Chinese family food, souped up with a modern edge. Banquets are good value and there are always beautiful flowers.

Blue Orange   V $$$

49 Hall St, Bondi Beach **Tel** *9300 9885*

You could spend your whole day here, starting with smoked salmon pancakes for breakfast, followed by chilli linguini and chicken for lunch. By night the casual café, loved by locals and tourists alike, transforms into an intimate restaurant with a menu drawing on African and Middle Eastern flavours. Best of all, there is jazz on Sunday nights.

Garfish $$$

2/21 Broughton St, Kirribilli **Tel** *9922 4322*

This is the best fishy place on the North side. Not many places offer breakfasts as exciting as smoked hiramasa kingfish omelette with crème fraîche and ciabatta toast. Diners are able to customize their dishes by selecting a type of fish, how they would like it cooked and can even select its garnish. Very busy during weekends.

Manly Wharf Hotel   V $$$

Manly Wharf Esplanade, Manly **Tel** *9977 1266*

Not much beats sharing a seafood platter packed with oysters, prawns, crab, salt and pepper squid, octopus, scallops and fish, while looking out over Sydney Harbour. Even better, this is a pub you can bring your kids to, keeping them happy with one of the well-priced offerings from the kids' menu. Perfect after a long day at the beach.

mu shu   V $$$

108 Campbell Parade, Bondi Beach **Tel** *9130 5400*

A very slick fit out makes this place the hippest at the beach. Kick off your shoes and jump onto a day bed, but do not be put off by signs prohibiting hanky-panky. There is a great range of cocktails and modern Asian food designed to be shared among friends. Try a selection of *yum cha* as appetizers, followed by the signature roast duck pancakes.

Pompei's   V $$$

126 Roscoe St, Bondi Beach **Tel** *9365 1233*

It is a mystery how the residents of Bondi survived Sydney's long hot summers before the arrival of this pizzeria and gelateria. Wood-fired, thin-based pizzas are scattered with the freshest toppings and although the *gelato* kicked off a city-wide craze, it is still the best in town. Seasonal flavours include blood orange, nectarine and roasted almond.

Restaurant Balzac $$$

141 Belmore Rd, Randwick **Tel** *9399 9660*

This local bistro, with its sandstone walls and think white tablecloth, is luxurious and yet relaxed. It has earned a reputation with gourmands for its excellent Anglo-French food, reasonable prices and great service. *Dégustation* menus and special deals are available. Also try treats from the tasting plate of tiny petit fours. Booking is essential.

Flying Fish   V $$$$

Pier 21, Lower Deck, Jones Bay Wharf, 19–21 Pirrama Rd, Pyrmont **Tel** *9518 6677*   **Map** *3 C1*

Glam meets clams, with fabulous modern Australian and Sri Lankan flavours, and a sculpture of 500 lights. Australian soldiers embarked for World War II from this Wharf and train tracks remain along its length. History evaporates as you stare out at the harbour views. Those with kids could try little sister, flying fish and chips.

Key to Price Guide *see p184* **Key to Symbols** *see back cover flap*

Hugo's

70 Campbell Parade, Bondi Beach **Tel** *9300 0900*

Perennially popular, this beachfront diner manages to be relaxed and glamorous simultaneously. It is a great place for a romantic dinner and has spawned other equally stunning venues: Hugo's Lounge and Hugo's Bar Pizza, both in Kings Cross. Here at the original, the best tables are outside, with cushioned banquettes overlooking the beach.

Icebergs Dining Room and Bar

1 Notts Ave, Bondi Beach **Tel** *9365 9000*

The first really swish restaurant to hit the surf at Bondi, this dining room is above the famous swimming pool. The decor gives a glamourous beach feel with a palette of ocean blues, giant rustic chandeliers and a scattering of silk cushions. Food is simple, modern Italian, such as char-grilled whole snapper with sauce *vierge*.

Longrain

85 Commonwealth St, Surry Hills **Tel** *9280 2888*

Chilli and ginger turn up the spice at Sydney's hippest restaurant, where the giant communal table was one of the first in town. The Thai food lends itself well to sharing, with dishes such as crispy-salted salmon salad with green mango and sweet pork and spiced curry of duck with peanuts and mandarin juice. It has a great bar as well.

Ravesi's on Bondi Beach

Cnr Campbell Parade & Hall St, Bondi Beach **Tel** *9365 4422*

Sit on the balcony to catch the sea breeze and enjoy fish and chips with house tartare or grilled-Atlantic salmon with miso pesto and coriander on a noodle salad. Finish with delicious Amaretto and bitter chocolate or cheese plate with lavosh and glazed fruits. The two- and three-course set menus are excellent, and brunch is served on Sundays.

Sean's Panaroma

270 Campbell Parade, Bondi Beach **Tel** *9365 4924*

Like an oversized family dining room, Sean's is intimate and friendly. Serving a small range of seasonal dishes, with a few constants such as linguine with shredded arugula, lemon, chilli and Parmesan and the famous white chocolate, fig and rosemary nougat. Next door, Aroma To Go sells that nougat and more to take away. Bookings essential.

Aqua Dining

Cnr Paul and Northcliff Sts, Milsons Point **Tel** *9964 9998*

Floor to ceiling windows afford fine views of the harbour and the Olympic pool immediately below. The often luxurious menu allows the produce to shine and includes dishes such as fillet of Tasmanian salmon on a crisp goat's cheese parcel, braised leek, potato and vodka sauce. Extensive wine list and weekend lunch deals are of great value.

Bathers' Pavilion Restaurant

4 The Esplanade, Balmoral Beach **Tel** *9969 5050*

This classic restaurant is housed in the historic beachside changing rooms. The atmosphere is relaxed and there is a sea view from every table. Flavours vary from Chinese to Greek, Middle Eastern to French, sometimes all in one dish. There are great set price three-course deals but the accompanying café has better vegetarian options and good breakfasts.

The Boathouse on Blackwattle Bay

End of Ferry Rd, Glebe **Tel** *9518 9011*　　　　　　　　　　　　　　　　　　　　**Map** 3 A3

Water taxi is the best way to arrive at this restaurant. Housed in the upper level of a boatshed, it looks out at the fish markets and busy traffic of trawlers and pleasure crafts. The menu changes daily, but if the chef were ever to remove his signature snapper pie, there would be a revolt. Try some oysters and other fishy offerings as well.

Catalina Rose Bay

1 Sunderland Ave, Lyne Park, Rose Bay **Tel** *9371 0555*

It has been described as Sydney's veranda and this restaurant, which hangs over the harbour's edge, certainly has one of the best views. High-flyers snooze at lunchtime, while dinner at Catalina is a classic Sydney big night out. The flavoursome modern Australian food offers plenty of variety, from the roast snapper signature dish to pan-fried pork.

Marque

355 Crown St, Surry Hills **Tel** *9332 2225*　　　　　　　　　　　　　　　　　　　　**Map** 5 A3

Although there are few vegetarian dishes on the menu at this much-lauded restaurant, the signature dish is as meatless as they come. The star of the famous beetroot tart is the vegetable, as well as a frothy horseradish cream which lifts it towards the sublime. You will taste complex dishes here, with flavours you would have never imagined.

Orso Bayside Restaurant

79 Parriwi Rd, Mosman **Tel** *9968 3555*

This luxurious waterfront restaurant is destined to impress, with freshest seafood and splendid views of the harbour. Take a seat on Orso's private jetty and be greeted by schools of fish and ducks as you enjoy seared Queensland scallops followed by Frangelico chocolate mousse and white chocolate sorbet.

Pier

594 New South Head Rd, Rose Bay **Tel** *9327 6561*

This restaurant is one long, timber-panelled room which runs the length of a small pier and juts out into the harbour. Yachts moored in the marina float all around and you would feel like you were on one if the food was not quite so good. Good quality fish is cooked to perfection in dishes such as carpaccio of tuna and roasted barramundi.

Light Meals and Snacks

The mercurial nature of Sydney's dining scene is visible in the multitude of establishments that open and close each year. With cafés, this situation is magnified and, as a result of this competition, the standards are high. Coffee is of good quality across Sydney and almost every eatery has its own espresso machine. A surge in the popularity of tea has made many places switch from teabags to boutique, loose-leaf black teas, tisanes and herbal brews. Tipping is unnecessary at takeaways. While it is not essential at cafés, many have a jar on the counter where patrons leave their change as a gratuity.

CAFÉS

Coffee culture was introduced to Sydney by Italian migrants, who flooded in after World War II. **Bar Coluzzi**, with its boxing pictures on the walls, has long been the capital of Darlinghurst's caffeine kingdom. Media types, lawyers and taxi drivers throng here both for the company and the coffee. **Toby's Estate**, a latecomer on the scene, imports, roasts and grinds its own beans. Stylish **Apartment** is the ideal home away from home in the CBD, as is Paddington's bookshop-cum-café **Gertrude & Alice**, named after Gertrude Stein and Alice B Toklas. The vegetarian **Badde Manors** in Glebe is frequented by students.

Nothing revives quite like a good pot of tea. **The Tea Centre** is an oasis of calm in a city shopping centre and can serve you a pot of any of the dozens of teas they import. In the Rocks, the **Gumnut Café** serves traditional Devonshire tea with scones and jam. Those looking for a chocolate fix might try **Max Brenner** or the **Lindt Concept Store and Café**, where treats come as dark, milk or white, and in both solid and liquid forms.

Most cafés offer a menu of sandwiches, salads, cakes and muffins throughout the day. The fabulous food at **Danks Street Depot** presents a serious challenge to some of Sydney's top restaurants. The Depot shares a converted warehouse in a rapidly gentrifying industrial area with a handful of galleries, and is more than worth the cab fare. As well as excellent food, **Yellow Bistro** (see p189) serves some of the best pastries in town, and their food store is a great place to buy supplies. The French **Café Sel et Poivre** is very popular, while **Sloanes** in Paddington is a great pit stop for those weary after a day of treading the Oxford Street strip and Saturday's markets (see p126).

Cafés at attractions vary, but generally, those at art galleries and museums are of a high standard, while those at sporting venues are not. **Opera Bar** (see p184) on the **Sydney Opera House** concourse is hard to beat (see pp74–7). The **Museum of Sydney Café** (see p85) is also very good. Its shaded outdoor tables look out on the museum's paved forecourt and office workers striding by. The **Art Gallery Café** is a smart eaterie at the **Art Gallery of New South Wales** (see pp108–11) that serves delicious sandwiches, good coffee and wine, and special lunchboxes for children. There is also a restaurant on the ground floor (see p188). Coveted outdoor tables offer a view over the Woolloomooloo fingerwharf. At the **MCA Café** (see p73), they do a brisk trade in breakfasts and lunches, served with wonderful Opera House views.

Lunch amid lush greenery is possible at the **Botanic Gardens Café** (see pp104–5), attached to the lovely restaurant (see p188), and at the breezy **Centennial Park Restaurant** (see p127), which also has a takeaway kiosk next door, a favourite of mothers with prams.

BEST BREAKFASTS

Many belive that the as showpiece of celebrity chef, Bill Granger, **bills2** serves the official best breakfast. Tuck into his famous ricotta hotcakes with honeycomb butter and a healthy sunrise juice. At Darlinghurst stalwart **Le Petit Crème**, breakfast consists of Parisian options, including traditional bowls of café au lait and *croque monsieurs*. For the ultimate Sydney start to the day, you have to head to the water. Watch the surfers at Bronte's **Swell**, or the swimmers at the **Sundeck Café** at Bondi Icebergs Club (see p193). At the **Marina Kiosk Café**, where the excitement is in the location more than the food, sit on the edge of the pier and dangle your feet over the harbour.

TAKEAWAY FOOD

All kinds of cuisine, such as Thai, Turkish, Afghani and Albanian, can be found in this very multicultural city. Most cheap local restaurants offer takeaway. Connoisseurs of ethnic cuisines might want to catch a train or bus and explore the areas specialising in them. While Leichhardt is Italian, you'll find Greek and Vietnamese restaurants in Marrickville, and Kosher cafés in Bondi. A cluster of Indian restaurants can be found on Cleveland Street in Surry Hills. At lunchtime, the food courts of city shopping centres offer a wide variety of quick, cheap meals. Try **Galeries Victoria** and **Sydney Central Plaza**. Above **Paddy's Markets** (see p99) at Haymarket, **Market City** offers a selection of Chinese, Japanese, Korean and Thai food. The famous Food Hall at **David Jones** (see p199) has the best supplies for any picnic, snack, sweet treat or takeaway dinner.

If you're craving fast food, try a Bondi burger from **Oporto**, a Portuguese chicken chain that has shops across Sydney, including one in Kings Cross and another in Galeries Victoria. Takeaway can be healthy too. top fish (maybe without the chips) comes from **A Fish Called Coogee**, where side dishes include barbequed corn on the cob and wok-fried greens. One of many sushi outlets, **Sushi Train** only serves the freshest fish and seafood. Juice bars, such as **Boost Juice**, have sprung up all over town, and most can add a shot of vitamins or wheatgrass

to your drink. Macrobiotics has become popular too. At **Iku** the food is flavourful as well as nutritious.

LATE-NIGHT SNACKS

Drop in to the long-standing **Harry's Café de Wheels** to sample an Aussie meat pie from the stand-up bar. Having satisfied the midnight cravings of locals and visitors for

decades, it is particularly popular with sailors from the adjacent naval dockyard.
BBQ King *(see p187)* is open until 2am most nights, as is noodle chain **Wagamama** *(see p187)* on weekends.

For real night owls, **City Extra** is open 24 hours. **Café Hernandez**, also open throughout the day, is famous for its Spanish short black tortillas and cakes.

DIRECTORY

CAFÉS

Apartment
155 Macquarie St.
Map 1 C4.
Tel 9241 1488.

Art Gallery Café
Art Gallery Rd,
The Domain.
Map 2 D4.
Tel 9225 1819.

Badde Manors
37 Glebe Point Rd,
Glebe. **Map** 3 B5.
Tel 9660 3797.

Bar Coluzzi
322 Victoria St,
Darlinghurst. **Map** 5 B1.
Tel 9380 5420.

Botanic Gardens Café
Royal Botanic Gardens,
Mrs Macquaries Rd.
Map 2 D4.
Tel 9241 2419.

Café Sel et Poivre
263 Victoria St,
Darlinghurst. **Map** 5 B2.
Tel 9361 6530.

Centennial Park Restaurant
Cnr Grand & Parkes
Drives, Centennial Park.
Map 6 E5.
Tel 9360 3456.

Danks Street Depot
1/2 Danks St, Waterloo.
Tel 9698 2201.

Gertrude & Alice
78 Oxford St, Paddington.
Map 5 B3.
Tel 9380 6617.

Gumnut Café
28 Harrington St,
The Rocks. **Map** 1 B3.
Tel 9247 9591.

Lindt Concept Store and Café
53 Martin Place.
Map 1 B4.
Tel 82571600.

Max Brenner
447 Oxford St,
Paddington.**Map** 6 D4.
Tel 9357 5055.

MCA Café
Museum of Contemporary
Art, Circular Quay West.
Map 1 B2.
Tel 9241 4253.

Museum of Sydney Café
Cnr Bridge and Phillip Sts.
Map 1 B3.
Tel 9241 3636.

Opera Bar
Sydney Opera House,
Bennelong Point.
Map 1 C2.
Tel 9247 1666.

Sloanes
312 Oxford St,
Paddington.
Map 5 C3.
Tel 9331 6717.

The Tea Centre
Shop 4005, The Glass
House, 135 King St.
Map 4 E2.
Tel 9223 9909.

Toby's Estate
6/81 Macleay St,
Potts Point.
Map 2 E5.
Tel 8356 9264.

Yellow Bistro
57 Macleay St, Potts Point.
Map 2 E4.
Tel 9357 3400.

BEST BREAKFASTS

bills2
359 Crown St,
Surry Hills.
Map 5 A3.
Tel 9360 4762.

Le Petit Crème
116 Darlinghurst Rd,
Darlinghurst.
Map 5 B1.
Tel 9361 4738.

Marina Kiosk Café
Rose Bay Marina, 594 New
South Head Rd, Rose Bay.
Tel 9362 3555.

Sundeck Café
Bondi Icebergs Club,
1 Notts Ave, Bondi Beach.
Tel 9130 3120.

Swell
465 Bronte Rd, Bronte.
Tel 9386 5001.

TAKEAWAY FOOD

A Fish Called Coogee
229 Coogee Bay Rd,
Coogee. *Tel 9664 7700.*

Boost Juice
15 Hunter St.
Map 1 B4.
Tel 9232 6678.

David Jones
Cnr Market and
Castlereagh Sts.
Map 1 B5.
Tel 9266 5544.

Galeries Victoria
2 Park St.
Map 4 E2.
Tel 9261 0456.

Iku
62 Oxford St, Darlinghurst.
Map 5 B3
Tel 9380 9780.

Market City
9-13 Hay St,
Haymarket.
Map 4 D4.
Tel 9212 1388.

Oporto
3C Roslyn St,
Kings Cross.
Map 5 C1.
Tel 9380 2975.

Sushi Train
570 George St.
Map 1 B3
Tel 9283 1622.

Sydney Central Plaza
100 Market St.
Map 4 E2.
Tel 8224 2000.

LATE-NIGHT SNACKS

BBQ King
18-20 Goulburn St.
Map 4 E4.
Tel 9267 2586.

City Extra
Shop E4, East Podium,
Circular Quay.
Map 1 B3.
Tel 9241 1422.

Café Hernandez
60 Kings Cross Rd, Potts
Point. **Map** 5 C1.
Tel 9331 2343.

Harry's Café de Wheels
Cowper Wharf Rd,
Woolloomooloo.
Map 2 E5.
Tel 9357 3074.

Wagamama
49 Lime St,
King Street Wharf.
Map 4 D1.
Tel 9299 6944.

Sydney Pubs and Bars

Confusingly for the overseas visitor, Australian pubs and bars are also known as hotels. This is because licensing laws originally required any place serving alcohol to provide accommodation too. In the cities, at least, hotels have changed radically and what were once the domains of beer-swilling males have now evolved into far more civilized spots. Pub menus have also undergone a metamorphosis. In place of the former meat pie and sauce, most pubs now offer hearty snacks at remarkably low prices. All pubs serve beer, basic mixed spirit-based drinks and wine by the glass, but cocktails tend to be the preserve of the more up-market venues. Pubs are also often good venues for live music *(see pp214-15)* and for watching telecasts of major international and local sporting matches.

RULES AND CONVENTIONS

The pubs and bars across Sydney operate under various licensing schemes. In general, those located in quiet neighbourhoods close at 10pm on weekdays and midnight on Friday and Saturday nights. Many pubs in busy tourist areas such as Darlinghurst, Kings Cross and near Central Station stay open much later; some even have 24-hour licences.

You must be at least 18 years of age to buy or consume alcohol, or to even enter many bars. Anyone under 30 should carry photo ID such as a driver's licence or passport. Children and teenagers under 18 are often allowed to join their parents in outdoor beer gardens and pub restaurants. It is also against the law for a hotel to serve alcohol to someone who is inebriated. The management can refuse service and may not allow people who seem drunk to enter a bar.

Dress requirements vary and these too are at the discretion of the publican. Up-market bars might require patrons to look stylish, sometimes banning sneakers, though very few insist on suit jackets. Local pubs might refuse entry to those in flip flops or shorts.

One aspect of traditional pub culture is the custom of "shouting", or buying drinks for your companions. When someone buys you a drink, it is considered bad form if you do not return the favour. However, it can become tricky if you are on a budget. Explain that you are only staying for one drink.

HISTORIC PUBS

Hotels have been part of Sydney life since the early days of the colony. Many of the town's old pubs are in The Rocks and while you will spot some on George Street, others are hidden in backstreets. The **Hero of Waterloo** *(see p69)*, built in 1843, has a maze of stone cellars underneath. First licensed in 1841, the **Lord Nelson** *(see p172)* now brews its own ales. It offers a bistro and a few guest rooms. **The Australian Hotel** *(see p184)* boasts a pizza menu that features crocodile, kangaroo and emu meat, making it a favourite with locals and visitors. The **London Tavern** *(see p124)*, the oldest pub in Paddington, opened in 1875. Underneath the glamorous new Hilton Sydney hotel *(see p174)* the ornate **Marble Bar** is much as it was when built in 1893.

BARS WITH VIEWS

In a city built around one of the world's most beautiful harbours, it will not be out of the ordinary to find a plethora of bars with magnificent views. Many restaurants have compact bars attached. The bar at **Guillaume at**

Bennelong is a destination in its own right. Other favoured venues are **Opera Bar** *(see p184)* and the **Bridge Bar** on the tenth floor of the infamous "toaster" building. On level 36 of the Shangri-La Hotel *(see p172)*, **blu horizon** is a flamboyant bar offering a range of cocktails as well as extra-ordinary views over the harbour, airport and city lights. The **Manly Wharf Hotel** *(see p192)* occupies a prime position in the ferry building. It is a great spot for a relaxed drink with friends and serves excellent food. Established in 1870, the **London Inn** *(see pp131, 142–3)* in Balmain enjoys the reputation of being the most atmospheric pub in Sydney. Those arriving early can grab a tractor seat on the balcony and sip local Red Back beer while soaking up the most unusual view.

STYLISH BARS

Sydney has no lack of beautiful people, or of places for them to play. Those who wish to dive into the social scene might head to the pricey **Hugo's Lounge**, **Mint Bar and Dining** at the luxurious Hotel InterContinental *(see p175)*, **Water Bar** at W Sydney *(see p176)* or the new **Zeta** at the Hilton Sydney *(see p174)*. Overlooking Taylor Square, **Middle Bar** is hip yet relaxed, as is **Longrain** *(see p193)*. The smart little bar at the tiny **Lotus** *(see p189)* continuously wins awards for serving the best cocktails in Sydney. Darlinghurst's **The Victoria Room** feels like an estate in colonial Singapore, and serves tapas-style food. In the CBD, the fashionable **Establishment Hotel** *(see p174)* is home to several bars, including the eponymous ground-floor spot, a post-work favourite for city suits. Also on the hotel grounds is the exclusive **Hemmesphere**, decorated like a Moroccan lounge. Contemporary chandeliers, chairs suspended from the ceiling, a scattering of silk cushions and endless ocean views make the ultra swish **Icebergs Dining Room and Bar** *(see p193)* the best of the lot.

LOCAL FAVOURITES

Join the locals at city nightspot, **Arthouse Hotel**, which hosts life-drawing classes and live music on some nights, DJs on others. The lovely Art Deco **Civic Hotel**, with a small cocktail bar and a large main bar, is low-key in the early evening, but turns into a club on weekend nights. Paddington has a surfeit of pubs and some of the best are the **Royal Hotel** at Five Ways *(see p126)*, the busy **Paddington Inn** *(see p190)* and, at the top of Oxford Street, the **Light Brigade Hotel**. The newly-renovated **Tilbury Hotel** *(see p189)* is another trendy pub in town and plays jazz on Sunday afternoons. The crowd here and at the **Green Park Hotel** is usually a mix of gay and straight. The **Bank Hotel** in Newtown hosts lesbian nights every Wednesday. In Bondi, suntanned locals frequent **Ravesi's**. Even after most other bars close, **Baron's** in Kings Cross offers drinks and backgammon long into the night.

TOURIST CENTRAL

Those who enjoy being surrounded by fellow travellers should try the **Bondi Hotel**, **Cargo Bar** in Darling Harbour, **The Coogee Bay Hotel** or Irish pub **Scruffy Murphy's**. **Forrester's** in Surry Hills is famed for its $5 steaks.

DIRECTORY

HISTORIC PUBS

The Australian Hotel
100 Cumberland St,
The Rocks. **Map** 1 B2.
Tel 9247 2229.

Hero of Waterloo
81 Lower Fort St,
Millers Point.
Map 1 A2.
Tel 9252 4553.

London Tavern
85 Underwood St,
Paddington.
Map 6 D3.
Tel 9331 3200.

Lord Nelson
19 Kent St, Millers Point.
Map 1 A2.
Tel 9251 4044.

Marble Bar
Level B1, Hilton Sydney,
488 George St.
Map 1 B5.
Tel 9265 6072.

BARS WITH VIEWS

Bridge Bar
Level 10, 1–3 Macquarie
St, Circular Quay.
Map 1 C2.
Tel 9252 6800.

blu horizon
Shangri-La Hotel Sydney,
176 Cumberland St.
Map 1 A3.
Tel 9250 6250.

Guillaume at Bennelong
See p185.

London Inn
234 Darling St, Balmain.
Tel 9555 1377.

Manly Wharf Hotel
Manly Wharf Esplanade.
Tel 9977 1266.

Opera Bar
Sydney Opera House,
Bennelong Point.
Map 1 C2.
Tel 9247 1666.

STYLISH BARS

Establishment Hotel and Hemmesphere
Levels 1 and 4, 252
George St. **Map** 1 B3.
Tel 9240 3000.

Hugo's Lounge
33 Bayswater Rd,
Potts Point. **Map** 5 B1.
Tel 9357 4411.

Icebergs Dining Room and Bar
1 Notts Ave,
Bondi Beach.
Tel 9365 9000.

Longrain
85 Commonwealth St,
Surry Hills. **Map** 4 F4.
Tel 9280 2888.

Lotus
22 Challis Ave, Potts Point.
Map 2 E4.
Tel 9326 9000.

Middle Bar
Kinsela's, 383 Bourke St,
Darlinghurst.
Map 5 A5.
Tel 9331 3100.

Mint Bar and Dining
Hotel InterContinental,
117 Macquarie St.
Map 1 C3.
Tel 9240 1220.

The Victoria Room
231a Victoria St,
Darlinghurst,
Map 5 B2.
Tel 9357 4488.

Water Bar
W Sydney, 6 Cowper
Wharf Rd,
Woolloomooloo
Map 2 D5.
Tel 9331 9000.

Zeta
Level 4, Hilton Sydney,
488 George St.
Map 1 B5.
Tel 9265 6070.

LOCAL FAVOURITES

Arthouse Hotel
275 Pitt St.
Map 4 E2.
Tel 9284 1200.

Bank Hotel
324 King St, Newtown.
Tel 9557 1692.

Baron's
5 Roslyn St, Kings Cross.
Map 5 C1.
Tel 9358 6131.

Civic Hotel
388 Pitt St
(Cnr Goulburn St).
Map 4 E4.
Tel 8080 7000.

Green Park Hotel
360 Victoria St,
Darlinghurst.
Map 5 B2.
Tel 9380 5311.

Light Brigade Hotel
2 A Oxford St, Woollahra.
Map 6 D4.
Tel 9331 2930.

Paddington Inn
338 Oxford St,
Paddington.
Map 6 D4.
Tel 9380 5913.

Ravesi's
118 Campbell Pde,
Bondi Beach.
Tel 9365 4422.

Royal Hotel
237 Glenmore Rd,
Paddington.
Map 5 C3.
Tel 9331 2604.

Tilbury Hotel
12–18 Nicholson St,
Woolloomooloo.
Map 2 D5.
Tel 9368 1041.

TOURIST CENTRAL

Bondi Hotel
Cnr Campbell Parade and
Curlewis St, Bondi Beach.
Tel 9130 3271.

Cargo Bar
52–60 The Promenade,
King St Wharf.
Map 4 D2.
Tel 9262 1777.

The Coogee Bay Hotel
Cnr Coogee Bay Rd and
Arden St, Coogee.
Tel 9665 0000.

Forrester's
336 Riley St,
Surry Hills.
Map 4 F5.
Tel 9211 2095.

Scruffy Murphy's Hotel
43–49 Goulburn St.
Map 4 E4.
Tel 9211 2002.

SHOPS AND MARKETS

The shopping options in Sydney is wide and the quality of merchandise is usually good. The inner city has innumerable elegant arcades and shopping galleries, with plenty of nooks and crannies to explore. The range of goods on offer is enormous – most international labels, Gucci, Vuitton and

Souvenir boomerangs

Chanel, are imported and local talent in many fields, notably jewellery, fashion and indigenous arts and crafts, is promoted. Nor does the most interesting shopping stop at the city centre; there are several "satellite" alternatives. Some of the best shopping areas are highlighted on pages 200–201.

A typical junk-shop-cum-café in Balmain (see p131)

SHOPPING HOURS

Most shops are open from 9am to 5:30pm Monday to Saturday, though some may close early on Saturdays. High-end boutiques open from 10am to 6pm. On Thursdays, most shops stay open until 9pm. Most shops in Chinatown are open late every evening and on Sundays.

HOW TO PAY

Major credit cards are accepted almost everywhere. You will need identification, such as a passport or driver's licence,

when using traveller's cheques. Department stores will exchange goods or refund your money if you are not satisfied, provided you have kept your receipt. Other stores will only refund if an item is faulty. There is also a Goods and Services Tax (GST) which is almost always included in the marked price.

SALES

Many shops conduct sales all year round. The big department stores of **David Jones** and **Myer** have two gigantic and chaotic clearance sales every year. The post-Christmas sales start on 26 December and last into January. The other major sale time is during July, after the end of the financial year.

TAX-FREE SALES

Duty-free shops are found in the centre of the city as well as at Kingsford Smith Airport *(see p228)*. You can save around 30 per cent on goods such as perfume, jewellery, watches and alcohol at duty-free shops but you must show your

passport and onward ticket. Some stores will also deliver your goods to the airport to be picked up on departure. Duty-free items must be kept in their sealed bags until you leave the city.

You can claim back the GST paid on most goods, purchased for (or in a single transaction of) \$150 or more, at the airport.

Chifley Tower, with the Chifley Plaza shopping arcade at its base

ARCADES AND MALLS

The **Queen Victoria Building** *(see p82)* is Sydney's most palatial shopping space. Four levels contain more than 200 shops. The top level, Victoria Walk, is devoted to merchandise such as silver, antiques, designer knitwear and high-quality souvenirs. The **Strand Arcade** *(see p84)* was originally built in 1892. Jewellery, chocolates, coffee shops and tea rooms are its stock in trade.

Pitt Street Mall has several shopping centres. **Sydney Central Plaza**, contains upmarket stores such as Calibre, selling designer menswear, Saba, a popular Australian fashion label, and Nine West, offering shoes and handbags.

Inside Gleebooks, popular with students and locals in Glebe *(see p131)*

Next door to the Hilton, the **Galeries Victoria** houses the fantastic Kinokuniya bookstore, which sells a variety of both Australian and American imprints as well as Chinese and Japanese language, anime art books and stationery. The Mooks store is packed with designer streetwear for men and women from the eponymous label, as well as international brands such as G-Star and Camper.

Nearby in Pitt Street, the marble and glass of **Piccadilly** houses more than 40 stores and flashy boutiques, including quality jewellers.

Facing onto Castlereagh Street, the **MLC Centre** and **Chifley Plaza** also cater to the prestige shopper. Gucci, Cartier, Tiffany & Co, MaxMara, Kenzo are just some of the shops here.

The **Harbourside Shopping Centre** has dozens of shops, plus several waterfront restaurants. The atmosphere is festive and the merchandise includes fine arts, jewellery, duty-free shopping, beachwear and Australiana.

DEPARTMENT STORES

David Jones and **Myer** compete fiercely, each snaring exclusive rights to stock various local design talents and international labels. The David Jones, or DJs, spring floral displays are legendary, as is the luxurious perfumery

Part of the spring floral display, David Jones department store

Greengrocer's display of fresh fruit and vegetables

and cosmetics hall on the ground floor. David Jones spreads out in two buildings, across the road from each other on Market and Elizabeth streets. The food hall on the lower ground floor is famous for its gourmet fare and fine wines. Myer has a ground floor packed with makeup and accessories, including a large MAC counter. Both stores sell women's clothing, lingerie, menswear, baby goods, children's clothes, toys, stationery, kitchenware, furniture, china, crystal and silver.

Gowings, a Sydney institution, has been operating since 1868. This unpretentious menswear store also sells such things as sunglasses, watches, Swiss army knives, fishing gear, miners' lamps and genuine Australiana such as kangaroo leather wallets and plaited leather belts.

Gowings menswear store logo

SHOPPING FURTHER AFIELD

Good shopping areas outside central Sydney are Balmain, for village-style shopping; Double Bay, with its chic, though pricey, boutiques; the new "black label" mega-mall at Bondi Junction; and Left Bank-style student haunts of Newtown and Glebe. Bargains can be found at the factory outlets in Redfern, **Market City** and at Birkenhead Point. **Shopping Spree Tours** can arrange outings to little-known outlets for the day.

DIRECTORY

Chifley Plaza
2 Chifley Square. **Map** 1 B4. *Tel* 9221 6111.

David Jones
Cnr Elizabeth & Market Sts. **Map** 1 B5. *Tel* 9266 5544. Also: Cnr Market & Castlereagh Sts. **Map** 1 B5. *Tel* 9266 5544.

Harbourside Shopping Centre
Darling Harbour. **Map** 3 C2. *Tel* 9281 3999.

Galeries Victoria
2 Park St. **Map** 4 E2. *Tel* 9261 0456.

Gowings
45 Market St. **Map** 1 B5. *Tel* 9287 6394.

Market City
9–13 Hay St, Haymarket. **Map** 4 D4. *Tel* 9212 1388.

MLC Centre
19–29 Martin Place. **Map** 1 B5. *Tel* 9224 8333.

Myer
436 George St. **Map** 1 B5. *Tel* 9238 9111.

Piccadilly
210 Pitt St. **Map** 1 B5. *Tel* 9267 3666.

Queen Victoria Building
455 George St. **Map** 1 B5. *Tel* 9265 6855.

Shopping Spree Tours
Tel 9360 6220.

Strand Arcade
412–414 George St. **Map** 1 B5. *Tel* 9232 4199.

Sydney Central Plaza
100 Market St. **Map** 4 E2. *Tel* 8224 2000.

Sydney's Best: Shopping Streets and Markets

Sydney's best shopping areas range from galleries, arcades and department stores selling expensive gifts and jewellery *(see pp198–9)*, to boutiques of extroverted or elegant cutting-edge fashion and its accessories. The range of styles is impressive – both international couture brands and acclaimed local designer labels *(pp204–5)*. The city's hip fringe areas are alive with street fashion and its accoutrements.

Colourful markets are a delight for collectors and bargain-hunters alike *(p203)*, while those who seek out the quirky and one-off items are well catered for, as are those looking to take home quality craft and indigenous art as mementos of their visit. Specialist browsers will find a tempting selection of book and music shops *(pp206–7)* from which to choose.

The Rocks Market
At weekends, the stalls offer affordable arts and crafts and jewellery. (See p203.)

THE ROCKS
AND CIRCULAR
QUAY

CITY
CENTRE

Queen Victoria Building
This elegant shopping gallery offers four floors of designer wear, gifts, and speciality stores amid cafés.

Darling Harbour
Quality Australiana, surf and beach wear, souvenir ideas, children's clothes, colourful knits and art and craft shops abound.

DARLING
HARBOUR

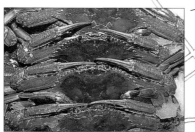

Sydney Fish Market
You can buy fresh seafood daily in the colourful fishmongers' halls or order from the cafés which spill out on to the sunny terrace alongside the marina. (See p202.)

Chinatown
This is the place to find discounts on watches, gold jewellery, opals and even fabrics. There are also Chinese butchers' shops, herbalists and supermarkets.

| 0 metres | 500 |
| 0 yards | 500 |

City Centre
Dazzling shopping arcades and smart malls are dotted throughout the city centre, notably Pitt Street Mall, Strand and Piccadilly Arcades, and Centrepoint.

Castlereagh Street
The city's designer row is home to Chanel, Gucci, Hermès and others. The most exclusive names cluster near the King Street intersection.

BOTANIC
GARDENS AND
THE DOMAIN

Darlinghurst and Surry Hills
These suburbs are the youth culture barometer: young designers, leather à la mode, gay fashion, hot music and gifts for those who love quirky collectables.

KINGS CROSS AND
DARLINGHURST

PADDINGTON

Paddington and Woollahra
Up-market clothing, shoes, homeware and gourmet food are on show here, while cafés and galleries add to the allure. Queen Street, Woollahra, is the antique shop strip.

Paddington Markets
Considered by many to be Sydney's best market and a showcase for the up-and-coming fashions, it is held every Saturday. (See p203.)

Sydney Fish Market

Each day, 65 tonnes (tons) of fresh fish and other seafood are sold at the Fish Market's Dutch Clock auction. According to this system, prices start high, and gradually descend on a computerized "clock", until a buyer puts in a bid. At this point,

Balmain bug

no other bids are accepted, and the deal is made. This unusually quiet auction starts at 5:30am every Monday to Friday, and runs for two to three hours until all the seafood is sold. Members of the public can follow the auction proceedings from a viewing area.

The waterfront cafés *offering fine seafood at reasonable prices make dining here a rare treat.*

Blue swimmer crabs *have a mild flavour and are found all around the Australian coastline.*

About 30 wholesalers, *many of them family concerns, buy bulk quantities of the day's catch; some also have retail outlets at the market itself.*

Local fishermen *send their fish to the market anytime between 4pm the previous day and 8am on the day of the auction. Most of the catch is from the far coasts of New South Wales.*

SELECTING YOUR FISH

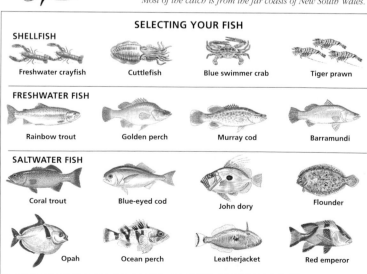

SHELLFISH

Freshwater crayfish · Cuttlefish · Blue swimmer crab · Tiger prawn

FRESHWATER FISH

Rainbow trout · Golden perch · Murray cod · Barramundi

SALTWATER FISH

Coral trout · Blue-eyed cod · John dory · Flounder

Opah · Ocean perch · Leatherjacket · Red emperor

Markets

Scouring markets for the cheap, the cheerful and the chic has become a popular weekend pastime in Sydney. Weekly or monthly markets that suit both the bargain-hunter and the serious shopper have sprung up all over the suburbs. Caps, souvenir t-shirts, leather jackets, high-class art – there is something to suit every taste. Even more popular are the Sydney Fish Market and the produce markets, which team with people from early in the morning and have turned shopping into a big event.

BALMAIN MARKET

Cnr Darling St and Curtis Rd, Balmain. 🚌 442, 434.
Open 7:30am–4pm Sat.

Held in the grounds of the Balmain Congregational Church in the shade of a fig tree said to be more than 150 years old, this compact market attracts both locals and tourists. Fees from stallholders contribute to the ongoing restoration of the church, which was built in 1853. As well as stalls selling children's wear, second-hand books, contemporary and antique jewellery, arty mirrors, recycled stationery, stained-glass mobiles and Chinese healing balls, there is a food hall where you can find fresh and aromatic Japanese, Thai, Indian and specialist vegetarian dishes in the making.

BONDI BEACH MARKET

Bondi Beach Public School, Campbell Parade, North Bondi. 🚌 380, 382, 389. **Open** 9am–5pm Sun in summer; 4pm in winter.

Many Sydney fashion labels start off here, as did current darlings **Sass & Bide** (see p204). There are also lots of second-hand clothing buys; funky 1970s gear is particularly popular. Arrive early as some of the stalls are all set up by 9am. The best bargain clothes are near the back of the market. Expect to see the odd actor or rock star among the browsers.

THE ENTERTAINMENT QUARTER

Lang Rd, Moore Park. **Map** 5 C5. 🚌
Oxford St or Anzac Pde routes. **Open** 10am–4pm Wed, Sat, Sun. (See p126.)

There is plenty of fresh produce and gourmet delicacies to sample at the Farmers' Market every Wednesday and Saturday, located next to the working Fox Studios, where films such as *Mission Impossible 2* and the *Star Wars* prequels were shot. There is also a Merchandise Market every Saturday and Sunday.

GLEBE MARKET

Glebe Public School, Glebe Point Road, Glebe. **Map** 3 B5. 🚌 431, 433. **Open** 10am–4pm Sat.

A treasure-trove for the junk shop enthusiast and canny scavenger, this market is bright, changeable and popular with the inner-city grunge set. Best buys are bric-à-brac and crafts made from recycled wood, metal and glass. Get there early for bargain porcelain and, if you are lucky, the odd undervalued lithograph. A few fashion students also sell their creations. You will also find handmade bags, hats and jewellery. Second-hand clothes are a good buy here, as are leather wallets, silver rings and pendants, books, CDs and records.

THE GOOD LIVING GROWERS' MARKET

Pyrmont Bay Park, opposite Star City Casino. Map 3 C1. 🚃 light rail from Central. **Open** 7–11am first Saturday of every month.

Get in early; by 8am long lines snake back from each of the stalls selling coffee, bread and pastries. This is the place to find native Australian bushfoods, such as lemon myrtle linguini, dried bush tomatoes, nutty wattleseed and pepperberries. There is everything you will need to cook a gourmet feast, including poultry, beef, pork and venison from around NSW; lesser-found vegetables such as wild mushrooms, cavolo nero and golden beetroot; and delicacies such as honey, cheese and fudge. Fresh flowers are available too.

THE OPERA HOUSE MARKET

Western Boardwalk, Sydney Opera House. **Map** 1 C2. 🚌 438. **Open** 9am–6pm Sun & public hols.

Under calico market umbrellas, you will find arts and crafts in a spectacular setting. Some call this a distillation of the best, and certainly you will not find T-shirts and cheap souvenirs, but rather goods that have been either hand-made or hand-finished.

PADDINGTON MARKETS

(See p126.)

From nouveau to novelties, there is always something tempting here, and it is unlikely you will come away empty-handed. Silver jewellery is abundant, so prices are very competitive; there are also children's clothes, leather goods, unusual buckles, belts and accessories, stationery, candles, and oddities such as babies' baseball caps and rubbery novelty masks.

PADDY'S MARKETS

(See p99.)

In the 19th century, Paddy's in the Haymarket was the city's fringe market and also the location of fairgrounds and circuses. Today, it has between 500 and 1,000 stalls under one roof. Early birds will get the best flowers, fruit, vegetables and seafood. There are also good buys in caneware, luggage, leather goods, tools, homewares, ornaments, souvenirs and toys.

THE ROCKS MARKET

George St, The Rocks. **Map** 1 B2. 🚌 431, 432, 433, 434. **Open** 10am–5pm Sat & Sun.

At weekends, rain or shine, a sail-like canopy is erected at the top end of George Street, transforming the area into an atmospheric marketplace. Get there early to beat the afternoon crowds. There are about 140 stalls, whose wares are unique rather than inexpensive. Quality is a priority here. Look out for wind chimes, pewter picture frames, pub poster prints, oils, leather goods, wooden toys, gold-plated bush leaves, and jewellery made from wood, shell, silver or crystal. Every Friday in November the Rocks Market hosts "Markets by Moonlight", a combination of night markets, live music and outdoor bars and food stalls.

SYDNEY FISH MARKET

(See p131.)

Sydney is famous for its fresh seafood and the Sydney Fish Market is the ideal place to buy it. The displays of seafood are arresting, with coral reds, marble pinks, greys, blacks and iridescent yellows to take your mind off the sloshy floors and the smell of the sea. The market also has a sushi bar, fish cafés, a bakery, a gourmet deli, a poultry and game specialist, a bottle shop, and a vegetable shop. The Sydney Seafood School operates above the market, offering lessons in preparing and serving seafood.

Clothes and Accessories

Australian style was once an oxymoron. Sydney now offers a plethora of chic shops as long as you know where to look. Top boutiques sell both men's and women's clothing, as well as accessories. The city's "smart casual" ethos, particularly in summer, means there are plenty of luxe but informal clothes available.

AUSTRALIAN FASHION

A number of Sydney's fashion designers have attained a global profile, including **Collette Dinnigan** and **Akira Isogawa**. Dinnigan's is filled with lacy evening gowns whereas Japanese-born Isogawa makes artistic clothing for women and men.

Young jeans labels such as **Tsubi** (for men and women) and **Sass & Bide** (women only) have also shot to fame, with celebrities wearing their denims. Nearby is **Scanlan & Theodore**, a stalwart of the Australian fashion scene.

Other shops are **Dragstar**, where women's and children's clothes come in the tradition of retro favourites, such as bright sundresses and minis. The quirky **Capital L** and **Fat** boutiques house the hottest names in Aussie fashion, while **Zimmermann** offers women's and girls' clothes and is famous for its swimwear. **Lisa Ho** is the place to go for a frock, with designs ranging from pretty sundresses to glam gowns. Head to **Farage Man & Farage Women** for quality suits and shirts.

High-street clothing can be found in and around Pitt Street Mall and Bondi Junction. Here you will find both international and homegrown fashion outlets. **Sportsgirl** sells funky clothes that appeal to both teens and adult women. The **Witchery** stores are a favourite among women for their stylish designs. **Just Jeans** doesn't just sell jeans; it stocks the latest trends for men and women.

General Pants has funky street labels such as One Teaspoon and Just Ask Amanda. Surry Hills is the place for discount and vintage clothing; check out **Zoo Emporium**. New designers try out their wares in Bondi, Glebe and Paddington markets.

INTERNATIONAL LABELS

Many Sydney stores sell designer imports. For the best ranges, visit **Belinda** – a women's and men's boutique – as well as others in Double Bay, including the **Belinda Shoe Salon**. In **Robby Ingham Stores** you will find women's and men's ranges including Chloé, Paul Smith and Comme des Garçons. For shoe addicts, **Cosmopolitan Shoes** stocks labels such as Dolce & Gabbana, Sonia Rykiel, Dior and Jimmy Choo. **Hype DC** also offers all the latest ranges. New Zealand designers **Zambesi** offer their own designs for women and men as well a range of Martin Margiela pieces.

LUXURY BRANDS

Many visitors like to shop for international labels such as **Gucci** and **Louis Vuitton**. You will find both in Castlereagh Street, along with **Chanel** and **Gianni Versace**. The Queen Victoria Building is home to **Bally**, and Martin Place has resident A-listers such as **Prada** and **Giorgio Armani**. **Diesel** is further afield on Oxford Street.

SURF SHOPS

For the latest surf gear, look no further than Bondi where the streets are lined with shops selling clothing, swimwear and boards of all sizes to buy and hire. Serious surfers and novices should check out **Mambo Friendship Store** and **Bondi Surf Co**. Besides stocking its own beachwear label, **Rip Curl** also sells Australian brands such as Tigerlily and Billabong. **Labyrinth** and **The Big Swim** are hugely popular swimwear shops packed with bikinis by designers such as Jet and Seafolly.

CLOTHES FOR CHILDREN

Department stores, **David Jones** and **Myer** (see pp198–9), are one-stop shops for children's clothes, from newborn to teenage. Look out for good quality

SIZE CHART

Women's clothes

Australian	6	8	10	12	14	16	18	20
American	4	6	8	10	12	14	16	18
British	6	8	10	12	14	16	18	20
Continental	38	40	42	44	46	48	50	52

Women's shoes

Australian	6–6½	7	7½–8	8½	9–9½	10	10½–11	
American	5	6	7	8	9	10	11	
British	3	4	5	6	7	8	9	
Continental	36	37	38	39	40	41	42	

Men's suits

Australian	44	46	48	50	52	54	56	58
American	34	36	38	40	42	44	46	48
British	34	36	38	40	42	44	46	48
Continental	44	46	48	50	52	54	56	58

Men's shirts

Australian	36	38	39	41	42	43	44	45
American	14	15	15½	16	16½	17	17½	18
British	14	15	15½	16	16½	17	17½	18
Continental	36	38	39	41	42	43	44	45

Men's shoes

Australian	7	7½	8	8½	9	10	11	12
American	7	7½	8	8½	9½	10½	11	11½
British	6	7	7½	8	9	10	11	12
Continental	39	40	41	42	43	44	45	46

Australian labels such as Fred Bare and Gumboots. Mambo, Dragstar and Zimmermann (see above) also sell fun and unusual kidswear.

ACCESSORIES

The team behind **Dinosaur Designs** are some of Australia's most celebrated designers. They craft chunky bangles, necklaces and rings, and also bowls, plates and vases, from jewel-coloured resin. **Collect**, the retail outlet of Object Gallery, is another place to look for handcrafted jewellery, scarfs, textiles, objects, ceramics and glass by leading and emerging Australian designers. At **Makers Mark** *(see pp206–7)* the jewels feature unique South Sea pearls, classic sapphires and diamonds or unusual materials, such as wood. In her plush store, **Jan Logan** sells exquisite jewellery, using all kinds of precious and semi-precious stones.

Australian hat designer, **Helen Kaminski**, uses fabrics, raffia, straw, felt and leather to make hats and bags. In a different style altogether, **Crumpler** use high-tech fabrics to make bags that will last a century. And in a street of designer names, **Andrew McDonald's** little studio shop doesn't cry for attention, but he does sell handcrafted shoes for men and women.

DIRECTORY

AUSTRALIAN FASHION

Akira Isogawa
12A Queen St, Woollahra.
Map 6 E4. *Tel 9361 5221.*

Capital L
333 S Dowling St,
Darlinghurst. **Map** 5 A3.
Tel 9361 0111.

Collette Dinnigan
33 William St,
Paddington. **Map** 6 D3.
Tel 9360 6691.

Dragstar
96 Glenayr Ave, Bondi.
Tel 9365 2244.

Farage Man & Farage Women
Shops 54 & 79, Level 1
Strand Arcade. **Map** 1 B5.
Tel 9231 3479,

Fat
18 Oxford St, Woollahra.
Map 6 D4.
Tel 9380 6455.

General Pants
Queen Victoria Building.
Map 4 E2. *Tel 9264 2842.*

Lisa Ho
2a–6a Queen St,
Woollahra. **Map** 6 D4.
Tel 9360 2345.

Just Jeans
Mid City Centre, Pitt St.
Map 4 E2. *Tel 9223 8349.*

Sass & Bide
132 Oxford St,
Paddington. **Map** 5 B3.
Tel 9360 3900.

Scanlan & Theodore
122 Oxford St,
Paddington. **Map** 5 B3.
Tel 9380 9388.

Sportsgirl
Skygarden, 77 Castlereagh
St. **Map** 1 B5.
Tel 9223 8255.

Tsubi
16 Glenmore Rd,
Paddington. **Map** 5 B3.
Tel 9361 6291.

Witchery
Sydney Central Plaza,
Pitt St. **Map** 4 E2.
Tel 9231 1245.

Zimmermann
1/387 Oxford St,
Paddington. **Map** 6 D4.
Tel 9357 4700.

Zoo Emporium
332 Crown St, Surry Hills.
Tel 9380 5990.

INTERNATIONAL LABELS

Belinda
39 & 29 William St,
Paddington. **Map** 6 D3.
Tel 9380 8728.

Belinda Shoe Salon
14 Transvaal Ave,
Double Bay.
Tel 9328 6288.

Cosmopolitan Shoes
Cosmopolitan Centre,
Knox St, Double Bay.
Tel 9362 0510.

Hype DC
Cnr Market St &
Pitt St Mall. **Map** 1 B5.
Tel 9221 5688.

Robby Ingham Stores
424–428 Oxford St,
Paddington. **Map** 6 D4.
Tel 9332 2124.

Zambesi
8 Cross St, Double Bay.
Tel 9363 1466.

LUXURY BRANDS

Giorgio Armani
4 Martin Place.
Map 1 B4. *Tel 8233 5888.*

Bally
Ground floor, Queen
Victoria Building.
Map 1 B5. *Tel 9267 3887.*

Chanel
70 Castlereagh St.
Map 1 B5. *Tel 9233 4800.*

Diesel
408–410 Oxford St,
Paddington. **Map** 6 D4.
Tel 9331 5255.

Gucci
MLC Centre, 15–25
Martin Place. **Map** 1 B4.
Tel 9232 7565.

Prada
44 Martin Place.
Map 1 B4. *Tel 9231 3929.*

Gianni Versace
128 Castlereagh St.
Map 1 B5. *Tel 9267 3232.*

Louis Vuitton
63 Castlereagh St.
Map 1 B5. *Tel 9236 9624.*

SURF SHOPS

Bondi Surf Co.
72-76 Campbell Parade,
Bondi Beach.
Tel 9365 0870.

Labyrinth
30 Campbell Parade, Bondi
Beach. *Tel 9130 5092.*

Mambo Friendship Store
17 Oxford St, Paddington.
Map 5 B3. *Tel 9331 8034.*

Rip Curl
82 Campbell Parade,
Bondi Beach.
Tel 9130 2660.

The Big Swim
74 Campbell Parade,
Bondi Beach.
Tel 9365 4457.

CLOTHES FOR CHILDREN

David Jones
Cnr Elizabeth &
Castlereagh sts.
Map 1 B5. *Tel 9266 5544.*

Myer
436 George St.
Map 1 B5.
Tel 9238 9111.

ACCESSORIES

Andrew McDonald
58 William St, Paddington.
Map 6 D3.
Tel 9358 6793.

Collect
88 George St, The Rocks.
Map 1 B2. *Tel 9247 7984.*

Crumpler
30 Oxford St, Paddington.
Map 5 B3.
Tel 9331 4660.

Dinosaur Designs
See pp206–7.

Helen Kaminski
Shop 3, Four Seasons
Hotel, 199 George St.
Map 1 B3. *Tel 9251 9850.*

Jan Logan
36 Cross St, Double Bay.
Tel 9363 2529.

Makers Mark
72 Castlereagh St.
Map 1 B5. *Tel 9231 6800.*

Specialist Shops and Souvenirs

Sydney offers an extensive range of gift and souvenir ideas, from unset opals and jewellery to Aboriginal art and hand-crafted souvenirs. Museum shops, such as at the Museum of Sydney *(see p85)* and the Art Gallery of NSW *(see pp108–11)*, often have specially commissioned items that make great presents or reminders of your visit.

ONE-OFFS

Specialist shops abound in Sydney – some practical, some eccentric, others simply indulgent. **Ausfurs** sells everything from luxurious sheepskin coats and jackets to pure wool handknits and mohair rugs.

Wheels & Doll Baby is a powder-room, 1950s chic, a mixture of rock'n'roll heaven and Hollywood glamour. **The Hour Glass** stocks traditional-style watches, while designer sunglasses such as Armani and Jean Paul Gaultier can be found at **The Looking Glass**.

For a touch of celebrity glamour, **Napoleon Perdis Cosmetics** sells a huge array of make-up and bears the name of Australia's leading make-up artist to the "stars". Or, for some eclectic fashion and homewares, try a branch of **Orson & Blake**, the one in Surry Hills has a good café.

AUSTRALIANA

Australiana has become more than just a souvenir genre; it is now an art form in itself.

Done Art and Design has distinctive prints by Ken and Judy Done on a wide range of clothes, swimwear and accessories, while at **Weiss Art** you will find tasteful, mainly black and white, minimalist designs on clothes, umbrellas, baseball caps and cups. **Makers Mark** is a showcase for exquisite work by artisans in wood, glass and silver. The Queen Victoria Building's Victoria Walk *(see p82)* is dominated by shops selling Australiana: souvenirs, silver, antiques, art and crafts.

The **Australian Museum** *(see pp88–9)* has a small shop on the ground floor. It sells slightly unusual gift items such as native flower presses, bark paintings and Australian animal puppets, puzzles and games.

BOOKS

The larger chains such as **Dymocks** and **Angus & Robertson's Bookworld** have a good range of guide books and maps on Sydney. For more eclectic browsing, try **Abbey's Bookshop**, **Ariel** and **Gleebooks**, while **Berkelouw Books** has three floors of new, second-hand and rare books. **The Bookshop Darlinghurst** specializes in gay and lesbian fiction and non-fiction. The **State Library of NSW** *(see p112)* bookshop has a good choice of Australian books, particularly on history.

MUSIC

Several specialist music shops of international repute can be found in Sydney. **Red Eye Records** is for the streetwise, with its collectables, rarities, alternative music and concert tickets. **Central Station Records and Tapes** has mainstream grooves, plus rap, hip hop, and cutting edge dance music. **Birdland** has a good stock of blues, jazz, soul and avant-garde. **Anthem Records** is Australia's oldest record and CD import store, selling funk, soul and R&B for over 30 years. **Folkways** specializes in world music, **Waterfront** in world and left-of-centre and **Utopia Records** in hard rock and heavy metal. **Michael's Music Room** sells classical music only, specialising in historical and contemporary opera recordings.

ABORIGINAL ART

Traditional paintings, fabric, jewellery, boomerangs, carvings and cards can be bought at the **Aboriginal and Pacific Art.** You can find tribal artifacts from Aboriginal Australia at several shops in the Harbourside Shopping Centre, Darling Harbour. The **Coo-ee Aboriginal Art Gallery** boasts a large selection of limited edition prints, hand-printed fabrics, books and Aboriginal music. The long-established **Hogarth Galleries Aboriginal Art Centre** has a fine reputation and usually holds work by Papunya Tula and Balgo artists and respected painters such as Clifford Possum Tjapaltjarri *(see p111)*. Works by urban indigenous artists can be found at the **Boomalli Aboriginal Artists' Cooperative**.

OPALS

Sydney offers a variety of opals in myriad settings. **Flame Opals** is a family run store, selling stones from all the major Australian opal fields. At **Opal Fields** you can view a museum collection of opalised fossils, before buying from the wide range of gems. **Giulian's** has unset opals, including blacks from Lightning Ridge, whites from Coober Pedy and boulder opals from Quilpie.

JEWELLERY

Long-established Sydney jewellers with 24-carat reputations include **Fairfax & Roberts, Hardy Brothers** and **Percy Marks**. World-class pearls are found in the waters off the northwestern coast of Australia. Rare and beautiful examples can be found at **Paspaley Pearls**.

Victoria Spring Designs evokes costume jewellery's glory days, with filigree and glass beading worked into its sumptuous pendants, rings, earrings and Gothic crosses. **Dinosaur Designs** made its name with colourful, chunky resin jewellery, while at **Love & Hatred**, jewelled wrist cuffs, rings and crosses recall lush medieval treasures. **Jan Logan** is an iconic Australian jewellery designer, with stores in Melbourne, Hong Kong, and London. Choose from beautiful and unusual contemporary pieces, otherwise the shop also carries antiques.

DIRECTORY

ONE-OFFS

Ausfurs
136 Victoria Rd,
Marrickville.
Tel 9557 4040.

The Hour Glass
142 King St.
Map 1 B5.
Tel 9221 2288.

The Looking Glass
Queen Victoria Building.
Map 1 B5.
Tel 9261 4997.

**Napoleon Perdis
Cosmetics**
74 Oxford St,
Paddington.
Map 5 A2. **www**.
napoleoncosmetics.com

Orson & Blake
78 and 83–85 Queen St,
Woollahra. **Map** 6 E4.
Tel 9326 1155.

Also at:
483 Riley St, Surry Hills.
Map 4 F5.
Tel 8399 2525. **www**.
orsanandblake.com.au

Wheels & Doll Baby
259 Crown St,
Darlinghurst.
Map 5 A2.
Tel 9361 3286.

AUSTRALIANA

**Australian Museum
Shop**
6 College St. **Map** 4 F3.
Tel 9320 6150
One of two branches.

**Done Art and
Design**
123 George St, The Rocks.
Map 1 B2.
Tel 9251 6099.
One of several branches.

Makers Mark
72 Castlereagh St. **Map**
1 B5. **Tel** 9231 6800.

Weiss Art
85 George St, The Rocks.
Map 1 B2.
Tel 9241 3819.

Also at: Harbourside
Shopping Centre, Darling
Harbour. **Map** 3 C2.
Tel 9281 4614.

BOOKS

Abbey's Bookshop
131 York St. **Map** 1 A5.
Tel 9264 3111.

**Angus & Robertson
Bookworld**
Pitt St Mall, Pitt St. **Map**
1 B5. **Tel** 9235 1188.
One of many branches.

Ariel
42 Oxford St, Paddington.
Map 5 B3.
Tel 9332 4581.

Berkelouw Books
19 Oxford St, Paddington
Map 5 B3.
Tel 9360 3200.

Also at:
70 Norton St, Leichhardt.
Tel 9560 3200.
www.berkelouw.com.au

**The Bookshop
Darlinghurst**
207 Oxford St,
Darlinghurst. **Map** 5 A2.
Tel 9331 1103.

Dymocks
424 George St.
Map 1 B5.
Tel 9235 0155.
One of many branches.

Gleebooks
49 Glebe Point Rd, Glebe.
Map 3 B5.
Tel 9660 2333.

**Lesley Mackay's
Bookshop**
346 New South Head
Road, Double Bay.
Tel 9327 1354.
One of two branches.

**State Library
of NSW Shop**
Macquarie St. **Map** 1 C4.
Tel 9273 1611.

MUSIC

Anthem Records
9 Albion Place. **Map** 4 E3.
Tel 9267 7931.

Birdland
231 Pitt St. **Map** 1 B5.
Tel 9267 6811.

**Central Station
Records and Tapes**
46 Oxford St, Darlinghurst.
Map 4 F4.
Tel 9361 5222.

Fish Records
350 George St
Map 1 B3.
Tel 9233 3371

Folkways
282 Oxford St,
Paddington. **Map** 5 C3.
Tel 9361 3980.

**Michael's Music
Room**
Shop 17, Town Hall
Square. **Map** 4 E3.
Tel 9267 1351.

Red Eye Records
66 King St, Sydney.
Map 1 B5.
Tel 9299 4233.

Utopia Records
Hoyts Cinema Complex,
505 George St. **Map** 4 E3.
Tel 9283 2423.

ABORIGINAL ART

**Aboriginal and
Pacific Art**
2 Danks St, Waterloo.
Tel 9699 2111.

**Boomalli Aboriginal
Artists' Cooperative**
191 Parramatta Rd,
Annandale. **Map** 3 A5.
Tel 9560 2541.

**Coo-ee Aboriginal
Art Gallery**
31 Lamrock Ave, Bondi
Beach.
Tel 9300 9233.

**Hogarth Galleries
Aboriginal Art
Centre**
7 Walker Lane, off Brown
St, Paddington.
Map 5 C3.
Tel 9360 6839.
One of two branches.

OPALS

Flame Opals
119 George Street,
The Rocks. **Map** 1 B2.
Tel 9247 3446.

Giulian's
2 Bridge St. **Map** 1 B3.
Tel 9252 2051.

Opal Fields
190 George St, The Rocks.
Map 1 B2.
Tel 9247 6800.
One of three branches.

JEWELLERY

**Dinosaur
Designs**
Strand Arcade. **Map** 1 B5.
Tel 9223 2953.
One of several branches.

Fairfax & Roberts
44 Martin Place.
Map 1 B4.
Tel 9232 8511.

Hardy Brothers
77 Castlereagh St.
Map 1 B5.
Tel 9232 2422.

Jan Logan
36 Cross St, Double Bay.
Tel 9363 2529.

Love & Hatred
Strand Arcade.
Map 1 B5.
Tel 9233 3441.

Paspaley Pearls
142 King St.
Map 1 A4.
Tel 9232 7633.

Percy Marks
60–70 Elizabeth St.
Map 1 B4.
Tel 9233 1355.

**Victoria Spring
Designs**
110 Oxford St,
Paddington.
Map 5 D3.
Tel 9331 7862.

ENTERTAINMENT IN SYDNEY

Sydney has the standard of entertainment and nightlife you would expect from a cosmopolitan city. Everything from opera and ballet at Sydney Opera House to Shakespeare by the sea at the Balmoral Beach amphitheatre is on offer. Venues such as the Capitol, Her Majesty's Theatre and the Theatre Royal play host to the latest musicals, while Sydney's many smaller theatres are home to interesting fringe theatre,

A Wharf Theatre production poster

modern dance and rock and pop concerts. Pub rock thrives in the inner city and beyond; and there are many nightspots for jazz, dance and alternative music. Movie buffs are well catered for with film festivals, art-house films and foreign titles, as well as the latest Hollywood blockbusters. One of the features of harbourside living is the free outdoor entertainment so, for children, a Sydney visit can be especially memorable.

Recently built Sydney Theatre (see p210) on Hickson Road, Walsh Bay

INFORMATION

For details of events in the city, you should check the daily newspapers first. They carry cinema, and often arts and theatre, advertisements daily. The most comprehensive listings appear in the *Sydney Morning Herald's* "Metro" guide every Friday. The *Daily Telegraph* has a gig guide on daily, with opportunities to win free tickets to special events. The *Australian's* main arts pages appear on Fridays and all the papers review new films in weekend editions.

Tourism NSW information kiosks have free guides and the quarterly *What's on in Darling Harbour*. Kiosks are found at Town Hall, Circular Quay and Martin Place. *Where Magazine* is available at the airport and the Sydney Visitor Centre at The Rocks. Hotels also offer free guides, or try **www. sydney.citysearch.com.au**.

Music fans are well served by the free weekly guides *Drum Media* and *3-D World* and *Brag,* found at video and music shops, pubs and clubs.

Many venues have leaflets about forth-coming attractions, while the major venues have infor-mation telephone lines and websites.

BUYING TICKETS

Some of the most popular operas, shows, plays and ballets in Sydney are sold out months in advance. While it is better to book ahead, many theatres do set aside tickets to be sold at the door on the night.

You can buy tickets from the box office or by telephone. Some orchestral performances do not admit children under seven, so check with the box office before buying. If you make a phone booking using a credit card, the tickets can be mailed to you. Alternatively, tickets can be collected from the box office

half an hour before the show. The major agencies will take overseas bookings.

Buying tickets from touts is not advisable, if you are caught with a "sold on" ticket you will be denied access to the event. If all else fails, hotel concierges have a repu-tation for being able to secure hard-to-get tickets.

CHOOSING SEATS

If booking in person at either the venue or the agency, you will be able to look at a seating plan. Be aware that in the State Theatre's stalls, row A is the back row. In Sydney, there is not as much difference in price between stalls and dress circle as in other cities.

If booking by phone with one of the agencies, you will only be able to get a rough idea of where your seats are. The computer will select the "best" tickets.

The annual New Mardi Gras Festival's Dog Show (see p49)

BOOKING AGENCIES

Sydney has two main ticket agencies: **Ticketek** and **Ticketmaster**. Between them, they represent all the major entertainment and sporting events. Ticketek has more than 60 outlets throughout NSW and the ACT, open from 9am to 5pm weekdays, and Saturdays from 9am to 4pm. Opening hours vary between agencies and call centres, so check with Ticketek to confirm. Phone bookings: 8:30am–10pm, Monday to Saturday, and 8.30am–5pm Sundays. For internet bookings, visit their website.

Ticketmaster outlets are open 9am–5pm Monday to Friday. Phone bookings: 9am–9pm Monday to Saturday and 10am-5pm Sunday. Agencies accept traveller's cheques, bank cheques, cash, Visa, MasterCard (Access) and Amex. Some agencies do not accept Diners Club. A booking fee applies, plus a postage and handling charge if tickets are mailed out. There are generally no refunds (unless a show is cancelled) or exchanges. If one agency has sold out its allocation for a show, it is worth checking with another.

The Spanish firedancers Els Comediants at the Sydney Festival

DISCOUNT TICKETS AND FREE ENTERTAINMENT

Tuesday is budget-price day at most cinemas. Some independent cinemas have special prices throughout the week. The Sydney Symphony Orchestra and Opera Australia *(see p212)* offer a special Student Rush price to full-time students under 28 but only if surplus tickets are available. These can be bought on the day of the performance, from the box office at the venue.

Outdoor events are especially popular in Sydney, and many are free *(see pp48–51)*. Sydney Harbour is a splendid setting for the fabulous New Year's Eve fireworks, with a

A busker at Circular Quay

display at 9pm for families as well as the midnight display.

The Sydney Festival in January is a huge extravaganza of performance and visual art. Various outdoor venues in the Rocks, Darling Harbour and in front of the Opera House feature events to suit every taste, including musical productions, drama, dance, exhibitions and circuses. The most popular free events are the symphony and jazz concerts held in the Domain. Also popular are the Darling Harbour Circus and Street Theatre Festival at Easter, and the food and wine festival held in June at Manly Beach.

DISABLED VISITORS

Many older venues were not designed with the disabled visitor in mind, but this has been redressed in most newer buildings. It is best to phone the box office beforehand to request special seating and

The highly respected Australian Chamber Orchestra *(see p212)*

other requirements or call **Ideas Incorporated**, who have a list of Sydney's most wheelchair-friendly venues. The **Sydney Opera House** has disabled parking, wheelchair access and a loop system in the Concert Hall for the hearing impaired. A brochure, *Services for the Disabled*, is also available.

DIRECTORY

USEFUL NUMBERS

CitySearch
www.sydney.citysearch.com.au

Sydney Visitor Centre
Tel 1800 067 676 or 9240 8788.
www.sydneyvisitorcentre.com

Ideas Incorporated
Tel 1800 029 904.

Sydney Opera House
Information Desk
Tel 9250 7209.
Disabled Information
Tel 9250 7185.

The Access Foundation
Tel 9310 5732.
www.accessibility.com.au

Tourism NSW
Tel 132 077.
www.visitnsw.com.au

TICKET AGENCIES

Ticketek
Tel 132 849.
www.ticketek.com.au

Ticketmaster
Tel 136 100.
www.ticketmaster.com.au

Theatre and Film

Sydney's theatrical venues are well known for their atmosphere and quality. There is a stimulating range of productions, ranging from musicals, classic plays and Shakespeare by the Sea to contemporary, fringe and experimental theatre. Comedy is also finding a strong niche as a mainstream performance art. Prominent playwrights include David Williamson, Debra Oswald, Brendan Cowell, Stephen Sewell and Louis Nowra.

Australian film-making has also earned an excellent international reputation. A rich variety of both local and foreign films are screened throughout the year, as well as during eagerly anticipated annual film festivals.

THEATRE

Sydney's larger, mainstream musicals, such as those of Andrew Lloyd Webber, are staged at the **Theatre Royal**, the opulent **State Theatre** (see p82) and the **Capitol Theatre** (see p99). The **Star City** entertainment and casino complex boasts two theatres, the Showroom, and the first-rate Lyric Theatre for musical productions and stage shows.

Smaller venues also offer a range of interesting plays and performances. These include the **Seymour Theatre Centre**, which has three theatres; the **Belvoir Street Theatre**, which has two; the **Ensemble Theatre**, a theatre-in-the-round by the water; and the **Footbridge Theatre**. The **Stables Theatre** specialises in works by new Australian playwrights, while the new **Parade Theatre** at the National Institute of Dramatic Arts (NIDA) showcases work by NIDA's acting, directing and production students throughout the year. It also hosts shows by other theatre groups. The well-respected **Sydney Theatre Company**

(STC) has just introduced an ensemble of actors, employed full time, who will perform a minimum of two plays each season. Most STC productions are at **The Wharf** or the new **Sydney Theatre** at Walsh Bay, though some are staged in the Drama Theatre of the **Sydney Opera House** (see pp74–7).

The **Bell Shakespeare Company** interprets the Bard with an innovative slant without tampering with the original text. Its productions are ideal for young or wary theatre-goers. While venues vary, there are two seasons in Sydney – one at the beginning of summer and one in autumn.

Street performances and open-air theatre are popular during the summer months when life in Sydney moves outdoors. **Shakespeare by the Sea**, at lovely Balmoral Beach (see p55), has no need for painted backdrops.

For the adventurous, the **Sydney Festival** (see p49) offers a celebration of original, often quirky, Australian theatre, dance, music and visual arts. Once considered somewhat frivolous, it has now developed the reputation of having serious artistic depth, while maintaining its unique flavour of Sydney in the summer.

CHILDREN'S THEATRE

Sydney thrives on spectacles that delight children, and their parents. You will often find jugglers, mime artists, buskers and magic shows at Circular Quay and around Darling Harbour (see p91).

The Sydney Opera House regularly has performances for children.

In the suburb of Killara, the **Marian Street Theatre for Young People** stages the occasional theatrical production. With luck, you may even be able to see a performance by the incredibly athletic **Flying Fruit Fly Circus**. This troupe, aged from eight to eighteen, excels in aerial gymnastics.

FILM

The city's main commercial cinema is in George Street, just one block south of Town Hall. The cinema behemoths, Greater Union and Hoyts join to form the **Greater Union Hoyts Village Complex**, which shows the latest films. Similar multiplexes can be found in the Entertainment Quarter on Driver Avenue, and in Bondi Junction on Oxford Street. The **IMAX Theatre** (see p92) in Darling Harbour has a giant, 8-storey screen and shows 2D and 3D films made specifically for the large screen. Many of these are suitable for children.

Cinephiles flock to **Palace Cinemas'** Academy Twin and Verona Theatres on Oxford Street, and to the **Dendy Cinemas** at Newtown and Opera Quays. **Cinema Paris** shows arthouse and indie films, and often screens Bollywood movies as well. The **Reading Cinema** regularly shows the latest Chinese films. Foreign films are usually screened in the original language with English subtitles.

For a movie and a meal, **Govinda's** (see p189), which is also an Indian restaurant, screens films that have just finished their run at the cinemas. The admission price includes a tasty vegetarian buffet dinner.

The latest screenings are usually at 9:30pm, although most major cinema complexes run shows up to as late as midnight. Commercial cinema houses offer half-price tickets on Tuesday, while Palace and Dendy do so on Monday.

FILM CENSORSHIP RATINGS

G For general exhibition
PG Parental guidance recommended for those under 15 years
M 15+ Recommended for mature audiences aged 15 and over
MA 15+ Restricted to people 15 years and over
R 18+ Restricted to adults 18 years and over

FILM FESTIVALS

The **Sydney Film Festival** is a highlight of the city's calendar (*see p51*), screening some 200 new features, shorts and documentaries from all over the globe. Tribute sessions and retrospectives are also presented. The main venue is the State Theatre but there are satellite screenings at other venues.

The **Flickerfest International Short Film Festival** (*see p49*) is held at the Bondi Pavilion Amphitheatre at Bondi Beach in early January. It screens shorts and animation films from around the world. In February, **Tropfest** (*see p49*) shows local short films that can be no longer than seven minutes. Each must feature the special Tropfest signature item, which in past years has included a rock, a pickle and a match.

Run by Queer Screen, the **New Mardi Gras Film Festival** (*see p49*), starts mid-February and continues for 15 days. Films dealing with issues relevant to the lesbian, gay and transgender community are shown at various inner-city venues.

COMEDY

Sydney's most established comedy venue, the **Comedy Store** is known for its themed nights. Tuesday is open-mic night; Wednesday, new comics; Thursday, cutting edge; Friday and Saturday are reserved for the best of the best. Monday is comedy night at **The Old Manly Boatshed**, where both local and visiting comics perform. Monday is also comedy night at the **Bridge Hotel**, where live entertainment is offered most nights of the week.

DIRECTORY

THEATRE

Bell Shakespeare Company
Tel 9241 2722. www.bellshakespeare.com.au

Belvoir Street Theatre
25 Belvoir St, Surry Hills.
Tel 9699 3444.
www.belvoir.com.au

Capitol Theatre
13 Campbell St, Haymarket. **Map** 4 E4.
Tel 9320 5000. Box office tel 136 100.
www.capitoltheatre.com.au

Ensemble Theatre
78 McDougall St, Kirribilli.
Tel 9929 8877. Box office tel 9929 0644.
www.ensemble.com.au

Footbridge Theatre
University of Sydney, Parramatta Rd, Glebe.
Map 3 A5. *Tel 9266 4800.*

Parade Theatre
215 Anzac Parade, Kensington. **Map** 5 B4
Tel 9697 7613.

Seymour Theatre Centre
Cnr Cleveland St & City Rd, Chippendale.
Tel 9351 7940.

Shakespeare by the Sea
Band Rotunda, Balmoral Beach. *Tel 9590 8305.*
www.shakespeare-by-the-sea.com

Stables Theatre
10 Nimrod St, Kings Cross.
Map 5 B1. *Tel 9250 7799.*

Star City
80 Pyrmont St, Pyrmont.
Map 3 B1. *Tel 9777 9000.*
Lyric Theatre Box office
Tel 9657 8500.
www.starcity.com.au

State Theatre
49 Market St.
Map 1 B5.
Tel 9373 6655.
Box office tel 136 100.
www.statetheatre.com.au

Sydney Festival
Tel 8248 6500. www.sydneyfestival.org.au

Sydney Theatre
22 Hickson Rd, Walsh Bay.
Map 1 A2.
Tel 9250 1999.

Sydney Theatre Company
Tel 9250 1777. www.sydneytheatre.com.au

Theatre Royal
MLC Centre, King St.
Map 1 B5.
Tel 9224 8444.

The Wharf
Pier 4, Hickson Rd, Walsh Bay. **Map** 1 A1.
Tel 9250 1777.

CHILDREN'S THEATRE

Flying Fruit Fly Circus
Tel 6021 7044.
www.fruitflycircus.com.au

Marian Street Theatre for Young People
2 Marian St, Killara.
Tel 9498 3166.

FILM

Cinema Paris
Entertainment Quarter, Driver Ave, Moore Park.
Map 5 C5. *Tel 9332 1633.*

Dendy Cinemas Opera Quays
Shop 9/2, East Circular Quay. *Tel 9247 3800.*

Newtown
261–263 King St, Newtown. *Tel 9550 5699.*

Govinda's
112 Darlinghurst Rd.
Map 5 A2.
Tel 9360 7853.
www.govindas.com.au

Greater Union Hoyts Village Complex
505–525 George St.
Map 4 E3. *Tel 9267 8666.*
www.greaterunion.com.au

IMAX Theatre
Southern Promenade, Darling Harbour. **Map** 4 D3. *Tel 9281 3300.*
www.imax.com.au

Palace Cinemas Academy Twin
3a Oxford St, Paddington.
Map 5 B3. *Tel 9361 4453.*

Verona
17 Oxford St, Paddington.
Map 5 B3. *Tel 9360 6099.*
www.palacecinemas.com.au

Reading Cinema
Level 3, Market City, 9 Hay St, Haymarket.
Map 4 E4. *Tel 9280 1202.*
www.readingcinemas.com.au

FILM FESTIVALS

Flickerfest International Short Film Festival
Tel 9365 6877.
www.flickerfest.com.au

New Mardi Gras Festival
Tel 9557 4332. www.queerscreen.com.au

Sydney Film Festival
Tel 9660 3844. www.sydneyfilmfestival.org

Tropfest
Tel 9368 0434.
www.tropfest.com

COMEDY

Bridge Hotel
135 Victoria Rd, Rozelle.
Tel 9810 1260.
www.bridgehotel.com.au

Comedy Store
Entertainment Quarter, Driver Ave, Moore Park.
Map 5 C5. *Tel 9357 1419.*
www.comedystore.com.au

The Old Manly Boatshed
40 The Corso, Manly.
Tel 9977 4443.

Opera, Classical Music and Dance

Music buffs cannot possibly visit Sydney without seeing an opera or hearing the city's premier orchestra perform in the Sydney Opera House. And that is just the start. Since the 1970s, music played in Sydney has considerably broadened its base, opening the door to all manner of influences from Asia, Europe and the Pacific, not to mention local compositions. For the visitor, there is a wealth of orchestral, choral, chamber and contemporary music from which to choose.

OPERA

Australia has produced a number of world-class opera singers, including Joan Sutherland, and eminent conductors such as Sir Charles Mackerras, Simone Young and Stuart Challender. The first recorded performance of an opera in Sydney was in 1834. For 120 years, most opera was performed by visiting international companies.

In 1956, the Australian Opera (now called **Opera Australia**) was formed. It presented four Mozart operas in its first year. But it was the opening of the **Sydney Opera House** (see pp74–7) in 1973 that heralded a new interest in opera. Opera Australia's summer season is held from early January to early March; the winter season from June to the end of October. Each season usually includes one accessible opera in English as well as more challenging shows. Every year at the hugely popular Opera in The Domain (see p49), members of Opera Australia perform excerpts from famous operas.

ORCHESTRAL MUSIC

Much of Sydney's orchestral music and recitals are the work of the famous **Sydney Symphony Orchestra** (SSO). Numerous concerts are given, mostly in the Opera House Concert Hall, the **City Recital Hall** and the **Sydney Town Hall** (see p87). A Tea and Symphony series is held mid-year on Friday mornings at the Sydney Opera House. Babies' Proms take place many times each year in the **Eugene Goossens Hall** for children under five.

The recently renovated Conservatorium of Music (see p106), set in the Royal Botanic Gardens, provides a wonderful atmosphere and location. It holds a number of concerts, where you can enjoy symphony and chamber orchestras, or jazz big bands.

Formed in 1973, the **Sydney Youth Orchestra**, is praised for its talent, enthusiasm and impressive young soloists. With a loyal following, it stages several performances in major concert venues throughout the year.

Aficionados of Baroque and classical music should try to catch a performance by the **Australian Brandenburg Orchestra**. Australia's first period instrument orchestra, this popular group appears regularly in Sydney's major concert halls.

CONTEMPORARY MUSIC

The first concert held by **Musica Viva** was in 1945, at the NSW Conservatorium of Music. Originally specialising in chamber music, it now presents string quartets, jazz, piano groups, percussionists, soloists and international avant-garde artists as well. Concerts take place at the Opera House and the City Recital Hall.

Synergy is one of Australia's foremost percussion quartets. The group commissions works from all over the world and gives its own concert series at the Sydney Opera House and at Sydney Town Hall. It also collaborates with dance and theatre groups.

Eastside Arts, held, like Paddington Markets (see p126), in the Uniting Church, hosts Café Carnivale every Friday night, showcasing some of the best world music, including rembetika, Indian, African, percussion, gypsy, salsa and tango music.

Fourplay is a group of classically-trained musicians who play electric string quartet versions of popular music at various venues.

CHAMBER MUSIC

Under director Richard Tognetti, the **Australian Chamber Orchestra** has won high acclaim for its creativity and interesting choice of venues, including museums, churches and even wineries. Its main concerts are held at the Opera House and the City Recital Hall, Angel Place.

The **Australia Ensemble** is the resident chamber music group at the University of New South Wales. It performs six times a year at the Sir John Clancy Auditorium and

---

FREE CONCERTS

Throughout the year, festivals provide free live music (see pp48–51). These are mostly held outdoors, to take advantage of Sydney's warm weather. During the Sydney Festival the city's favourite outdoor concerts take place, including Opera in the Park, Symphony in the Domain and the Australia Day Concert, all held in The Domain, as well as Latin music in the Aquadome at Darling Harbour and events in the Sydney Opera House forecourt.

The Conservatorium of Music holds a weekly series of inexpensive concerts in their Verbrugghen Hall (see p106) during the university semester, entry is by gold coin ($1 or $2) donation. Staff and students present classical, modern and jazz music in ensemble, soloist and chamber performances. Buskers, jazz bands, string ensembles, guitarists or dancers perform most weekends and during school holidays at Circular Quay, The Rocks and Darling Harbour.

also appears for Musica Viva. Many choral groups and ensembles, such as the **Macquarie Trio** of violin, piano and cello, like to book **St James Church** because of its atmosphere and acoustics. This talented group also performs at the theatre in Macquarie University.

CHORAL MUSIC

Comprising the 120-strong Sydney Philharmonia Symphonic Choir and the 40-member Sydney Philharmonia Motet Choir, the **Sydney Philharmonia Choirs** are the city's finest. They perform at the Opera House. December is the focal point of Sydney's choral scene, with regular massed choir performances of Handel's *Messiah*.

The **Australian Youth Choir** is booked for many private functions, but if lucky, you may catch one of their major annual performances.

One of Sydney's most impressive vocal groups is the **Café of the Gate of Salvation**, described as an "Aussie blend of *a capella* and gospel."

DANCE

There is an eclectic variety of dance on offer in Sydney. The **Australian Ballet** has two seven-week Sydney seasons at the Opera House: one in March/April, the other in November/December. The company's repertoire spans traditional through to modern, although it is perhaps most noted for classical ballets such as *Swan Lake* and *Giselle*.

Sydney Dance Company is the city's leading modern dance group, often combining its vigorous productions with innovative musical scores. It has performed in Italy, New York, London and China. Productions are mostly staged at the Sydney Opera House, but are, on occasion, held at The Wharf or the new Sydney Theatre *(see pp210–11)*. Acclaimed choreographer and artistic director, Graeme Murphy, often collaborates with international luminaries to put up fantastic shows.

The **Performance Space**, which consists of a theatre, two galleries and a studio, is very popular for its experimental dance and movement theatre. Artists with backgrounds in everything from dance, mime and circus work to Butoh and performance art are likely to appear here.

Bangarra Dance Theatre uses traditional Aboriginal and Torres Strait Islander dance and music as its inspiration, infused with contemporary elements. It makes outback interstate and international tours, but is based in Sydney.

The startling and original **Legs on the Wall** are a physical theatre group who work all over the world, combining circus and aerial techniques with dance and narrative to form a heady mix, often performed while suspended from skyscrapers.

The smaller experimental companies rely on year-to-year funding or community-based work. These include the collaborative **One Extra Dance Company**. They perform contemporary and exploratory dance, in youth theatre, at concerts, for communities and at venues all over Sydney.

DIRECTORY

Music Venues and Nightclubs

Sydney attracts some of the biggest names in modern music all year round. Venues range from the cavernous Sydney Entertainment Centre to small and noisy back rooms in pubs. Visiting international DJs frequently play sets at Sydney clubs. Some venues cater for a variety of music tastes – rock and pop one night, jazz, blues or folk the next. There are several free weekly gig guides available, including *Drum Media*, *3-D World* and *Brag (see p208)*, which tell you what is on.

GETTING IN

Tickets for major shows are available through booking agencies such as Ticketek and Ticketmaster *(see p208)*. Prices vary considerably, depending on the shows that are going to take place. You may pay from $30 to $70 for a gig at the Metro, but over $150 for seats for a Rolling Stones concert. Moshtix also sells tickets for smaller venues across Sydney and their website gives a good idea of the various venues and what is on. Buying online also prevents you from having to queue early for tickets from the door.

You can also pay at the door on the night at most places, unless the show is sold out. Nightclubs often have a cover charge, but some venues will admit you free before a certain time in the evening or on weeknights.

Most venues serve alcohol, so shows are restricted to those at least 18 years of age. This is the usual case unless a gig is specified "all ages". It is advisable that people under 30 years old carry photo identification, such as a passport or driver's licence, because entry to some venues is very strict. You are also not allowed to carry any kind of bottle into most nightclubs or other venues. Similarly, any cameras and recording devices are usually banned.

Dress codes vary, but generally, shorts (on men) and flip flops are not welcome. Wear thin layers which you can remove when you get hot instead of a coat, and avoid carrying a big bag, because many venues do not have a cloakroom. For more information on rules and conventions, which are followed in Sydney bars and pubs see pages 196–7.

ROCK, POP AND HIP HOP

Pop's big names and famous rock groups perform at the **Sydney Entertainment Centre**, **Hordern Pavilion**, and sports grounds such as the Aussie Stadium at **Sydney Olympic Park** *(see p138)* in Homebush Bay. More intimate locations include the **State Theatre** *(see pp210–11)*, **Enmore Theatre** and Sydney's best venue, **The Metro Theatre**. Hip Hop acts usually play in rock venues rather than in nightclubs. You are almost as likely to catch a crew rapping or a band strumming and drumming at the Metro Theatre, the **Gaelic Club**, **@Newtown** or the **Hopetoun Hotel**. It is not unusual to catch a punk, garage or electro-folk band at **Spectrum** or the **Annandale Hotel** on Parramatta Road.

Pub rock is a constantly changing scene in Sydney. Weekly listings appear on Fridays in the "Metro" section of the *Sydney Morning Herald* and in the street press *(see p208)*. Music stores are also full of flyers and gigs by international acts and popular Australian bands, on every week at the Metro Theatre and Gaelic Club, usually sell out.

JAZZ, FOLK AND BLUES

For many years, the first port of call for any jazz, funk, groove or folk enthusiast has been **The Basement**. Visiting luminaries play some nights, talented but struggling local musicians others, and the line-ups now also includes increasingly popular world music and hip hop bands.

Soup Plus, Margaret Street, plays jazz while serving reasonably priced food, including soup. Experimental jazz is offered on Fridays and Saturdays at the **Seymour Theatre Centre** *(see pp210–11)*. **The Vanguard**, a newer venue, also offers dinner and show deals, as well as show-only tickets, and has been drawing an excellent roster of jazz, blues and roots talent. Annandale's **Empire Hotel** is Sydney's official home of the blues, and the **Cat & Fiddle Hotel** in Balmain of acoustic music and folk. **Wine Banq**, a plush CBD bar and restaurant, dishes up smooth jazz most nights of the week.

HOUSE, BREAKBEATS AND TECHNO

Sydney's only super club, **Home Sydney** in Cockle Bay features three levels and a gargantuan sound system. Friday night is the time to go, as the DJs present house, trance, drum and bass and breakbeats. A mainstream crowd flocks to the nearby **Bungalow 8** on King Street Wharf. Once the sun has set, house DJs turn the place into a club. At the swank **Tank** on Bridge Lane, the emphasis is on pure house music and the decor is a throwback to Studio 54 in New York. **Cave**, at Star City, is another mainstream house club.

For something a little more hip, try **Candy's Apartment** on Bayswater Road, or the fashionable tech-electro **Mars Lounge** on Wentworth Avenue, with its red lacquered interior. Enter **Goodbar** on Oxford Street in Paddington by a barely marked door, descend a flight of stairs, and you will find yourself in one of Sydney's longest established nightclubs. There is hip hop some nights, house others. Down the road, **Q Bar** on Oxford Street, Darlinghurst, has arcade games for when you need a breather. Or try the low-ceilinged **Chinese Laundry** on Sussex Street, tucked under the gentrified pub, **Slip Inn** *(see p186)*.

GAY AND LESBIAN PUBS AND CLUBS

Sunday night is the big night for many of Sydney's gay community, although there is plenty of action throughout the week. A number of venues have a gay or lesbian night on one night of the week and attract a mainstream crowd on the other nights. Wednesday is lesbian night at the **Bank Hotel** in Newtown and some Sundays are queer nights at Home Sydney and Mars Lounge. **Club Kooky**, on

William Street, offers an alternative to the mainstream gay clubs with a mixed crowd, excellent DJs and live electronic music, and an anything-goes vibe on Sunday nights.

ARQ on Flinders Street is the largest of the gay clubs, with pounding commercial house music. The main dance floor is overlooked by a mezzanine for watching the writhing mass of bodies below. **Midnight Shift** on Oxford Street is for men only, and **Stonewall** plays camp

anthems and is patronized mostly by men and their straight female friends. At **The Venus Room**, on Roslyn Street, cabaret club, drag shows are performed every night.

The **Colombian** is the best of the Oxford Street bars, with a mock-Central American jungle and large windows that open out to the street. The **Oxford Hotel** and its upper-level cocktail bars are popular too. Both the **Newtown Hotel** and **Imperial Hotel** have drag shows on most nights of the week.

DIRECTORY

ROCK, POP AND HIP HOP

Annandale Hotel
17–19 Parramatta Rd, Annandale.
Tel 9550 1078. **www.**annandalehotel.com

Enmore Theatre
130 Enmore Rd, Newtown.
Tel 9550 3666. **www.**enmoretheatre.com.au

The Gaelic Club
64 Devonshire St, Surry Hills. *Tel 9211 1687.*
www.thegaelicclub.com

Hopetoun Hotel
416 Bourke St, Surry Hills.
Tel 9361 5257.

Hordern Pavilion
Driver Ave, Moore Park.
Map 5 C5.
Tel 9921 5333.
www.playbillvenues.com

The Metro Theatre
624 George St. **Map** 4 E3.
Tel 9264 2666. **www.**metrotheatre.com.au

Moshtix
Tel 9209 4614.
www.moshtix.com.au

@Newtown
52 Enmore Rd, Newtown.
Tel 9557 5044.
www.atnewtown.com.au

Spectrum
34 Oxford St, Darlinghurst. **Map** 4 F4.
www.pashpresents.com

State Theatre
49 Market St. **Map** 1 B5.
Tel 9373 6655.
Box office tel 136 00.
www.statetheatre.com.au

Sydney Entertainment Centre
Harbour St, Haymarket.
Map 4 D4.
Tel 9320 4200.

Sydney Olympic Park
Homebush Bay.
Tel 9714 7958.
www.sydneyolympicpark.nsw.gov.au

JAZZ, FOLK AND BLUES

The Basement
29 Reiby Place.
Map 1 B3.
Tel 9251 2797. **www.**thebasement.com.au

Cat & Fiddle Hotel
456 Darling St, Balmain.
Tel 9810 7931.
www.thecatandfiddle.net

Empire Hotel
Cnr Johnston St & Paramatta Rd, Annandale.
Tel 9557 1701.
www.sydneyblues.com

Seymour Theatre Centre
Cnr Cleveland St & City Rd, Chippendale.
Tel 9351 7940.

Soup Plus
1 Margaret St (cnr Clarence St). **Map** 4 E1.
Tel 9299 7728.
www.soupplus.com.au

The Vanguard
42 King St, Newtown.
Tel 9557 7992. **www.**thevanguard.com.au

Wine Banq
53 Martin Pl. **Map** 1 B4.
Tel 9222 1919.
www.winebanq.com.au

HOUSE, BREAKBEATS AND TECHNO

Bungalow 8
The Promenade, King St Wharf.
Tel 9299 4660.

Candy's Apartment
22 Bayswater Rd, Kings Cross. **Map** 5 B1.
Tel 9380 5600.

Cave
Star City, Pirrama Rd, Pyrmont. **Map** 3 C1.
Tel 9566 4755.

Chinese Laundry
Slip Inn 111 Sussex St.
Map 1 A3. *Tel 8295 9999.*

Goodbar
11a Oxford St, Paddington. **Map** 5 B3.
Tel 9360 6759.

Home Sydney
Wheat Rd, Cockle Bay, Darling Harbour.
Map 4 D2.
Tel 9266 0600.
www.homesydney.com

Mars Lounge
16 Wentworth Avenue, Darlinghurst. **Map** 4 F4
Tel 9267 6440.

Q Bar
Level 2, 44 Oxford St, Darlinghurst.
Map 4 F4.
Tel 9360 1375.

Tank
3 Bridge Lane.
Tel 9240 3094.

GAY AND LESBIAN CLUBS AND PUBS

ARQ
16 Flinders St, Taylor Square. **Map** 5 A2.
Tel 9380 8700.

Bank Hotel
324 King St. Newtown.
Tel 9565 1730.

Club Kooky
77 William St, East Sydney.
Map 5 A1.
Tel 9361 4981.

Colombian
Cnr Oxford and Crown Sts, Surry Hills. **Map** 5 A2.
Tel 9360 2151.

Imperial Hotel
35 Erskineville Rd, Erskineville.
Tel 9519 9899.

Midnight Shift
85 Oxford St, Darlinghurst.
Map 5 A2.
Tel 9360 4319.

Newtown Hotel
174 King St, Newtown.
Tel 9557 1329.

Oxford Hotel
134 Oxford St, Darlinghurst. **Map** 5 A2.
Tel 9331 3467.

Stonewall
175 Oxford St, Darlinghurst. **Map** 5 A2.
Tel 9360 1963.

The Venus Room
2 Roslyn St, Kings Cross.
Map 5 C1.
Tel 8354 0888.

Casual dress at a beachside café

ETIQUETTE AND TIPPING

While Sydney customs are generally casual, there are a few rules to follow. Eating and drinking is frowned at on public transport, and also when travelling in taxis.

Dress code is generally smart casual, but is more relaxed in summer – although people do like to go all out for formal occasions. Topless bathing is accepted on many beaches, but not at public swimming pools.

People do not depend on tips for their livelihood so this is generally optional. However, it is the custom to leave a little extra for good service in cafés and restaurants (see p179), to tip hotel porters (see p169) and to leave any small change for bartenders and taxi drivers.

GUIDED TOURS AND EXCURSIONS

Tours and excursions offer the visitor many different ways of exploring the city and its surroundings – from bus tours of the city's night spots, jaunts on the back of a Harley Davidson, guided nature walks, cruises on a replica of the *Bounty*, to aerial adventures by hot-air balloon, seaplane or

helicopter. As well as being an easy way to take in the sights, a tour can help you to get a feel for your new surroundings.

Perhaps the most economical and flexible introductions to Sydney's attractions are the unregimented tours provided by the State Transit Explorer Buses (see p231). The **State Transit Tourist Ferries** also run special sightseeing routes. In addition, commuter ferries (see pp234–5) provide a less costly alternative to all-out commercial harbour cruises.

Top-sail schooner

STUDENT TRAVELLERS

Student travellers carrying the International Student Identity card are eligible for discounts in museums, theatres and cinemas, as well as a 40 per cent reduction on internal air fares and 15 per cent off interstate coach travel.

Overseas visitors who are full-time students in Australia can purchase an International Student Identity card (there's a guidebook included) for $18 from Sydney branches of **STA Travel**.

DIRECTORY

COACH AND MOTORCYCLE TOURS

Newmans Coach Tours
Tel 1300 300 036.

Bikescape Motorcycle Rentals and Tours
Tel 1300 736 869.
www.bikescape.com.au

HARBOUR AND RIVER CRUISES

Captain Cook Cruises
Wharf 6, Circular Quay.
Map 1 B3. *Tel* 9206 1111.

Matilda Cruises
Pier 26, Darling Harbour.
Map 4 D2. *Tel* 9264 7377.

State Transit Tourist Ferries
Wharves 4 and 5, Circular Quay.
Map 1 B3. *Tel* 131500.

WALKING TOURS

Blue Mountains Guides
PO Box 145, Katoomba NSW 2780. *Tel* 4782 6109. www.bluemountainsguides.com.au

Maureen Fry Sydney Guided Tours
15 Arcadia Rd, Glebe.
Tel 9660 7157.

The Rocks Walking Tours
23 Playfair St, The Rocks.
Map 1 B2. *Tel* 9247 6678.
www.rockswalkingtours.com.au

AIR TOURS

Cloud 9 Balloon Flights
Tel 9679 2899.
www.cloud9balloonflights.com

Sydney Seaplanes
Tel 1300 732 752.
www.sydneyseaplanes.com.au

Sydney Helicopters
Tel 9637 4455.

STUDENT INFORMATION

STA Travel
855 George St, Sydney.
Tel 9212 1255.

Seaplane moored at Rose Bay, available for scenic flight charter

DISABLED TRAVELLERS

Sydney has recently made much-needed advances in catering for the disabled. State Transit is phasing in specially designed buses with doors at pavement level and ramps that allow people in wheelchairs to use the bus service. There is also priority seating for those with a disability and bus hand-rails and steps are marked with bright yellow paint to assist visually impaired passengers.

The Circular Quay railway station is completely accessible to wheelchair users. Several other stations have wide entrance gates and most have ramps installed. The Transport Infoline *(see p230)* can give details on disabled access at each station.

Museums, newer hotels and some major sights cater to the less mobile, including those in wheelchairs, as well as people with other disabilities. You are strongly advised to phone all sights in advance to check on facilities, allowing the most effective forward planning.

For detailed information on accessible services and venues, *Access Sydney (see p170)* is available from Spinal Cord Injuries Australia. A map and directory for those with limited mobility can be obtained from the **Sydney City Council One-Stop Shop**.

Sydney City Council One-Stop Shop

Town Hall House, Sydney Square, George St. **Map** 4 E3. **Tel** 9265 9255.

SYDNEY TIME

Sydney is in the Australian Eastern Standard Time zone (AEST). Daylight saving in New South Wales starts on the last Sunday in October and finishes on the last Sunday in March. The Northern Territory, Queensland and Western Australia do not observe daylight saving, so check time differences when you are there.

City and Country	Hours + or – AEST
Adelaide (Australia)	*–½*
Brisbane (Australia)	*same*
Canberra (Australia)	*same*
Darwin (Australia)	*–½*
Hobart (Australia)	*same*
Melbourne (Australia)	*same*
Perth (Australia)	*–2*
London (UK)	*–9*
Los Angeles (USA)	*–17*
Singapore	*–2*
Toronto (Canada)	*–14*

IMMIGRATION AND CUSTOMS

All visitors to Australia, except New Zealand passport holders, must hold a valid passport and visa, an onward ticket and proof they have sufficient funds for their visit. However, visitors should always check requirements before travelling.

The customs allowance per person over 18 entering Australia, is up to the value of A$400, 1.125 litres (about 2 pints) of alcohol and a carton of 250 cigarettes.

Quarantine regulations in Australia are strict because of the debilitating effect that introduced pests and diseases would have on agriculture, and the country's unique flora and fauna. The importation of

Overseas cruise ship in port at Circular Quay passenger terminal

fresh or packaged food, fruit, vegetables, seeds, live plants and plant products is prohibited. It is also illegal to bring in any items or products made from endangered species. Because of these restrictions, all personal luggage, including hand luggage, is x-rayed before you can leave the baggage reclaim area. The penalties for importing illegal drugs of any sort are severe.

On all international flights to Sydney, the customs declaration forms issued on the plane must be filled out and given to customs officers as you enter the country. The practice of spraying the cabin with insecticide before landing has been discontinued.

DEPARTURE TAX

As in many other countries, Australia has a departure tax. All passengers aged 12 or over are required to pay a departure tax when leaving the country. This tax is usually included in the cost of your airline ticket.

Entrance gates with wheelchair access at Circular Quay railway station

MEDIA

Sydney's chief daily morning newspaper is the *Sydney Morning Herald*. It includes a comprehensive listing of local entertainment on Fridays and Saturdays. The other Sydney daily is the *Daily Telegraph*.

The *Australian* is a daily national paper with the most comprehensive coverage of overseas news, and the *Australian Financial Review* largely reports on international monetary matters. *Time* magazine is Australia's leading international news magazine. Most of the major foreign newspapers and magazines are widely available at many newsstands.

Sydney is well served with AM and FM radio stations. The state-run ABC (Australian Broadcasting Corporation) stations cater for various tastes from rock to classical, as well as providing a range of services, including news, rural information for farmers, arts commentary and magazine-style programmes. There are also community radio stations that cater to local cultural and social interests. Details of current programming are available in local newspapers.

Sydney has two state-run television stations. The ABC's Channel 2 provides news and current affairs coverage, children's programmes and high quality local and international drama. The multicultural Special Broadcasting Service (SBS) caters to Australia's many cultures with foreign language programmes. In addition, there are three commercial television stations, Channels 7, 9 and 10, offering a variety of entertainment from sport and news to soap operas. Many more stations are available on the cable network, Foxtel.

PUBLIC TOILETS

Free public toilets are to be found in Sydney's public places, galleries and museums, department stores and all bus and railway stations. They are generally well serviced and clean. Baby changing facilities

Drinking fountain in the city

are also quite common, particularly in department stores and major museums and galleries.

Clean drinking fountains can be found throughout the city. Spring, or distilled, water is also freely available from dispensers in waiting areas of chemist shops, travel agents and offices.

Standard Australian three-pin plug

ELECTRICAL APPLIANCES

Australia's electrical current is 240–250 volts AC. Electrical plugs can have either two or three pins. Most good hotels will provide 110-volt shaver sockets and hair dryers, but a flat, two- or three-pin adaptor will be necessary for other appliances. These can be bought from electrical stores.

CONVERSION TABLE

Imperial to Metric
1 inch = 2.54 centimetres
1 foot = 30 centimetres
1 mile = 1.6 kilometres
1 ounce = 28 grams
1 pound = 454 grams
1 pint = 0.6 litres
1 gallon = 4.6 litres

Metric to Imperial
1 centimetre = 0.4 inches
1 metre = 3 feet, 3 inches
1 kilometre = 0.6 miles
1 gram = 0.04 ounces
1 kilogram = 2.2 pounds
1 litre = 1.8 pints

DIRECTORY

EMBASSIES AND CONSULATES

Canada
Level 5, 111 Harrington St.
Map 1 B3. *Tel* 9364 3050.

New Zealand
55 Hunter St, **Map** 1 B4.
Tel 8256 2000.

Republic of Ireland
20 Arkana St, Yarralumla
ACT 2600. *Tel* 6273 3022.

United Kingdom
Level 16, The Gateway,
1 Macquarie Place. **Map** 1 B3.
Tel 9247 7521.

USA
MLC Centre, 19–29 Martin Place.
Map 1 B4. *Tel* 9373 9200.

RELIGIOUS SERVICES

Anglican
St Andrew's Cathedral,
Sydney Square, George St.
Map 4 E3. *Tel* 9265 1661.

Baptist
Central Baptist Church,
619 George St. **Map** 4 E4.
Tel 9211 1833.

Catholic
St Mary's Cathedral, Cathedral St.
Map 1 C5. *Tel* 9220 0400.

Interdenominational
Wayside Chapel of the Cross,
29 Hughes St, Potts Point.
Map 2 E5. *Tel* 9358 6577.

Islamic
Surry Hills Mosque,
175 Commonwealth St.
Map 4 F4. *Tel* 9281 0440.

Jewish Orthodox
The Great Synagogue,
187 Elizabeth St. **Map** 1 B5.
Tel 9267 2477.

Presbyterian
St Peters Presbyterian Church,
Cnr Blues Point Rd & Blue St,
North Sydney.
Tel 9955 1662.

Uniting
St Stephen's Church,
197 Macquarie St. **Map** 1 C4.
Tel 9221 1688.

Personal Security and Health

Street crime in Sydney is less prevalent than in many other large cities, but it does exist. You can minimize your risk of becoming a victim of crime by exercising reasonable caution. Members of Sydney's police patrol the city's streets and public transport system in pairs. Mobile police stations, set up at crowded tourist areas and at public events, have proved particularly successful and are popular with the public. Further afield, the surf beaches and natural bushland can present a few dangers of their own, and the following information offers some practical advice for coping with environmental hazards.

Police vehicle

Fire engine

Intensive care ambulance

LOOKING AFTER YOUR PROPERTY

Leave valuables and important documents in your hotel safe, and don't carry large sums of cash with you. Traveller's cheques are generally regarded as the safest way to carry large sums of money. It is also worth photocopying vital douments in case of loss or theft.

Be on guard against purse snatchers and pickpockets in places where big crowds gather. Prime areas for petty theft are popular tourist areas, beaches, markets, sporting venues and on public transport.

Never carry your wallet in an outside pocket where it is an easy target for a thief, and wear shoulder bags and cameras with the strap across your body and the bag or camera in front with the

clasp fastened. If you have a car, always try to park in well-lit, reasonably busy streets. Remember to lock the vehicle securely. It is also important not to leave any valuables or property visible inside the car that might attract a thief.

PERSONAL SAFETY

Sydney has no definite off-limit areas during the day, but it is probably wise to avoid the more unsavoury side streets and lanes of areas such as Kings Cross. If you take reason-able care, you can go into most areas at night, although visitors are advised to stay clear of deserted, poorly lit streets and toilets in parks.

Ambulance paramedic

When travelling by train at night, stay close to security points on platforms and use those parts of the train in the

marked "Nightsafe" area of the platform. Although more expensive, taxis are probably the safest, most efficient means of travel at night, especially for shorter journeys.

MEDICAL TREATMENT AND INSURANCE

Sydney has excellent medical services, with highly trained doctors and modern hospitals. However, overseas visitors are not covered by Australia's "Medicare" government health scheme, and medical, dental and ambulance costs are quite expensive. Before leaving your own country, be sure to purchase adequate insurance for any medical, hospital or dental costs you may incur during your stay. Under a reciprocal arrangement, British passport holders are entitled to free basic emergency medical and hospital treatment.

If you are in need of urgent medical attention, dial 000 for an ambulance or go to the emergency department of the nearest main public hospital. For less urgent treatment, look under "Medical Centres" in the Yellow Pages of the Sydney telephone directory.

The **Travellers' Clinic** offers medical treatment for travel-related illnesses as well as a vaccination service. For non-urgent dental treatment, look under "Dentists" in the Yellow Pages of the telephone directory. The **Emergency Dental Service** has an after-hours phone line for urgent cases.

Policewoman

Policeman

Fire officer

PHARMACIES

Pharmacies are generally known as "chemist shops" in Sydney and are liberally scattered throughout the city and suburbs. They sell a wide range of unrestricted drugs and other medical supplies over the counter. Pharmacists can be a source of advice on simple ailments such as colds and stomach upsets. You can ring **After-Hours Pharmacy Information** if you need to find one that is open outside normal business hours.

Doctor's prescriptions from your own country cannot be filled by an Australian pharmacist unless they are first endorsed by a medical practitioner practising locally.

Chemist shop in The Rocks

ENVIRONMENTAL HAZARDS

Take care when going out in the sun – the ultraviolet rays are very intense, even on cloudy days. You should wear SPF 30+ sun block at all times. A hat and sunglasses are also recommended, as is staying out of the sun between 10am and 2pm (11am and 3pm during daylight saving). When swimming at an ocean beach, check that there are lifesavers

on patrol and swim within the "flagged" areas. In their red and yellow caps, surf lifesavers keep an eye out for changing surf conditions, people in difficulty and surfers coming too close to areas set aside for swimmers only. Lifeguards from district councils are dressed in blue (*see p54*). Look out for signs on the beach indicating that it is dangerous to swim, and do not go in under any circumstances. Popular beaches have loudspeakers to warn people of sudden hazards. If you plan to bushwalk, do

Lifesaving flag not hike alone. Always tell someone where you are going and when you will be back. It is wise to take a map and a basic first-aid kit, as well as food and fresh water, and warm, waterproof clothing.

When walking through the bush, be aware that you are passing through the habitat of native animals, including some poisonous snakes and spiders. It is very unlikely that you will encounter any, but you should wear substantial footwear, keep a close eye on where you step and check around logs and rocks before sitting on them.

Snake bite victims should be kept calm and, most important, remain still while emergency medical help is sought. Try to identify the snake by size and colour so that the correct antivenom can be administered.

The funnel-web (*see p89*) and the redback spider are both poisonous species found in the Sydney region. Anyone bitten by either of these should seek urgent medical attention.

DIRECTORY

EMERGENCY SERVICES

Emergency Dental
Tel 0417 603 322 (after hours, Darling Harbour area). **Dental Hospital** 2 Chalmers St, Surry Hills. *Tel 9293 3200.*

Police, Fire and Ambulance
Tel 000 from any phone. Calls are free (24-hour phoneline).

GENERAL HELP

After-Hours Pharmacy Information
Tel 9966 8377.

HIV/AIDS Information Line
Tel 1800 451 600.

Alcoholics Anonymous
Tel 9488 9820.

Lost Property
State Rail and CityRail trains
Tel 8202 2000.
Sydney Buses
Tel 131 500.
Sydney Ferries
Tel 9207 3101.

NRMA (National Roads and Motorists Association)
Tel 132 132.

Poisons Information Centre
Tel 131 126.

Translating and Interpreting Service
Tel 131 450.

Travellers' Clinic
Suite 1, 13 Springfield Ave, Potts Point. **Map** 2 E5. *Tel 9358 3376.*

Victims' Support Line
Tel 9374 3000.

HOSPITAL EMERGENCY DEPARTMENTS

St Vincent's Hospital
Victoria St (cnr Burton St), Darlinghurst. **Map** 5 B2. *Tel 8382 1111 or 8382 2520.*

Sydney Hospital
Macquarie St (near Martin Place). **Map** 1 C4. *Tel 9382 7111.*

Surf lifesaving sign indicating a dangerous undertow or "rip"

Banking and Local Currency

Sydney is Australia's financial capital. In the central business district are the imposing headquarters of several of the country's leading banks, as well as the Australian head offices of major foreign banks. Visitors will find local, state and national bank branches dotted at convenient intervals throughout the city and suburbs.

There is no limit to the amount of personal funds that visitors can bring into Australia. Most currencies can be exchanged on arrival at the airport (beyond immigration and customs). Although banks generally offer the best exchange rates, money can also be changed at bureaux de change, larger department stores and major hotels.

in smaller outlets. Foreign currency cheques can be cashed at banks, bureaux de change and established hotels.

Banks are generally the best places to go as their fees are lower. Some banks will cash traveller's cheques in Australian dollars without charge. Other banks have varying transaction charges, so shop around.

BUREAUX DE CHANGE

Sydney has many bureaux de change in the popular shopping districts. Most are open Monday to Saturday from 9am to 5:30pm. It can be hard to change money on Sundays.

While their extended hours can make bureaux de change a convenient alternative to a bank, their commissions and fees are generally higher than those charged by major banks.

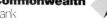

High street bank logos

BANKING

Bank trading hours are generally from 9:30am to 4pm Monday to Thursday, and 9:30am to 5pm on Fridays. Some are also open to midday on Saturdays. Major city banks open 8:30am to 5pm on weekdays.

A valid passport or another form of photographic ID is usually needed if you are cashing

Automatic cash dispenser

traveller's cheques. The current exchange rates, which can vary considerably from day to day, are displayed in the windows or foyers of many banks.

AUTOMATIC CASH DISPENSERS

Automatic cash dispensers can be found in most bank lobbies or on an external wall near the bank's entrance. Ask your own bank which Sydney banks and cash dispensers will accept your card and what the transaction charges will be.

Australian currency (in $20 and $50 denominations) can be withdrawn from your bank

or credit account. Most cash dispensers will accept various Australian bank cards, Visa and MasterCard (Access), as well as certain others. They are not only convenient, but may also provide a better exchange rate than cash transactions.

CREDIT CARDS

All well-known international credit cards are widely accepted in Australia. Major credit cards such as American Express, MasterCard (Access), Visa and Diners Club can be used to book and pay for hotel rooms, airline tickets, car hire, tours and concert and theatre tickets. Credit cards are accepted in most restaurants and shops, where the logos of all recognized cards are usually shown on doors and counter tops. You can also use credit cards in automatic cash dispensers at most banks to withdraw cash.

Credit cards are a convenient way to make phone bookings and avoid the need to carry large sums of cash. They can be especially useful in emergencies or if you need to fly home at short notice.

CASHING TRAVELLER'S CHEQUES

Australian dollar traveller's cheques issued by major names like Travelex and American Express are usually accepted (with a passport) in larger shops in Sydney. You may have problems, however,

LOCAL CURRENCY

The Australian currency is the Australian dollar ($ or A$), which breaks down into 100 cents (c). The decimal currency system now in place has been in operation since 1966.

Single cents may still be used for some prices, but as the Australian 1c and 2c coins are no longer being circulated, the total amount to be paid will be rounded up or down to the nearest five cent amount.

It can be difficult to get $50 and $100 notes changed, so avoid using them in smaller shops and cafés and, more particularly, when paying for taxi fares. If you do not have change, it is always wise to tell the taxi driver before you start your journey to avoid any misunderstandings. Otherwise, when you arrive at your destination, you may have to find change at the nearest shop or automatic cash dispenser.

To improve security, as well as increase their circulation life, all Australian bank notes have now been plasticized.

Bank Notes

Australian bank notes are produced in denominations of $5, $10, $20, $50 and $100. There are two types of bank note in circulation: the older paper notes, which are still legal tender, and plasticized notes in similar colours.

$100 note

$50 note

$20 note

$10 note

$5 note

5 cents (5c)

10 cents (10c)

20 cents (20c)

50 cents (50c)

1 dollar ($1)

2 dollars ($2)

Coins

Coins currently in use are 5c, 10c, 20c, 50c, $1 and $2 (shown here at actual sizes). There are several 50c coins in circulation; all are the same shape, but have different commemorative images on the face. The 10c and 20c coins are useful for local telephone calls (see p226).

Using Sydney's Telephones

Sydney's public payphones are generally maintained in good working order. Their prevalence on streets throughout the city and suburbs – as well as in hotels, cafés, shops and public buildings – means that users seldom have to queue to make calls. To save money, avoid making calls from hotel rooms. Hotels set their own rates and a call from your room will invariably cost more than one made from a payphone in the hotel lobby.

Using a mobile phone at Bondi

Telstra Corporation logo

PUBLIC TELEPHONES

Most payphones accept both coins and phonecards, although some operate solely on phonecards and major credit cards.

Phonecards can be bought from selected newsagents and news kiosks displaying the Telstra sign. All public telephones have a hand receiver and 12-button key pad, though they may vary in shape and colour, as well as instructions (in English only) and a list of useful phone numbers. The **Telstra Phone Centre** is open 24 hours and **Global Gossip** is open until midnight, but you can also send a fax from there.

Telstra payphones

PAYPHONE CHARGES

Local calls (those with the 02 area code) are untimed and cost 40 cents. Charges for long-distance calls can be obtained at no cost by calling 012 (for within Australia) and 0102 (for international). Phonecard and credit card phones debit 40-cent units in the same way as other telephones; however, all credit card calls have a $1.20 minimum fee, making them uneconomical for local calls. Long-distance calls are less expensive if you dial without the help of an operator. Most international calls can be dialled direct and there is little need for operator assistance unless you wish to make a reverse-charge call. Savings can be made on both national and international calls

by phoning during off-peak periods. In general, peak and discount calling times fall into three ascending price brackets: economy, 6pm Sat–8am Mon, or 10pm–8am daily; night rate, 6pm–10pm Mon–Fri; day rate, 8am–6pm Mon–Sat. Special rates and times may apply to calls to certain countries.

MOBILE PHONES

Mobile telephones are used extensively in Australia. You can rent one from Vodafone at the airport international arrivals hall. Rates cost $4–10 a day (calls are extra), and you'll need a credit card and your passport. Other rental companies are listed in the Yellow Pages telephone directory under "Mobile Telephones". Ask your service provider about whether your own digital mobile phone will work in Australia.

FAX SERVICES

Most Sydney post offices offer a fax service. There are also many copy shops that will send or receive faxes on your behalf. Look under the heading "Facsimile &/or Telex Communication Services" in the Yellow Pages phone directory for an agency near you.

Post offices charge per-page fees to send a fax to another fax machine within Australia. The cost per page is reduced after the first page. A fax can be sent to a postal address for the same charge, in which case the fax is sent to the local post office and delivered with the mail, usually the following day. A same-day fax to a postal

USING A COIN/PHONECARD OPERATED PHONE

1 Lift the receiver and wait for the dialling tone.

2 Insert the coins required or insert a Telstra phonecard in the direction of the arrows shown on the card.

3 Dial the number and wait to be connected.

5 Replace the receiver at the end of the call and withdraw your card or collect any unused coins. Payphones do not give change.

6 When you finish your call, the phonecard is returned to you with a hole punched in it showing the approximate remaining value.

4 The display shows you how much value is left on your phonecard or coins. When your coins or phonecard run out you will hear a warning beep. To continue, insert more coins if using coins. If using a phonecard, remove the old card and insert a new one.

Phonecards
Telstra phonecards are available in $2, $5, $10, $20 and $50 denominations.

address must be dispatched by 1pm, and there is a delivery fee. Delivery within 2 hours is available for a higher charge.

Overseas faxes can also be faxed to another fax machine or sent to a postal address. The cost is on a per-page rate, as with faxes to local numbers.

USEFUL INFORMATION

Telstra Phone Centre
231 Elizabeth St. **Map** 4 F3.

Global Gossip
790 George St. **Map** 4 E5.

REACHING THE RIGHT NUMBER

- To ring Sydney from the UK, dial 0061 2, then the local number.
- To ring Sydney from the USA and Canada, dial 011 61 2, then the local number.
- For long-distance direct-dial calls outside your local area code, but within Australia (STD calls), dial the appropriate area code, then the number.
- For international direct-dial calls (IDD calls): dial **0011**, followed by the country code (USA and Canada: 1; UK: 44; New Zealand: 64), then the city or area code (omit initial 0) and then the local number.
- International directory enquiries: dial **1225**.
- Local directory enquiries: dial **12455**.
- STD directory enquiries: dial **12455**.
- International operator assistance: dial **1234**.
- Local operator assistance: dial **1234**.
- Reverse charge calls within Australia: dial **12550**.
- International reverse charge calls: dial **12550** or **1800 801 800** to access operator in home country.
- Numbers beginning with **1800** are toll-free numbers.
- Numbers with the prefix **0414, 0415, 0418, 0421**, etc are mobile or car phones.
- *See also* Emergency Numbers, *p223*.

Postal Services

Australia Post logo

Post offices are open 9am–5pm week days. Almost all post offices offer a wide range of services, including poste restante, fax, money orders, electronic post, express delivery, parcel post and telegrams, as well as stamps, envelopes, packaging, stationery and postcards. Stamps can also be bought from hotels and shops where postcards are sold, and from some newsagents.

Australia Post postman

POSTAL SERVICES

All domestic mail is first class and usually arrives within one to five days, depending on distance. Be sure to include postcodes on mailing addresses to avoid delays in delivery.

Express Post, for which you need to buy one of the special yellow and white envelopes sold in post offices, guarantees next-day delivery in designated areas of Australia. International air mail takes from five to ten days to reach most countries.

Labels used for overseas mail

Typical stamps used for local mail

Stamp from a scenic series issue

There are two types of international express mail. EMS International Courier is the fastest service and will reach nearly all overseas destinations within two to three days. Alternatively, Express Post International will reach most destinations throughout the world in four to five days.

Standard and express postboxes

POSTBOXES

Sydney has both red and yellow postboxes. The red boxes are for normal postal service; yellow boxes are for Express Post within Australia.

POSTE RESTANTE

Address poste restante letters to Poste Restante, GPO Sydney, NSW 2000, but collect them from 310 George St, Hunter Connection, opposite Wynyard Station. The GPO is purely a retail shop and mail centre. You will need to show your passport or other proof of identity before collecting mail sent to you poste restante.

USEFUL INFORMATION

General Post Office (GPO)
1 Martin Place. **Map** 4 E1.
Tel 131 318 (enquiries). 8:15am–5pm Mon–Fri. **Poste Restante** 8:15am–5:30pm Mon–Fri. **Tel** 9244 3732.

TRAVEL INFORMATION

Travelling to Sydney can involve a long and tiring flight. Visitors from Europe can take advantage of stopovers in Asia; those from the United States could break their journey in Hawaii or one of the other Pacific Islands. A break can mean the difference between arriving in Sydney jet-lagged or stepping off the plane refreshed and ready to take in the sights. Sydney is linked to Australia's other state capitals

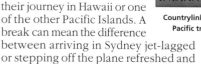

Countrylink and Indian Pacific train logos

by efficient air, rail and coach connections. Long-distance coach travel is comfortable and relatively inexpensive; interstate trains are more expensive, but they are generally a great deal faster. People travelling by coach should consider taking one of the scenic routes with stopovers offered by some coach companies. Car travellers can also plan their journey to Sydney to pass through scenic areas.

ARRIVING BY AIR

International flights to Sydney can be expensive. They are also often heavily booked, especially between the months of December and February. December is peak season, and therefore the most expensive time to fly. Shoulder season, from 1 January to 12 April, is slightly less costly.

APEX fares are often the cheapest. Some stipulate set arrival and departure dates, or carry penalties if you cancel your flight. Round-the-world fares can be good value and are increasingly popular. **Qantas Airways** Virgin Blue and Jetstar, Australia's international and major domestic carriers, link Sydney with other cities and major tourist destinations. Other domestic airlines service shorter routes. Flights within Australia are not cheap, but you can save by booking in advance (although restrictions apply). Overseas visitors with international tickets are eligible

for discounts on internal flights. You can book cheap domestic and international flights at Sydney airport's website.

ARRIVING AT SYDNEY AIRPORT

The main gateway to Australia is Sydney (Kingsford Smith) Airport. As a result of this, congestion, especially at peak periods, can sometimes cause irritating delays. There is a duty-free shop for arriving passengers on the incoming side of the baggage collection and customs area. Just beyond this is Tourism NSW's information kiosk *(see p218)*, where you can book accommodation. The terminal also has a range of other services including shops, a bureau de change, internet facilities, ATMs and car hire desks.

Flight arrivals and departures are displayed on TV monitors and the whereabouts of toilets and other airport facilities are indicated using internationally recognized symbols.

Queueing for taxis at the Sydney Airport domestic terminal

GETTING INTO THE CITY

Sydney airport is about 9 km (5½ miles) from the CBD, 10 minutes on the new rail link or a 30-minute express bus journey. Catch a bus or taxi outside the terminals, or CityRail from underground stations at both terminals.

State Transit has three routes serving the airport: Metro route 400 from Burwood to Bondi Junction via the airport, Metro route 100 to Dee Why and Metro route 353 to Bondi Junction.

KST Sydney Airporter leaves for Darling Harbour, the city and Kings Cross every 20-30 minutes from 5am until the last flight. It will drop you off anywhere in these areas, but only picks up from accommodation. You should ring to book a seat 24 hours before you want to depart.

ARRIVING BY SEA

The most delightful way to arrive in Sydney is by ship. Passenger ships berth at the overseas passenger terminals at Circular Quay and Darling

International flight arriving at Sydney Airport

The *QEII* passenger ship berthed at Circular Quay

Harbour. At either terminal, you will find the city on the doorstep. Information booths, tour booking centres, buses, trains, ferries, taxis and water taxis are all close at hand.

ARRIVING BY COACH

Most long-distance bus or coach services arrive at the **Sydney Coach Terminal** at Central Railway Station. The terminal has left-luggage lockers, while shower facilities and food outlets are found in the station above.

Competition between the coach companies is fierce, so it is worth shopping around to get the best price.

ARRIVING BY CAR

The four major routes into Sydney are the Pacific Highway from the north; the Great Western Highway from the west; the Princes Highway, which follows the coast from Melbourne; and the Hume Highway, which runs inland from Melbourne.

As they approach Sydney, these routes feed into freeways or motorways, which in turn lead to priority routes known as "Metroads" (marked by blue and white hexagonal badges). When you reach the city out-skirts, look for the Metroad signs and stay in the lanes as marked for the city centre.

ARRIVING BY TRAIN

All interstate and regional trains arrive at Central Railway Station. Australia's nationwide rail network is known by a different name in each state, but it still operates cohesively. The **Countrylink** reservations line will answer queries and take bookings (6:30am–10pm daily) for train services throughout Australia.

CityRail also has slower, but cheaper, services from nearby centres on which seats cannot be booked. The Bus, Train & Ferry Infoline *(see p230)* has information about CityRail's country services.

Country service passenger train waiting at Central Railway Station

DIRECTORY

SYDNEY AIRPORT

Airport Information
Tel 9667 9111. **www.**
sydneyairport.com.au

AIRLINE INFORMATION

Air New Zealand
Reservations
Tel 132 476.
Arrivals and departures
Tel 1800 147 332.

Air Canada
Reservations
Tel 1300 655 767.
Arrivals and departures
Tel 131 223.

American Airlines
Reservations
Tel 1300 650 747.

British Airways
Reservations
Tel 1300 767 177.
Arrivals and Departures
Tel 131 223.

Japan Airlines
Reservations and flight information
Tel 9272 1111.

Qantas Airways
Reservations
Tel 131 313.
Arrivals and departures
Tel 131 223.

Singapore Airlines
Reservations *Tel 131 011.*
Arrivals *Tel 131 223.*

Thai Airways
Reservations
Tel 1300 651 960.
Arrivals and Departures
Tel 131 223.

United Airlines
Reservations and information
Tel 131 777 or 9317 8933.

AIRPORT HOTELS

Hilton Sydney Airport
Tel 9518 2000.

Stamford Sydney Airport
Tel 9317 2200.

LONG-DISTANCE COACH SERVICES

Sydney Coach Terminal
Cnr of Eddy Ave & Pitt St.
Map 4 E5. *Tel* 9281 9366.

McCafferty's Greyhound
Tel 132 030 or 131 499.

Premier Motor Service
490 Pitt St.
Tel 133 410.

TRAIN INFORMATION

Central Railway Station
General inquiries
Tel 131 500.
Lost property
Tel 9379 3341.

Countrylink
Reservations *Tel 132 2*
Arrivals *Tel 132 232.*

AIRPORT BUS

KST Sydney Airporter
Tel 9666 998
www.kst.cc

Getting Around Sydney

SydneyPass ticket

In general, the best way to see Sydney's many sights and attractions is on foot, coupled with use of the public transport system. Buses, trains and the new light railway will take visitors to within easy walking distance of anywhere in the inner city. They also serve the suburbs and outlying areas. Passenger ferries provide a fast and scenic means of travel between the city and harbourside suburbs. The best selection of maps, plus fascinating aerial and satellite views and historical maps, can be found at **Map World**.

People crossing at pedestrian lights in the centre of the city

WALKING

Take care when walking around the city. Vehicles are driven on the left and often move quickly. It is wise to use pedestrian crossings. There are two types. Push-button crossings are found at traffic lights. Wait for the green man signal and do not cross at lights if the red warning sign is on or flashing. Zebra crossings are marked by yellow and black signs. Make sure vehicles are stopping before you cross.

̄OMPOSITE TICKETS

 ̄velling on Sydney's trains
 ̄s and harbour ferries is
 ̄xpensive, especially if
 ̄e one of the composite
 ̄or TravelPasses that
 ̄ly available.
 ̄an be bought from
 ̄ses Transit Shop,
 ̄ons, newsagents
 ̄ds where the
 ̄ack "bus tickets

sold here" sign is on display. For some visitors, TravelTen or FerryTen *(see p234)* tickets, which can be used on buses and ferries respectively, may prove useful.

TRAVELTEN TICKETS

Travelten tickets entitle you to make ten journeys on State Transit buses. Bus routes are divided into parts, or "sections". Tickets are colour-coded according to the number of sections for which they can be used on each journey.

These tickets are useful if you need to travel the same route a number of times. Most visitors use a Blue TravelTen, valid for 1–2 sections, a Brown TravelTen valid for 3–5 sections or a Red TravelTen, valid for 6–9 sections.

TravelTen tickets can be transferred from one user to another and can be shared on the same journey.

A Blue Weekly TravelPass, Red TravelTen and Blue TravelTen

TRAVELPASSES

The most economical of th ̄ composite tickets are the TravelPasses. These allow you unlimited seven-day travel on Sydney's public buses, trains and ferries as long as you travel within stipulated zones.

They are sold in "bus only" or "bus–ferry" and "bus–ferry–train" combinations. The Red TravelPass, a combined bus–ferry–train ticket, covers all zones included in the usual tourist jaunts. The slightly more expensive Green TravelPass allows for bus, train and ferry travel over a wider area.

SydneyPass

The SydneyPass allows either three or five days' use in any eight-day period, or seven consecutive days of unlimited bus and ferry travel, including trips on the Manly Jetcat, three Sydney Harbour cruises *(see p235)*, the Sydney Explorer and the Bondi Explorer buses and the Airport Express services *(see p228)*.

You can buy a SydneyPass direct from the driver on any Airport Express or Explorer bus, travel agents where you see the SydneyPass sign on display, Circular Quay ferry wharf and State Transit Information and Ticket Kiosks.

All-Day Tickets

If you have only one day for sighseeing, a Daytripper ticket may be useful. Travel on a Daytripper includes unlimited rides on all blue and white STA buses, CityRail suburban area trains and all STA Sydney Ferries. It is not valid on tourism services.

USEFUL INFORMATION

Map World
280 Pitt St. **Map** 4 E3. *Tel* 9261 3601. **www**.mapworld.net.au

Sydney Buses Transit Shop
Railway Square
Cnr George and Lee Sts.
Map 4 D4.
Circular Quay
Cnr Loftus and Alfred Sts.
Map 1 B3.
Tel 9244 1990
Queen Victoria Building
York St. **Map** 1 A5.
Wynyard Park
Carrington St. **Map** 1 A4.

Bus, Train & Ferry Infoline
Tel 131 500.

Sydney Ferries Information Office
Opposite Jetty No. 4, Circular Quay.
Map 1 B3. *Tel* 9207 3166.

Travelling by Bus

Sydney buses provides a punctual service that links up conveniently with the city's rail and ferry systems. As well as covering city and suburban areas, there are three regular bus routes that serve the airport *(see p228)* and two excellent sightseeing buses – the Sydney Explorer and the Bondi Explorer. The **Transport Infoline** can advise you on routes, fares and journey times for all Sydney Buses. Armed with the map on the inside back cover of this book and a composite ticket, you can avoid the difficulties and expense of city parking.

Automatic stamping machine for validating composite bus tickets

USING SYDNEY BUSES

Route numbers and journey destinations are displayed on the front, back and left side of all Sydney buses. An "X" in front of the number means that it is an express bus. Daytripper and single-journey tickets can be purchased on board regular buses. Single fares are bought from the driver. Try to have coins at hand as drivers are not always able to change large notes. You will be given a ticket valid for that journey only – if you change buses you will have to pay again.

If using a TravelTen ticket or TravelPass, you must insert it in the automatic stamping machine as you board. Ensure the arrow is facing you and pointing downwards. If sharing a TravelTen, insert it into the machine once for each person. Front seats must be given up to elderly or disabled people. Eating, drinking, smoking or playing music is prohibited on buses. To signal that you wish to alight, press one of the stop buttons – they are mounted on the vertical handrails on each seat – well before the bus reaches your stop. The doors

BUS STOPS

Bus stops are indicated by yellow and black signs displaying a profile of a bus and a boarding passenger. Sometimes the numbers of the buses travelling along the route are listed below this symbol.

Timetables are usually found on the bus stop sign or nearby shelter. The Sunday timetable also applies to public holidays. While efforts are made to keep bus stop timetables as up-to-date as possible, it is always best to carry a current bus timetable with you.

Express bus

They may be collected from some tourist information facilities and are also available at Sydney Buses Transit Shops in the city, as well as at Bondi Junction and the Manly ferry wharf.

SIGHTSEEING BY BUS

Two Sydney bus services, the distinctive red Sydney Explorer and the blue Bondi Explorer, offer flexible sightseeing with informative commentaries. The Sydney Explorer bus covers a 36-km (20-mile) circuit and stops at 26 of the city's most popular sights and attractions. The Bondi Explorer travels through a number of Sydney's eastern suburbs, taking in much of the area's coastal and harbour scenery along the way.

Sydney Explorer Red buses run daily every 20 minutes, the blue every 30 minutes. The great advantage of these services is that you can explore at will, getting on and off the buses as often as you wish in the course of a day.

The best way to make the most of your journey is to choose the sights you most want to see and plan a basic itinerary. Be sure to note the opening times of museums, art galleries and shops; the bus drivers can advise you about these. Explorer bus stops are clearly marked by the colours of the bus (red or blue).

Tickets can be bought on the buses or from Sydney Buses Transit Shops.

A typical Sydney Bus used for standard services

The Bondi Explorer bus

The Sydney Explorer bus

Travelling by Train and Monorail

CityRail logo

As well as providing the key transport link between the city and suburbs, Sydney's railway network also serves a large part of the central business district. The City Circle loop is the main line running through the city centre stopping at Central, Town Hall, Wynyard, Circular Quay, St James and Museum. All suburban lines connect with the City Circle at Central station. A convenient alternative for exploring the museums and shops of Darling Harbour is to use the Metro Light Rail (MLR).

FINDING YOUR WAY AROUND BY RAIL

Operating in the Darling Harbour Area, Sydney's newest transport system is the Metro Light Rail (MLR). It runs from Central Railway Station, along the harbourside and through Pyrmont and Glebe to Star City or Lilyfield. These environmentally friendly trains offer a quicker and quieter way of visiting places of interest between Glebe and Darling Harbour, and there are plans in the pipeline to extend the MLR to Circular Quay.

Buy tickets on board from the conductor. The daily service runs trains every eight to ten minutes at peak times, every 15 minutes between 10pm and midnight, and every 30 minutes until 7am.

Use CityRail to get to outlying suburbs and to the airport. Trains run from 4:30am to about midnight. At night, stand in the "Nightsafe" areas marked on the platform and use carriages near the train guard, signalled by a blue light. After midnight, night-ride buses travel along rail routes, and all routes pick up from George St and Town Hall. Your return rail ticket is valid.

SIGHTSEEING BY MONORAIL AND METRO LIGHT RAIL (MLR)

More novel than practical, the Monorail runs along a 12-minute scenic loop through central Sydney, Chinatown and Darling Harbour. It is an easy way to travel and sightsee if you do not feel like walking.

There are seven stops on the Monorail route: City Centre, Darling Park, Harbourside, Convention, Paddy's Markets, World Square and Galeries Victoria. Trains run from 7am–10pm, Mondays to Thursdays, 7am–midnight Fridays and Saturdays and 8am–10pm Sunday. A Monorail Day Pass allows

Pedestrian concourse outside Central Railway Station

USING THE CITYRAIL ROUTE MAP

The different CityRail lines are colour-coded and route maps are displayed at all CityRail stations and inside train carriages. Distances shown on the map are not to scale and the routes that lines are seen to take should not be relied upon when working out the direction of travel.

Station for changing between lines

Station serving two lines

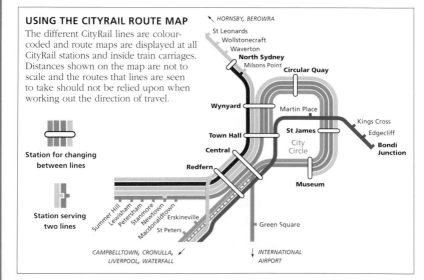

unlimited rides all day.
It can be bought at any of the monorail information booths.

The MLR stops at many places around the Pyrmont area, including Paddy's Markets, Chinatown, Darling Harbour, the Maritime Museum, Star City, and the Fish Market.

Monorail leaving the city centre, with Sydney Tower in background

COUNTRY AND INTER-URBAN TRAINS

State Rail has **Countrylink Travel Centres** throughout the city and suburbs, which provide information about its country rail and coach services and also take bookings. The NSW Discovery Pass, valid for one month, allows unlimited economy travel by rail and coach in New South Wales.

Inter-urban trains run to the Blue Mountains to Sydney's west, Wollongong in the south and Gosford and Newcastle to the north (see p229).

USEFUL INFORMATION

CityRail Information
Central Railway Station
Map 4 E5.
Tel 131500.
Circular Quay Railway Station
Map 1 B3.
Tel 9224 3553.
www.cityrail.info

Countrylink Travel Centres
Central Railway Station Sydney Terminal. **Map** 4 E5.
Tel 132232.
www. metrolightrail.com.au

Metro Light Rail and Monorail *Tel* 9285 5600.

MAKING A JOURNEY BY CITYRAIL

1 Study the CityRail route map. Route lines are distinguished by colour, so simply trace the line from where you are to your destination, noting where you need to change and make connections.

2 Buy tickets from ticket dispensing machines or ticket booths at stations (TravelPass tickets can only be bought at stations). To obtain your ticket from a dispensing machine, press the button to indicate destination, then the ticket type (single, return, etc). Insert money into the slot, then collect your ticket and any change.

3 To pass through the ticket barrier, insert your ticket (arrow side up) into the slot at the front of barrier machines (indicated by green arrows). Take your ticket as it comes out of the machine and the barrier gates or turnstile will open.

4 To find the right platform, follow the signs with the same colour code as the line you need and the name of the line's final station.

Platform 20 City Circle via Museum
Platform 21 City Circle via Museum

5 On the platform, display signs show all the stations the line travels through. Stations at which the next train will stop are lit up and are announced as the train arrives at the station.

indicates train stops at that station.

Town Hall	Gordon	*Berowra
Wynyard	Pymble	Cowan
Milson's Point	Turramurra	Town Hall
North Sydney	Warrawee	Wynyard
Waverton	Wahroonga	Circular Quay
Wollstonecraft	Waitara	St. James
St. Leonards	Hornsby	Museum
Artarmon	Change at	Special
Chatswood	Hornby for	Terminates
Roseville	Asquith	8 Car Train
Lindfield	Mount Colah	6 Car Train
Killara	Mt. Kuring-gai	4 Car Train

Tickets
Keep your ticket – you will need it at the end of your journey and possibly to show a ticket inspector on the train. A TravelPass (left) and a single-fare ticket (right) are shown.

Travelling by Ferry and Water Taxi

For more than a century, Sydney Ferries have been a picturesque, as well as a practical, feature of the Sydney scene. Today, they are as popular as ever. Travelling by ferry is both a pleasure and an efficient way to travel between Sydney's harbour suburbs. Sightseeing cruises are operated by various private companies as well as by Sydney Ferries Corporation (see p219). Water taxis can be a convenient, but pricey, alternative to the ferry.

A State Transit harbour ferry

SIGHTSEEING BY FERRY

Sydney Ferries offers well-priced harbour cruises that take in the history and sights of Sydney Harbour. They are a cheap alternative to the commercial harbour cruises. There are morning, afternoon and evening tours, all with a commentary. Tickets can be purchased from the ferry ticket offices or from local travel agents. Food and drinks are available on board, or you can bring your own.

Sydney ferries coming and going at Circular Quay Ferry Terminal

USING SYDNEY'S FERRIES

There is a constant procession of Sydney Ferries traversing the harbour between 6am and midnight daily. They service most of Sydney Harbour and several stops along the Parramatta River. Frequent services run to and from Manly, Darling Harbour, Balmain, Parramatta, Taronga Zoo, Neutral Bay, Pyrmont Bay, Balmain/Woolwich, Mosman and Rose Bay, with numerous stops en route. Sydney Buses (see p231) provide convenient connections at most wharves.

Staff at the Sydney Ferries Information Office (see p230), open 7am–6pm daily, will answer passenger queries and provide ferry timetables. You can also phone the Transport Infoline on 131500 (see p230) for advice about connections, destinations and fares between 6am and 10pm daily.

MAKING A JOURNEY BY FERRY

All ferry journeys start at the Circular Quay Ferry Terminal. Electronic destination boards at the entrance to each wharf indicate the wharf from which your ferry will leave, and also give departure times and all stops made en route.

Tickets can be bought from ticket booths located on the wharves at Circular Quay. You can also buy your ticket from the vending machines. At Circular Quay and Manly Wharf there are automatic ticket barrier machines. Put your ticket into the slot with the arrow-side up and the arrow pointing into the slot, to board your ferry.

Manly's large ferry terminal is serviced by ferries, Jetcats and SuperCats. Tickets and information can be obtained from the ticket windows located in the centre of the terminal. No food or drink is permitted on JetCat or SuperCat ferries.

Most, but not all, wharves have wheelchair access. Passengers should check before travelling.

Morning Harbour Cruise

This 1-hour cruise takes you through the main reach of Sydney's harbour. The cruise goes past Shark and Clarke Islands, travelling close to

A State Transit SuperCat

Manly Ferry Collaroy

A State Transit RiverCat ferry

Electronic destination board for all ferries leaving Circular Quay

Sydney Opera House, the Royal Botanic Gardens and Fort Denison. You will also pass beautiful bays and homes with waterfront gardens. You cruise under Harbour Bridge before returning to Circular Quay.
Departures Wharf 4, Circular Quay. 10am & 11:15am daily.

Afternoon Harbour Cruise
This cruise to Watsons Bay and Middle Harbour takes around 2½ hours. The ferry passes the Opera House and Royal Botanic Gardens, then follows the southern shore past Elizabeth Bay, Double Bay, Rose Bay and Watsons Bay. You can view some stunning waterfront gardens and homes and harbour beaches on the way. In the upper reaches of Middle Harbour, the ferry passes between the dense bush covered sandstone hills.
Departures Wharf 4, Circular Quay. 1pm Mon–Fri, 1:30pm Sat, Sun & pub hols.

Evening Harbour Lights
Spectacular night-time views of the city feature on this 1½-hour cruise, which travels as far as Shark Island and Goat Island. This is the best way to see the colourful lights that illuminate the Opera House and Harbour Bridge, and to enjoy the glorious sunsets of summer as they silhouette the city. You will cruise past the Opera House and Fort Denison, beneath the Harbour Bridge, skirting Goat Island and old Balmain and glimpsing the lights of vibrant Darling Harbour before finally returning to Circular Quay.
Departures Wharf 4, Circular Quay. 8pm Mon–Sat.

Other Cruises
There is also an abundance of commercial sightseeing cruises. **Australian Travel Specialists** has information on all river and harbour cruises

from Circular Quay and Darling Harbour. They do not charge a booking fee.

WATER TAXIS

Small, fast taxi boats will carry passengers to any number of destinations on the harbour. You can flag them down like normal cabs if you spot one cruising for a fare. Try Circular Quay near the Overseas Passenger Terminal or King Street Wharf. You can also telephone for a water taxi. They will pick up and drop off at any navigable pier. Rates vary, and some charge for the boat (about $40) and a fee per person (about $10).

A water taxi on Sydney Harbour

USEFUL INFORMATION

Australian Travel Specialists
Wharf 6, Circular Quay; Harbourside Shopping Centre, Darling Harbour. *Tel* 9211 3192.

Sydney Ferries Lost Property
Wharf 3, Circular Quay. **Map** 1 B3. *Tel* 9207 3101.

Water Taxi Companies
Harbour Taxi Boats *Tel* 9555 1155.
Harbour Water Taxis *Tel* 9299 0199.

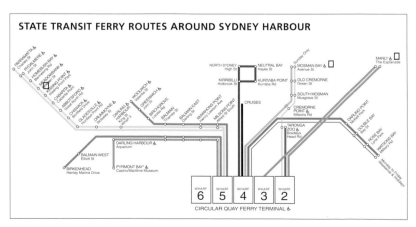

STATE TRANSIT FERRY ROUTES AROUND SYDNEY HARBOUR

Travelling by Car and Bicycle

Driving is not the ideal way to get around central Sydney, although cars can be very convenient for journeys into the suburbs and further afield. The city road network is confusing, traffic is congested and parking can be expensive. If arriving in Sydney by car, make sure that your hotel provides parking. Cycling in the city can also be difficult and dangerous for those unfamiliar with Sydney's traffic and road conditions.

Petrol station with full driveway service in Balmain *(see p131)*

DRIVING IN SYDNEY

If you are planning to use a car to drive around greater Sydney, you will need a good street directory. It is best to avoid the peak-hour traffic periods (about 7:30–9:30am and 5–7:30pm). Regular traffic update reports are broadcast on many radio stations.

On a positive note, petrol is relatively cheap, being a little more expensive than in North America, but about half the price of petrol in Europe. Dispensed by the litre, it comes in super, regular unleaded, premium unleaded and diesel grades. Most petrol stations are self-service and many of them accept major credit cards.

Kerbside Traffic Signs
Always pay strict attention to Sydney's parking and traffic signs as fines for infringements can be very expensive.

DRIVING REGULATIONS

Overseas visitors can use their usual driving licences to drive in New South Wales, but must have proof that they are simply visiting. When driving ensure you have your licence or an International Driver's Permit.

Australians drive on the left-hand side of the road and overtake on the right. Speed limits and distances are given in metric measurements. The speed limit is 50 km/h (30 mph) in the city and most suburbs, and 100–110 km/h (60–65 mph) on motorways, freeways and highways, unless otherwise indicated. Drivers and passengers must wear seatbelts.

Drivers must give way to all police vehicles, fire engines and ambulances. At some clearly marked intersections, drivers are allowed to make a left-hand turn at a red light after stopping, but must give way to pedestrians.

The 0.05 per cent maximum blood alcohol level for drivers is enforced by random breath tests. Drivers who are found to be over the legal limit will incur heavy fines, suspension or loss of licence, and even prison sentences. Should you be involved in an accident while over the limit (whether or not you are at fault), your insurance may be invalidated.

The NRMA *(see p223)* has a free 24-hour roadside service for members. Most car hire companies provide free roadside emergency service.

A toll is charged every time you use the new Cross City Tunnel, you can buy 1–7 day passes, set up an account or charge a tag online.

Traffic on the Harbour Bridge

PARKING

Parking in Sydney is strictly regulated with fines for any infringements. In certain areas, particularly along clearways (indicated by signposts), vehicles are towed away if parked illegally. Contact the **Sydney Traffic Control Centre** to find out where your vehicle has been impounded if this happens. There are car parks scattered around the city area. They vary widely, both in how much they charge and their opening hours. Most close after midnight, but many close earlier – check carefully before parking your car for the evening.

Look out for the blue and white "P" signs or seek out one of the metered parking zones. Many metered parking zones apply 7 days a week and as late as 10pm. This varies from council to council.

Beware of kangaroos crossing

CAR HIRE

Metropolitan rates offered by the major agencies (**Avis, Budget, Hertz** and **Thrifty**) range from about $75 a day for a small car to $100 a day for a large car. These rates usually include comprehensive insurance. However, many of the other agencies listed in the Yellow Pages telephone directory offer highly competitive prices, and rentals can be obtained for as little as $35–$40 a day. Be sure to read the fine print on hire agreements as deals may not be as attractive as they first seem – and be aware of the costs you could incur in the event of an accident if you opt for less than full insurance cover.

Generally, rates are lower if you hire for more than three days, or if you take a limited, low-kilometre deal. Charges may apply if you drive over 100 km (60 miles) a day, travel over rough rural roads or for late returns. You must over 21 years old to hire a car from some companies and if you do not have a credit card, you will need to leave a deposit. Make sure you return the car full of fuel, as you will be charged a premium rate for filling it.

TAXIS

Taxis are plentiful in Sydney in the city and inner suburbs, although they can be scarce "bewcen shifts" at 2:30–3:15pm. There are taxi ranks at many city locations and taxis are often found outside the large city hotels. The four main taxi companies provide a reliable telephone service; book your taxi at least 15 minutes before you need it.

Meters indicate the fare plus any extras, such as booking fees and waiting time. Fares, as well as extra charges, are regulated and are more expensive after 10pm. Tips are not normally expected, but it is customary to round the fare up to the next dollar.

Taxis designed to accommodate disabled passengers can be booked through any of the

Cycling in Centennial Park

major companies. Smoking in taxis is forbidden by law in New South Wales.

SYDNEY BY BICYCLE

Visitors would be well advised to restrict their cycling to designated cycling tracks, or to areas where motor traffic is likely to be light. Helmets are compulsory by law.

Keen cyclists who wish to take advantage of Sydney's undulating terrain and pleasant weather can seek advice from **Bicycle New South Wales**. It publishes a handbook, *Bike It, Sydney*, which has a map of good cycling routes. **Bonza Bike Tours** offers entertaining and energetic guided cycling tours, which take in many of Sydney's best sights.

Centennial Park is one of the most popular spots; on weekends and every evening packs of riders can be seen cycling through the park. You can take your bicycle on CityRail trains *(see p232)*, but you may have to pay an extra child's fare.

Cabcharge is for account customers only, but some taxis also accept American Express and Diners Club.

The orange light, when lit, shows the taxi is available.

The taxi company name and phone number are displayed on front driver and passenger doors.

Taxi licence number

The taxi driver's photo licence must be on clear display within the taxi.

DIRECTORY

CAR HIRE COMPANIES

Avis
Tel 9353 9000 or 136 333

Budget
Tel 132 727.

Hertz
Tel 133 039.

Thrifty
Tel 1300 367 227.

TAXI COMPANIES

Legion Cabs
Tel 131 451.

Premier Cabs
Tel 131 017

RSL Cabs
Tel 9581 1111.

Taxis Combined
Tel 8332 8888.

CYCLE HIRE AND INFORMATION

Bicycle New South Wales
Level 5, 822 George St (entrance on Little Regent St).
Map 4 D5. *Tel* 9281 4099.

Bonza Bike Tours
Tel 9331 1127.

Centennial Park Cycles
50 Clovelly Rd, Randwick (near Centennial Park).
Tel 9398 5027.

Inner City Cycles
151 Glebe Point Rd, Glebe.
Tel 9660 6605.

Woolys Wheels
82 Oxford St, Paddington.
Map 5 B3. *Tel* 9331 2671.

USEFUL NUMBERS

Infringement Processing Bureau
130 George St, Parramatta.
Tel 1300 138 118.

Sydney Traffic Control Centre
Tel 132 701 (24-hour service).

Taxi Complaints
Department of Transport,
418a Elizabeth St, Surry Hills.
Map 4 E3. *Tel* 1800 648 478.

Cross City Tunnel
www.crosscity.com.au

SYDNEY STREET FINDER

The page grid superimposed on the *Area by Area* map below shows which parts of Sydney are covered in this *Street Finder*. Map references given for all sights, hotels, restaurants, shopping and entertainment venues described in this guide refer to the maps in this section. All the major sights are clearly marked so they are easy to locate. A complete index of the street names and places of interest follows on pages 246–9. The key, set out below, indicates the scale of the maps and shows what other features are marked on them, including railway stations, bus terminals, ferry boarding points, emergency services, post offices and tourist information centres.

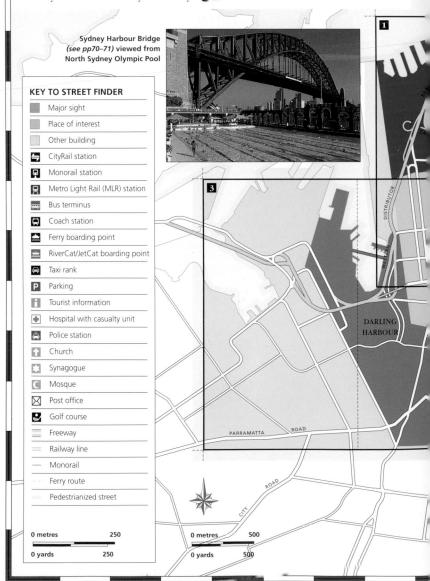

Sydney Harbour Bridge *(see pp70–71)* viewed from North Sydney Olympic Pool

KEY TO STREET FINDER

	Major sight
	Place of interest
	Other building
	CityRail station
	Monorail station
	Metro Light Rail (MLR) station
	Bus terminus
	Coach station
	Ferry boarding point
	RiverCat/JetCat boarding point
	Taxi rank
P	Parking
i	Tourist information
	Hospital with casualty unit
	Police station
	Church
	Synagogue
C	Mosque
⊠	Post office
	Golf course
	Freeway
	Railway line
	Monorail
	Ferry route
	Pedestrianized street

0 metres	250
0 yards	250

0 metres	500
0 yards	500

DARLING HARBOUR

PARRAMATTA   ROAD

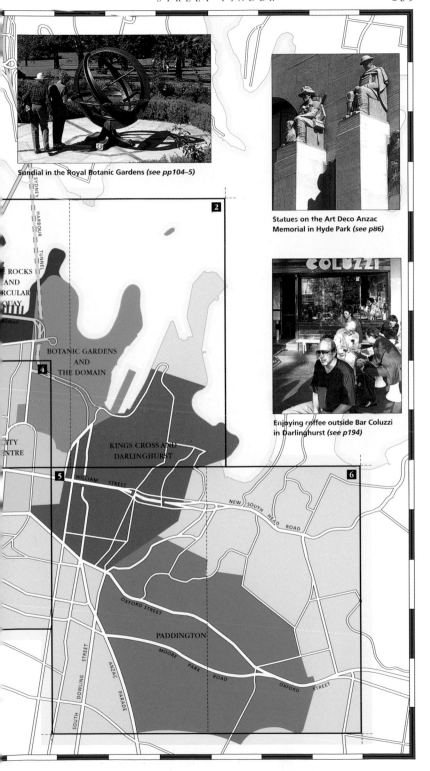

Sundial in the Royal Botanic Gardens *(see pp104–5)*

Statues on the Art Deco Anzac Memorial in Hyde Park *(see p86)*

Enjoying coffee outside Bar Coluzzi in Darlinghurst *(see p194)*

BOTANIC GARDENS
AND
THE DOMAIN

KINGS CROSS AND
DARLINGHURST

PADDINGTON

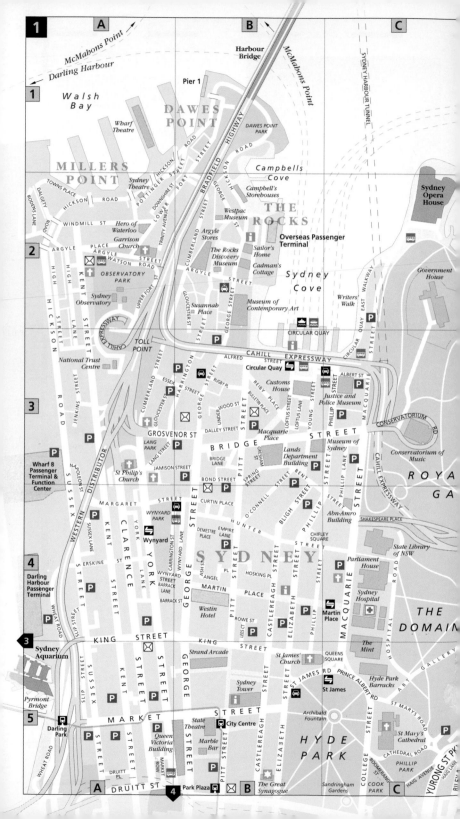

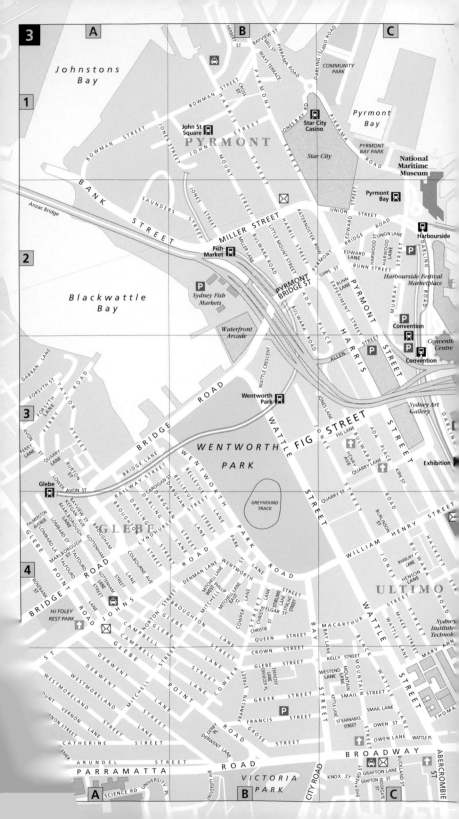

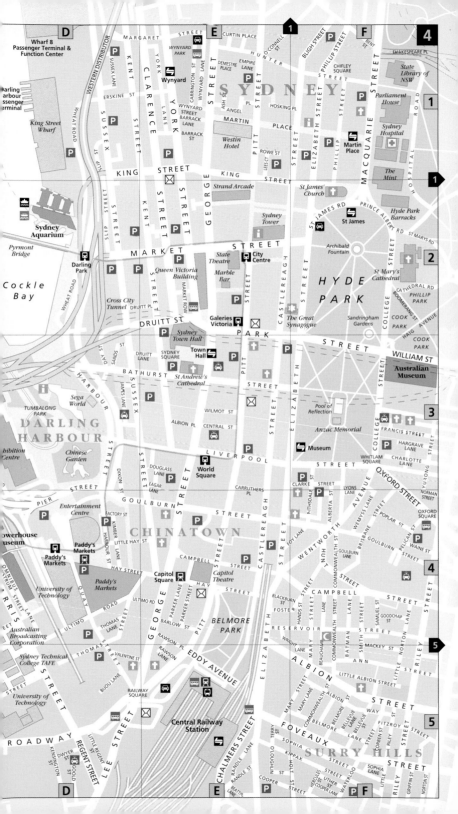

Street Finder Index

General Index